A History of Scotland's Landscapes

A History of Scotland's Landscapes

Fiona Watson with Piers Dixon

First published in 2018
Printed in paperback in 2024 by
Historic Environment Scotland
Enterprises Limited SC510997

Historic Environment Scotland
Longmore House
Salisbury Place
Edinburgh EH9 1SH

British Library Cataloguing-in-Publication Data.
A catalogue record for this book is available from
the British Library.

ISBN 978 1 84917 333 9

© Historic Environment Scotland 2018

All rights reserved. No part of this publication
may be reproduced, stored in or introduced
into a retrieval system, or transmitted, in any
form, or by any means (electronic, mechanical,
photocopying, recording or otherwise) without
the prior written permission of Historic
Environment Scotland. Any unauthorised act
in relation to this publication may be liable to
prosecution.

Designed by Oliver Brookes
Typeset in Garamond and Gill Sans
Printed and bound in Italy by L.E.G.O. S.p.A.

front cover
Linhope, Teviothead, the Borders
HES, DP266259

back cover
Friarton Bridge, River Tay, Perthshire
HES, DP220515

frontispiece
**Church and cemetery,
Teampull Eion, Isle of Lewis**
HES, DP109574

Contents

- 7 **Preface**
  A Road Well Travelled

- 13 **Introduction**
  Where Stands Scotland?

- 19 **Chapter One**
  Settlement

- 79 **Chapter Two**
  Farming

- 131 **Chapter Three**
  Industry and Infrastructure

- 175 **Chapter Four**
  Leisure

- 203 **Conclusion**

- 207 **Land-use Maps**

- 230 End Notes
- 238 Glossary
- 242 Bibliography
- 248 Historic Land-use Assessment
- 251 Acknowledgements
- 252 Index

The Red Field by Sir William Gillies, 1950
Sir William Gillies's watercolour invites us to enter a well-ordered, cheerful lowland farming landscape with its neat houses and fields newly ploughed for winter wheat or barley. It is in many ways the antithesis of Landseer's *Highland Landscape* on the cover.
The Fine Art Society in Edinburgh

Preface

A Road Well Travelled

Living as I do in a small Perthshire village, I spend a lot of time driving to Crieff, our nearest town. It is a twenty-minute journey, the road meandering up over one hillside before plunging down into the neighbouring valley, cattle and sheep rooting around in the rough pasture higher up, great arable fields kilting the carseland beside the River Earn. Birch, beech, oak, larch and a mixed bag of evergreens cloak the lower slopes of the surrounding hills, neat little farms and villages hug the roads, while red kites soar overhead and red squirrels can be glimpsed in patches of woodland.

It would be easy to imagine that this land has changed little, or at least that any past transformations must have eased their way in slowly, cautiously, in a manner unlikely to upset anyone. Not like the upheavals that have dug so deep into the central belt some 40 miles further south or the cleared landscapes of the far north.

But that twenty-minute journey is littered with the remains of all kinds of human activity from the mundane to the extraordinary, stretching back not just hundreds of years, but thousands: evidence that suggests there has been far more going on in this quiet corner of Scotland than first meets the eye. And I don't need a spade or a metal detector to find it – all it takes is a glance out of the car window.

So let us take a closer look. My journey starts in Braco, where I almost immediately pass two churches in quick succession, though one is reduced now to its clock tower. The original Ardoch Church was a chapel of ease, built in the 1770s to spare the scattered inhabitants of this part of the parish the five-mile trek to Muthill further north. In 1844, however, a section of the congregation, led by Reverend Samuel Grant, left in high dudgeon to found their own United Free Church. They were determined that the local landowner should not appoint the minister, a dramatic moment replicated throughout much of Scotland. Feelings ran so high that there were even two separate schools right next door to each other. The congregations did not reunite until 1929, though there had been doubts about the safety of the Free Church building since its spire was struck by lightning in 1874.

The original chapel of ease did not serve a village; Braco came into being only in 1815. Planned, like many across the length and breadth of the country, by the local laird (in this case, Sir James Masterson of Braco Castle), the new settlement was designed to attract tradesmen and agricultural workers for the surrounding estates. By 1837 it was described as 'a very thriving village' with 384 inhabitants. It has expanded since, but not too dramatically. Today there are over 500 of us, though, like many places in rural Scotland, we find it hard to sustain one local business, never mind the plethora of them, from grocers to farriers, that used to flourish here.

And despite some quarrying on Braco Castle estate in recent years, there is little or no industrial activity to compare with previous centuries either. But the remains are still there – two mills (one superseding the other) on the River Knaik and another near the Keir Burn on the western side of the estate, together with a threshing mill at Nether Braco. Alas, evidence for the mysterious gunpowder factory that supposedly gave the name 'Snuff' to a local path still proves elusive.

Turning sharp right going north out of the village, I cross the Knaik. A few yards upstream of the road bridge sits a narrow two-arched packhorse bridge that I certainly would not like to wrestle any animal across. Though largely rebuilt in the 1980s, parts of this bridge have been there since at least 1743, though it was upgraded as part of the eighteenth century determination to drive roads through Scotland beyond the 'civilised' south.

On the eastern side of the bridge lies the Ardoch estate. Like its neighbour on the western side of the Knaik, the land is used for a combination of arable farming, livestock rearing and sport. Unlike Braco Castle, however, Ardoch's splendid Georgian mansion house, set in a pleasant landscape of exotic trees and shrubs with a walled garden nearby, was abandoned in the 1960s and demolished by 1989.

But that is not what Ardoch is famous for. As I continue along the A822, a grassy bank leads up to a stone wall on my right. Beyond are the stalwart peaks and troughs of one of the best preserved Roman forts in Scotland and an ideal place for schoolchildren to hone their attacking skills. Built in the last decades of the first century AD by a Spanish cohort surely well out of its comfort zone, then abandoned but briefly occupied again some 60 years later, this fort was once a major defensive component of Rome's most northerly frontier. Now its biggest threat comes from rabbits, which have made themselves at home among the ditches, much to the agitation of the local dogs.

But already the road begins to cut through a long stretch of rough grazing with such fabulous views across Strathallan to the Ochils that, on my return, it is an easy matter to spot the next weather system blowing in from the west, along with the annual honking legions of greylag and pink-footed geese intent on finding their winter quarters. This kind of wet, tussocky grass can be found all over upland Scotland, divided into large fields and controlled, often at some considerable distance, from a farmhouse with its barns and outbuildings arranged around the obligatory farmyard.

We all know what a farm is, even if it is only through the nursery rhyme 'Old MacDonald'. But even in my own lifetime, farms are not what they used to be – though it should become apparent that one of the main points made in this book is that nothing ever is. Individual farmhouses go up for sale as one holding swallows up another; barns and steadings are 'made over' into beautiful rural retreats for those seeking the benefits of country life. Change is all around us, even in this most fundamental and ancient of human activities.

As I crest the hill I can see, at regular intervals, the wire fences that divide one field from another. If I look closer, however, the grassed-over remains of the old stone walls that came before slumber right next to them, even under them. Technologies alter our lives, but also our landscapes; economics makes sense out of a new way of doing things. But then, as I round a corner to find a stone wall standing proud against the horizon, it strikes me that sometimes we choose to make do with what has gone before or perhaps it is that 'old ways' have come back into fashion.

I drive on, catching a glimpse of one of the newest landscape features in this part of Scotland – the tall, spindly pylons of the Beauly to Denny line that will take electricity generated from renewable energy in the outer reaches of the National Grid down to the more populous areas of Scotland and on into England. The dumpy remains of the old pylons that have criss-crossed the land since the 1930s lie in the surrounding fields waiting to be carted off for scrap like the skeletons of huge prehistoric creatures. Though there were protests against the new line, especially for its potential impact on some of Scotland's most picturesque landscapes, it must have been far more shocking to watch the original pylons go up. And what did swallows and house martins do before the arrival of the handy wire perches strung between them? (They presumably used trees like everyone else.)

After ten minutes or so, I reach Muthill, another neat little village, but one that is far older than Braco. Though there are no traces left of the Culdees – a 'back-to-basics' form of monasticism that flourished in Ireland, Scotland and England in the latter half of the first millennium – you can still see a twelfth century bell tower attached to the ruins of the late medieval church. There was a school here too, from at least the thirteenth century; if it were attached to the church (as was surely the case) then it lay only a stone's throw from the current primary.

The curious Z-shaped layout of the main thoroughfare through Muthill was not originally designed to test drivers' ingenuity when confronted with an approaching lorry or tractor in a narrowing gap between parked cars. Rather, it is a direct reflection of the settlement's history over the last thousand years. Coming from Braco, I start at the wrong end from a chronological point of view; Willoughby Street, which forms two-thirds of the Z, bears witness to the expansion of the village from the 1770s. In these busy decades about 80 houses were built while others were renovated and enlarged to cope with the multitude of hands then needed for the new scientific forms of agriculture that arrived in this part of Perthshire in the wake of the Agricultural Revolution. It is only when I have eased my way round the sharp bend onto Drummond Street (and the final bit of the Z) that I find myself in the old part of Muthill, its medieval core, having survived the narrow pinch-point between the two.

Beyond the village limits it is plain sailing straight ahead to Crieff. On my right are arable fields – pale, ruffled gold in summer – taking advantage of the better soils down on the valley floor. To my left a stone wall tracks me until it is punctuated by a magnificent pair of wrought-iron gates from which a majestic drive, escorted by a phalanx of beech trees, stretches on to the horizon. Deep inside is Drummond Castle. In 1723 it was described as 'much neglected',[1] because its owner, the Earl of Perth, had chosen the losing side in the Jacobite Rebellion of 1715. But its splendid seventeenth century gardens were revitalised in the early nineteenth century. The local minister, James Walker, noted their renown in 1837, enthusing that 'Scarcely a breath of wind can injure the most delicate flower in it; for on all sides it is protected from the blast; and everything about it, as its lofty trees, its descending stairs, its little ponds and its lovely walks with varied flowers on every hand, render it truly enriching.' Even Queen Victoria remarked approvingly that it 'is really very fine, with terraces, like an old French garden'.[2]

Soon enough I must slow down as I approach the outskirts of Crieff, but not before I mentally salute a lonely standing stone marooned in an arable field, sole survivor of an ancient circle. Two sister monoliths were still to be seen up until 1909, when a new tenant farmer removed them, 'much to the surprise and indignation … of the neighbours'.[3] I wonder what stories the remaining one could tell from the thousands of years it has stood – just one of countless others – in this fertile valley.

I am very glad to live where I do, but if I happened to have put down roots somewhere else or not moved from my childhood home, then there too it would be possible to layer back the centuries. Even where the activities of the last few hundred years have hit much harder – flattening, straightening, digging, damming with ever more powerful machinery – we can still catch glimpses of our ancestors in the lines of our streets, beneath patches of woodland, on the shoreline, etched into hillsides, at the boundary between field and moorland, in the outline of a retail park or the grounds of a stately home.

Ah, you might say, but you have been trained to read a landscape. Well, the truth is that, as a historian, my natural professional habitat is the library or the records office and the only landscapes I read are mountains of words. But I was fortunate to go on a jaunt across Rannoch Moor in Argyll one Sunday several decades ago, along with other members of the Scottish History Department at Glasgow University. Stopping for our picnic lunch, Allan Macinnes – who had been brought up not so far from where we were sitting – pointed out a number of rich green patches of grass dotted among the paler, less vibrant sward. This, he explained, was evidence for shielings – the temporary summer shelters once used for taking animals up to the better grass and away from the growing crops. Animals and people produce dung, which enriches the soil, hence the difference in colour.

I was astonished and delighted with this revelation. I was fortunate too that, over the following years, my subsequent work on woodland history in particular brought me into contact with archaeologists, palaeoecologists, foresters and ecologists, who do insist on going out and looking at the things they are researching. Although I am no expert, I can recognise things like a coppiced hazel or a charcoal platform or the site of a long-gone farmstead given away by the trees planted to shelter it in an otherwise open moorland.

But, perhaps more importantly, my eyes were opened to the idea that this land is tattooed with reminders of its past. And now, thanks to the latest research that informs this book, we have a good idea of not only just how much remains, but also the extent to which the activities of our predecessors have shaped, and still shape, the places we live and work in today, even in the depths of our biggest cities. Some of them are obvious – standing stones or brochs are hard to miss. But others are more discrete – lumps and bumps on the ground, discolourations, street patterns or the footprint of one building maintained in the outline of its successor.

This book is intended to be a celebration of what remains of the nation's historic landscapes and the work that has gone into revealing them. It is not meant to be an elegy to what has been lost, though many of those whose voices we are about to hear certainly found the disappearance of what they were used to disquieting, even heart-breaking, just as others celebrated the potential benefits that it was hoped change would bring. It is often tempting to feel nostalgic about the nation's past just as we tend to remember only the sweeter, more pleasurable landscapes of our own childhoods – when even the weather seemed to be better. As we will see, the past is just as complex and many-sided as the present; change created winners and losers then just as it does now. Or, even more difficult to evaluate, change pursued in the interests of desperately needed material wellbeing might also herald the loss of less tangible things that proved necessary, at least in the short-term, to other aspects of health and happiness.

But this book's main purpose is to explore how to 'read' a landscape, how to notice, even in passing, the depths of the past all around us and to understand how and why our predecessors did what they did to the places where they lived and worked; how some ways of using the land came to be abandoned while others survived, even if they had to adapt. It is another way of telling Scotland's story, but in this history everywhere is equal and will often have a quite different contribution to make to the whole. I am aware that some of the language that has developed among landscape specialists may not be familiar, so a glossary has been added to the end of the book, where you will find words marked with an asterisk on their first appearance.

What follows are accounts of ways, both scientific and instinctive, of getting the most out of what this land has had to offer over millennia; of homes built to flaunt status or just to keep families safe and warm; of landscapes designed to be enjoyed or to provoke awe or to make it easier to connect with the wider world; of formidable hard work and decisions taken on how to use the land with long-term consequences even beyond what might have been anticipated. As we look out from our windows we may be reassured by the familiarity of what we see or we may lament the removal of well-loved landmarks, just as we might feel moved to lambast or applaud what is put up in their places. In that we are no different to our predecessors.

And perhaps, too, some day in the future our successors will wonder about what made us live the way we do; whether our homes and offices, our transport systems and our energy supplies fulfilled our needs; what we demanded of the places we enjoyed in our leisure time; how we projected our sense of self and our position in the world; what we built to protect ourselves from external threats; what we put in place to allow us to live – or not – in harmony with each other; and how we felt about it all. Because one day much of what you can see from your window will have vanished. Though not without trace.

The Borders of Loch Fyne by Alfred Fontville de Breanski
Alfred Fontville de Breanski's painting is a Romantic Highland landscape full of dramatic light and the equally dramatic scenery that has enticed visitors to Scotland for centuries.
Estate of Alfred Fontville de Breanski. Crown copyright: Government Art Collection, UK

Introduction

Where Stands Scotland?

In this parish was lately discovered a singular road through a morass, made of wood, consisting of split oak planks, eight feet long, fastened down by long pins or stakes, driven through the boards into the earth. It was found out by digging of peat, and at that time lay six feet beneath the surface.[1]

Thomas Pennant
A Tour in Scotland and Voyage to the Hebrides, 1772

In the ten thousand years since the glaciers retreated at the end of the last Ice Age, Scotland has been transformed not once, but many times. As the ice sloped off, it left in its wake great boulder fields and rivers of rubble. The removal of the heavy weight of ice also allowed the downtrodden land to rise. But then glacial melt-waters pouring into swollen seas began to lap up the shoreline and along sea lochs and rivers – especially around 7,000 years ago when a great tsunami, set off by a vast chunk of collapsing Norwegian mountain, hit Scotland's east coast. It took another thousand years before the land finally began to outrun the sea.

With the ice gone, the first tentative plant life began to drift in. Hardy herbs and shrubs like juniper and dwarf willow took root among the rock, providing nourishment to the great beasts – mammoth, bison, woolly rhinoceros, giant fallow deer, reindeer, giant elk – that lumbered across the land bridge from Europe. But still the temperatures rose, sending these plants higher up the

A History of Scotland's Landscapes   13

hillsides away from the heat; lower down, tree species like birch, followed by hazel, pine and oak, moved in to a height of around 500 metres, though even these natural forests contained areas of heath and grassland. Smaller creatures, from wolves to voles, moved with them as their larger predecessors began to die out.

By then humans had arrived too, dodging the rising waters which occasionally wiped out settlements on the coast and, in the right seasons, flitting from place to place, island to island, hillside to seaside, to hunt, collect and fish. They soon knew how to manage the great forests that surrounded them, cutting back branches to encourage shoots to grow straight and produce more fruit (hazelnuts were a particular favourite) and perhaps even burning out clearings to make it easier to hunt.

But in terms of material culture these earliest settlers have left us almost nothing apart from huge middens* containing phenomenal quantities of shells, the bones of fishes, birds and mammals, and bone and antler tools, many of which are still to be found covered in grass (though often at some distance from the current shoreline). Fourteen middens have been found between Bo'ness and Falkirk at the western end of the Firth of Forth alone, measuring up to 160 metres long by 23 metres wide and nearly 2 metres deep. They are so huge that they perplexed eighteenth century commentators, who could only conclude that they had once been part of the Forth's riverbed rather than a manifestation of the protein-rich diet and hoarding instincts of many generations of hungry hunter-gatherers.

But then the warmer climate started to give way to wetter, windier and colder conditions. This led to yet another significant change to the landscape, one that was to make a huge difference to the lives of succeeding generations until modern times. With the decline in temperature, as well as pressure from rising human populations and their accompanying livestock, trees began to die and not spring up again, decaying into peat. Meanwhile farming, which originated in the Near East, had spread slowly west until, by c2000 BC, our camp-based, semi-nomadic predecessors began to settle down permanently. By then, parts of the north and west Highlands were already losing their pinewoods, open heath and grasslands taking their place. But from around 500 BC, it is clear that humans were also presiding directly over the more systematic and permanent removal of trees to make way for the cultivation of crops and the pasturing of livestock.

Peat continued to spread over succeeding millennia, transforming much of Scotland and its agricultural potential, mostly in the north and west, until the scientific revolutions of the last few hundred years gave modern farmers the wherewithal to remove large swathes of it. Time and again prehistoric and even medieval communities were obliged to avoid the creeping, glutinous bogs and adapt to new conditions. And time and again, their descendants would wonder at what they found in the depths of the peat, from ancient roads to houses to ploughed fields to huge tree trunks where woods no longer existed.[2]

Climate change and human activity were both responsible for the dramatic loss in tree cover, but the next major change to the landscape that we can still see today came about through technological innovation. The earliest types of plough – known as ards – were simple affairs, in essence a cutting blade made of stone or iron (the *share*) attached to a wooden beam (the *mainshare*), the end of which acted as a handle (the *stilt*) held by the ploughman to direct its course; another beam was attached to oxen or other beasts of burden who would pull the ard along. This only really rips up the soil rather than turning it over, as we would now expect a plough to do.

Such implements were perfectly good for the dry sandy soils of the Near East and the Mediterranean, but they weren't much use in the heavy, clay-based soils that dominated northern Europe. However, that is what our predecessors were stuck with for thousands of years and some have even argued that this helps to explain why urbanisation and economic development advanced at a much slower pace here than in the south.[3]

This was to change with the invention of the mouldboard plough, one of history's under-appreciated heroes. 'Iron technology in the later first millennium AD was used to make a shoe for a plough, which could turn the sod over with the help of a heavy iron coulter and a mould board. Such a plough could produce a plough ridge (or rig) by pulling the plough up and down on either side of the centre of a strip so that the soil was consistently pushed to the middle.[4]

The benefits of a mouldboard plough were numerous. In the first place, it allowed far greater areas of land to be brought into cultivation than had previously been possible. Secondly, the act of turning the earth over not only brought to the surface nutrients that had been washed down through the soil, but pushed weeds underground. This saved a lot of time and effort in cross-ploughing (going over the ground again at right angles to the first set of furrows) to get rid of unwanted plants. Thirdly, the farmer could now mix in manure and the remains of previous crops, which would improve his yields. And lastly, the broad high-backed ridges – tell-tale signs of this new style of ploughing still visible in the landscape today – made for an effective drainage system.[5] Ridging, as we will see, still survives from prehistoric times, but the difference is that those ridges had to be created by hand spades after the soil was broken up with the ard, a labour-intensive and time-consuming process (albeit one that was used to great effect until relatively recently in places where labour was still plentiful but the land too rocky and difficult for anything else).

The evidence for the broad ridge and furrow produced after the introduction of the mouldboard plough dates from the twelfth century (though there are tantalising earlier possibilities from both the south-east and the south-west). Knowledge of the new technology was probably brought in from English territory to the south (where it was certainly in use before AD 1000) by the Norman friends of the Scottish king David I, many of whom were settled by him in the Lothians. Monasteries, with their European-wide connections, were also likely to have been in the vanguard of this agricultural revolution.

The farming that went along with the mouldboard plough was essentially communal in both the cultivation of crops and the grazing of animals and this became the basic form of agriculture right up until the next agricultural revolution, which began in the eighteenth century. The new plough was not suitable for all parts of the country; hand-spades continued to be the only way to cultivate the water-logged soils of much of the north-west. But from Orkney down the east coast and across to Galloway in the far south-west, the broad and distinctive reverse-S-shaped rigs ploughed over and over again by generations of oxen, horses and men stand as testament to the enduring influence of the mouldboard plough on the Scottish landscape.

It would be pointless, however, to deny the impact of modern agricultural practices on the appearance of the land today and the survival – or otherwise – of what went before. With the application of science to almost every aspect of agricultural life, from the crops planted to manuring and draining techniques to the layout of farms and fields, the landscape was once more transformed from the eighteenth century onwards. Above all, the agricultural improvers liked order, encouraging the removal of weeds and the construction of mile upon mile of straight hedgerows or stone walls, first of all around the new amalgamated farms and then separating fields within them. They liked trees too, and hundreds of acres were planted to beautify the view and protect the soil from wind and rain.

Many agricultural workers had already been attracted by the job opportunities offered by the fast-growing industries of the Lowlands, either moving into the cities, towns and industrial villages lock, stock and barrel or travelling to and from their homes during the spring and summer months. Others faced no choice but to look for work elsewhere as the communal system of agriculture that had endured for so long was abandoned in the face of new agricultural methods, the open rigs of the mouldboard plough fenced off and parcelled up among a far smaller number of individual farmers, rendering large numbers of former tenants, agricultural workers and landless labourers surplus to requirements. But this is not one simple, single story; in the north-east and the north-west particularly, small-holdings for farm workers remained an important part of the landscape.

New improved breeds of animals arrived too, sometimes from south of the border, like the Cheviot sheep. Or particular regions developed a reputation for the superiority of their own animals – Ayrshire for dairy cows; Aberdeenshire for its beef – and exported them all round the country. Large expanses of the uplands were soon patrolled by only a few shepherds and their dogs as their flocks pushed out the previous inhabitants to the coastal margins, the cities or the colonies.

As I have already suggested, however, Improvement was not a single, all-encompassing revolution, but a stop–start, phased series of transformations that, as with everything else, reflected the particular environmental and historical conditions of the landscapes that it touched. The Sutherland Clearances, with their horror stories of so many families forcibly removed for sheep in a comparatively short time, have captured the modern imagination precisely because they were such an unusually concentrated, violent and disruptive example of the processes that had been at work across both the Highlands and Lowlands before and since. Sometimes, too, it became abundantly clear that even the most up-to-date scientific techniques were no match for certain environmental conditions and the new ways of doing things were abandoned, leaving us, as we will see, with the evidence for failure as well as success.

This agricultural revolution continues even now, with advancing technology, the development of farming at an industrial scale in some parts of the country and new breeds of animals introduced not just from these islands but abroad – the popular Texel sheep, which arrived in Britain in the 1970s, originally came from the Netherlands, having been crossed with a number of English breeds in the nineteenth century. Climate change will also alter what can and can't be done in both the lowlands and the uplands, as has always been the case; so too will any dramatic changes in farming subsidies beyond the current commitment to replicate European Union levels until 2020.

Having outlined key aspects of nearly 10,000 years of history that have a bearing on the evolution of Scotland's landscapes and what has survived to bear witness to the past, now we must begin to fill in the gaps. The following chapters will peel back the layers of this basic chronology. We will also hear, where we can, from those who lived through aspects of what is being discussed, or who had opinions on them (sometimes extremely pronounced even if based on limited experience), or who looked back, just as we are doing, to try to explain what they could see of the past around them. If, in reading this book, you feel that we should appreciate and value the remains of what has gone before – not least because they make such an important contribution to the rich and colourful 'personality' of the place we call Scotland – then I, for one, will count that a success.

* * * *

Stands Scotland where it did?
Alas, poor country, almost afraid to know itself[6]

William Shakespeare
Macbeth, c1606

Before we go on, I have a confession to make. It is no easy task, when writing any history of Scotland, to give proper consideration to the very different experiences of all parts of this small but diverse country if you want to tell a reasonably coherent story.

But to confine oneself to 'Great Historical Events' or 'Trends' leaves the writer open to the charge that he or she is only interested in a very limited Scotland, mentioning other areas only when they impinge on certain interests mostly emanating from the Lowlands. There are exceptions, of course – T C Smout's beloved *A History of the Scottish People* manages this delicate tightrope with sensitivity and rigour. But most writers, myself included, either know quite a bit about a limited geographical area or focus on the influential activities of those involved in government or other national bodies, the machinations of select, albeit powerful, individuals.

This will certainly not suffice if we wish to explore the many and varied remains of past human activity across Scotland's disparate landscapes from the border with England right to the tip of Shetland and the humps of St Kilda in the Outer Hebrides. Instead, we really should acknowledge that this particular piece of land (as anywhere else) is elusive almost to the point of disintegration if we try to define it in terms of common (by which I mean national) characteristics, whether we are describing its towns and cities, its farmland, forests and hillsides, its industrial complexes and leisure spaces, or its inhabitants. And this has been at least as true at any point in the 9,000 years since humans began to spread across Scotland after the last Ice Age as it is today.

But perhaps this is essentially a tale of two nations? Certainly it has been believed from as early as the twelfth century[7] that the country is essentially split into the Scotland of the Lowlands and the Scotland of the Highlands. It was long agreed (by Lowland writers at least) that the great mountainous barrier that stretches from Arran off the Ayrshire coast to Stonehaven in Kincardineshire divided not only the arable plains of the south and east from the pastoral uplands of the west and north, but also represented an intractable gulf between two peoples separated by language, culture, dress and way of life.

However, the Highland–Lowland divide is far too blunt an instrument to take us very far. The imprint of the past sets the scene for the outline of the present, and both the original structures and what survives are ultimately products of local circumstances. Responses to national or even international forces (such as the spread of new materials, ideas and technologies) were never exactly the same across either the uplands or the valleys, never mind the whole country. Culture, historical experience and economic and social realities, as well as more specific geology and geography, have all played their part, combining to a greater or lesser extent to ensure that no-one would ever mistake being in Sutherland for Argyll (upland) or Angus for Orkney (lowland), to suggest but two examples.

And because there is such a wealth and complexity of remains scattered across this land, I need to be clear: this is not a walk through time tracing the evolution of Scotland's many and varied landscapes, a painstaking ravelling of how and why soil and settlement, woods and waterways, highways and byways evolved from a point in the distant past until now. Some of those histories will certainly find their way onto the following pages, but only when they help to describe and explain aspects of the jumble of historic debris that has accumulated and lies still all around us.

What follows is more like a jigsaw, an intricately layered and often exasperating puzzle with a great weight of missing pieces similar to what the Orcadian poet Edwin Muir found when he toured Scotland in the 1930s:

When one comes to the end of a journey one feels a desire to turn back and cast a last glance over all the impressions one has gathered, even though they should be as casual as a collection of shells picked up on a sea-shore. Scotland itself could only be known by someone who had the power to live simultaneously in the bodies of all the men, women and children in it. I took a chance cut through it, stopping here and there, picking up this or that object, gathering shells whose meaning was often obscure or illegible to me. I did not find anything which I could call Scotland; anything, that is to say, beyond the vague and wandering image already impressed upon me by memory …[8]

But when we bring together those pieces that remain from the past, we might come to see, however imperfectly, a rich tapestry of shape and colour. Not one Scotland, but a vibrant, full-blooded and rather different prism through which to view life as it has been played out, perched on the far north-western edge of Europe.

The City of Edinburgh, John Clark, published in *View in Scotland*, 1824

Edinburgh's Old Town grew up around the castle rock, which had been occupied for countless generations. By the end of the eighteenth century the Old Town was critically overpopulated and plans were underway for the nobility and aspiring middle classes to break out of its confines into a spacious New Town. Clark's view of Edinburgh clearly shows the neo-classical lines of this genteel addition to the city.

Crown copyright: Government Art Collection, UK

Chapter One

Settlement

... we seemed now to be on the edge of a very large, almost circular, lake, the town of Inveraray before us, a line of white buildings on a low promontory right opposite, and close to the water's edge; the whole landscape a showy scene, and bursting upon us at once. A traveller who was riding by our side called out 'Can that be the Castle?' Recollecting the prints which we had seen, we knew it could not; but the mistake is a natural one at that distance.[1]

Dorothy Wordsworth
Recollections of a Tour made in Scotland AD 1803

In 1803 Dorothy Wordsworth, her brother William and the poet Samuel Coleridge spent six weeks touring Scotland, enduring considerable hardship in order to pay homage to some of the northern nation's literary heroes and its Romantic scenery. On Tuesday 30 August, she and her companions reached Inveraray on the banks of Loch Fyne in Argyll, a new town built a quarter of a mile west of the original settlement over the previous 30 years. Miss Wordsworth did not quite know what to make of it, acknowledging that, at a distance, it looked 'pretty', though 'the mixture of regularity and irregularity of the buildings' made her think of theatrical depictions of Venice or 'representations in raree-shows' (displays or scenes contained within a box, like a peep-show).

   Her initial enthusiasm turned to dismay on closer inspection, however; as they walked through the town she concluded that it was 'a doleful example of Scotch filth' (she was somewhat obsessive about dirt, as were many of her class and upbringing, considering cleanliness as very much next to godliness). Though the new houses were deemed perfectly comfortable even by English standards, their windows and doorways 'were as dirty as in a dirty by-street of a large town' something she was prepared to forgive in a Highland hut, with (to her mind) all its inherent inadequacies, but not here. For such slovenliness denoted only one of two things; either 'vice or the extreme of wretchedness'.[2]

Perhaps the people of Inveraray did feel a little wretched; they had, after all, been forced out of their homes, which were then demolished for spoiling the Duke of Argyll's view from his own remodelled castle. But since they have not left us their opinion, it is impossible to say. The new houses of Inveraray were undoubtedly more robust and weather-resistant than those they had lived in previously, but they were not necessarily more comfortable, as Dorothy and many others presumed.

There is, however, evidence that the women she was presumably criticising for their slovenly habits were, at that very moment, extremely busy doing something far more essential than cleaning their windows and doorsteps – bringing in and drying peat, the only affordable fuel for most families while a heavy tax on carrying coal remained in place. Ten years earlier, the local Church of Scotland minister, Paul Fraser, reported that they were so completely occupied with this back-breaking task for several months of the year (usually during the summer) that they were not able to take advantage of the lucrative opportunity to spin for the woollen factory at Douglas Water some 27 miles east towards Loch Lomond. 'This', Reverend Fraser lamented, 'unavoidably interferes with, and retards, the business of the whole year, and is, in fact, a very great obstacle to all improvement in this country.'[3] Peat also produces notoriously dirty smoke, which only added to the difficulty of keeping surfaces smut-free.

Dorothy Wordsworth's vivid and fascinating account of her trip to Scotland highlights some of the difficulties we have, many centuries later, in understanding what lay behind descriptions of, and opinions about, the buildings and settlements in which Scots have lived and worked. The essence of the problem lies in the fact that we so rarely hear directly from those who actually occupied them and must pick our way through the words of those who were either outsiders with very different experiences and expectations or who, like the local ministers, may have lived in the places they were describing, but usually came from a different social class from their neighbours.

Then again, for most human history, we have no documentary evidence at all for the most fundamental and ubiquitous structures around which humans organised their daily lives. The remains on the ground, from soil to stone, must therefore speak volumes and we are fortunate that so much of them survive.

* * * *

It appears that these first farmers built a hefty enclosing wall, and within it several discrete houses with yards and passageways and 'activity areas'. Then they just kept building on top of it. 'How many layers of occupation have you gone down already?' I asked Hazel and she sucked in her breath. 'A simple answer? Three or four layers, within the enclosure. A metre and a half in depth. But they didn't raze the place then start again. Buildings just fell out of use, or were closed, or robbed of stone or re-invented and rebuilt. It was in use for about seven hundred years.[4]

Kathleen Jamie, 'Diary',
London Review of Books, 2016

The return of hunter-gatherers[5] to these shores after the last Ice Age between 11,000 and 9,000 years ago is known only from finding broad-bladed pieces of flint used to prepare what could be found or caught on sea or coast. Technological developments over the following centuries led to more sophisticated tools, still made from flint, but also antler and bone, which are found in greater numbers, suggesting that the population was increasing. As we have already seen, these early Scots (although they were not really Scots, as we are many thousands of years from the formation of the kingdom of Scotland) often left middens or detritus in caves. Together with their tools, these provide evidence for an impressive protein diet of creatures of the land, sea and air. Some of these settlements may have been more or less permanent wooden huts, while others were clearly used in particular seasons. Unfortunately no burial sites have been found to tell us something about the culture of these early peoples or their physical characteristics.[6]

The process of settling down permanently – to accommodate the needs of farming, which spread west from the Near East – took many hundreds of years. Beginning in Scotland around 4000 BC, it may not have been fully accomplished until around 2000 BC. It took a long time to persuade Scotland's early post-Ice Age settlers that giving up entirely on the hunting and gathering that had sustained them for generations in exchange for such a labour-intensive approach to getting food was a good idea. Indeed, some hunter-gatherers may never have made the move, but eventually found themselves pushed out (they probably weren't asked nicely) once agriculture began to take over the landscape. Even then we must imagine small communities of early farmers still moving from time to time to get the best out of the soil, rebuilding their hut homes as they went, as recent excavation at Roslin in Midlothian seems to suggest.[7]

These early farmers have left us a little more to go on, even if it is only the scratch of the point of an ard on a stone or narrow ridges formed by ploughing, again now covered with peat or turf; these cry out 'People lived here!' Though much has undoubtedly been disturbed or even obliterated by the spread of peat or subsequent farming, cropmarks* of, for example, timber-built halls such as those excavated at Balbridie and Crathes, Aberdeenshire, suggest that their inhabitants lived together communally before smaller rectangular houses (of timber or stone, depending on local availability) became typical. The timber halls may also have influenced the design of places for the dead (mortuary houses), although the latter were often finally covered in earth or stone; but their influence may have extended further, to the plan of those enigmatic ceremonial spaces known as cursus monuments*. To begin with (c4000–3500 BC) these long rectangular ceremonial enclosures were made of timber, with only the post-holes for large upright posts surviving. The fashion then moved towards earthworks of banks and ditches for another thousand years or so.

Such monuments were by far the biggest structures ever built in Scotland by that date, stretching up to 2 kilometres in length and 100 metres in width and involving the sacrifice of considerable amounts of potential agricultural land (though others, such as Kirkmabreck North, Kirkcudbrightshire, and Douglasmuir, Angus, were only 60 metres and 65 metres in length respectively). So far – and the study of cursus monuments in Scotland is relatively recent – they would seem to be particular to lowland Scotland and are often situated on gravel terraces overlooking rivers.

Modern ploughing has flattened the earthworks, and time has destroyed the massive posts, but at least 50 cursus monuments have been found, 29 of which were the timber kind. They appear mainly as cropmarks in current arable fields, often as part of a mosaic of earlier and later cropmark features indicating the use of these landscapes over a considerable period of time.[8]

The astonishing Cleaven Dyke near Blairgowrie in Perthshire, which may be classed as a form of cursus, can still be seen on the ground – two parallel ditches set up to 51 metres apart with a central mound as a spine and stretching for over a kilometre. It seems to have been built in stages, perhaps over many centuries, but its earliest sections have been dated to before 3600 BC. Yet many who saw it, even in the twentieth century, presumed its banks to be of Roman construction or even, in the case of Thomas Pennant, a Welsh naturalist and writer who visited Scotland in 1769 and 1772, the outer walls of a Pictish '*oppidum* or town' in the vicinity of the nearby Roman fort of Inchtuthil. He presumed (with good reason) that both were situated on a flat outcrop sitting 18 metres above the valley of Strathmore for strategic reasons, commenting that 'Two nations [ie the Romans and the Picts] took advantage of this natural strength…'[9]

It is not difficult to believe that these impressive cursus monuments 'embodied deeply held spiritual or religious beliefs', but it is harder to say exactly what these might have been. Some, including Cleaven Dyke, did have burials associated with parts of them, but this does not seem to have been their main purpose. It has even been suggested that they might have been regarded as a kind of spiritual river, confronting the life-giving and life-quenching attributes

Maeshowe Chambered Cairn, Orkney
One of the most significant achievements of prehistoric Europe, Maeshowe was built around 4,000 years ago. Even now, bereft of its interior treasures and covered in turf, Maeshowe dominates its surroundings, just as its builders intended. HES

of real rivers and nature as a whole that both plagued and nurtured these early communities. Such monuments, like the churches that came later, perhaps provided a safe space in which to consider the big questions of human existence, to provide a fleeting sense of being in control. Certainly the communal decision-making and effort to construct such impressive monuments (even piecemeal) and the shared experience of the ceremonies that took place within their boundaries must have played a crucial role in forging stronger links among these scattered farming communities.[10]

However, the most enduring monuments of the early farmers are the barrows* and chambered cairns* that housed their dead. These ancestral places were often visited as part of a ritual response to questions of life and death. Over time they developed distinct regional characteristics, and in Caithness became increasingly complex and imposing.

After 3000 BC communal burial places were neither built nor used and inhumations began to be

made more often than not under smaller cairns and barrows designed to contain the remains of just one individual.

Other ritual monuments soon followed (around 3000 BC), particularly various types of enclosure. These are often described as henges*, and one of the earliest, Stenness, can be found on Orkney. Because these circular sites were usually surrounded by a ditch and bank with large timber or stone circles inside, they may represent an attempt to exclude some members of the community from seeing the ceremonies that took place within and, at the same time, to enhance the status of those who participated in them. Alternatively, they may represent 'closure',

essentially marking and preserving a space where certain activities of significance had once taken place. Some were truly monumental, as at Strathallan in Perthshire or the Ring of Brodgar on Orkney, but they too may not have been built all at once.

A part of the immense Neolithic monument at Callanish on Lewis in the Outer Hebrides must always have been known to local people, but its wonders were given a wider audience in the 1690s when Martin Martin, a writer from Skye, also in the Outer Hebrides, 'enquired of the inhabitants what tradition they had from their ancestors concerning those stones; and they told me, it was a place

appointed for worship in the time of heathenism, and that the chief druid or priest stood near the big stone in the centre, from whence he addressed himself to the people that surrounded him'. He also noticed that there was more than one site: 'Upon the same coast also there is a circle of high stones standing on one end, about a quarter of a mile's distance from those above-mentioned.'[11]

The true extent – in terms of the height of the stones and the number of them scattered around the area – only began to be revealed once peat cutting exposed their hidden depths in 1837. Now we know that the site was developed between 2900 and 2600 BC and that it adds up to a complex design incorporating a huge central monolith, a chambered tomb, radiating lines of smaller stones on an east, west and south axis and an avenue of stones stretching 83 metres to the north. There are also another six stone circles and seven standing stones within a three mile radius, many of them situated on prominent ridges so as to be easily seen from land and sea for some considerable distance.

Most stone circles were small. They can be found throughout Scotland and in particularly high numbers in the north-east after 2500 BC, where they are often distinguished by a large recumbent stone on the south. These spectacular structures were known as 'altar stones' in popular folklore and have been described as 'blocked doorways to another world, a world sprung from the imaginations and beliefs of peoples who lived some 4,000 years ago'.[12] These are sites where cremations had originally taken place, yet these monumental doorways harken back to the entrances of earlier chambered tombs and so forge a link across time.

Although there is no evidence for the involvement of 'wise men' or druid-type priests with complex astronomical and geometrical knowledge (despite what Martin Martin was told), most archaeologists are prepared to accept that Callanish and other such ritual spaces were roughly aligned 'on lunar rising and setting points, particularly the extremes of their ranges', as well as 'solar alignments on the winter solstice' (a feature particularly associated with Maeshowe on Orkney).[13] But like henges, stone circles can be associated with the idea of closure.

After 2000 BC, there is an increasing wealth of material from which to tease out the complexity and diversity of settlement across both the uplands and the lowlands. These remains are spread across the country far more evenly, if thinly, than settlements are today, implying that the population was still comparatively small.

In north-east Perthshire, for example, settlement sites have been found up to 500 metres above sea-level (more than half-way up a Munro!). Building on slopes was not only possible but desirable in many places, to avoid boggy, waterlogged valley floors. In the drier moorlands of the north and north-east, the imprints of hut circles* can still be seen, while in the wetter west, they are hinted at only by shallow hollows in the peat. They were not necessarily all occupied or even built at the same time, but represent different phases of expansion and contraction, remodelling, reuse, decay and abandonment, just like farms in more recent times. Given that these farmers were dependent to such a high degree on the kindness, or otherwise, of the seasons, and had only rudimentary means at their disposal to overcome limitations in the soil or the weather, it was sometimes easier to move and start again than pit themselves against nature in a deadly game of diminishing returns.

Nor do the surviving remains represent a single building design or settlement type. In the Southern Uplands near the border with England, for example, the huts were made of timber rather than stone (presumably reflecting what was most readily available) and sat on a platform made from material dug out of the uphill side of the slope, presumably to help with drainage. This was also true in Sutherland, but there stone was the building material of choice.[14]

Around the end of the first millennium BC a period of wetter, cooler weather encouraged the spread of peat, leading to the abandonment of farms at higher elevations. The desire, or perhaps the need, to exclude was adopted in settlement

Stenness, Orkney, with Maeshowe in the foreground

Maeshowe's close proximity to the Ring of Brodgar and the Standing Stones of Stenness must surely have been highly symbolic. Although these monuments were built in the third millennium BC (slightly predating Maeshowe), all three are clearly part of the ceremonial landscape. HES, DP083284

patterns in the centuries after 1000 BC, when it became more common to build stockades in and around existing farming communities. This was not always about defence; building fences or stone walls also made it easier to manage the competing needs of arable farming and livestock.[15]

These impressive and blatantly high status sites now, for the first time, seem to fall into broad regional types – brochs* largely concentrated in the far north-west, duns* in the centre-west and other types of hill-fort in the south-east. Despite some differences in outward appearance, however, the communities that built them surely shared much in terms of maturing economic and social structures, including a move towards hierarchies, with some individuals and families clearly enjoying higher status than their fellows. We can perhaps also see early forays into the wielding of power beyond local tribal groupings.

Despite regional differences, forts of one kind or another can be found throughout Scotland except for the highest ground. They often took advantage of naturally defensive sites and added man-made ditches, ramparts and walls, the remains of which can still be seen dug into rocky outcrops, cliff edges and hillsides today. Some could have housed large numbers of people.

There can be no doubt that these forts were designed to be seen and to show off the ability of groups or individuals to control the natural resources and the people of the surrounding area, as well as to protect these resources from others. Most presided over the nearby agricultural systems that sustained them and so, like the castles that eventually replaced them on the same or similar sites, must be seen as part of the surrounding landscape rather than looking down on them in lofty, privileged isolation.

They are perplexing, however, because there is no obvious pattern to their development. They can change from unenclosed to palisaded, from single to many defensive ramparts and then back to unenclosed, which might helpfully imply an increasingly violent and defensive society before the Romans forcibly calmed things down, as was once thought. That raiding against other tribes was a part of the lives of at least some of these communities was gruesomely proved in 2013 by analysis of bones excavated from Broxmouth fort in East Lothian in the 1970s. These belonged to men, women and children from elsewhere who had been killed by sword and axe blows and parts of them perhaps brought back home as trophies.[16]

But perhaps it is only to be expected that any type of settlement that endures for such a long time would go through several phases of construction and that the scale of activity and the order in which defences grew, declined, or were even done away with altogether varied according to local conditions, both natural and human-inspired. It is also the case that large swathes of the country were entirely or largely unaffected by the Roman invasions, so what might be true for the south is unlikely to have dictated the way people lived beyond the line formed by the Rivers Forth and Clyde. Having said that, the evidence suggests that enclosed sites were already going out of fashion *before* the Imperial armies arrived,[17] which may say something about the ability of certain groups or individuals to enforce peace on their terms over neighbouring peoples.

The survival of these forts for hundreds of years beyond their active lives depended partly on their sheer size and partly, as ever, on how likely the site was to be used and reused in the coming millennia. Many survived right up until the 1800s, only to be ploughed out or their stone viewed as fair game for quarrying. Not everyone was appalled by their destruction, however. In 1834, George Tough, the minister at Ayton in Berwickshire, noted, with regard to the fort at nearby Habchester (see page 29), that 'Some modern antiquarians have lamented that so perfect a specimen of the ancient British encampments has not escaped the mutilation of the plough, especially as no ancient relics have been discovered by the process of ploughing it down to compensate for the deed. Enough, however, remains to mark the judgement and the industry with which such places had been selected and constructed, both with a view to observation and defence.'[18]

The archaeologist Strat Halliday agrees. Because Habchester happened to be split between two modern farms, only half of it was destroyed and so, as he says:

Standing within the sweep of its twin ramparts and ditches today one can really get this sense; seeing and being seen, securing the power and aspirations of the people who lived there. It does not take much imagination to repopulate the interior with round-

26 Chapter One – Settlement

houses and to rebuild the tumbled earthen banks with timber-faced walls perhaps three or four metres high. All that is missing are the sounds of everyday life, lost in the wind and the drone of traffic in the valley below.[19]

Habchester rather neatly sums up the kind of imprint on the ground to look out for, whether it is ditches and built-up banks (they may not be as complete) or a suspiciously regular shape beneath the turf. Sometimes you can still see the steps of their large ramparts or tumbled stone walls set on a prominent hill, as at Bennachie in Aberdeenshire or White Cathertun in Angus. While there is a wealth of prehistoric monuments still out there, most of them are to be found in moorland or areas of rough grazing where the plough hasn't reached. They also tend to be in well-drained situations (ie, on a ridge or terrace), though there would usually need to be a water-source nearby for both the inhabitants and their animals.

The brochs of the north-west are, if anything, even more impressive than their hill-fort contemporaries, but their history and provenance have proved rather more difficult to fathom until comparatively recently. From at least the 1690s right up into the nineteenth century, they were commonly described as 'Danish forts', rather than what they in fact were, being of much earlier and – so far as we know – native construction.

Earlier writers also liked to advance various theories to explain what they were for. Martin Martin, at the end of the seventeenth century, began circumspectly enough, saying only, with regard to those he saw on Harris in the Outer Hebrides, that the locals had told him they were Danish and that 'they are of a round form, and have very thick walls and a passage in them by which one can go round the fort'.

By the time he got to his home island of Skye, however, he was prepared to assert – presumably on the grounds of a much deeper local knowledge – that they were used to communicate by fire, being 'so disposed that there is not one of them which is not in view of some other … and this hath always been observed upon sight of any number of foreign vessels or boats approaching the coast', a statement which says as much about his own times as that of the broch inhabitants.[20] It also illustrates the fact that such ancient dwellings could remain useful to local communities long after they were abandoned.

By the time Thomas Pennant saw the fourteen-foot-high beauty at Dun Bhoraraig on Islay in the Inner Hebrides in 1772, the level of speculative detail had blossomed, emphasising above all what he and his contemporaries imagined to be the brochs' military *raison-d'etre*, which sounds remarkably like that reflected in the design of a medieval castle:

… the walls are twelve feet thick; and within their very thickness is a gallery, extending all around, the cavern for the garrison, or the place where the arms were lodged secure from wet. The entrance is low, covered at top with a great flat stone, and on each side is a hollow, probably intended for guardrooms, the inside of the fort is a circular area, of fifty-two feet diameter, with a stone seat running all round the bottom of the wall, about two feet high, where might have been a general resting-place of chieftains and soldiers.

Pennant, echoing Martin, was also led to believe that Dun Bhoraraig was part of a chain of forts designed to be able to transmit warnings of impending danger, but not just with fire.

Each was the centre of a small district; and to them the inhabitants might repair for shelter in case of any attack by the enemy: the notice was given from the fort, at night by the light of a torch, in the day by the sound of trumpet: an instrument celebrated among the Danes, sometimes made of brass, sometimes of horn. The northern bards speak hyperbolically of the effect of the blast blown by the mouth of the heroes.

By the nineteenth century, there was sufficient understanding of the nature of brochs to call them 'Pictish Towers'.[21] But even this emphasises a predominantly military or defensive purpose behind their construction, while archaeologists today are far from agreed that this is what prompted their structure and location. As with the hill-forts and even medieval castles, we will have to settle, for the time being at least, for a range of possible reasons, from the vaunting of wealth and status to the protection of people and animals. What we can say with confidence is that brochs and hill-forts, as well as crannogs* built on lochs, bear witness to the power and sophistication of the communities

that built them, whilst acknowledging that there was likely to be a marked inequality between those who lived in them and those who toiled on their construction.

* * * *

A thousand-foot slog, then a cairn of old stones –
hand-shifted labour,
and much the same river, shining
    way below
as the Romans came, saw,
    and soon thought the better of.
Too many mountains, too many
    wanchancy tribes
whose habits we wouldn't much care for
(but could probably match),
too much grim north, too much faraway snow …[22]

Kathleen Jamie, 'Glacial'
The Bonniest Companie

In AD 79 Gnaeus Julius Agricola, the Roman governor of southern Britain, sent a fleet north to map the unconquered parts of the island as a prelude to invasion, the results of which were written up by his son-in-law, Tacitus, to provide us with the earliest written description of Scotland's coastal geography. Four years later, Agricola reputedly defeated an army of Caledonian tribes at the battle of Mons Graupius (no-one knows for sure where that was), consolidating his hold over southern Scotland. At the same time, at least four forts were constructed – including the one in my village – between Camelon on the Forth in West Lothian and Bertha, near modern-day Perth, with an intended headquarters begun at Inchtuthil, also in Perthshire, hinting at an occupation that was soon given up.

These symbols of occupation and any prospect of the conquest of the rest of mainland Britain were abandoned, because soldiers were needed elsewhere in the Empire. Forty years later, in AD 122, the Emperor Hadrian ordered the construction of a wall at the northern limits of Roman power across the entirety of what is now northern England, but they had not given up on the idea of going further. Around AD 141, the British governor, Lollius Urbicus, advanced beyond Hadrian's Wall, building forts and roads along a new frontier that swept across Scotland between the Firths of Clyde and Forth. But in AD 142 another wall was begun, to be named after the current Emperor, Antoninus Pius – the Antonine Wall. Even the Romans thought it was a bad idea to venture beyond the Highland–Lowland line.

This new frontier was abandoned only twenty years later and, though one final attempt at conquest was launched around AD 200, they finally gave up on the idea for good. For the next 200 years, until the Romans permanently left these islands in AD 411, there was contact, mostly in the form of trade, between those living south of Hadrian's Wall and those beyond it. But the remains of the Roman presence in southern and eastern Scotland slowly disappeared, swallowed up by earth and grass, though memory of them lived on. It was only Roman roads that proved of lasting value to the natives.

But there was another legacy of Imperial attempts at conquest that did affect the future of those who resisted the Romans. Indeed, it was the very act of resistance that may have made the difference, as native tribes joined together to cross the wall and attack the invaders. These pragmatic alliances may well have intensified the consolidation of power in the hands of dominant individuals across broader stretches of territory whose descendants, by the sixth century, were called Picts, possibly learning from the Scots/Irish, who already had provincial kings.

Recent archaeology is finally shedding light on the complex native societies – both Pictish and Gaelic-speaking – of the early first millennium AD. As ever, presumptions of a lack of sophistication, of crude social and therefore physical structures, are being exposed as almost entirely the product of one-sided propaganda and prejudice (the Romans rarely saw anything of value in the cultures they came up against and we've been far too willing to believe their narrow-minded judgements – the most easily understood evidence we have – ever since).

Habchester Fort, Berwickshire
The remains of this Iron Age fort beautifully illustrate the different fates that may befall our ancient structures. Split between two landowners, one half has been ploughed under, obliterating the ditches and walls, while the other half has been conserved. HES, SC993205

The Pictish site at Rhynie in Aberdeenshire has, for example, been recently revealed as 'a sophisticated Pictish power centre of international significance, which enjoyed long-distance trade contacts with Anglo-Saxon England, Frankia and the Byzantine world' suggestive of 'complex, highly stratified societies with developed strategies of rulership and governance'. Archaeologists working there found pottery from the Mediterranean, glass from France and Anglo-Saxon metal-work, as well as evidence to suggest there were craftsmen on site producing their own intricate examples. Excavation revealed the remains of four separate enclosures surrounding the Craw Stane (depicting a salmon above a Pictish 'elephant', believe it or not), which once stood alone in an arable field, the only visible sign of the riches below. Post and beam settings found nearby seem to be parts of an elaborate entrance to the fort and there are two more symbol stones – one of which is the very charming Rhynie Man – downhill of the Craw Stane.[23]

The site at Rhynie has been dated to the fifth and sixth centuries AD, which ties in neatly with the emergence of kings in the written record. According to the text (the source was actually compiled many centuries later, which is why we can't necessarily rely on it), kings first appear in the Scottish/Irish kingdom of Dalriada (established by invaders, called Scots, from Ireland who settled in modern Argyll and the islands) and then, a decade or so later, in Pictland itself.[24] The splendid hill-fort at Dunadd in Argyll dates from the sixth century (though such an outstanding site may have been occupied long before, even if no traces remain) and is generally viewed as the main centre of Scottish Dalriada. Here too there is evidence for metal-working, including beautiful and ornate brooches to adorn the clothing of the powerful men and women who lived or visited here, as well as goods likely to have come some considerable distance, including from the Mediterranean.

Dunadd's natural terraces, which reach ever upwards towards an 'inner sanctum' at the top, may well have been used to restrict access to the increasingly prestigious areas (just as only the chosen few would have been allowed to progress from the outer hall to the inner hall to the king's bed-chamber in the sixteenth century palace of Stirling). And then there are 'the two outsized human feet', along with other symbols, carved into the rock and usually interpreted as marking the place where a mystical ceremony would have turned ordinary mortals into kings. With its easy access to the sea, Dunadd was somewhere at which 'an astonishing assortment of people, including merchants, sailors, clerics and warrior-potentates seems to have mingled … at the height of Dalriada's power'. The citadel was occupied until the ninth century, by which time the Vikings had begun to terrorise the west coast.[25]

In the same period there is evidence for the advance of perhaps the Roman Empire's most enduring legacy – Christianity – which spread west after a ban on the middle-eastern sect was lifted by the Emperor Constantine in AD 313. It was Irish monks, the most famous of whom was Columba, who took the word of God across both southern and northern Pictland in the sixth and seventh centuries. Signs of their presence on the ground are mostly confined now to the small stone huts and chapels they built on islands off the western and northern coasts in which to spend their lives of contemplation, though documentary evidence and recent excavation have revealed the presence of more complex monastic sites on the coast at Rosemarkie and Portmahomack in Ross and Cromarty and Kinnedar in Moray, as well as Columba's Iona in the far west. There may, of course, have been many more.

The remains of these early monastic sites, which were mostly built of timber, have largely disappeared or been subsumed beneath later structures. It is a similar story for settlement remains which, as ever, tend now to be found mostly in the relatively undisturbed upland fringes. Not surprisingly, major landscape features continued to be used as places of strength. By the middle of the first millennium AD, hill-forts found a new lease of life, some of them built from scratch but others re-occupied, as was the case at Craig Phadrig, near Inverness, supposed to have been the place where St Columba visited the Pictish king, Bridei, son of Maelchon (AD 555–584), in whose territories three of the above monasteries were founded.[26] Along the coast, the hill-fort at Burghead on the southern bank of the Moray Firth was also a major Pictish centre for the best part of half a millennium from around AD 400.

In the south, the castle rock in Edinburgh, topped with a timber hall, is generally supposed to have been home to the leaders of the Gododdin,

Chapter One – Settlement

a British tribe whose territory stretched across the border counties of Berwickshire, Roxburghshire, Selkirkshire and Peeblesshire through the Lothians towards Stirling; in the west the stronghold of Alt Cluath (Dumbarton Rock) in Dunbartonshire played host to kings of another British tribe from at least the seventh century;[27] about the year 839 the Pictish king Giric died at Dundurn, deep in the valley of the River Earn in Perthshire; and in the hills looking out across the vast plain of Strathmore north of Perth, a prominent knoll was crowned with 'a massively defended citadel' called Dunsinane, reputedly the infamous site of a battle between the Scottish king Macbeth and Earl Siward of Northumbria in the mid eleventh century.[28]

These are clearly strongholds occupied now and again by peripatetic kings and noblemen, though even here much of the accommodation would have been wooden and so has long since disappeared. The inhabitants of the Northern Isles (Pictish) and the many islands off the west coast (Scottish) continued to build in stone, but, unlike much of the mainland, the era of monumental building there was over long before AD 500. In their place the Picts and Scots built much smaller, cellular houses of various designs but eventually standardised to some extent as a figure-of-eight and often cowering beneath the mighty brochs and wheelhouses of their predecessors.[29]

Norse raiders first hoved into terrifying view in the north and west in the 790s, returning year after year to plunder and kill before establishing themselves more permanently in and around these coastal zones in the following centuries. It was Dalriada in the west and northern Pictland that bore the brunt of the attacks, though the south and east were certainly not left in peace. As the Norse began to settle down, it is not at all surprising to find the Pictish cell-houses replaced by the newcomers' longhouses.

The Norse were not the only ones to like longhouses; examples up to 30 metres in length have also been found in Perthshire dating from around AD 600–900, but their inspiration may have been Frisian rather than Scandinavian. With rounded ends, they had turf walls and, like later homes, sheltered both humans and animals in separate quarters with a specially built pit or drain added to the byre end. Frisian influence in early medieval Britain stemmed from the fact that Anglo-Saxons used Frisia, now part of the Netherlands, as a stepping-stone to the invasion of England, and East Anglia in particular, in the fifth century AD as part of the migrations and upheavals that helped to bring an end to the Roman Empire in Western Europe. The Frisians were also enterprising traders of luxury goods from Sweden to the Rhine and across to Britain – a Frisian coin dated to AD c 715 was found in a metal-working workshop established on the site of the monastery at Portmahomack in Ross and Cromarty several centuries later.[30]

By then a new kingdom had been born away from the Norse frontline; in AD 900 the Irish annals recorded the death of Donald, ri Albann – king of Scotland.[31] Donald's grandfather was Kenneth mac Alpin, who took over first the kingdom of Dalriada in the west and then southern Pictland in the aftermath of a catastrophic defeat of an alliance of Picts and Scots against the invading Norse that wiped out both kings and many of their nobles in AD 839.

This new Scotland only reached as far south as the River Forth. Beyond its southern border (in the Lothians and the Borders today) lived the Anglo-Saxons of the kingdom of Northumbria, who had, in the mid seventh century, forced the Gododdin – the native Britons – to flee west to the British kingdom of Strathclyde. Both the Britons and the Anglo-Saxon elites liked extensive timber hall palaces and traces of such complexes have been found at Doon Hill in East Lothian (British), Philiphaugh and Sprouston in Selkirkshire (Anglo-Saxon). In fact, 'it is likely that, isolated or grouped, imposing rectangular buildings will form a component of aristocratic architecture in much of Scotland away from the Atlantic coastlands';[32] certainly the Pictish/Scottish palace complex at Forteviot in Perthshire – situated in the heart of a prehistoric ritual landscape – fits such a description.[33] But there is little or no trace of most of them now, though they may be revealed as cropmarks when conditions are right.

In the south-east the vast majority of the population probably lived in timber huts either on platforms or with floors sunk into the ground, traces of which show up as cropmarks. Elsewhere all we can say is that most Scots lived in houses that have left little or no trace, their flimsiness amply illustrated by a throw-away remark in a Norse saga:

Castle Law Fort, Midlothian
This site shows signs of three building phases, culminating in a fort surrounded by ditches around AD 79/80. HES, DP146304

Reconstructed Wheelhouse, Old Scatness Broch, Shetland
Late Iron Age wheelhouses were stone built except for the central hub which was roofed with timber and thatch.
Davy Cooper, Shetland Amenity Trust

Kilphedir Broch, Sutherland
The Iron Age broch on a prominent knoll at Kilphedir, with its surrounding small cairns and hut circles, commands an excellent view down the valley of the River Helmsdale. HES, DP080106

Dun Carloway Broch, Lewis, Outer Hebrides, 1900
This well-preserved broch was built and occupied in the first millennium BC. Opinion remains divided as to whether brochs were primarily for defence, status, or both. HES, SC1113130

Phopachy Crannog, near Inverness
Situated on the Beauly Firth, the Phopachy crannog is 250 metres from the shore. Crannogs were Iron Age loch dwellings either built over the water or on islands. HES. DP191478

Scottish Crannog Centre, Loch Tay, Perthshire
After seventeen years of research, this reconstructed crannog opened its wattled timber doors in 1997, providing a glimpse of life in an Iron Age loch dwelling. Peter Carroll / Alamy Stock Photo

Dun Anlaimh Crannog, Coll, Inner Hebrides
Local tradition links the site to the last generations of Norwegians, successors of the Norse invaders who first appeared on these shores in the later eighth century AD. HES. SC875184

The Broch of Gurness, Orkney
The broch village at Gurness is one of the most extensive examples of an Iron Age settlement in northern Scotland. HES

A History of Scotland's Landscapes

'Dwellings perished, when they burned – peril that day did not fail – there sprang into smouldering thatch red flame – the Scots' realm …'[34]

* * * *

The Picts devoted themselves to tilling their fields, and to the construction of fortifications and castles, for in these things they placed all hope for preserving and enhancing their commonwealth.[35]

Hector Boece
Historia Gentis Scotorum, 1527

The Picts didn't really build castles, but it is not much of a stretch of the imagination to conjure up such fortresses – as the sixteenth century author of the above quote rather imaginatively did – out of earlier elite structures like hill-forts. Although these various 'power centres' differ in outward appearance, they have much in common in terms of function. Indeed some of the earlier crannogs and hill-forts continued to be used long after what we might regard as the classic medieval castle made its appearance.

Having said that, there is no single model for a castle any more than there is for a hut circle, and fashions in their design vary across both time and place. Introduced by the Normans when they were invited into Scotland by King David I (1124–1153), these fortresses started out as motte and bailey* – a keep built on a mound with an adjacent enclosed flat area – originally built of timber but later in stone. To begin with David and his successors transplanted nobles of Norman origin into areas, like Moray in the north and Galloway in the south-west, that either resisted the authority of the kings of Scots or fought to provide alternatives to individual monarchs. Those areas still under Scandinavian control (the north and north-west islands), on the other hand, were entirely castle-free.

The earliest stone-built walled castles in Scotland were constructed from the last decades of the twelfth century by the Crown and aristocratic lords, both Anglo-French and Gaelic in origin. They can be found in places like the western coastal mainland (the west was slowly recovered from the Norse, a process completed in 1266), where building materials and ideas were more easily transported by sea. Their walls could be square, as at Castle Sween and Castle Tioram in Argyll, or round, as at Rothesay on the island of Bute off the Ayrshire coast.

Throughout the thirteenth century, stone castles spread throughout Scotland. Timber – obviously a fire hazard – was becoming scarce in many places, but was still used for impressive internal features, including intricate and marvellous hammer-beam roofs. The royal forest at Darnaway in Moray provided oak for a roof put into the nearby castle of the same name in 1387 and was still capable of producing beams of sufficient size and quality for the Great Hall at Stirling before 1450, though this was probably its last gasp at providing such large timbers.[36]

Sites that had previously been hill-forts, as on the castle rocks of Edinburgh and Stirling, often became royal residences. However, the fact that the earliest buildings within them have not survived, despite recent excavation, means that it is now impossible to tell what, if anything, differentiates them from earlier structures. It was, as we will see, the relationship between these particular castles and the growing urban centres at whose heart they lay that had really changed.[37]

Castles served a number of purposes, as well as sending out a message that their owners were men of substance and authority. Some were effectively manors of agricultural estates, whilst others, in more remote locations, were designed to take advantage of good hunting opportunities, one of the most important social aspects of aristocratic life. They were not usually occupied for much of the time – medieval elites moved around both in order to exercise lordship and to freshen things up – but such was the symbolic authority of the castle that they might act as the backdrop to land transactions long after they had been abandoned.[38]

One Scottish king – Robert I, otherwise known as Robert the Bruce – was so convinced that,

Caerlaverock Castle, Dumfriesshire

The thirteenth century Caerlaverock Castle replaced an earlier fortification, visible in a clearing in the trees, which sat beside a harbour on the River Nith (the river has since retreated). It is likely that such a low-lying site was chosen for its easy access to ships that sailed out to the Irish Sea via the Solway Firth. HES

Chapter One – Settlement

Smailholm Tower, Roxburghshire
The Pringle family built Smailholm Tower in the fifteenth century to offer protection against English raids. It sits on the top of Lady Hill, giving its occupants a superb view of the surrounding area and boldly asserting the Pringles' possession of these lands in the hotly contested Border region.
HES

from a military point of view, castles were of more use to his enemies than his own regime that he proceeded to throw down the walls of those that fell into his hands. His feelings ran so deep that he built a manor house, not a castle, at Cardross in Dunbartonshire (not the modern Cardross) for his own semi-retirement. But Bruce's castle-phobia did not catch on and his successors, including his son, David II, set about rebuilding what had been lost with walls now entirely in stone.

We should also remember that most castles still standing today have lost the designed landscapes – parks, woods, gardens and orchards – intended to enhance the impression of cultured sophistication provided by the buildings' external design and internal furnishings. Some later examples have been restored, as at Edzell in Angus and Drummond in Perthshire, and visitors to Stirling Castle can look out to the south-west over the turfed-over remains of what was once, among other things, a royal park and tournament ground. Few, if any, castles were ever the bare, barren islands they sometimes seem today.

Castles were not the only Grand Designs of medieval Scotland; abbeys and monasteries could more than compete in terms of architectural splendour (though bishops usually lived in castles and palaces of their own). Since their main purpose was to serve God and exploit His bounty here on earth, the new monastic orders invited in by Scottish kings in the twelfth century sought out fertile sites on low-lying plains. The monks' knowledge of draining, ditching and dyking enabled them to get the best out of these boggy haughs* and other, often extensive, possessions granted to them by royal and noble patrons.

Urquhart Castle, Inverness-shire
The thirteenth century Urquhart Castle sits on a low promontory jutting out into Loch Ness, a place of paramount strategic importance at the northern end of the Great Glen. Control of this major route has long been highly prized – the remains of an earlier fort have also been found there.
HES

Like their castle-counterparts, the stone cathedrals, abbeys and churches of the later middle ages were either a new incarnation of an established religious site, as at Muthill in Perthshire, St Andrews and St Serf's in Fife, or a completely new foundation, as seems to be the case at Dunfermline, also in Fife. They were also, like castles, part of larger complexes housing the activities of those who lived there, those who came to visit and those who provided for their needs. These could include guest houses, kitchens, stables, mills, barns and burial grounds. At both Holyrood in Edinburgh and Dunfermline, the abbey's guest house later developed into a royal palace, while crypts below the churches formed the final resting places of kings and noblemen (everyone else had to settle themselves eternally outside).

But despite all this elite attention, the fortunes of ecclesiastical sites – reflected in their physical condition – ebbed and flowed, not least because the Border abbeys in particular found themselves in the frontline of the wars with England that lasted, on and off, from the end of the thirteenth century to the middle of the sixteenth. Even Scotland's foremost ecclesiastical centre, St Andrews in Fife, was said to have seen better days by the early sixteenth century. Its decline was only arrested in the 1520s by 'the abbot John Hepburn (whom they call its prior), who restored the fabric to its pristine appearance when it was in a tumbledown condition because of old age, and built many other structures from the foundations upward, together with a larger basilica (and there is none fairer for divine offices) decorated with interior ornamentation acquired at great expense, and surrounded the abbey with a wall made of dressed

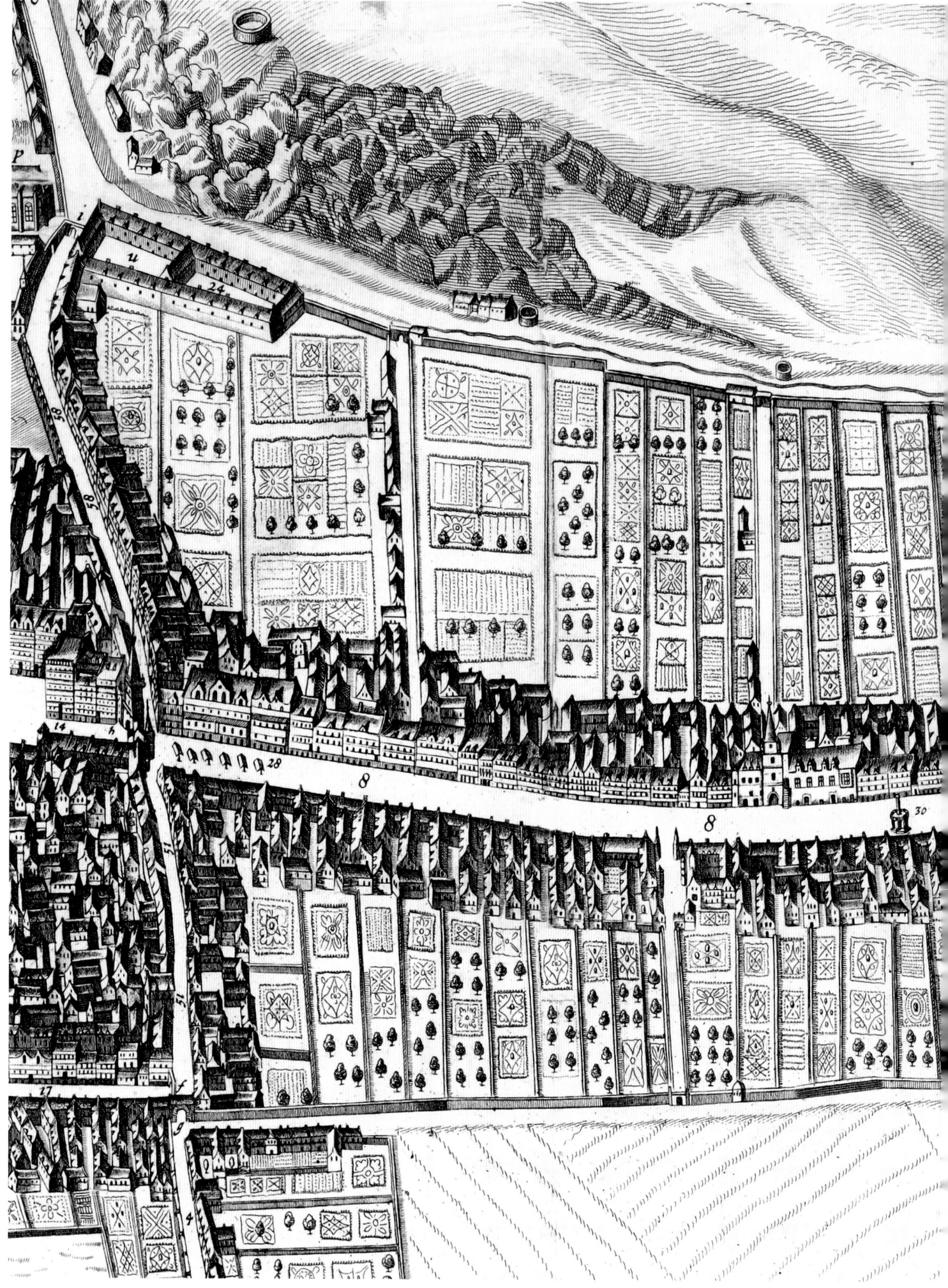

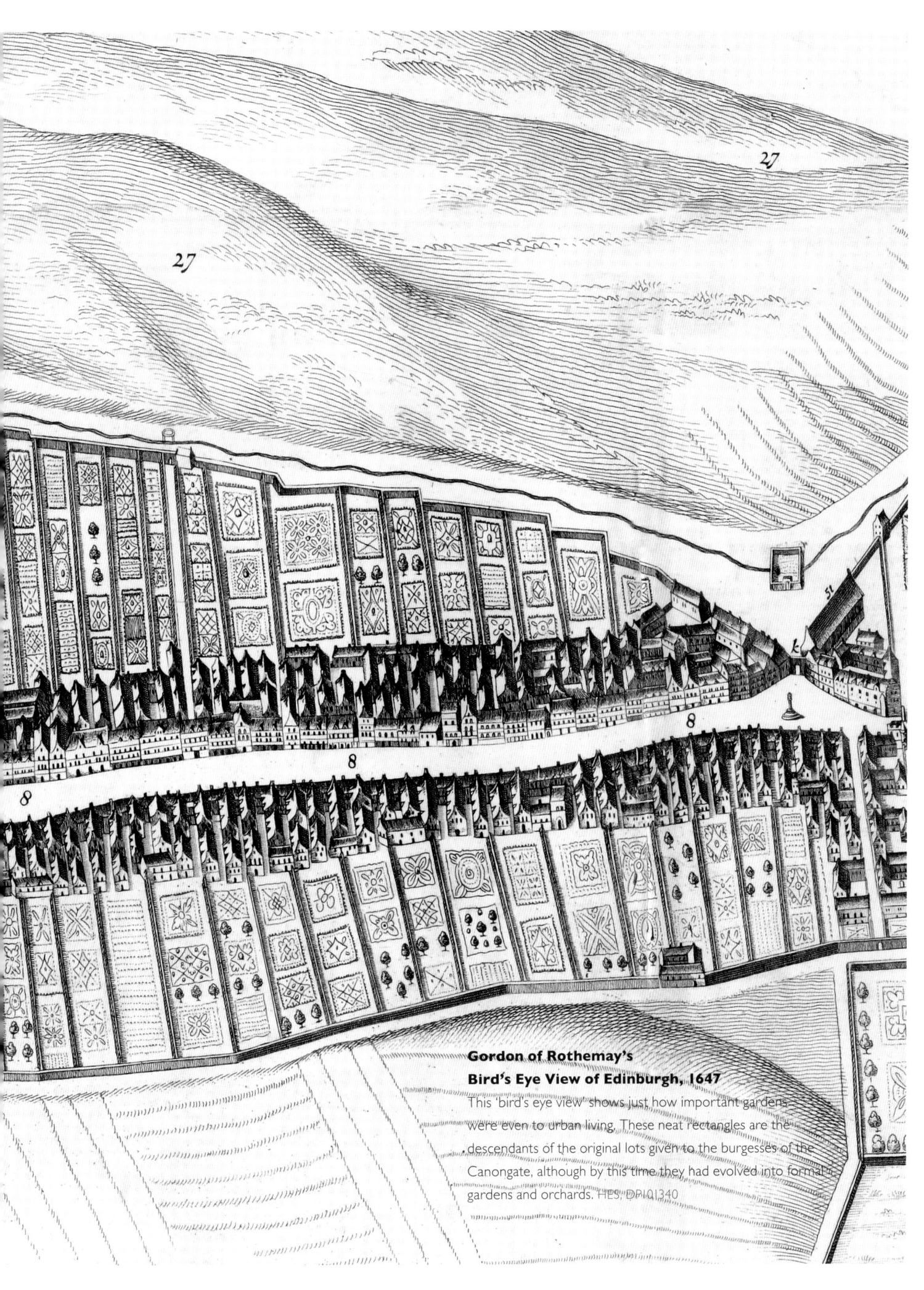

Gordon of Rothemay's Bird's Eye View of Edinburgh, 1647

This 'bird's eye view' shows just how important gardens were even to urban living. These neat rectangles are the descendants of the original lots given to the burgesses of the Canongate, although by this time they had evolved into formal gardens and orchards. HES, DP101340

stone and wonderfully adorned with many towers and ramparts'.[39]

These renovations were completed just in time for the destruction unleashed by the Protestant Reformation* 40 years later, when many abbeys and churches, including the great cathedral at St Andrews, were smashed and looted. The nobles, who profited most by acquiring former church lands, were not above pilfering stone for their own creations either. In 1723 John Macky, a Scottish spy for the British government who conducted a tour of his native land, visited Cambuskenneth Abbey near Stirling. 'It is now a heap of ruins, the stones being carried away by that Earl of Mar who turned protestant at the reformation to build his fine palace at Stirling; and the superstitious people give that for the reason why that palace has never had the luck to be inhabited.'[40]

According to Edmund Burt, an English engineer posted to Scotland in the 1720s, the Reformation also supposedly brought about a complete change in how the dead were treated; in describing the churchyard in Inverness, he notes that it is 'where, as is usual in Scotland, the monuments are placed against the wall that encloses it, because, to admit them into the church, would be an intolerable ornament'.[41] It is true, as noted above, that, once the medieval church had appropriated to itself the where and the how of burial, kings and nobles would command pride of place within the buildings whose construction and upkeep many of them had contributed to. The most obvious example is Dunfermline Abbey, founded by David I, who was then buried in front of its high altar. His successors and their families then took their places near him in a hierarchy that treated death in exactly the same way as life, with the obvious caveat that those that came later might find their desired spot already taken.

But, despite what Burt thought or the fact that the Reformation fathers ordained that everyone should be buried outside in ground selected for that purpose, those that could afford it were still able to spend their eternal rest within a church's four walls well into the nineteenth century. In the end, it seems to have been the health of the living that brought about a change of policy, resulting in the abandonment even of the burial aisles that various families had added on to their local kirks as a way round the prohibition. At Dairsie in Fife in 1845, it was noted that 'within these few years a vault was discovered in the east end of the church, near the pulpit, and found to contain coffins and bones being used as a place of interment. It is understood that this practice of burying in the inside of churches is in future to be done away with, as prejudicial to the health of
the sitters.'[42]

Standing in the ruins of Melrose Abbey in Roxburghshire or Inverlochy Castle in Argyll, it takes a considerable stretch of imagination to conjure up the vivid colouring and remarkable spectacle, the bustle and noise, not to mention the smell, in and around these remarkable buildings in the days when they were not open to the sky. Though many of these impressive medieval establishments, both lay* and ecclesiastical*, have survived in the landscape in some shape or form, they have long since lost their place at the heart of the communities that usually grew up around them.

Although castles themselves had begun to adapt, perhaps from as early as the thirteenth century, to an increasing desire on the part of their owners for privacy, there came a point when these great stone buildings could be adapted no longer. It was a long withdrawal that nonetheless gathered speed, like so much else, in the eighteenth century.

Now that there was little need for strong defences, the nobility generally preferred more elegant houses of modern design, either by remodelling their draughty old castles or starting afresh, perhaps in part because the Union of 1707 brought them into close contact with the kinds of buildings occupied by the nobility of England. Indeed, Macky the spy was at pains to make as many positive comparisons between the stately piles of his countrymen and those down south – the park of the palace of Yester in East Lothian was 'larger, as well walled and more regularly planted than Richmond in Surrey'; its hall and salon shared a gallery for music 'exactly as at Blenheim House in Woodstock'; the Duchess of Buccleuch's house at Smeaton, also in East Lothian, 'is as large as Ham [House near Richmond]'; nearby Dalkeith Palace 'is the very model of King William's Palace at Loo in Guelderland [this is William III of England and II of Scotland, who was originally Prince of Orange in the

Netherlands and married to Mary Stuart, daughter of James VII and II, whose throne he forcibly seized in 1688]; only that is of brick and this is of stone'; the royal apartments at Holyrood in Edinburgh are almost exactly like St James's Palace in London, and so on.[43] (Edmund Burt, the English surveyor who published his own journeys round Scotland a few years later, remarked somewhat cattily, but with some justification, that Macky's work 'might with more propriety be called, *A Journey to the Heralds Office*, and the *Seats of the Nobility and Gentry of North Britain*'.[44]) Their parks and pleasure-gardens – inspired initially by Louis XIV's extravagant geometric wonder at Versailles – were usually given at least as much attention as the house itself.

By the later eighteenth and nineteenth centuries, wealthy merchants and industrialists joined the aristocracy in building large country mansions well away from the noisy, insanitary conditions where they made their money and where their employees were forced to reside. But many in the twentieth century found that the upkeep of these large estates became impossible, especially once the government began to levy considerable taxes on the transfer of property on the death of its owner from 1894. Many great houses have thrown open their doors to the paying public, been bought for the nation or completely reinvented, often as hotels. Whichever, it is the hoi polloi – once deliberately kept at a safe distance – who have been the saving of them.

* * * *

He did not think there had been so many people in the world as in the city of Glasgow; and it was a great mystery to him to think what they could all design by living so many in one place. He wondered how they could all be furnished with provision; … and when he observed horses with shoes on their feet, and fastened with iron nails, he could not forbear laughing, and thought it was the most ridiculous thing that ever fell under his observation.[45]

A St Kilda man goes to Glasgow, c1695

The urban settlements of medieval Scotland were very different in scale and organisation from the ones that came before and, while much has changed since then, they still form the core of many villages, towns and cities down to the present day. To begin with, they grew up to cater for the needs of elite households, but soon developed as markets for craftsmen and merchants all over the lowlands from Dumfries in the south-west to Tain in Ross and Cromarty in the north-east. Attracting goods and customers from a wider hinterland and often importing and exporting commodities to and from Europe, such centres were a striking new phenomenon in the landscape, not least because of the plethora of roads and tracks that radiated from them, though it was usually rivers with access to the sea that provided the main thoroughfares.

Their continuing success was given official sanction and encouragement by the granting of burgh status, a legal framework for conducting trade introduced by David I in the twelfth century. By the later fourteenth century, the four main towns – Berwick, Roxburgh, Stirling and Edinburgh – formed a governing body over the rest. In 1357 the burghs' importance to the Scottish economy in general and crown finances (in the form of the Great Customs levied on trade) in particular was acknowledged by their permanent admittance to parliament as the third estate.[46] Burghs were technically abolished by local government reorganisation in 1975, but many remain proud of their historic origins.

The inhabitants of a burgh were not automatically burgesses; that term was restricted to merchants or craftsmen who could freely trade within its jurisdiction. They had to own property there in order to qualify and there was a roughly standard, if geographically variable, size to the burgess plots. They tended to be long and narrow, their width (and thus their fronts on the street side) based on the ancient units of pole or perch (c5.5m to 11.6m). Their gardens stretched behind them some considerable distance towards a back lane that marked the outer boundary of the settlement. The houses formed long terraces usually organised around a central market square or along the length of a broad main street that opened up into an even wider section for the market. A total of 482 burghs have been identified, including 70 royal burghs, with over half still forming a part, however small, of the current landscape.

Though we have lost many medieval settlements over the past few hundred years, as field systems requiring straight lines began to overtake them or landowners decided to obliterate them and build anew, large numbers can still be identified in the rural landscape, as well as in towns and cities that have long since spilled out of their earliest boundaries. You're likely to have found a medieval village or the original core of a town if you spot a collection of stone houses sitting somewhat randomly along the sides of roads, curving or straight, radiating from a central point, be it a church, main street or market square. Many are built in rows on an east–west axis to shelter them from the prevailing wind and tend to be situated on higher ground to avoid the perennial problem of flooding. The oldest surviving houses are traditionally harled with small windows, again to keep the winds at bay.

Sometimes they are heavily disguised. In the nineteenth century there was a tendency to replace the old structures with new houses with larger windows, but still on the original site. In some places the original back plots are also still there, accessed via a back lane. The western end of the village of Freuchie in Fife centred on its High Street is still essentially medieval in plan, even if the buildings themselves have mostly been rebuilt and extra ones inserted in between. General Roy's maps, compiled between 1747 and 1755, contain valuable evidence for what has been lost, though some places occasionally make their presence felt as cropmarks.

Of those that have disappeared, the most striking has to be Roxburgh, which was a major trading centre second only to Berwick (which acted as its port) in the Middle Ages. Fought over during the wars with England and vulnerable to the vagaries of the wool trade supplying the cloth manufacturers of the Low Countries, Roxburgh died a death when Berwick was permanently annexed by the southern kingdom in 1482. The remains of its impressive and majestic castle – called Marchmont – can still be found, while the outline of the town's streets and houses and rubbish pits are sometimes still visible as cropmarks. They were investigated by *Time Team* in 2003.[47]

By 1707, when the parliaments of Scotland and England were united at Westminster, Edinburgh was well established as the capital city, the recognised centre of government, though the removal of the royal court to London on the accession of the Scottish king, James VI, to the throne of England (as James I) in 1603 had deprived it of some of its pomp and splendour. On the other hand, access to England's colonies after the Union of 1707 was to prove the making of Glasgow, which remained a relatively small city until the mid eighteenth century. The impact of these singularly Scottish political developments is hard to gauge, though, as always, there were winners and losers.

Despite losing kudos and economic opportunity as the seat of government, Edinburgh continued to impress visitors, who were both wowed by the original Old Town and incredulous at its physical limitations. We can almost feel the open-mouthed wonder of John Taylor, the English 'Water Poet', when, in 1618, he 'descended lower to the City, wherein observed the fairest and goodliest street that ever eyes beheld, for I did never see or hear of a street of that length …'. Though he was less taken with the merchants and tradesmen's houses on the High Street, he was certainly pleased with the gentlemen's mansions down the adjoining lanes: 'the walls are eight or ten foot thick, exceeding strong, not built for a day, a week, or a month, or a year; but from antiquity to posterity, for many ages'.

Nevertheless, Taylor expressed his dissatisfaction – often repeated by others – at the city's location, lamenting that it was not built towards the shore at Leith only one mile distant, whereby it would soon have 'been comparable to many a one of our greatest towns and cities in Europe, both for spaciousness of bounds, port, state, and riches'. Using Leith as its port had never been a drawback for Edinburgh before and the problem was less the lack of direct access to the sea and more the fact that it would be 150 years before the city finally broke out of its medieval walls, despite a rising population, which forced the inhabitants to build their houses ever higher. The poet, continuing his penniless journey round Scotland on foot, also noted that Perth, although a 'fine town', was nonetheless 'much decayed, by reason of the want of his Majesty's yearly

Kilconquhar, Fife
The houses which front the main street, with their narrow strips of land, reveal the village's medieval origins.
HES, DP227151

coming to lodge there' after the departure of the court to London in 1603.[48]

Most towns, however, were tiny by today's standards, little more than villages even by 1700. Maybole, in Ayrshire, for example, was just a couple of streets with vennels (alleys) in between. It was, however, equipped with a green, probably near its medieval castle, where there 'is a pleasant plot of ground enclosed around with an earthen wall wherein they were wont to play at football but now at the golf and Byasse bowls'.[49]

Montrose, a port on the east coast north of Dundee, was essentially only one street, but its suburbs were the site of constant building – 'not just houses, but kilns, malthouses and corn granaries' – which it was thought would soon rival the original town.[50] In the south-west, Dumfries, too, was thriving in the early eighteenth century, a situation imputed by the writer and government spy Daniel Defoe, who visited Scotland in the 1720s, squarely on the Union and its trading opportunities.

But he also admitted that not every burgh was proving able to take advantage of it. Further west Kirkcudbright was in the doldrums, as were the rest of the ports all the way up to Ayr, with its 'fine river' and 'handsome stone bridge'. The exception was Irvine, also in Ayrshire, despite being a harder harbour to access. As a result it could boast 'two handsome streets, a good key [quay], and not only room in the harbour for a great many ships, but a great many ships in it also'.

It was a similar story of decline from former glories intermingled with the odd success on the east coast south of Dundee. With the exception of Kirkcaldy – 'one street running along the shore, from east to west, for a long mile and very well built, the streets clean and well pav'd; there are some small by-streets or lanes, and it has some considerable merchants in it' – the Fife ports were in a shocking state. Dysart was 'a most lamentable

Hopetoun House, West Lothian

Begun in 1699, Hopetoun House was magnificently expanded from the 1720s by the famous Scottish architect William Adam and his sons, John and Robert. What followed was the transformation of a traditional country seat with an extensive designed landscape into a palace which was dubbed the Scottish Versailles. HES, DP107101

object of a miserable, dying Corporation', an impression corroborated a year or so earlier by John Macky: it 'has been by its buildings a celebrated town, but now like Pisa in Italy: the structures remain, but hardly a glass window, or any furniture in any of the houses … however their streets are all pav'd with stone';[51] Buckhaven was 'a miserable row of cottage-like buildings, and people altogether meer fishermen'.

Even the cities had their low-quality housing well away from their splendid civic centres. Edmund Burt, who also came to Scotland in the 1720s, noted that 'the extreme parts of the town [Inverness] are made up of most miserably low, dirty hovels, faced and covered with turf, with a bottomless tub, or basket, in the roof for a chimney'; while 'Even the best sort of street houses, in all the great towns of the low country, are, for the most part contrived after one manner, with a staircase withoutside, either round or square, which leads to each floor …'

Nevertheless, the largest towns – Edinburgh, Glasgow, Perth, Dundee, Aberdeen, Linlithgow in West Lothian and, a little grudgingly, Stirling and Inverness – received a largely positive report from Defoe on the state of their broad, clean streets, their well-built stone houses and, most importantly, their civic buildings (such as market places and tollbooths*). He reserved his particular admiration for Perth – found to be on the way down by Taylor in 1618 – which had been 'unhappily' at the heart of the Jacobite* rebellion in 1715, 'but I cannot say it was unhappy for the town: For the townsmen got so much money by both parties [the Jacobites and the government] that they are evidently enrich'd by it … particularly a new Tolbooth or Town-hall … The town was well built before, but now has almost a new face; … here are abundance of new houses, and more of old houses new fitted and repair'd which look like new.'

Defoe's experiences led him to think through the problems that Scotland faced in modernising its commercial foundations and he drew a conclusion that some later native writers would also suggest held the nation back when it came to overhauling its agricultural methods.

…'tis evident [these sea-port towns] have made a much better figure in former times, owing to the removing of the court and nobility of Scotland to England; for it is

most certain, when the court was at home, they had a confluence of strangers, residence of foreign ministers, being of armies, etc and consequently the nobility dwelt at home, spent the income of their estates, and the product of their country among their neighbours.[52]

It was not that simple, for there were many urban centres and, later, estates, which managed to modernise despite the lack of a resident nobility, who, seeing at first-hand what was happening in England, might therefore bring back new ideas to Scotland; equally those landowners who still lived at home did not always provide the kind of support likely to help those beneath them to take advantage of developments after 1707. It is hard to generalise; all we can say for sure is that the eighteenth century would herald dramatic changes for both town and country.

* * * *

[Near Edzell, Angus] I lay at an Irish house, the folks not being able to speak scarce any English, but I supped and went to bed, where I had not laid long, but I was enforced to rise, I was so stung with Irish musquitoes, a creature that hath six legs, and lives like a monster altogether upon man's flesh, they do inhabit and breed most in sluttish houses, and this house was none of the cleanest.[53]

John Taylor
The Pennyless Pilgrimage, 1618

A quite different story surrounds Highland settlements, even those that surely congregated around castles, because there were almost no towns or burghs and scarcely any that could be described even as villages. Few places there today have medieval origins, partly because – as at Inveraray in Argyll – they have been rebuilt elsewhere, or because they didn't exist in the first place. There certainly were settlements; it's just hard to find them on the ground now.

Indeed, the organic, intrinsically temporary nature of most Scottish homes beyond the burghs and the big elite complexes means that we often have far less to find for the period during and immediately after the Middle Ages than for more ancient times. It does not help that, in many cases, later structures were built immediately on top of flimsy, older ones.

In Perthshire the archaeological evidence suggests that prehistoric sites such as hill-forts in the uplands were re-occupied by people in the early Middle Ages (cAD 800), but eventually changes we can only guess at led to these uplands being turned into summer grazing grounds. The basic pattern of rural settlement became scattered townships or small hamlets lying beside large, open strip fields undefended from wind and rain by hedge or tree and within reach of moors or hills for pasturing animals. There is also considerable evidence for the splitting of farms or townships well before the major changes of the eighteenth and nineteenth centuries, probably due to population pressure.[54] This was no static, moribund society, but one that already made a tremendous impact on the landscape.

After 1500 we have a few descriptions of the inside and the outside of ordinary houses that suggest some similarities with later centuries. The historian and scholar George Buchanan was a big fan of the health benefits of natural materials, writing in 1582 in tones worthy of a luxury bedding advert today that the people of the Hebrides:

… lie upon the ground; strewing fern, or heath, upon the floor, with the roots downwards and the leaves turned up. In this manner they form a bed so pleasant, that it may vie in softness with the finest down, while in salubrity it far exceeds it; for heath, naturally possessing the power of absorption, drinks up the superfluous moisture, and restores strength to the fatigued nerves, so that those who lie down languid and weary in the evening, arise in the morning vigorous and sprightly.[55]

As we will see, this is not an opinion usually shared by later commentators.

A century after Buchanan, Martin Martin described houses on the island of Ronay off North Uist in the Outer Hebrides in terms that would not have been inappropriate much later still, noting that 'every tenant has his dwelling-house, a barn, a house where their best effects are preserved, a house for their cattle, and a porch on each side of the door to keep off the rain or snow. Their houses are built with stone, and thatched with straw, which is kept down with ropes of the same, posed with stones.'[56] Ronay is now uninhabited but there is evidence for at least 22 buildings in and around what has been described as the township of Buaile-mhor.[57]

However, his voyage round the Outer Hebrides brought Martin sight of dwellings that even he, a native of Skye, found suggestive of 'extreme poverty'. And yet the houses of St Kilda sound as if they followed the same basic model as those on Ronay, stone-built, their thatched roofs weighted down with heavy stones, 'of a low form, having all the doors to the north-east, both on purpose to secure them from the shocks of the tempest of the south-west winds.'[58] When we have accounts written only by visitors to a particular community, we must be careful not to presume that what they believed to be essential for a comfortable life was automatically shared by the natives. The people of St Kilda built their houses to accommodate the conditions they found themselves in and they were not necessarily as poverty-stricken as they seemed, *choosing*, for example, to 'lie on straw, although they have plenty of down and feathers'.[59]

Nevertheless, it was Martin Martin who witnessed the gobsmacked reaction of the St Kildan who visited Glasgow quoted above, a passage that ended with a remark that foretells the difficult choice facing many remote communities between ties to home and hearth and the material wealth that many soon discovered was available elsewhere: 'He longed to see his native country again, and passionately wished it were blessed with ale, brandy, tobacco and iron, as Glasgow was.'[60]

There is, however, one type of housing that connects the more recent past both to the Middle Ages and indeed, in terms of seasonal migration, to our earliest predecessors. Shielings were the temporary dwellings inhabited by at least some members of the surrounding communities during the summer months, when they moved with their beasts up into higher ground in search of better grass and to preserve the growing crops from hungry mouths. It is an ancient form of animal husbandry found across the globe and known formally as transhumance.

The history of shielings is, however, curiously divided between Highlands and Lowlands. The practice of transhumance was common in the Lowlands from the twelfth century, but had died out by the seventeenth century at the latest (though place-names, such as Galashiels in Selkirkshire, memorialise their former presence). In contrast, shielings were not established in the north and west until they were already disappearing in the south and east, despite the fact that animals played such a crucial role in the Highland economy.

Excavation of shieling sites on Loch Tayside in Perthshire, which date from at least the fifteenth century, have found both oval and rectilinear forms in use at the same time, the former perhaps explained as temporary structures for stashing things like cheese or peat (and possibly even children!), compared with the latter more enduring, inhabited ones.[61] Thomas Pennant provides us with a charming, if condescending, peek at the shielings of 'some peasants who attend the herds of milk cows' when he crossed the island of Jura in the Inner Hebrides in 1772.

These formed a grotesque group; some were oblong, many conic, and so low that entrance is forbidden, without creeping through the little opening, which has no other door than a faggot of birch twits, placed there occasionally: they are constructed of branches of trees, covered with sods; the furniture a bed of heath, placed on a bank of sod; two blankets and a rug; some dairy vessels, and above, certain pendent shelves made of basket work, to hold the cheese, the produce of the summer. In one of the little conic huts, I spied a little infant asleep, under the protection of a faithful dog.[62]

The remains of more than 6,000 shielings have been found and recorded, 1,700 of them in groups of more than five huts. Given that they have, at one time or another, been everywhere, they are to be found everywhere, but we are most likely to come across them now in the Highlands and Islands (especially Lewis in the Outer Hebrides, where they were later turned into permanent settlements) and the Cairngorm and Grampian mountains in the north-east (Shetland, despite being an upland landscape, doesn't have any because the peat grew too deep where they would otherwise naturally have been situated).

They are almost always located near a stream or other water-source essential for both animals and people, and likely to produce better grass. If made entirely of turf, they are given away only by particularly vibrant patches of grass; but if the

Blackhouses, Eilean a'Ghiorr, North Uist, 1906
Though these blackhouses (*tigh dubh* in Gaelic) on the tiny island of Eilean a' Ghiorr probably date only from the nineteenth century, their basic structure reflects a far more ancient system of living and working, including the open hearth and housing of animals next to the family living quarters. HES, SC746292

turf was set on stone footings, these are often still embedded in the ground. Since shielings were regularly rebuilt in and around the same place, there are often considerable remains to be found.

Dorothy Wordsworth enjoyed her experience of discovering shielings just as much as I did nearly 200 years later. She and her brother were travelling south from Glendochart towards Loch Katrine in Stirlingshire with a Highland guide when:

> … *we were passing, without notice, a heap of scattered stones round which was a belt of grass – green, and, as it seemed, rich, where all else was either poor heather and coarse grass, or unprofitable rushes and spongy moss. The highlander made a pause, saying, 'This place is much changed since I was last here twenty years ago.' He told us that the heap of stones had been a hut where a family was then living, who had their winter habitation in the valley and brought their goats thither in the summer to feed on the mountains and that they were used to gather them together at night and morning to be milked close to the door, which was the reason why the grass was yet so green near the stones. It was affecting in that solitude to meet with this memorial of manners passed away; we looked around for some other traces of humanity, but nothing else could we find in that place. We ourselves espied another of those ruins, much more extensive – the remains, as the man told us, of several dwellings.*[63]

Miss Wordsworth continued to shieling-spot along the banks of Loch Katrine; after that she was back in the Lowlands and had to give it up.

It was unusual for there to be but one shieling. Like so many of the physical remains before

Catherine MacDonald, Morar, Inverness-shire, c1905

This early twentieth century photograph shows Mrs MacDonald calling to her hens at feeding time. The out house is built in the same manner as the blackhouses – stone walls without lime mortar and a weighted-down thatched roof.

National Museums Scotland, licensor Scran

the later eighteenth century, they testify to the communal nature of life, which, though hard, was certainly not lonely. A most romantic description of a trip to the summer grazings is recorded in *The Lairds of Glenlyon*, written some 80 years after Dorothy Wordsworth passed nearby, but supposedly referring back to 1727 (and so carries a reliability health warning, though the essence of it, including the carrying with them of household items, is corroborated elsewhere):

June was the time for the second and more universal flitting. The young women and children, and a few old men to keep all in order, accompanied the herds; most of the matrons and grown-up males remained at home for the harvest work. It was a happy day of bustle and anticipation that for setting out to the sheilings. The old men and boys, driving the cattle, went first. The girls followed guiding or leading horses, laden with their household goods, churns, cheese-presses, crocks, dairy utensils of all shapes and sizes, but mostly all of one material, birchwood pots, crooks, small bags of meal, and old hose metamorphosed into salt-cellars, in short, the whole household goods and gear of the mountain hut, and that was not bulky, for one horse carried it, and perhaps on the top of all, the presiding deity, the laughing maid, with ribbon or snood round her long twining tresses, who proudly anticipates her temporary rule over beast and man, and the joyful greeting from friends in the neighbouring sheiling.[64]

There were benefits for the ground too, of a kind that has only recently come to be appreciated once more. In Sutherland it was noted in the 1790s that the grass near the shielings 'is richly variegated with clover, daisies, and other valuable grasses and wild

A History of Scotland's Landscapes

Arnisdale, Inverness-shire, c1898
The township of Arnisdale stretched along the shore of Loch Hourn. By this time a new type of housing had begun to appear – the 'white house' (or *tigh geal* in Gaelic), with lime mortar and slate roofs. However, the older blackhouses still visible nearer to the shoreline provide us with a glimpse of a community in transition, although we should be careful about judging the traditional accommodation, as so many visiting commentators did. HES, SC748658

flowers'.[65] Such contributions to biodiversity would soon be condemned by the Improvers as 'weeds' and resolutely extirpated.

Highland transhumance continued into the nineteenth century (even the twentieth century on the isle of Lewis), but many shielings had already been abandoned as these ancient hill pastures were turned over to large-scale cattle droving and, most particularly, sheep-farming. This was one of the many new and improved approaches to agriculture, based on scientific methods and, to begin with at least, heavily influenced by what was already happening in England. Though Improvement* encompasses a vast array of activities introduced at different times in different places, one of its most profound impacts was on settlement patterns across the country. Time and again those describing the effects of Improvement mention, often with profound misgiving, the numbers of people from first the Lowlands and then the Highlands who were either forced into the growing towns and cities or overseas as farms were amalgamated into much larger holdings held by just one tenant.

* * * *

… but on reaching the small village of Ayton [Berwickshire], the scene was greatly altered; the wretched cottages, or rather the hovels of the country, were vanishing; good comfortable houses arise in their stead; the lands are enclosing, and yield very good barley, oats, and clover; the banks are planting: I speak in the present tense; for there is still a mixture of the old negligence left amidst

Mission House, Coll, Inner Hebrides, c1898
This Mission House is typical of cottages throughout rural Scotland during this period. Usually built by farmers and fishermen, their neat walls and roofs provided a marked contrast to earlier housing. HES, SC740706

the recent improvements, which look like the works of a new colony in a wretched impoverished country.[66]

Thomas Pennant
A Tour in Scotland and Voyage to the Hebrides, 1769

In the two hundred years between 1700 and 1900, Scotland's population increased from around 1 million to nearly 4.5 million,[67] putting even more pressure on the subsistence* agriculture that lingered in some parts of the country. In 1782 the potato crop failed, grain refused to ripen and cattle died, causing a severe famine in many areas. Dredging up deep-seated memories of the 'Seven Ill Years' of the 1690s, this famine was known as *Bliàdhna na peasrach* (pease-meal year), and prompted many from the Highlands to seek work in the south as day-labourers or domestic servants (though the effects were felt in the Lowlands too).[68] For those promoting the radically different methods of Improvement agriculture, 1782 underscored the urgent need to move away from subsistence and depressingly regular food shortages.

The potential for improvement was not restricted to agriculture, however, as voices were raised in protest against the huts and cottages occupied by much of the rural population. It proved very easy for visitors and even local commentators to condemn these 'hovels'; when they were found in the Highlands, racial stereotyping by Lowlanders and the English was another factor in the near-universal condemnation, to the point that Thomas Pennant was astonished, on entering one of these turf dwellings, at the politeness of the owner and his wife.[69]

In truth, however, as late as the 1790s there was not always much difference between the design of houses in the Highlands and the Lowlands – in Kilmarnock in Ayrshire farmers still lived with their animals, their quarters separated only by a wooden partition, and slept on the dirt floor, with their roofs liable to catch fire or be blown off; at Maybole, also in Ayrshire, the schoolhouse was an 'old mean thatched house'; at Libberton in Lanarkshire the cottages and even some of the farmhouses were 'fitter for the habitation of beasts than of human beings'. On the other hand, stone houses had been newly built at Rannoch in Highland Perthshire instead of the old 'stake and rice'* huts.[70] Even where walls were rebuilt in stone, roofs might still be thatched since slates – and the timber frames to place them on – were expensive or hard to come by.

It would be a mistake, however, to imagine that these 'huts' were constructed in such an apparently rudimentary fashion only because the occupants knew no better. For a start, they were often built 'on some rising rocky spot at the foot of a hill, secure from any burn or springs that might descend upon them from the mountains; and, thus situated, they are pretty safe from inundations from above or below, and other ground they cannot spare from their corn.'[71] There was also a lot more to them than mere speed or ease of construction. In 1833 the minister of Stornoway on Lewis described the homes of many of his rural parishioners in the usual terms – 'indescribably filthy'. And yet he goes on to detail the logic behind their design, which, despite his sometimes scathing tone, implies considerable ingenuity:

Where a sufficient supply of stones can be found, the walls of the houses are from 4 to 6 feet thick, and consist of an outer and inner face, the intervening space being crammed with earth or pounded moss. … The thatch, in general, is made of stubble or potato stalks which are spread on the scanty wooden roof, and bound by heather or straw ropes, which again are … fastened by stones called anchors, resting on the top of the broad wall. On this wall it is no unusual sight to see sheep and calves feeding. … The thatch is not expected at first to keep out much rain … but to compensate for this defect, the inmates are practical chemists; they keep plenty of peats on the fire; … the smoke and increasing heat repel the rain … by evaporation. These houses, after a smart shower, appear like so many salt pans or breweries in operation.*[72]

These Lewis folk were clearly ahead of their time – I have seen sheep grazing on the grass roof of a rather nice farmshop and café on the A66 between Penrith and Scotch Corner. And this was not the end of the ingenuity; every summer, the soot-soaked thatch was taken off and 'carefully carried' to the growing crops of potato or barley, on which it was spread. The minister admitted that this 'gives a wonderful stimulus to the vegetation', but warned that 'the soot, as an excessive stimulant, is doubtless injurious to the soil'. In fact, it is still used by some gardeners today.[73]

The horror that so many commentators felt towards Scottish houses overlooked the fact that they were designed to be as warm as possible in the face of Atlantic gales and cold, damp winters. This, as much as any principled attachment to 'ancient prejudices and mistaken ideas', explains why there was resistance to, for example, moving their animals into separate accommodation, or even to putting up partitions between them.[74] In essence, these houses were cheap, making use of local materials, and it was a simple and pleasant enough matter for communal elbow-grease to put them up:

[Dornock, Dumfriesshire, 1792] The farm-houses in general and all the cottages are built of mud or clay; yet these houses, when plastered and properly finished within … are exceedingly warm and comfortable … In the first place, they dig out the foundation of the house, and lay a row or two of stones, then they procure, from a pit contiguous, as much clay or brick-earth as is sufficient to form the walls: and … upon a day appointed, the whole neighbourhood, male and female, to the number of 20 or 30, assemble, each with a dung-fork or spade, or some such instrument. Some fall to working the clay or mud, by mixing it with straw; others carry the materials; and 4 or 6 of the most experienced hands build and take care of the walls. In this manner, the walls of the house are finished within a few hours; after which they retire to a good dinner and plenty of drink which is provided them, where they have music and dance with which, and other marks of festivity, they conclude the evening. This is called a daubing, and in this way they make a frolic of what would otherwise by a very dirty and disagreeable job.[75]

For many, the new stone houses were cold, cheerless places, especially without a cheap, easy supply of fuel. (Though I can't help wondering what the move away from communal living – everyone, from cows to kids, sleeping in the same room – to separate bedrooms might have done for the sex lives of most adults. Not that they seemed to have a problem before.)

This is not meant to imply that there were no improvements to be made in the housing of much of the rural population – apart from anything else, though these turf houses were wonderfully cosy, they were also a breeding ground for flies and bacteria, and they must have been hellish to live in for anyone with a chest complaint. But, given that leases were either non-existent or extremely short and that there was no such thing as a mortgage in our sense of the word, building more substantial houses was often neither practicable (because the inhabitants might not retain possession when leases shortly came to be renewed) nor possible (they did not have the capital to invest in such an expense). The Duke of Sutherland found his attempt to keep his people from emigrating through a house-building programme at Tongue in the far north scuppered by the fact that 'the houses were upon a scale far too expensive for [his tenants'] slender means.'[76]

If landowners wanted housing to improve, then they had to find a way to advance the capital; they also needed to feu* the land on which new housing might sit, so that the house owner had more or less permanent possession of it. Some landowners did put their money into such improvements, but others were only interested in siphoning off a share of any increasing wealth without doing anything to encourage the enterprise that produced it.

Dorothy Wordsworth began to understand that things weren't necessarily as simple as she first thought when her friend Coleridge, on seeing yet another miserable cottage on Loch Lomondside in Dunbartonshire, which 'admitted the rain at the door and retained it in the hollows of the mud floor…', told the lady of the house how easy it would be to remove these inconveniences and to contrive something, at least, to prevent the wind from entering at the window-places, if not a glass window for light and warmth. The woman replied that this was very true, but if they made any improvements the laird would conclude that they were growing rich, and raise their rent.[77]

The only way to increase living standards, it was generally agreed by university men and the land managers they taught, was by allowing individuals to own their farms and run them for profit, which could then be reinvested in further improvements, whether this was crop types and their rotations, breeding stock or field systems. The days of communal living were coming to an end. The old runrig* system of unenclosed strips of land vulnerable to wandering animals had to go, and with it the clusters of homes or the dispersed townships of those who farmed them.

The clearing of the uplands for sheep began in the Border hillsides (and especially the vast Buccleuch estates that stretched from Dumfriesshire to Liddesdale in Roxburghshire) in the seventeenth century. Two centuries later, the practice had reached Sutherland in the very north of the Scottish mainland. In the 1720s Daniel Defoe noted that the gentlemen of Galloway were 'the greatest sheep-masters in Scotland, (so they call themselves) and the greatest breeders of black cattle and horses'.[78] But they could only become so by placing the hillsides into the care of a few shepherds and their dogs rather than the tenants and their families who once worked together to control their beasts.

From the middle decades of the eighteenth century, a similar story began to play out in earnest down on the valley floors, as arable land was consolidated into single farms, forcing many tenants and cottars* to find employment elsewhere or move away from agriculture altogether. At the same time, the gathering pace of technological innovation brought about an increase in both the type and the scale of industrial activity, even in sectors like coal-mining that had been practised for centuries. These industries needed men, women and often even children to help them expand.

Those farmers with sufficient capital to become the sole tenants of the amalgamated farms – especially with encouragement from their landlords – were in the vanguard of a revolution that would reshape the entire landscape, much of which we have inherited today. Though the main focus was on the way that agriculture was practised, Improvement encompassed just about anything that scientific enquiry might have an answer to, including how to create more substantial farm-houses and the outbuildings that would support the new improved methods of cultivation.

As we have already seen, farmers throughout Scotland traditionally lived in houses very similar to those of their landless neighbours. Now some of

Scarp, Outer Hebrides

The uninhabited island of Scarp lies off the coast of Harris. It once had a population of around 200 people, but the last of them left in 1970. This image clearly shows the remains of the nineteenth century crofting township. Across the north and west, these remains pay silent testimony to the scale of depopulation over the last two centuries.

HES, DP110773

the new sole tenants began to build much better accommodation, though it was a slow process due to a lack of capital. Even at the end of the eighteenth century, it was often a question of finding a better method of roofing – slates were viewed as ideal, but they were often too expensive, so proper thatch (with straw and mortar or clay, rather than reeds or turf) was recommended.

However, where the landowner was willing and able to put his hand in his own pocket, change could come quickly – Mr Scott of Gala in Selkirkshire had, for example, commissioned six new farmhouses with 'complete office buildings', as well as 'thirty-two good dwelling houses' in the village of Galashiels by 1792. Building in stone was deemed best, with lime mortar, bringing a new demand for quarries. Such farmhouses had, often for the first time, more than one storey, as well as tile or slate roofs, all of which had the desired effect of looking 'neat and commodious'. Large numbers of the older 'mean' houses were pulled down to help to create 'a decent appearance.'

Good farm-steadings were also part of this drive for substantial neatness, though they were not yet necessarily built in the courtyard style, but might be out in the middle of the holding (though some were adjacent to one another so that they seemed 'almost as large as a small village or hamlet'). Even the Duke of Argyll had his stables, outhouses and farmhouses 'in different parts of the ground behind the Castle', much to the disgust of Dorothy Wordsworth, who found them 'broad, out-spreading, fantastic and unintelligible buildings'.

She did, however, approve of those farmhouses she found beyond Roslin in Midlothian, which resembled 'those of the farming counties of England'. She noted, too, that, in contrast to the large numbers of huts scattered throughout the glens that she found in the Highlands, here the farmhouses were 'at a considerable distance from each other', a pattern that would eventually become standard.[79] While Miss Wordsworth seems to have found beauty in familiarity and a heartfelt belief in the efficacy of English methods, there were many in Scotland who lamented the derelict cottages and the steady flow of people away from the land of their ancestors (though the writers were not usually the ones who left).

In the decades after 1800, the spirit of Improvement turned most farmhouses and their outbuildings in the Lowlands and parts of the Highlands into stone; slate roofs were also becoming common, though at Caskieben and Dyce in Aberdeenshire, the landowner built his farmhouses in the 'cottage ornée' style, which was more common in England as part of the Romantic movement, harking back to older rustic ways (including thatched roofs). Here the farm outbuildings were arranged 'in the figure of a square', with their threshing mills* attached, a configuration that would spread across the country.[80]

The story of Improvement, despite the general optimism that anything could be overcome with the right attitude, industry and investment, was far from an unmitigated success. Many farms failed and were abandoned, partly because there was in fact a limit to what the ground could sustain in more marginal areas of Galloway, Ayrshire, North Lanarkshire, Argyll, Caithness and the Outer Hebrides, not least once an international grain market began to open up from the 1870s, making competition even fiercer.

Elsewhere, in the good farming areas, the trend has been to create ever larger farms with ever bigger fields, especially once many labour- and time-intensive agricultural activities became mechanised in the twentieth century. The kind of social upheaval described by those who witnessed the first flush of Improvement, when the communal system was dismantled and farms amalgamated, happened again, but this time we can hear directly from those who experienced it. During his trip round Scotland in 1934, the poet Edwin Muir met up with some friends, who were farmers in Angus. They described to him what they had witnessed in the decades since 1900:

Before that the servants on a farm were more or less members of a family and ate in the kitchen at one long table along with their master and mistress. In the larger farms this has now completely changed, and my friends put this down partly to the increased commercialisation of farming, and partly to such mechanical devices as the motor-car, the use of which automatically translates the man who owns it into a different world from other people.

But one of the most eloquent expressions of yet another dying world can be found in Lewis Grassic Gibbon's classic 1932 novel, *Sunset Song*, which, along with the other books in his A Scots Quair trilogy, is an elegy to the disappearance of the sights, sounds and smells of the author's rural childhood, the loss of an entire way of life.

Blawearie hadn't had a tenant for nearly a year, but now there was one on the way … The biggins of it stood fine and compact one side of the close, the midden was back of them and across the close was the house, a fell brave house for a little place, it had three storeys and a good kitchen and a fair stretch of garden between it and Blawearie road. There were beech trees there, three of them, one was close over against the house, and the garden hedges grew as bonny with honeysuckle of a summer as ever you saw; and if you could have lived on the smell of honeysuckle you might have farmed the bit place with profit.

This was an Improvement farm, with a good farmhouse, hedges and trees. But its day too was almost done. According to Grassic Gibbon, 'We are repeating here what the border men did in Badenoch and the Highlands – eating away the land and the crofter, killing off the peasant as surely as in Russia …'[81]

There is another quiet social revolution going on these days; where once surplus farmhouses and steadings would fall into ruin, now they are viewed as prime real estate for urban dwellers seeking the peace and quiet of the countryside. In a village like mine, founded two hundred years ago to provide housing for agricultural workers and associated trades needed by the surrounding estates, very few people work on the land anymore and most commute, sometimes considerable distances. And yet the farming goes on.

* * * *

The old people remember double the number of ploughs in the parish than are at present; and the ruins of demolished cottages are to be seen in every corner … Since 1760 the plan, in this country, has been to destroy the villages and cottages and throw the lands into as few hands as possible … Some defend this plan by asserting … the people [are] only changing the country for the town. But it ought to be considered, that towns never supply themselves with inhabitants … It is a truth generally admitted that, in large cities, fewer children come into the world, and immensely fewer arrive at maturity, than in the country …[82]

Old Statistical Account, Libberton and Quothquan, South Lanarkshire, 1792

As Improvement took hold, many landowners did not, in fact, want to lose the labour on their estates and employed a number of strategies to keep their people housed and occupied. One such was planned villages for both agricultural and industrial purposes (coal-mining, fishing and textiles). Between 1700 and 1840 two hundred of them were founded, replacing or adding to older communities. Many tiny places began to expand and flourish because landowners were prepared to feu the land for new housing.[83]

Most were situated around the coast or across the central belt. Larkhall in Lanarkshire, Newton Stewart in Wigtownshire, Dalswinton, Wanlockhead and Leadhills in Dumfriesshire, Straiton in Ayrshire, Newtyle in Angus, Buckie in Moray, Macduff in Banffshire, Tobermory on Mull in the Inner Hebrides and Ullapool in Ross and Cromarty are a few examples of villages entirely or partly laid out in this period, often on a far more regular pattern (both streets and houses) than what might have been there already.

These new settlements were mainly built in stone, though they were not always good quality – the miners' houses in Wanlockhead were described as 'huts, all alike and all thatched' as late as 1804, though a greater number in neighbouring Leadhills were more substantial.[84] Some, like Turriff in Aberdeenshire and Hamilton in South Lanarkshire, grew to be significant towns in their own right, while others were abandoned and have since disappeared. In the 1770s the old village of Eaglesham in East Renfrewshire was completely replaced by a new one at the instigation of the landowner, the Earl of Eglinton, earning a reputation – at least according to its minister – as ' one of the most delightful places in Great Britain':

It consists of two rows of houses opposite to, and distant from each other thirty-two falls (about 200 yards). Down the middle of that space runs a small rivulet

to which there is a gentle descent from each row … and the whole area on each side of the rivulet consists of grass for the use of the inhabitants. There they may bleach their linen etc etc but no cattle are allowed to graze or tread on it. A number of fine trees planted along both sides of the rivulet adds to the beauty of the scene.

A cotton mill was built by the Glasgow firm Maclean and Brodie at the higher end of the stream in the 1790s; in 1840 there were 400 weavers living in the village besides the cotton spinners at the mill.[85] The outline of this new creation can easily be found on the ground today along with at least part of the area allocated to each family in quarter acres to grow crops and vegetables. These allotments were typical of planned villages, though most elsewhere were between two and four acres each. One of their most attractive features must have been the way that these villages brought together most things that their inhabitants might need, from places of worship and employment to shops and hotels, a feature still obvious in north-east planned villages like Tomintoul in Banffshire and Fochabers in Moray, and Inveraray in the west.

Inevitably, however, these brand new settlements began to show signs of wear and tear and failed to meet changing expectations, not least in comfort and sanitation. And so they too were replaced. Fortingall in Perthshire, which had its origins in the Middle Ages, was re-established as a planned agricultural village. However, it was again rebuilt in the 1890s – on the same layout – in an Arts and Crafts style that remains attractive today, not least because of the thatched roofs of some of the houses, the reintroduction of which would no doubt have perplexed and appalled our friend Dorothy

Ullapool, 1988

The grid-like layout of Ullapool reveals its origins as an early planned village. Prior to the Jacobite rebellion, there does not seem to have been a pier, jetty or even community in the vicinity. However, following the governmental road-building efforts, in 1787 the area's commercial potential came to the attention of the British Fisheries Society. Having purchased a 1,300-acre site, the Society hoped to discourage emigration by attracting the Highland population to the new port.
HES NCAP

Wordsworth, and numerous contributors to the *Statistical Accounts*.

Planned villages were not the only form of social engineering employed by landowners to attempt to stem the flow of people to the towns and the colonies. Smallholdings were another way to deal with tenants and farm workers surplus to requirements following the amalgamation of agricultural holdings. Landowners also became used to the idea of giving returning soldiers a livelihood at the end of a number of wars from the mid eighteenth to the mid twentieth century, though such attempts to mop up redundant labour met with a mixed degree of success.

Crofting is the most famous form of Scottish smallholding, because of its association with the whole terrible experience of clearance from Highland estates. Crofts in fact have a medieval origin and were to be found far more often – at least in terms of official documentation – in the Lowlands. They were often associated with the word 'toft' – the site of a house – and the term means 'a piece of enclosed land, or small field, used for tillage or pasture',[86] in other words, a smallholding. There could be large numbers of them in one place and, though we rarely catch a glimpse of their size, Turner's Croft lying next to Dundrennan Abbey, Kirkcudbrightshire, was said to be roughly four acres.

Indeed, crofts are so ubiquitous in the written records of medieval and early modern land transactions as to imply that almost everyone had one (even if the owners did not always farm themselves, but received income from those who lived and worked on them) and that their precise definition is hard to pin down.[87] It's a similar story with another medieval hang-over – the marvellous term 'pendicle' that originally meant a piece of land or other property regarded as subsidiary to a main estate[88] and found pretty much all over Scotland. In more recent centuries, however, it has come to denote a smallholding almost entirely restricted to Perthshire.

The history of crofts after their early pervasive presence as Lowland smallholdings diverged, depending on which part of the country we are talking about. In much of the Highlands, crofting townships – houses and other buildings spread out next to each other rather than clustered together – were the usual form of farming community created

Ullapool and Loch Broom
In 1794, once housing, a pier and a breakwater had been constructed (and inspected by the engineer Thomas Telford), advertisements declared Ullapool to be an 'excellent harbour'. Within 50 years, however, Ullapool began to fail, partly because its boats were not designed for deep-sea fishing.
David Robertson/Alamy

for small tenants during the Improvement period. By the 1840s the improved townships in Farr on the Sutherland coast ranged from eight to forty-five houses, which 'stand at a considerable distance from each other, not in the manner of a regularly formed village'. That such numbers were probably already too many to be sustainable is suggested by the fact that in some places around thirty tenants occupied land formerly possessed by twelve, added to which some of them were given ground that had never been cultivated.[89] Many new crofting townships replaced old ones and so used land that had already been cultivated – in the Uists crofters were given strips of machair* to dig out, manure and plough, soils that had been used for millennia. However, it was also hoped that modern farming methods might bring marginal land into cultivation.

Dorothy Wordsworth came across some crofts near Dalmally in Argyll in 1804: 'Lord Breadalbane had lately laid out a part of his estate in this way as an experiment, in the hope of preventing discontent and emigration.'[90] Those who lived in the new townships at Farr, as elsewhere in Sutherland, had been cleared from the valleys of the interior to make way for sheep in 1818–19. Their landowner, the Countess of Sutherland and her husband, the Marquess of Stafford, were not (yet) at all keen to encourage emigration, especially since industries such as kelp* and herring fishing were very lucrative.

In the new townships, each tenant was allocated his own croft with a share of newly divided and enclosed fields, often taking in some of the old infield*, so that the meaning of the word 'croft' had evolved to include the house of these smallholdings as well as the land. The townships themselves tended to be spread along a road, with croft houses, farm buildings and other roads mostly built parallel to it, often at the landowner's expense. This is the basic pattern underpinning the current landscape of much of the north and west Highlands and Islands, though it was not necessarily how townships had been previously laid out.

It was a similar story on Shetland, though here landowners needed to keep their tenants from going elsewhere so that there were enough hands to go fishing, the primary economic activity. The communal field systems were broken up, as usual, but, instead of being amalgamated, they were used to create small individual holdings, each with their own house, arable land and pasture. As the population grew, new plots were created on land that had never previously been farmed (though the preponderance of peat limited where this was possible). Nevertheless, elements of pre-Improvement townships were sometimes incorporated into these new holdings and still survive, despite the landowners' general success in keeping the land occupied and well used.

Landowners did not always succeed in stemming the flow of emigration with these new smallholdings, however. In 1841, the minister of Tongue, on the far north coast of Sutherland, lamented the poverty of the crofters, caused in his view by the fact that their holdings were half the size needed for a proper farming rotation, so that they were only actually producing enough to sustain their inhabitants for seven or eight months of the year. Some had no land at all, making them quite destitute, and it should have come as no surprise that many went south annually 'because so little encouragement is given them at home'. The minister expected permanent emigration to follow soon enough. Part of the problem stemmed from the collapse of the kelp industry after 1825 (because the duty on the import of an alternative – barilla* – was abolished), a source of employment that had helped many of the crofters to pay their rents.

Some landowners tried desperately to help their small tenants by allowing the subdivision of land, though many would decry these attempts as only making the problem worse. These crofters were called lotters (particularly in the Outer Hebrides), because they rented tiny lots of land and lived in the kind of 'inferior' dwellings we have already encountered. While the majority held their lots independently, others still worked together in what sounds like a very ancient and sensible system:

These divide their spots of corn land as they are detached upon the farm, giving each other a proportion according to their respective rents; and that each may have his just share of the pasture also they restrict each other to a proportion of cattle corresponding with the amount of their rents; so share produce of farm proportionate to what they pay.

Their houses resisted the straight lines beloved of the Improvers, being placed 'more promiscuously'.[91]

At Kilmuir in Skye in the Outer Hebrides, the land and its people were soon groaning under the weight of numbers; in 1837 the population exceeded 4,000, having increased dramatically over the previous fifty years and particularly the last sixteen, despite some emigration; 421 families lived on 190 lots, crofts and farms, while a further 231 were landless, working as cottars or under-tenants 'who held shares of the said 190 divisions under the baneful system of sub-letting. As this process of sub-letting was annually progressing, the population, as a matter of course, was rapidly increasing until it accumulated to an amount by far too large for being comfortably supported by the produce or agricultural returns of the parish.' The practice had now been stopped by the landowner and his managers, so the lotters could no longer give 'a few shreds and patches' to sons and daughter when they got married, meaning that the latter would almost certainly have to move away. The same thing was noted as happening on Lewis, in Gairloch in Ross and Cromarty and Durness in Sutherland, suggesting the practice was widespread.[92]

Not surprisingly, this rise in population and pressure on the land led to tensions and, eventually, unrest. The crofters often had to endure the same insecurity of tenure and short leases that had beset them previously and therefore had no incentive to break their backs or invest in improving what was ultimately not theirs. As well as withholding rents and occupying land, particularly on the island of Skye, they also organised themselves politically over the following decades, winning five parliamentary seats in 1885.

A year later, an act of parliament enshrined in law a definition of the crofting counties (Argyll, Caithness, Cromarty, Inverness, Orkney, Ross, Shetland and Sutherland) and established the Crofters Commission to fix fair rents and approach landowners with proposals to enlarge holdings.[93] Crofters now had security of tenure, longer leases and the right to pass on their holdings to their successors. Though the Crofters Commission didn't yet have sharp enough teeth to deal with all that needed fixing, it laid down the basic crofting structure that still exists today and is emblematic of the difficult and particular history of smallholding in the Highlands.

However, the failure of successive governments to heed the crofters' demands to give them enough land to make their holdings viable led to continued agitation and land raids right into the twentieth century. The best known of these agitators were the cottars of Barra and Mingulay in the Outer Hebrides who, desperately needing ground on which to grow potatoes, took over the neighbouring island of Vatersay in 1902. These Vatersay Raiders had, until that year, been able to cultivate the island, and the prohibition on their doing so meant that many of them faced starvation. After many years of strife, which spread to other parts of the Highlands, Vatersay was finally purchased by the Congested Districts Board (set up in 1897 and given government cash to deal with overpopulation in some parts of the Highlands and Islands), allowing the crofters legal access to the island.

Though this might seem a victory for decency and common sense, it was actually not ideal, since the Congested Districts Board inherited the same problems that afflicted many of these islands and the coastal townships resettled by those forced to leave the inland valleys – they were often not big enough or on sufficiently fertile land to sustain their new inhabitants. Eight years after the purchase of Vatersay, the crofters still could not afford to pay any rent. The whole business struck at the heart of the problem of these smallholdings; the 1886 Crofters Act was based on the notion of secure and effective tenancies (rather than outright possession) to make the smallholdings more financially stable, but many landowners now wanted to get rid of these unproductive, overpopulated parts of their estates.[94]

Nevertheless, government purchase of land for smallholdings continued during the first half of the twentieth century in the Inner and Outer Hebrides. By now a far greater degree of central planning went into the new crofting townships, including the form of the croft house itself.

From the 1920s onwards, the Board of Agriculture for Scotland subsidised the construction of the typical two-up, two-down, storm-windowed croft houses that sit solidly and harmoniously in the crofting landscape. These usually were built with thick stone walls, but

Upper and Lower Barabhas (Barvas), Lewis
Within the landscape surrounding the modern Barabhas townships is a complex history of settlement and land-use, including pre-Improvement settlement, and crofts with long thin field patterns. HES, DP111150

Dun Carloway, Lewis
With lazy bed ridges on the rocky outcrop, crofters' strips running down to the sea, former blackhouses, modern housing, and even a broch (on the right), there is a real sense of several thousand years of settlement at Dun Carloway. HES, DP110857

could be of poured concrete in areas where aggregates were plentiful. Other designs also attracted assistance, such as the single-storey dwellings with stone gables and timber-frame construction clad with corrugated iron, intended to be built quickly in areas of land resettlement such as at Portnalong and Fiscavaig in Skye. Following World War II, crofters were encouraged to build very substantial, state-of-the-art homes. These bungalows can still be seen throughout the Highlands and Islands with their hipped roofs and tall chimney stacks. They have three bedrooms (which originally had fireplaces) and a bathroom, and were being built at a time when very many crofters still lived in blackhouses*.[95]

The scheme on Skye was ambitious – 68 new holdings – though the houses were not built all at once. The single-storey timber huts supplied by the Board as temporary accommodation were to be turned into barns later, though this took much longer than intended for the simple reason that they were far too comfortable. Nevertheless, the scheme was successful, proving popular perhaps because they copied the style and ethos of their predecessors. Such townships are easily found in the Outer Hebrides, surviving as working communities.

Nevertheless, there are differences among the crofting counties. Argyll, for example, has very few townships still occupied today because their paternalistic dukes generally preferred to sponsor other types of settlement; Harris's crofting townships, in contrast to those of neighbouring Lewis, do not conform to the regular pattern described above, simply because its topography is too rugged and uneven and the smallholdings had to adapt to the landscape as best they could; Caithness, being largely lowland, was capable of sustaining the kind of large, amalgamated farms more likely to be found further south and so has very few townships. Some were completely abandoned for a variety of reasons – subsequent changes of ownership brought change or they were created on land that was just too poor or too remote to provide a viable future for its inhabitants, as was the case at Erisko on Skye, abandoned in 1875.[96] Though more modern farming techniques (including Improved strains of crops, breeds of animals and crop rotations) might well be found on crofting townships, the latter did not, generally speaking, look like lowland smallholdings simply because of the topography and their particular evolution.

Where landowners decided to create planned smallholdings themselves (rather than giving their tenants money off their rent or other incentives to build houses or create holdings or taking advantage of government schemes), the design could prove different again, depending on their personal preferences and the amount of money they were prepared to spend on the project. Some were able to lay down equal-sized plots (usually square or rectilinear), regardless of conditions on the ground. The result was a regimented landscape of small farmsteads with more land than was usual in the crofting townships scattered across a wide area. They can be found within the crofting counties (Caithness, Wester Ross, the Black Isle north of Inverness, the islands of Arran off the coast of Ayrshire and Islay in the Inner Hebrides, the north coast of Moray) and also beyond them (the north coast of Aberdeenshire and Loch Tay in Perthshire).

The eighteenth century owners and managers of the Gairloch estate in Ross and Cromarty were keen to get to grips with the general impoverishment of their tenants without resorting to the evictions common elsewhere, having already turned part of the estate into a deer forest. After the death of Francis Mackenzie of Gairloch in 1843, his brother, Dr John, began to create four and a half acre portions of land whose variable rents reflected their variable quality. As well as supplying the roofing timbers (larch), Mackenzie also brought in a mason to show the crofters how to construct a model cottage; they then built their own under the mason's beady eye.

Not everyone approved of these efforts; many Lowlanders thought that only large farms would do and, if these were not possible, preferred emigration to smallholdings, which, they said, only encouraged overpopulation.[97] The crofters themselves don't seem to have appreciated Dr John's determined efforts to turn them into Improvers and once the heir, his nephew Kenneth, took over in the 1850s, many decided to leave rather than live in such poverty. Nevertheless, there are about 135 crofters still living on the Gairloch estate today.[98]

In the 1790s the Earl of Breadalbane planned and laid out crofts of around 50 acres of land each on both sides of Loch Tay in the Perthshire part of his estate. Given that Dorothy Wordsworth saw similar smallholdings on the Earl's Argyll lands around Dalmally in 1804, this was clearly something he rolled out right across his lands. By the 1850s, however, they had mostly been amalgamated into larger farms.[99] On Islay in the Inner Hebrides, where the smallholders were lotters rather than crofters, some of these lots failed despite great efforts to put in drainage; they are now cut for peat. But elsewhere on the island their outline still survives in field boundaries, though the houses are long gone.

In the early nineteenth century the establishment of crofts, which are found most commonly in the north-east Lowlands, the north-west Highlands and the Northern Isles, intensified. Many of these are now to be found on the fringes of farms established in the later nineteenth century (which often took in rough ground previously broken up and improved by the crofters). Many croft houses, if not abandoned and allowed to fall into ruin, have been converted into private dwellings or farm outbuildings. Their field systems leave distinctive patterns in the landscape, whether they are neat squares and rectangles or more organic shapes dictated by the ground.

Though mostly outwith the crofting counties, the north-east is another area where smallholdings have survived in the landscape. In Aberdeenshire we can still see the remains of those from the pre-Improvement period, which were usually attached to a farm and built to house the labour for rural industries, such as a mill, or to take in new land. Later, such smallholdings formed part of the Improvement landscape – the 1790s Monymusk parish in Aberdeenshire, for example, comprised 35 large farms; 61 smaller farms; 62 inhabitants with houses with gardens only; and 85 subtenants (smallholders with small crofts) – as well as the planned village of the same name built by the local landowner in the 1750s to house agricultural workers and craftsmen needed by the estate.[100]

On the other hand, smallholdings have effectively disappeared in the south-east, where crofts were once everywhere, though their presence is sometimes kept alive in other ways. In the village of Chirnside in Berwickshire, street-names include South Crofts and Croftsfield, lying very close to the medieval settlement.

There was one other group that numerous governments (as opposed to landowners) felt should be given the opportunity to live and work on smallholdings often specially created for them. From as early as the 1750s, returning soldiers were offered 'quiet retreats' as a reward for their service. In the 1760s George III's government decided 'on the Utopian project of establishing colonies (on the forfeited estates*) of disbanded soldiers and sailors.'

It was actually John Campbell of Barcaldine, factor on the lands confiscated from the Duke of Perth, who wrote to the Commissioners of the Forfeited Estates 'that several Perthshire men who had served in America[101] with the Highland regiments had lately returned home wounded and unfit for further service. They had applied to him for smallholdings for themselves and their families and he thought they were quite able to manage a small farm.'

The Commissioners agreed and, though Barcaldine's scheme came to nothing (because, apparently, the returnees strongly objected to being flung together in their various states of incapacity), they reported to the king in 1763 that they intended to spend £3,000 on providing for 300 married and 200 unmarried soldiers. 'Each of the soldiers was to be allotted three acres of ground for spade cultivation, the ground adjoining the houses was to be enclosed and laid down in grass for pasture for cows, allowing two acres for a cow. Houses were to be rent-free for life, the farms for three years and thereafter only 5 shillings an acre was to be asked, while unmarried men were to be paid £1 per annum for three years.'[102] A veteran's village was even founded in the grounds of Drummond Castle which is now submerged under a pond! Others, like Strelitz in Perthshire, which was named after Queen Charlotte, wife of George III, give themselves away by the novelty of their names and the traces of their lots in the modern fields.

Thomas Pennant, during his visit to Scotland in 1772, saw some of these neat little houses as he travelled along the military road between Perth and Crieff. But, as he caustically remarked, they were 'as usual, deserted by the colonists', Even as the plan had been unveiled nearly ten years earlier, James Small, the factor on the Struan estate near Kinloch

Rannoch, also in Perthshire, who had himself been a soldier, predicted 'that five-sixth of the soldiers would be the greatest blackguards in no way amenable to civil discipline, "only the rod having kept them under control"'. Further, he anticipated that they would sell their whole possessions and squander their money on drink.[103] Whether or not his assessment of those who were to benefit from the scheme was accurate, these particular smallholding colonies were not a success.

The most famous scheme to provide for war veterans came immediately after the First World War in the Land Resettlement Act of 1919, more usually remembered as Prime Minister Lloyd George's promise to build 'Homes fit for Heroes'. Though many were to be found in the suburbs of large cities throughout the UK, there was also a need for smallholdings in the countryside, where further change was taking hold, this time because mechanisation was reducing the agricultural workforce in fertile lowland areas. 1919–27 was their heyday. They were concentrated in the Central Belt, so as to be close to the main cities and large towns with available markets. Nevertheless, Caithness, parts of Dumfries and Galloway, and the Borders also have significant numbers.

Farms were initially purchased, whenever appropriate ones came onto the market, by the Department of Agriculture (Scotland), before being split up into smallholdings of two to four acres, depending on the quality of the land. A simple wire fence was usually put up round each plot, though the original field boundaries were kept. This was enough to plant potatoes and market garden crops and to keep a few pigs and poultry.

Houses for the new smallholders were built to a standard government design – usually one or one and a half storeys with a hip-roof,* four rooms and – luxury! – an inside toilet. There was usually a shed painted white nearby, though its size and design could vary; most involved blockwork*, while some

Castle Street, Aberdeen c1880

Aberdeen was one of the original Scottish burghs. The city as a whole began to grow in the nineteenth century once improvements had been made to its harbour to accommodate the expanding fishing and shipbuilding industries. However, it was the discovery of oil in the North Sea that has given Aberdeen its modern identity. HES, DP073918

68 Chapter One – Settlement

were timber-framed and clad with corrugated iron. If the original farm-steading had been included in the sale, this was shared by the smallholders, though sometimes they were converted into houses with attached barns.

In keeping with the general ethos of government policy in the 1980s, these smallholdings were sold off, usually to their sitting tenants (though eight were still in government hands as late as 2005). Though most have disappeared, absorbed into neighbouring farms or adapted for housing, industry or recreational purposes (golf or horse-riding), some can still be picked out by the distinctive patterns they make in the landscape – a smattering of modern houses (built after 1919) with small fields in front of them and a network of roads joining them to the rest of the urban environment. On the other hand, these field patterns were soon lost if modern farming took over.

The houses belonging to the smallholdings, once easily recognisable by their uniform design, have usually been extended or altered or replaced altogether, and it is their sheds that are more likely to have survived. Sometimes these older steadings can be spotted among late twentieth century housing, with the fields that used to surround them preserved in the road pattern, as towns and cities continue their creeping assault on the countryside.

* * * *

Everything in it breathes spaciousness, order and good sense; the houses present a dignified front to the world; they suggest comfortable privacy and are big enough for large parties, and seem admirably planned to withstand the distractions and allow the amenities of a rational city life.[104]

Edwin Muir
A Scottish Journey, 1935

Prior to the 1770s, as we have seen, visitors to Edinburgh experienced a curious mix of admiration and disgust towards the city as it grew to impressive heights (along with its dirt and squalor) within its medieval walls. As elsewhere in Scotland, any increase in population had to be accommodated by filling in existing gaps or building alongside roads and highways; for a while, this remained true as people began to migrate from the countryside into the towns in search of work, a trickle that became a torrent in the first decades of the nineteenth century. Not surprisingly, it soon became clear that this was quite unsustainable.

Thomas Pennant, the Welsh naturalist, arrived in Edinburgh just in time to witness the beginnings of the great changes that would transform the city as it began to spread to the south (George Square and the Meadows) and to the north, where the gracious lines of the New Town were about to emerge. The first of its many elegant squares – St Andrew's – was, as Pennant approvingly declared, 'planned with great judgement, and will prove a magnificent addition to Edinburgh'. Houses cost the equivalent of between £200,000 to over £500,000 in today's money (£1,800 to £5,000). 'They are all built in the modern style, and are free from the inconveniences attending the old city.'[105] It was all very impressive and Glasgow and Aberdeen soon began to plan their own Classically inspired New Towns, with broad streets, squares and crescents.

Glasgow's development reversed that of Edinburgh. To begin with, everybody loved the place – even Daniel Defoe, who found so much lacking in Scotland, declared ''tis the cleanest and beautifullest, and best built city in Britain, London excepted'; Macky agreed that it was 'the beautifullest little city I have seen in Britain;' as did Burt, who said it 'is, to outward appearance, the prettiest and most uniform town that I ever saw; and I believe there is nothing like it in Britain'. Fifty years later, the city was starting, like Edinburgh, to expand well beyond its medieval boundaries, the wealthy entrepreneurs fleeing the Merchant City for the leafy suburbs to the west once better transport links made commuting possible. Pennant described their villas set in woods as 'the best of any modern second rate city I ever saw'.[106]

It was a different story if you approached from the east, as Dorothy Wordsworth did, for here were the homes of the urban poor: 'The suburbs of Glasgow extend very far, houses on each side of the highway – all ugly, and the inhabitants dirty.' She was better pleased as she walked on – the 'picturesque' Trongate, the New Town of the west end, in 'the best style of the very best London streets' and the 'citizen-like houses' of the western suburbs with their brand-new pine plantations. By the 1930s, the poet Edwin Muir was so appalled by the extent to which the city had been overwhelmed by the needs of industry that he paused to consider the nature of the urban environment, as well as the key difference between Scotland's two main cities:

A town was once as natural an expression of a people's character as its landscape and fields; it sprang up in response to a local and particular need; its houses, churches and streets were suited to the habits and nature of the people who lived in it. Industrialisation, which is a mechanical cosmopolitan power – and the same in Prague as in Glasgow – has changed this. It makes people live in houses which do not suit them, work in places which two hundred years ago would have been considered as mad as a nightmare, and destroys their sense even of ordinary suitability; and it does all this because its motive force is a mechanical and not a human one … Edinburgh is not predominantly an industrial town, and so one does not find in it the universal massacre of style that one finds, for instance, in Glasgow.[107]

Muir felt the same about the towns he visited further west, though he viewed houses built in 'an extraordinary variety of shapes and sizes' as preferable to 'the vertical, high, gaunt tenement slums of Glasgow'. He was not even particularly impressed by the new suburban housing in places like Knightswood – 'These boxes are certainly more comfortable to live in than the old-fashioned tenements of twenty or thirty years ago; but they are extraordinarily unattractive.'[108] It was the wholesale disregard for the place of architecture within its environment that disturbed him most, something that marked out the expanding towns and cities of the Industrial Revolution – with advancing technology, they were freed from topographical restraints. For others, this heralded unlimited possibilities and such developments had their own aesthetic value.

The change heralded by the break away from the confines of the medieval city was surely as much social as architectural; from now on the rich and the poor were pushed apart, living often as if they were on their own islands, a development that might be as much psychological as physical. Muir points out that, at the junction of Leith Walk and Princes Street in Edinburgh, 'two different streams of promenaders are brought within a few yards of each other; yet they scarcely ever mingle, so strong is the sense of social distinction bred by city life … The prostitutes are the sole class who rise superior to this inhibition.'[109]

And yet this was not true in Glasgow, where, in the centre of town at least, the writer H V Morton gloried in the fact that 'in the Bond Streets of this city, with their business heads under the biggest assembly of bowler hats in Great Britain and their crowds of perfectly lovely, fresh young girls, I shall see the stooped shoulders of some ancient wreck, the insolent swing of a youth with a cap over his eyes, the slow walk of a hatless woman from a neighbouring tenement … In Glasgow, there are no frontiers.'[110]

By the end of the nineteenth century, the balance between rural and urban had shifted forever; now more than 60 per cent lived in towns with a population of more than 5,000. At the same time, the distribution of people had also changed; where once they were scattered across the Scottish mainland, now most were concentrated in the towns and cities of the Central Belt stretching from Edinburgh to Glasgow, and up the east coast to the Dornoch Firth. There was a bit of a slowdown in the first few decades of the twentieth century, but after the Second World War urban overpopulation and an aging housing stock were again a serious problem.

As we have seen, smallholdings formed a small part of the solution. So too did the creation of a new generation of New Towns entirely independent of any mother city – Cumbernauld in eastern Dunbartonshire, East Kilbride in Lanarkshire, Livingston in West Lothian and Glenrothes in Fife – and designed to give the inhabitants of the overcrowded urban slums a better life, as well as, in some cases, housing workers where they were needed by expanding industries such as coal-mining. Considerable thought went into these new towns, so that, like the earlier planned villages, they would provide almost everything their inhabitants might need, combining housing with schools, shops and community centres, the whole wrapped up in a healthier and more pleasingly green environment. A range of new social housing schemes within existing urban centres, from high-rise flats to houses with gardens, completed this programme of rejuvenation

Cumbernauld

Incorporating two existing villages, Cumbernauld was designated one of Scotland's 'New Towns' in 1955.
The Scotsman Publications Ltd, licensor Scran

Craigshill, Livingston

Craigshill was the first residential district to be developed in Livingston after it was designated a New Town in 1962.
West Lothian Archives and Records Centre, licensor Scran

Aberdeen Royal Infirmary, 1933

In 1900 the elevated site was selected to combine the city's main hospitals and its medical school in an integrated public health resource. HES, SC1257941

Glenrothes, Fife

Glenrothes is one of Scotland's five twentieth century New Towns. Newsquest (Herald & Times), licensor Scran

72   Chapter One – Settlement

Whitfield Development, Dundee
Built between 1967 and 1972, the development used pre-fabricated panels and sections to construct a range of housing arranged in a hexagonal pattern. HES, SC682572

Stirling Royal Infirmary
The hospital was built one mile out of the town centre to provide larger facilities in a healthier environment.
HES, SC1438068

Cumbernauld, early 1960s
Flats in a New Town housing estate.
The Scotsman Publications Ltd, licensor Scran

Hutchesontown, Glasgow, 1965
Designed by Sir Basil Spence this estate replaced Victorian tenements. However, the high flats turned out to be short lived, being demolished in 1993. HES, SC1052311

A History of Scotland's Landscapes **73**

Dundee and the River Tay, 1988

Dundee's medieval centre (located at the end of the bridge) has expanded and developed hugely since the Industrial Revolution. But the looming presence of Dundee Law, with its remains of an Iron Age hill-fort and late medieval fortifications, is a reminder of the past in a resolutely modern city.

HES NCAP

and regeneration. This time it was often the poor being moved out of city centres to make way for gentrification (in which case, the more affluent moved back in).

These days, great new hub hospitals are built on the outskirts of towns and cities so that their antiquated inner-city sites with too little parking can make way for even more housing. In taking themselves out of town, they are replicating an earlier development, though for different reasons. Cottage hospitals, for example, were built in the later nineteenth century to provide medical care for villages and towns situated too far from cities at a time when car ownership and public transport were still limited.

But others were deliberately removed from the smoky, disease-ridden inner cities. Once the Victorians understood that some diseases could spread quickly and easily, especially among the inhabitants of overcrowded slums, fever hospitals were built well away from the squalor, a trend that continued into the twentieth century. Some were in the vanguard of new treatment methods and innovative architectural design – Nordrach-on-Dee Sanatorium at Banchory in Aberdeenshire, which opened in 1890, was built on the top of a hill in the middle of a pine forest and named after the German hospital recently visited by its founder, Dr David Lawson. He was very clear about the benefits:

It is essential for patients to spend the whole of their time in pure air. In order that they may do this with a maximum of comfort, the buildings have been specially designed. All bedrooms face south, and are heated by steam pipes, lighted by electricity, and fitted with hot and cold water supply; the floors being covered with a material which readily ensures absolute cleanliness.

Nordrach was soon renowned for its success in treating tuberculosis; Somerset Maugham was even a patient there in 1917, paving the way for his short story 'Sanitorium', published in 1923.[111]

Lunatic asylums too were specifically designed to cure, or at least improve, the conditions of their patients. Though poorhouses had long taken in the mentally ill (and would continue to do so), the state began to give more consideration to their specific needs with the renovation or building of district asylums under the 1857 Lunacy (Scotland) Act.

These large, impressive buildings, like sanatoriums, reflected the growing awareness of the positive benefits of a pleasant, healthy and productive environment – doctors and staff lived on site with their patients, who were encouraged to grow fruit and vegetables for the kitchens in an 'open-door' policy that sounds remarkably progressive and ahead of its time.

In 1962 Dingleton Hospital, a former asylum in Melrose in Roxburghshire, went a step further when it was transformed into an 'open hospital' by Maxwell Jones, a South African psychiatrist. Jones had treated soldiers suffering from combat stress during the Second World War and discovered 'that once he had explained the physiological basis of their condition to the patients, most of them recovered rapidly', after which they obviously no longer needed to be kept in 'regimented wards'.

At Dingleton, where many of his patients came from socially deprived backgrounds, Jones dealt with any obvious biomedical conditions, but 'believed it was more productive to treat mental illness as the result of adverse social forces', getting rid of white coats and giving his patients proper responsibilities within the hospital. He was visited on a number of occasions by Franco Basaglia, the recently appointed governor of the grim municipal asylum at Gorizia in north-western Italy. Basaglia returned enthused by what he had seen and ready to go even further, to close down the asylums entirely.[112]

Changes to treatment methods, as well as the expense of running and repairing such large establishments, eventually led to their demise. Nordrach-on-Dee became a hotel in 1934, before returning to the Health Service as a convalescent hospital in 1955, known as the Glen O' Dee Hospital, followed by a stint as a home for the elderly with physical disabilities. It closed in 1998 and is still empty, despite having featured on BBC 2's *Restoration* programme. Dingleton survived until 2001, when it was converted into flats with modern houses built in the grounds. Even when they are demolished, as happened to Bangour General Hospital west of Dechmont in West Lothian, the outline of the site, along with its pattern of roads, still remains.[113]

Even the dead are not immune to the evolving tastes and requirements of the living.

If Protestantism needed the best part of three centuries to persuade everyone to accept burial in graveyards outside the church, it took scarcely any time at all for the sheer weight of numbers of a dramatically increasing population to outgrow them. The solution was new cemeteries, originally run by private companies but later by the municipal authorities, who sold plots in return for the promise of perpetual preservation and maintenance. Most were originally built on the edges of towns and cities, but were eventually swallowed up by them, as with everything else.

More recent cemeteries tend to be rather formal, with paths and plots laid out in straight rows. Older ones, on the other hand, had ambitions towards the picturesque, based on the celebrated Père Lachaise Cemetery in Paris, begun in 1804. This was certainly the case with the very first Scottish cemetery, Glasgow's Necropolis, set on a hillside overlooking the Cathedral, which opened in 1832.[114] Its grand monuments or *mausolea* were replicated elsewhere, sometimes with the addition of a chapel for services, as at Edinburgh's Warriston Cemetery, which opened ten years after the Necropolis. In 1929 tastes changed, along with cost considerations, prompting the company to convert East Warriston House into a crematorium.

The pressure of ever more people on our towns and cities shows no signs of abating. In more recent decades, new housing, along with shops and entertainment zones, has been focused on the outskirts of existing towns and cities. Many developments have been built on former industrial complexes, either by converting the buildings or completely replacing them. Areas of former deprivation or abandonment in desirable waterfront locations, as in Leith, Dundee and Stirling, have now been targeted for renovation.

All this change can be, as it always has been, bewildering for those whose familiar sights and sounds are altered beyond almost all recognition. I have heard a few friends and acquaintances express that feeling – that large numbers of new houses bringing in large numbers of new people, or brand new civic and commercial buildings, dilute, if not destroy, local ties. It is the same feeling that Edwin Muir's friends in Angus shared with him and Lewis Grassic Gibbon expressed so poignantly in his depiction of the fictional Kinraddie of the Mearns.

* * * *

Heartbreak and opportunity have been the twin themes underpinning this brief history of where and how people have lived in Scotland over the past ten thousand years. In the earliest times, Nature itself dictated the places where people began to settle and, as time went on, whether they needed to adapt or move. But soon enough the demands of a chief or army began to compete for attention, reshaping farmsteads and villages just as much as the advance of peat or the need to build on drier ground.

The growth of towns was both the cause and the effect of an opportunity, as trade – under the protection of the king's law – allowed the economy to expand. But most Scots were still farmers, subject to the vagaries of weather and climate and the feuds or wars that interfered with the peaceful cultivation of the land. Sometimes the population grew, bringing about a need for new settlements; at other times there was a retreat. It is hard, now, to truly understand how interconnected most people's lives were with those of their neighbours; and therefore to appreciate how difficult it must have been to choose to leave or to be uprooted.

And yet leave they did, in their thousands, to the towns and cities of the Lowlands or to unknown shores. Improvement thinking was meant to make people's lives better, but, as ever, there were unforeseen consequences. This was not, however, a single transformation, a painful but rapid revolution; rather, it was a series of evolutions that slowly but surely laid down a landscape that we can begin to recognise today – overwhelmingly urban with a well-ordered rural landscape of individual farms set within ever larger fields.

But the deeper past lies still there.

Sheepwashing by Sir David Wilkie, c1815
Sir David Wilkie, one of the best-known Scottish painters of the early nineteenth century, took great interest in rural scenes and the profound agricultural changes that he witnessed. National Galleries of Scotland, licensor Scran

Chapter Two

Farming

The Scots, who were more devoted to rearing cattle, and hunting, betook themselves to the mountainous districts, not adapted to agricultural pursuits, while the Picts supported themselves by cultivating the more fertile coasts along the German Ocean*.[1]

George Buchanan
History of Scotland, 1582

When the Scottish historian and thinker George Buchanan penned these lines, he could not possibly have had any direct evidence for the agricultural practices of the Picts and the Scots from the best part of a thousand years before. What he was really reflecting was the essential distinction made by Lowlanders between themselves and their Highland neighbours in his own and more recent times.[2]

This distinction was not just a crude shorthand for the difference in the way the land was predominantly used between the two regions; it carried moral implications too. Buchanan had read about the character of the inhabitants of these two distinct areas in John of Fordun's chronicle from around two centuries earlier: 'The coastal people are of domestic and civilised habits, trustworthy, patient and courteous …' while 'the island or mountain people, on the other hand, are a savage and untamed nation, uncouth and independent, much given to theft, ease-loving …'[3] Growing crops, in other words, carried with it connotations of a peaceful, settled lifestyle, while raising animals made for sloth and rowdiness.

As with housing and settlement, judgements on the effectiveness or otherwise of farming practices very much depend on who is judging and their preconceptions. Given the number of impressive prehistoric settlement remains,

not to mention medieval power-centres, in areas inhabited by 'island or mountain people', they were clearly capable of generating at least as much wealth as anywhere else and of working extremely hard.

Unlike their predecessors, the early farmers did not just clear the land; they had at their disposal an ever increasing arsenal of tools and methods to help them organise and control the resources at their command. This ranged from the use of dung spread on fields as manure through the controlled burning of moorlands for better grazing to the use of enclosures separating different land-uses. As a consequence, the impact of farming on the landscape was also increasing. Additionally, the spread of peat in northern and western regions after 1000 BC restricted the ability of those areas to produce both crops and good grass for grazing.

On the upside, from our point of view at least, the peat has helped to preserve some of the earliest agricultural landscapes, especially on Shetland. Here excavation at Scord of Brouster in the west of the main island has revealed not only the clusters of vaguely round plots already known to archaeologists (and assumed to be fields), but also networks of walls sometimes several kilometres long, separating off extensive pieces of ground, presumably for grazing. They date from around 2500 BC and are a unique survival (so far) in Scotland of a wider agricultural landscape, implying that these early Shetlanders were in the habit of growing crops and pasturing animals on their farms, as they were to do over the millennia to come.[4]

Elsewhere, it is extremely difficult to identify the remains of prehistoric cultivation in the landscape today. But there are signs. Clearance cairns are one fairly obvious one – large, low piles of stones collected from the surrounding field and dumped together to get them out of the way of the plough. Stone field boundaries might also be recognisable on the ground, as well as lynchets – the tell-tale ridges formed on the downhill side of a field ploughed over a considerable period of time and eventually building up into obvious terraces. Archaeologists might

Iron Age fields at Hut Knowe, Roxburghshire
The small fields and cord rig of prehistoric agriculture are rarely visible in the Scottish landscape because of modern land-use. These fields survive on a high ridge of the Cheviot Hills, beyond the reach of the modern plough. HES, DP249911

also find the remains of gulleys formed by ards preserved now beneath the peat or the grass. There are also likely to be the remains of a prehistoric settlement or burial mound nearby.

Given the extent to which the better arable land has been worked and reworked for thousands of years, it should come as no surprise that so few echoes of the earliest farming remain. But there is one important exception. Cord rig is an ancient method of tilling the soil that is sometimes still visible today, surviving on the surface as furrows roughly 1.2 to 2 metres apart, usually with a slightly raised section in between. There is much debate as to whether these were created by plough or spade, but the most likely scenario is the use of an ard to break up the soil and mix it, followed by the mounding up and maintaining of the raised parts using a spade.

Because mouldboard ploughs made it unnecessary to use a spade, we can assume that cord rig predates their introduction to some parts of Scotland around AD 1000. Though first discovered *under* the Roman fort at Habchester in Berwickshire (meaning it is older than the fort), a number of examples of cord rig have been found in southern and eastern Scotland, mostly as part of the agricultural landscapes associated with palisaded settlements in the Border uplands and later field systems feeding hill-forts, perhaps in the Roman period.

One of the best examples is at Hut Knowe, on the Scottish side of the Cheviot Hills in the far south-east. Here there was an enclosed settlement surrounded by a trackway next to which lay enclosures of long, rectangular plots of cord rig. Such remains have survived, as ever, because cultivation in the past reached much higher up into the hills than in more recent centuries, so they have largely been left alone since they were abandoned. There is some cord rig to be found in the Highlands too, where the practices that created them seem to have continued for a while after AD 1000.

The main crops wherever such field systems have been found were barley (which makes sense for our Atlantic climate, especially if it was planted at higher altitudes) and some wheat, along with spelt* and oats, processed by the rotary querns* found in increasing numbers from this period.

River Brora, Highlands

At one stage in Scotland's history (following technological innovations in the Middle Ages), the rig pattern seen beside the River Brora could be found throughout Scotland.
HES, DP080218

What is clear from the remaining evidence is that, although the grazing of animals was very important, especially in the uplands, arable farming was practised on a wide scale and often intensively; faint traces of cultivation in the vicinity of more obvious sections of rig suggest that the ploughed-up area was moved around the landscape, presumably in order to give the ground a rest (and explaining why permanent field boundaries are not more

common). In the Northern and Western Isles, on the other hand, farmers used various substances, from manure to turf, to deepen and improve the soil (that was probably happening elsewhere too, but later disturbance makes it extremely difficult to find).[5]

Many later rural communities lived near the remains of their ancient predecessors' labours, which could prove most intriguing. In 1845, the minister at Aboyne and Glentanar in Aberdeenshire noted that:

… traces of the plough are visible far up the brows of the hills and at greater elevations than it is thought any grain would now ripen. These alpine rigs are all straight, arising, it is presumed from the plough [single handle], having been drawn by the amlinmor (great yoke) to which the cattle were attached abreast. In connection with these rigs, the more limited operations of the spade or cas-chrom appear in small cleared patches, from which the grubbed up stones have been collected into heaps.

From the mountain's brow, cultivation would appear to have gradually descended to the richer and stiffer soils of the glen, as it became cleared of wood and water, and there the straight rig of the amlin-mor appears to have been succeeded by the curvilinear of the ten-oxen-plough.[6]

These may be medieval, but they are most likely to be much earlier, with clearance cairns to boot; there is evidence of large swathes of prehistoric settlement and agriculture to the north and west of Aboyne.

Because of the continued reuse of the lowland landscape, often the only hints of early agriculture come in the form of cropmarks that emerge during particularly dry seasons, briefly exposing traces of ditches and pits. As their name suggests, cropmarks tend to be found among arable fields, especially on those soils, such as gravel or sand, that drain well and do not experience too much rain – essentially the east coast from Berwick to Inverness, and pockets along the major rivers, including the Clyde, and lowland parts of the south-west. As already noted, fields seem to have moved around, making them even harder to spot, though the woodlands and grazing areas that form part of the wider agricultural landscape are easier to identify. The exception is East Lothian, where pits were dug around fields to prevent livestock straying into crops, complementing the enclosures that surrounded nearby settlement.

There is little or no difference in terms of agricultural remains – essentially still cord rig – as we move out of prehistory and into the early documented centuries of the Middle Ages. But the written evidence tells a different story, of a warrior culture based on raiding neighbouring territory and driving off cattle, which were viewed as a testament to the wealth of a man and a people. The sixth century poet Taliesen (who probably lived in the British kingdom of Rheged, which extended over a large part of modern-day Cumbria) describes the return of a war-band from a raid into Manaw (Lothian today):

Each went on campaign
Eager for combat,
His steed beneath him,
Making for Manaw
And greater gain,
Profit in plenty,
Eight score, the same colour,
Of calves and cattle,
Milch cows and oxen,
And each of them comely.
… There would be no famine:
Herds of cattle surround him.

He waxed lyrical about another northern British king, Gwallawg, in similar terms: 'A beginning, my praise in verse, Of lords faultless in warfare: Men who fill byres with cattle …'[7] Crops would almost certainly have been destroyed in a raid, but bringing back large quantities of grain does not seem to have been the point of the exercise, despite the fact that Manaw/Lothian contains some of the best arable land in the north. Only a thundering herd of cattle would apparently add to a man's reputation and help to feed his people.

And yet nurturing the fruits of the ground was clearly a vitally important skill even for a warrior. One of the most famous British poems, *The Gododdin*, written in the sixth century about the people living in south-east central Scotland, contains the usual eulogies. But as well as being 'wolfish', 'champion' and a 'slayer', Eithinyn ap Boddw Adaf was also the 'war-band's herb-garden',[8] presumably meaning he had healing skills capable of dealing with the inevitable sword scratches (and worse) likely to be picked up on a raid.

Gardens, generally speaking, were a very necessary part of almost everyone's lives, serving a practical purpose, more like an allotment than a modern flower garden; the ability to grow vegetables in no time at all, as St Nynia supposedly did, was deemed understandably miraculous. (Nynia is better known as St Ninian, who was reputedly at work in the early fifth century but, if he can be identified with St Finnian of Moville, was actually born at the end of that century.) The eighth century description of his horticultural efforts suggests that gardens were often cultivated in a similar way, if on a smaller-scale, to the fields we have already met:

It happened once, when the Lord's servant [Nynia] and his brothers sat indoors at table, there were found to be no greens. And so he spoke to a certain man: 'Run now to the garden, as fast as your feet will carry you to our well-watered rigs, and bring to us whatever you find growing from the ground.' But the brother replied who had care of the garden, and uttered true words to the holy man: 'I have sown, only today, vegetables planted in furrows and from the green sod they have not yet grown those dewy shoots which flower from within.' But the priest spoke to the servant out of his chaste heart: 'Run, therefore, and look, believing in the Lord, for God almighty can perform all things ...'

Needless to say, the monk brought back 'herbs springing up to grow as much in one day as if they had grown green the whole summer season'.[9]

Even kings, whose job description included leading the army in war and giving justice for most of the Middle Ages, could also earn praise, from their monastic chroniclers at least, for being good gardeners. David I, whose early years in England brought him into contact with many innovations that he later helped to introduce into Scotland, earned himself a fulsome lament when he died in 1153. This included praise for the fact that 'he looked after not only the great affairs of state, but all things down to the very least – such as gardens, buildings, or orchards – in order that he might, by his example, stir his people up to do likewise'. King David's interest in gardening was far from just a token, encouraging gesture, however:

And that nothing might be wanting in him for a seemly life, he even, at a meet hour, busied himself in some seemly task, such as planting herbs or grafting upon another stock slips cut off from their own roots.[10]

It is generally accepted that the mouldboard plough was introduced to Scotland under his auspices, when he invited some of his Norman friends to take up estates in the Lothians in the twelfth century and brought in the first of the reformed monastic orders, who were well versed in making the most out of the soil.[11]

But even as the mouldboard plough was beginning to make its presence felt, the existence of the cultivated world among the tales of derring-do remain far more fleeting than their actual presence on the ground would seem to warrant. A poem about Arran celebrates the island's fertility with one quick reference to its arable land that seems to seek to reassure the reader of its quality:

Frisky deer on its mountains, moist bogberries in its thickets, cold waters in its rivers, acorns on its brown oak-trees. Hunting dogs and keen greyhounds, brambles, sloes of dark blackthorn; close against the woods its dwellings; stags sparring in its oak-groves ... Smooth its plain, well-fed its swine, glad its fields – believe the story! – nuts upon its hazels' tops, the sailing of longships past it.

Another passing reference comes in a twelfth century song written by a clerk of Glasgow about the recent death of Somerled of Argyll, the Norse–Gaelic king of the Isles, which notes that the cathedral's 'Gardens, fields and plough-lands were laid waste and destroyed' by his invading army.[12] The cultural obsession with livestock (not to mention warfare) even encompassed the use of cattle in an assessment of the compensation to be paid for the wounding or killing of a man, depending on status, and general breaches of the peace in the tenth and eleventh centuries.[13]

But even if farmland was not the focus of songs and poems, this was a complex, well-cultivated landscape and had been for hundreds, if not thousands, of years. Since Pictish times, the land north of the Forth seems to have been divided up into a unit known as a *dabhach* (plural, *dabhaichean*), usually anglicised to *davoch* or *davach*. This area was the original Scotia or Alba, known to historians as 'Scotland proper'. It did not extend as far as the kingdom of Strathclyde in the south-west, which was British, Galloway in the far south-west, which had been colonised by Gaelic-speakers from Ireland, the former Dalriada, then Norse territory, in the west, or the Lothians and Borders, which was Anglo-Saxon until a Scottish victory in 1018.

What seems extraordinary is that considerable efforts were made, certainly in the large medieval province of Moray (which formed much of what had been northern Pictland), to ensure that most *dabhaichean* were provided with all the necessities of life, from arable land to pasture to forest; where that wasn't possible, 'detached portions' were added to make sure that no-one missed out, particularly on high mountain grazing. A number of them were later put together to form both lordly estates and church parishes (in this last case, again in the reign of David I). Given that most of these *dabhaichean* endured, more or less unchanged, into the

Miniature from the Rochester Bestiary, 1200s
In this detail from a medieval manuscript, a man guides a mouldboard plough pulled by oxen. Although the plough is wooden, the coulter (which dug vertically into the soil) and the tip of the ploughshare are made of iron.
British Library Board/Bridgeman Images

eighteenth century, it would seem that the deliberate carving up of the landscape by Pictish kings into useful units survived in some parts of the country into the Improvement period.[14]

The mouldboard plough seems to have reached as far north as Sutherland by the fourteenth century, though it was not necessarily adopted in places where much of the ground was too difficult to plough or where it was hard to produce the quality of wrought iron needed for the ploughshare (the mouldboard's cutting edge) and coulter (a knife or spike-shaped component used to cut into the soil before the ploughshare turned it over). These iron pieces were valuable. In 1329, it was noted that: 'Theft was so frequent, that husbandmen housed their ploughshares every night. Randolph [Thomas, Earl of Moray], nephew of King Robert Bruce and a loyal and effective lieutenant who became regent in the minority of David II, ordered that all ploughshares should be left in the fields; and, if stolen, that the country should refund their value. The ironwork of a plough was estimated at two shillings.'[15]

The rig itself, its boundaries forming a curving reverse-S-shape created by the broad turning semicircle required by the large ox team, could measure up to 20 metres in width; however, there doesn't seem to have been a standard size and many were considerably smaller, generally between 6 and 9 metres. The basic system of runrig was described by Thomas Pennant in 1772 when he witnessed it in operation on the island of Arran:

The tenants annually divide the arable land by lot; each has his ridge of land, to which he puts his mark, such as he would to any writing: and this species of farm is called runrig, ie 'ridge'. They join in ploughing;

86　Chapter Two – Farming

Hunting scene from *Le Livre de la Chasse* by Gaston III, Comte de Foix, 1300s
This image of mounted huntsmen pursuing a stag epitomises the prestigious relationship between aristocrats and the chase. During the Middle Ages there were around fifty royal hunting forests in Scotland, ideal for showing off horsemanship.
The Print Collector/Alamy

everyone keeps a horse or more; and the number of those animals consume so much corn as often to occasion a scarcity; the corn and peas raised being (much of it) designed for subsistence, and that of the cattle, during the long winter. The pasture and moorland annexed to the farm is common to all the possessors. All the farms are open. Enclosures of any form, except in two or three places, are quite unknown: so that there must be a great loss of time in preserving their corn, etc. from trespass.[16]

In fact medieval farmers seem to have operated a more sophisticated system (though Pennant did not necessarily understand its eighteenth century intricacies either). They could and did use enclosures of various kinds, of stone or turf, depending on how permanent they wanted the walls to be, but also of hedging; in 1236, for example, a dispute between the monks of Melrose and a local landowner, Richard Avenel, makes mention of 'crops, hedges [and] meadows …'[17]

These enclosures were intended primarily to separate the 'infield' (the main arable rigs given the most attention in terms of manure provided by humans, animals and the regular removal and replacement of the organic parts of houses, such as turf walls or bracken thatch) from the 'outfield'*, where the animals were mostly kept and which was ploughed once in a while. The outfield soil could also be improved by 'tathing' – the pasturing of animals on the next section to be ploughed in small enclosures so that, again, their dung would go to good use. A variation on this theme of manuring the outfields is described by the Buchan laird, Alexander Garden of Troup, in 1683: 'Some of our grounds for keeping cattle in the night time we enclose in

A History of Scotland's Landscapes   **87**

summer and before the later end of harvest they dung this enclosed ground, so that it is as fruitful for the first and second crops as the best of our Intowns …'[18]

Outfield is a pretty sophisticated way of maintaining the productivity of less favourable land, whilst also allowing for the feeding of stock. The crumbling leftovers of earthen head-dykes and outfield enclosures litter deserted field systems in many parts of Scotland, especially in the west where outfields were often distinct pieces of arable land. They are less evident in the east where they tended to be dismantled and brought back into the common field, though some remains have been found in Menstrie Glen near Stirling.[19] In contrast, many upland areas do not seem to have had any outfield at all and depended on the manure produced during summer grazing.

A surprising number of reverse-S-shaped plough rigs, or at least the outline of them, survive today. Most fascinatingly, they are not just to be found in the usual boundary zone between the well-ploughed valley floors and the unploughed uplands (which might well have been cultivated in the warmer conditions of the Middle Ages); fossilised traces of medieval rig have also been recognised in the pattern of modern fields in lowland areas from Galloway in the south-west to Aberdeenshire in the north-east.

In other words, when the Improvers began to amalgamate farms and enclose the communally held rigs from the eighteenth century, they sometimes stuck with the original shape of their outer borders. A similar thing happened on the edges of some burghs, when the communal burgess plots were also divided up. But perhaps the most surprising place in which to find this distinctive reverse-S-shape is in the outline of modern streets.

At West Cornton Vale between Stirling and Bridge of Allan, both the surviving fields and the streets to the north of them have kept their medieval curves; the same is true in and around Academy Street on the south side of Elgin; in St Andrews, urban expansion meant that the twentieth century houses of Hepburn Gardens still sit in plots that have fossilised the shape of the fields that preceded them; while at Abernethy in Perthshire, the burgh's expansion brought about the division of the old rigs, which were then added to house plots and turned into gardens or orchards or paddocks.[20] For those lucky enough to live in or near such places, perhaps, in the dead of night, the shouts of ploughmen or the bellowing complaint of oxen might still be heard. Or at least imagined.

* * * *

1301. To Michael Whitton, valet of Scotland, who lately by the king's command [Edward I of England] caused his houses and other possessions within the Forest of Selkirk to be burned, help with his expenses by the king's gift during the truce between the English and the Scots in the current year, in money issued to him by the treasurer and chamberlain of the Exchequer, 22 November, 100 shillings.[21]

Book of the controllers of the king's wardrobe receipts, year 29 (1300–01)

Feeding a rising population in the twelfth and thirteenth centuries as well as trying to generate a profit was not easy, so any opportunity to expand the amount of land under the plough was welcome, whether that was up hillsides or in areas designated as forest. Since the word 'forest' in the Middle Ages had a precise legal definition relating to the ownership and management of the plant and animal life within a certain hunting area, a formal process was needed in order to convert any part of it into arable. This was known as an assart, which came from the Latin verb *exsartare* – to weed out.

Grants of assart were usually very specific, which strongly suggests that they were written to cater for the individual needs of the granter and grantee (other types of medieval charter can be woefully generic when it comes to outlining the components of a piece of land, so that we can never be sure without in-depth study if they really were all there on the ground, and sometimes not even then). As well as cutting down trees and whatever else was growing beneath them, assarters might also be allowed to build houses, create areas for grazing animals, cut peat and turf or gather wood – in other words, to carve out everything that was needed to live and work on this new piece of cleared ground. Equally, they might be specifically told what they could not do, since the purpose of the agreement was to balance the needs of the farmer with those of the deer, boar and game prized for the hunt by the owner.

Assarting became less common from the fourteenth century, partly because of another deterioration in climate (after a warmer spell) and the economy, which made arable farming less attractive. Nevertheless, this drive to create more and more arable land made even greater inroads into the tree cover of these lowland areas, coming on top of thousands of years of human activity that had already, together with climate change, decimated many of Scotland's woodlands. It would not be long before the alarm bells began to go off, particularly in the south.

On the other hand, the fruit trees of a wealth of orchards were thriving. They, like gardens, were an integral part of life across the country, even being used as a metaphor for an honourable lineage – 'Clann Somhairlidh, Sil Gofraidh' said the mid thirteenth century poet, referring to the ancestors of the man he was addressing, Angus mor Macdonald, 'whence you're born, they hoarded no herds; well-plotted orchard, apple branch, noble all blood from which you come'.[22]

But these medieval orchards were still subject to the kinds of problems that modern gardeners will sympathise with; in 1266, according to a much later report, 'there was such an abundance of caterpillars throughout all Scotland and England that they consumed all the fruit of trees such as apples, pears, plums, and whatever other fruit was growing, and ruined every manner of garden vegetable by eating them down to their stalks'.[23] Given that the produce of orchards and gardens was surely a major source of vitamins for much of the population, this must have had a significant, if temporary, effect on the nation's health.

By the end of the Middle Ages, their worth to the noble bottom line was underscored by the draconian measures taken against those who dared to interfere with them. In 1504 James IV's government published legislation ordaining a fine of £10 (over £6,000 today) 'regarding those who steal pike from ponds, break dovecotes, orchards or yards, or those who steal hives and destroy them, and also regarding those who kill enclosed deer, roes or roebucks from the lord's own woods'. But that was not the end of it, for further penalties were enacted against children caught stealing an apple or a fish – their father or master (if they were an apprentice) was to pay 13s 4d (around £400) for *each* one caught 'or else deliver the said child to the judge to be lashed, scourged and flogged according to his faults'.[24]

However, orchards could themselves pose problems as they were a convenient place for rooks, crows and other birds of prey (eagles, buzzards, kites and the unidentified mittels are mentioned) to build their nests, which then 'destroy both corn and wildfowl such as partridges, plovers and others'. The owners of the orchards were to get rid of the birds (something that would cause outrage today) on pain of forfeiting the tree to the king and paying him five shillings. This legislation was first promulgated by the Scottish parliament in 1424, but had to be reissued in 1458, suggesting that this was a battle the government was failing to win. However, this time it was as much about providing slaughtered wildfowl 'for man's sustenance' as protecting the growing crops, suggestive of famine.[25]

Although wildfowl and the other beasts of the hunt, as well as the prized cattle, were certainly the focus of much parliamentary and poetic attention, it was sheep that arguably contributed most to the economy of late medieval Scotland, certainly in the south. With the cloth industry flourishing in cities like Bruges and Ghent in Flanders, wool was an extremely valuable commodity and one well suited to Scotland's topography. Scottish monasteries, especially those of the eastern borders, created vast sheep runs in the hills of the southern uplands where the outline of their enclosures (called granges) can still be seen.

Disease posed a significant economic threat, but with such intensive farming that was probably to be expected. The terrible sheep scab, where mites cause the infected animal to become so obsessed with scratching that it forgets even to eat, arrived in England in 1272 and reached the border three years later. By 1294 the Scottish king, John Balliol, ordered his sheriffs to find out how far this *murrain* had spread throughout his kingdom and to order a ban on keeping and moving infected stock, which was to be slaughtered.[26] But by then it was already endemic.

Despite the riches to be won off the back of sheep, there were some parts of the country unwilling or unable to turn their grass over to

Ploughing, Orkney, c1900

Oxen were used for ploughing for millennia before being entirely replaced by horses.

George Washington Wilson, University of Aberdeen, licensor Scran

Ploughing, Fair Isle, 1936

On Fair Isle the use of oxen continued until the end of the Second World War. The first tractor or 'iron horse' arrived in 1947. Fair Isle Bird Observatory Trust

Sowing seeds, North Ronaldsay, Orkney, 1930s

A demonstration of how seed was broadcast before seed drills.

North Ronaldsay Heritage Trust, licensor Scran

Milking, Fair Isle, c1950

Mrs Stout milks her small cow from the right, as is traditional, into a metal pail. National Museums Scotland, licensor Scran

90   Chapter Two – Farming

Ploughing, near Peebles, 1936
While oxen were being used on Fair Isle, horses were ploughing fields outside Peebles.
The Scotsman Publications Ltd, licensor Scran

Farmer and harnessed horses, Leuchars, Fife, 1928
Though horses were gradually replaced by machinery, it speaks volumes that many farmers chose to be photographed with them.
National Museums Scotland, licensor Scran

Crofters with foot plough, Skye, c1900
The *cas-chrom* (literally 'bended foot') was once commonly used on boggy or stony ground throughout the north and west of Scotland. National Museums Scotland, licensor Scran

Grinding corn, Skye, c1900
Rotary querns had been used to grind corn since prehistoric times. Although the crofters' machine was more advanced, the principle remained the same. Chronicle/Alamy

A History of Scotland's Landscapes

Stone cleits and dry-stone walls, St Kilda
Even an island as remote as St Kilda was affected by agricultural improvement. The land was divided into crofts in the mid 1830s. Each croft included fields and cleitean – stone huts used for storing food and fuel. These fields were for growing hay and overlie former lazy bed rigs.
HES, SC1463898

them, mainly because, although wool exports were high, there was also a flourishing market for leather produced from cattle hides. In 1368, the Scottish king, David II, who needed money for his own living expenses while he was raising money for his ransom (having inconveniently got himself captured during a battle in England), discovered – and one can almost feel his surprise – that 'in certain parts there are no sheep, but other animals are abundant there'. Those animals were cattle, on whose carcasses a levy was to be taken.[27] Given the type of beasts involved and the fact that this was news to the king, these 'certain parts' were most likely to be the far north and west.

But nothing lasts forever, though no doubt the monasteries, the southern nobles and the royal exchequer imagined that it was inconceivable that the wealth from wool would ever disappear, just as Highland nobles surely banked on continuing returns off the backs of their cattle. But, of course, markets did change, not least in the aftermath of the arrival of the Black Death in the mid fourteenth century. Wool and hide exports peaked in the 1380s, but it was mainly downhill after that. Rents fell dramatically once the plague had carried away large swathes of the population, particularly around the east coast burghs; this was a good time to be a peasant, providing you survived the recurring onslaughts of the disease. Given the impact of a wetter, cooler climate, which affected the height at which grain could be grown, together with the increasing cost of labour (because of fewer peasants), it was much cheaper for landowners to focus on farming livestock.[28]

It is, of course, harder to trace how this affected the shape of things on the ground. Nevertheless, that there had been considerable changes wrought on the landscape in the two hundred years after the casual mention of hedges in 1236 is perhaps hinted at in parliamentary legislation of 1458, which aimed to strenuously encourage tenant farmers to 'make

View of Culross House, Fife, by John Slezer, c1719

The grounds of Culross House, which date from 1693, demonstate the geometric order of a typical Renaissance garden with its well-ordered fruit trees. The parkland sandwiched in the middle of the picture was once Culross Abbey's orchard, highlighting the long history of fruit-growing in Scotland. HES, SC1129171

hedges and sow broom',[29] This lack might have been in part a result of previous land clearance, including the assarting we have already seen, as well perhaps as the upheaval that southern Scotland endured during the wars with England, from marauding armies to displaced farmers, at a time when some border nobles successfully petitioned the king for lands much further north.

The 1458 legislation was repeated in 1504 and 1535, but finally seems to have had some effect, for a while at least, judging by the lack of further parliamentary interest and the odd reference to hedges in the south. However, in 1661, a year after Charles II was restored to his thrones of Scotland and England after the civil wars that had cost his father, Charles I, his head, an act was passed 'for making parks and enclosing of ground [by planting hedges or dykes] …' The strong hint that this was an attempt to get back to what had been tried before is contained in the reference to the 'many laudable laws [that] have been made by his majesty's royal progenitors'.

Eight years later, Charles, metaphorically rolling his sleeves up to deal with the shocking state of Scottish roads and highways after over twenty years of war and occupation, ordered 'that where laboured land lies upon the sides of highways that the said laboured land shall be fenced with dyke and ditch or hedge …'

In 1686, his brother, King James VII and II, went further in trying to protect planted trees and hedges, ordering 'that all heritors, liferenters, tenants, cotters and other possessors of lands or houses shall cause herd their horses, nolt*, sheep, swine and goats the whole year, as well in winter as in summer, and in the night time shall cause keep the same in houses, folds or enclosures, so as they may not eat or destroy their neighbours' ground, woods, hedges or planting'.[30]

Whether this had a practical effect is difficult to gauge, partly because turf or timber enclosures will have long since disappeared and any hedges from this period are likely to have been replaced. However, at the end of the eighteenth century, the minister of Libberton in Lanarkshire tells us that: 'On the south and east it [the village] has been surrounded with a strong dyke or earthen mound, the foundation of which is still visible; and which separates the arable from the waste lands.' He also mentions pens in all the villages, which he asserts were for keeping cattle safe from the depredations of the men of the lords of Douglas and Buccleuch.[31]

It is worth noting, too, that drainage was well understood long before the arrival of the Improvers. The monastic orders which were invited into Scotland from the twelfth century were certainly well-versed in such technological matters. In 1218, for example, the monks of Inchaffray Abbey near the village of Madderty in Perthshire founded their monastery on land that was mostly marsh; they were allowed to reclaim as much as they needed and soon got to work ditching and draining what became known as the Pow Water.

In 1696, the landowners were given permission to drain and ditch the Pow of Inchaffray, a 'long tract of level ground subject to unseasonable inundations and overflowings of the water, whereby the adjacent ground and meadows become marsh, and the grass and corns of several heritors* of the said lands are frequently lost and rendered useless'. Fifty years earlier, in 1641, they had agreed amongst themselves that they would clear away the turf and grass clogging up the Pow; unfortunately the outbreak of civil war a year later probably put paid to such sensible and far-sighted thinking. The Scottish government is currently being asked by the Pow of Inchaffray Commissioners to update legislation regarding a drainage system that is still crucial to the control of flooding over the surrounding area.[32]

In 1500 George, Bishop of Dunkeld, granted to John, Lord Drummond, and his heirs 'an aqueduct or watergang upon the Kirk lands of Larotoun and Buttergask with full power to dig and fence the same and to bring water through it from the burn of Lawton to his mill situated beneath his barony of Cargill …' (near Coupar Angus). In 1641 a charter, referring to lands near Dunfermline in Fife, makes mention of a 'sheuch', meaning a trench or ditch (though we cannot be entirely sure this was for drainage). By 1704, only three years before the union of the parliaments of England and Scotland, an act was passed 'for draining lochs and marshes'.[33]

The point here is not even that these kinds of improvements were clearly part of the arsenal of land management in at least some parts of the kingdom long before the eighteenth century, but that use of that knowledge seems to have waxed and waned across the years. It is curious that Daniel Defoe, visiting the northern kingdom in the 1720s, lamented that lowland farmers neither folded their sheep nor left their ploughed land fallow, both of which 'would increase and enrich them'.[34] And yet we know that they knew how to do both.

At first glance, it would be tempting to doubt that much was done in the way of proactive land management in the Highlands before Improvement. Certainly the culture among many of the Highland nobility in the sixteenth century in particular was focused on acquiring as many enemy beasts as possible and not the peaceful application of brawn to agricultural matters.

This is illustrated by the infamous story of Donald the Hammerer (born around 1525) that fascinated Sir Walter Scott. 'Once, as Donald was walking upon the green of Invernahyle [north of Loch Creran in Appin], he looked across the river, and saw several men working upon the farm of Inverfalla [his son Duncan's farm]. In the meantime Duncan came out, and took a spade from one of the men, seemingly to let him see how he should perform the work in which he was employed.' This indignity was too much for the old warrior, who rowed across the river with murder in his heart.[35]

And yet there was much in Highland society and economy to encourage those not involved in raiding and feuding, not least the habit of granting leases of up to 90 years, if not several lifetimes,[36] which surely fostered a degree of forward-thinking among at least some of these tenants. There is certainly evidence for collective action that suggests, at the very least, there was a wealth of knowledge and know-how that was surely applied to agriculture more generally.

At Loch Bi, on South Uist, it was noted in the mid sixteenth century that: 'An arm of the sea has worn the earth that was at the one end of this loch, which the sea has gotten entrance to the said fresh water Loch; and in that narrow entrance that the sea has gotten to the said Loch foresaid, the countrymen have built up a thick dyke.' Along the coasts, it was common – as it had been since prehistoric times – to use seaweed (called sea-ware) as a manure, including on some islands off the west coast that are uninhabited today – Pabay, for example, was 'inhabited and manured' as well as being 'good for thieves' and 'full of woods'.[37] It is none of these things today.

Interestingly, such knowledge was closely entwined with what would later be condemned as superstition. One of the most fascinating aspects of Martin Martin's voyage round the Western Isles is his description of belief on Raasay, an island off the east coast of Skye, in the power of the waxing and waning of the moon. This impelled the inhabitants to:

never dig their peats but in the decrease: for they observe that if they are cut in the increase they continue still moist and never burn clear, nor are they without smoke, but the contrary is daily observed of peats cut in the decrease. … They make up their earthen dykes in the decrease only, for such as are made at the increase are still observed to fall.[38]

Edmund Burt also noted the views of Highlanders more generally on the efficacy of the moon on ripening corn, while the author of the *Old Statistical Account* for the parish of Kilmuir on Skye went further, stating in 1796 that 'They imagine that an increasing moon communicates a growing quality to most substances, while a decreasing moon has an opposite tendency, and causes such substances to decay or wither.' On Orkney the inhabitants would not get married or kill their cattle except at the moon's waxing.[39]

Given the influence of the moon on tides, this is perhaps not entirely surprising and, while modern scientific studies have not managed to pinpoint any relationship between its phases and human physiology, there is some evidence for its effect on animal behaviour, as well as a full-blown branch of farming and wine-growing called biodynamics, which recognises the role of natural rhythms, including lunar activity, in agriculture.[40]

Putting the moon to one side, there is another point to be made, for the above contains clear evidence from Martin Martin for earthen dykes on Raasay, an assertion corroborated by Pennant 80 years later, who saw the country of northern Skye (Coire-chattachan) 'divided by low banks of earth'. He goes on to say that: 'Here a wet sky brings a reluctant crop: the ground, enclosed only with turf mounds, accessible to every animal. A continual watch employs numbers of his people.'

This labour-intensive approach was what didn't make sense to many southern observers. They did not think that this was effective land management; whereas in the Highlands, having many hands was still viewed as highly desirable. It is also possible that these low banks of earth were topped with wooden fencing in the right season (Pennant himself mentions that the inhabitants knew how to fence). Traces do survive; a survey of Waternish on Skye in 1990, for example, found and mapped many earthen banks that served either as head-dykes or outfield dykes.[41] So we should certainly not imagine that the pre-Improvement landscapes of either the Highlands or the Lowlands were always large prairies of open rig. It is also worth noting that the lazy beds* that were typical of many parts of the west coast and the Western Isles were constructed with deep ditches between their heaped-up ridges so as to provide the drainage essential in such a wet climate.

Donald Monro, a clergyman from the Black Isle north of Inverness who was posted to a parish on the island of Skye in 1526, toured the Hebrides in 1549. Unlike Martin Martin, he was not, therefore, completely native, but was more so than many who wrote about the Highlands. Certainly there was much about the agriculture of the far west that was very different from the area around Dingwall where he grew up; he seems to have been both astonished and impressed, for example, by what could be produced by the *cas-chrom* (foot spade). On the island of Taransay, 'all this tillage is dug with spades, except so much as a horse plough will till; and yet they have a great abundance of barley and most wealth of corn, store and fishing'; Bernera Beg, off the coast of the island of Lewis, 'will give yearly more than 200 bolls* of barley with digging only'.

The *cas-chrom* was described in detail three centuries later. This very ancient and effective instrument consisted 'of a crooked piece of wood, the lower end somewhat thick, about two-and-a-half feet in length, pretty straight, and armed at the end with iron made thin and square to cut the earth. The upper end of this instrument is called the "shaft", and the lower the "head". The shaft above the crook is pretty straight, being six feet long, and tapering towards the end which is slender. Just below the crook or angle, there must be a hole wherein a straight peg must be fixed, for the workman's right foot in order to push the instrument into the earth; while in the meantime, standing on his left foot, and holding the shaft firmly with both hands, when he

A History of Scotland's Landscapes

Linlithgow, West Lothian, detail from General Roy's Map (Lowlands), 1752–55

The land around Linlithgow is clearly covered in the open rigs of pre-Improvement agriculture, and reverse-S-shaped fields are also recorded. Since the rigs were worked communally, there was no need for fences or walls to demarcate fields, though enclosures were certainly used in order to manage livestock. British Library Board/Bridgeman Images

has in this manner driven the head into the earth, with one bend of his body he raises the clod by the iron-headed part of the instrument, making use of the "heel" or hind part of the head as a fulcrum. In so doing, he turns it over, always to the left hand and then proceeds to push for another clod in the same form.'[42]

Monro also stated that, on Lewis, '… all is peatmossland at the sea coast, and the place where he wins his peats this year there he sows his beir

Linlithgow, detail from first Ordnance Survey Map, 1843

In contrast to General Roy's map, the OS map shows the area covered in the regular rectilinear fields that superseded the runrig system during the Improvement period. This involved fencing-in sections of rig to be worked by a single tenant.

Reproduced by permission of the National Library of Scotland

[barley] the next year: after that he improves (guids) it well with sea ware'. The peat bog here cannot have been very deep (though it certainly was around the nearby stone circles of Callanish), but even so, it is unusual to find one being used for the growing of crops. The minister also tells us that gardens were certainly not unheard of; nor were orchards, which he found on Iona and Raasay. Later writers mention them on Barra, Skye and Islay (where there were even strawberries).[43]

On the subject of orchards, George Buchanan, writing 40 years after Monro, gave first prize to Moray – 'So abundant is this district in corn and pasturage, and so much beautified, as well as enriched, by fruit trees, that it may be truly pronounced the first county in Scotland.'[44] Gardens and orchards seem to have been more or less ubiquitous across both town and country right to the far north – the township of Learable in Sutherland, cleared for sheep in 1815, provides evidence on the ground for farms with kale-yards* attached.[45]

In the village of Maybole in Ayrshire at the end of the seventeenth century, too: 'The houses of this town on both sides of the street, have their several gardens belonging to them, and in the lower street there be some pretty orchards that yield store of good fruit.' A few decades later, the Carse of Gowrie between Perth and Dundee – renowned today for its fruit-growing – was described as 'all a perfect garden'. Aberdeen too was so well provided with these green spaces that 'the whole city, to those that approach it, seems the resemblance of a wood', while Buchan, on the other hand, didn't go in for it at all (in complete contrast to neighbouring Moray), though it made up for the lack with 'an abundance of good cheer'.

Even the doughtiest Highlanders had time for them – Edmund Burt, the engineer, visiting one particular (unnamed) chief, noted him 'walking alone, in his garden, with his dirk and pistol by his side, and a gun in his hand'. However, as we might expect, there was no fruit in some of the more mountainous glens, judging by the fact that a landlord there could not tell an apple from a lemon.[46]

Tarting up or entirely rebuilding their castles and big houses with lavish parks and gardens was an endeavour that nobles and lairds* set to with relish – usually on credit. And this perhaps explains why time-consuming, expensive and, let's face it, less glamorous maintenance schemes, such as dyking and draining, slipped down the 'to do' list in some periods of the seventeenth century, which also witnessed bitter warfare throughout the country during its middle decades. There was also a very different political environment now that the king, resident in England, sat at a distance from Scottish affairs, making him much more reliant on particular Scottish nobles with their own specific agendas; if they were not interested in improving schemes, then it was unlikely that their royal master would be. At the same time, English ways of doing things often proved temptingly attractive, whether or not they were appropriate in a Scottish context.

This was a period, too, when noble debts even in the Highlands began to spiral out of control, usually thanks to a serious increase in conspicuous consumption, as well as the impact of warfare. At the same time, the union of the crowns of England and Scotland in 1603 brought greater Scottish access to southern markets, the English – and especially Londoners – proving very keen on the succulent meat of the cattle and sheep of the north. The efforts of the Crown to 'civilise' the Highlands, as well as the carrot provided by these new opportunities to make money from black cattle meant the region began to move away from the violent feuding that had so blighted the previous century and earned the region such a bad name in the south.[47]

After 1707, this became even easier as Union brought free access not only to England but to its colonies. So there was more money to be made, but also more to spend it on. Not only that, but many Scottish nobles began to follow their kings' example and live south of the border, which later commentators claimed made them less knowledgeable about, and willing to spend money on, their original Scottish estates. As we saw with settlement, the reality is more complicated. But increasing contact with England in particular and a changing European world in general made certain developments irresistible.

* * * *

The open country continues as far as Lunan [near Montrose], where the enclosures commence ... After crossing that water, the country becomes enclosed, and divided into fields of about eight or ten Scotch acres [c40,000–50,000 m²] in size, fenced with walls or banks, planted with French furze [gorse], or with white-thorn.[48]

Thomas Pennant
A Tour in Scotland, 1769

The improvement of agriculture – the mainstay of the early modern economy – was just one, albeit key, aspect of a more general Enlightenment desire to discover through scientific study and experimentation the best way of doing things and to overcome whatever obstacles were to be found in nature in pursuit of scientifically proven methods. The founding of the Society of Improvers in the Knowledge of Agriculture in Scotland in 1723 was a crucial step in allowing the newest ideas and best practice (to use modern jargon) to circulate widely; smaller, local organisations on the same lines popped up all over the country in the following decades.

But before much could be done, a revolution was required in the way that the land was held. This began in the later seventeenth century, most particularly with the 1695 Division of Commonties Act, which permitted the breaking up of lands held in common (apart from those belonging to the king or the royal burghs), among those who could claim ownership of them.[49] Once that had happened, tenants could no longer, for example, graze animals or take turf or peat from these former common lands, as they had done for generations.

Apart from the avowed aim of this legislation to 'ease discords' over access to commonties (by excluding just about everyone), the logic of simplifying landownership to a single identifiable person with clear-cut rights and responsibilities soon spread to other aspects of farming life. As leases came to an end in some parts of lowland Scotland from as early as the later seventeenth century, but more generally from the middle of the eighteenth century, enclosure – the process whereby lands held in common by a number of tenants were put together and let out to a single tenant – began to change both the look of the landscape and the social structure of local communities.[50] Because many landowners in the Highlands were now moving away from the long-term leases that had prevailed in earlier centuries to very short ones or none at all, it was even easier to move people off one piece of land to another, if, as in Sutherland, that was deemed desirable.

It was believed – with good reason – that the communal system of runrig acted as a huge deterrent to investment and innovation; anyone tempted to make changes was unlikely to reap the rewards since his rig(s) would be allocated to someone else in subsequent years (which was fair, because it meant the good, middling and poor ground was regularly rotated among the tenants). But how, then, wondered the Improvers, could agriculture be geared towards the demands of the market rather than the needs of the farmers and their countless cottars and servants?

Within the space of a century, an utter transformation had been worked across most of the country, its scale and depth captured by the comparison between what was recorded by General Roy's cartographers working before most of the changes (1747–55) and the first Ordnance Survey maps (1843–82), which set down the shape of the new landscape in unprecedented detail.

Out of the great lengths of unenclosed strip fields with their characteristic reverse-S-shapes clearly visible on Roy's maps emerged the neat, straight blocks of modern farming of the OS maps, just as the clusters of old-style settlements gave way to sturdy stone farmhouses flanked by outbuildings arranged round a courtyard. The only landscape features that the two sets of maps share are the medieval burghs and the noble houses set within their designed landscapes.

It is powerful indeed to be able to chart these changes on such beautiful artefacts, but their contours provide us with only the bare bones of what happened in this remarkable century of change. For many, life was never the same again, whether they were a farmer and his family without a tenancy forced to find work elsewhere or the successful single tenant looking forward to a rising standard of living. There was, in other words, a lot of pain and anguish on the way, but for many it was a price worth paying if it would bring an end to cycles of famine and living conditions that seemed woefully inadequate. At the same time, the rise of increasingly large-scale modern industries helped to mop up many of these redundant rural workers, which marked the beginning of the long-term shift towards the overwhelmingly urban population we know today.

But, as we have seen, Improvement was not a straightforward, overnight revolution, transformative though it certainly was. The pace of change might be different from valley to valley, never mind region to region, usually reflecting the interest in modernisation or otherwise of individual landowners. There were different phases of Improvement too; the first phase was mostly focused on the amalgamation of farms and their enclosure;

later activity concentrated on drainage and the finer details of stock breeds and grain species. It was also true that some Improvers overreached themselves, imagining that science could overcome anything, even poor, cold, water-logged soils, ultimately abandoning their efforts, which remain as a fossilised testament to their failure. In such cases, Improvement was no such thing and the sweeping away of despised old ways, which might in fact be perfectly adapted to local conditions, was a really bad idea.

As already mentioned, the earliest modernisation came not to the runrig of the valleys, but the communal pasturelands of the southern uplands, particularly the huge estates of the Dukes of Buccleuch, in the seventeenth century. The turning over of vast swathes of Scottish hillside to the bigger, meatier breed of Cheviot sheep was the first quiet revolution to creep across much of the uplands (though cattle were still important away from the sheep-walks).

The trend had reached Argyll by the mid eighteenth century, though the sheep were not the only incomers to the area, since their shepherds were often from 'Southland' or Ayrshire. At the end of the century in Laggan in Inverness-shire, it was only sheep grazings that attracted the high rents, though the Duke of Gordon, one of the parish's main landowners, wasn't interested in letting to shepherds because 'that nobleman is attached to his people and fond of nourishing and rearing them'.[51]

The Duke was not alone in questioning the overall wisdom of turning so dramatically away from a system of farming that brought profit to more than just the landowner and single tenant. Thomas Pennant, seeing the hills round Crianlarich covered in southern sheep where once there had been cattle, was not at all sure, though his thoughts were partly turned to the needs of the British state:

Sheep are found to turn more to the advantage of the proprietors; but whether to the benefit of the community, is a doubt. The live stock of cattle of this kingdom decreases: from whence will our navy be victualled? Or how will those, who may be able to purchase animal food, be supplied, if the mere private interest of the farmer is suffered universally to take place? Millions at this time look up to legislature for restrictions, that will once more restore plenty to these kingdoms.[52]

Given that the law was very much on the landowners' side, however, resistance was futile – the harsh methods used to evict tenants on the Sutherland estate in particular are well-documented.[53] But some were still prepared to take a stand against these alien beasts and their often equally foreign shepherds. In the summer of 1792 two sheep farmers (brothers from Lochaber) who rented land in the hills north of Alness in Inverness-shire seized a number of cattle – not for the first time – that had wandered in from a nearby grazing. These belonged to local men, who had been forced out of their farms when the land was given over to sheep; this time, however, their outraged owners decided to liberate them from the folds the shepherds had put them in without paying the fine for the trespass. The incident nearly turned very ugly when the sheep farmers pursued them with guns, but they were disarmed and the cattle brought home.

Shortly afterwards the cattlemen were all at a wedding, and, encouraged by the convivial company, worked up a head of steam against 'the sheep-farming system [which] was progressing in every part of the North Highlands, and the people driven year after year from the fields of their fathers'. Without perhaps thinking too much about the potential consequences, they decided 'to raise the war-cry against sheep and sheep-farming'. Thousands of the beasts were rounded up and marched towards the border of the county until the 42nd Regiment of Foot (the Black Watch), despatched from Fort George, arrived on the scene.

Starving, exhausted and entirely unprepared for such a well-armed response, the Alness cattlemen abandoned their woolly captives (none of which had suffered beyond the rigours of the journey) and headed for home. The soldiers were reportedly relieved not to have to deal harshly with their fellow countrymen, but they did manage to capture three unfortunates, two of whom were sentenced to

Carse of Stirling and Stirling Castle
In the Middle Ages, much of the land forming the carse of Stirling was boggy and peaty, though even then parts had been drained for agriculture. The major reclamation of this land began in the eighteenth century, creating 10,000 acres of farmland. HES, DP079016

transportation (the third was declared insane). These two escaped from the tollbooth in Inverness with the connivance of its keeper, the authorities also turning a blind eye so long as they remained in exile in neighbouring Moray. The insurrection was over; the sheep farmers and the landowners had won, as was probably inevitable.[54]

The impact of sheep-farming was dramatic and entirely obvious to everyone concerned. In parts of the Lowlands, the transformation of the system of arable farming was just as revolutionary, though elsewhere it proceeded more cautiously. Although the runrig system was swiftly abandoned during the eighteenth century, that did not necessarily mean that farms were then all neatly enclosed, their fields turned into squares or rectangles and their crops perfectly manured.

Sometimes Improvement took place only on the home farms of the great estates, as Daniel Defoe noted in Galloway in the 1720s, 'where you have neither hedge or tree, but about the gentlemen's houses'. He was most pleasantly surprised when he arrived in Carrick in Ayrshire, however, where 'you have beautiful enclosures, pleasant pastures, and grass grounds, and consequently store of cattle well fed and provided. The whole country is rich and fruitful, fill'd with gentlemen's seats and well-built houses: It is said this enclosing the country was owing to the English soldiers, who were placed here and in Kyle by Oliver Cromwell …'[55]

Whether or not Cromwell, whose armies conquered and held Scotland between 1650 and 1660, can be credited with setting the ball rolling, individual landowners could and did adopt some of the most up-to-date farming practices on their estates; the 5th Earl of Loudoun, whose main lands were also in Ayrshire, enclosed and subdivided his lands, paid for new farmhouses, roads and a bridge, planted trees, brought in coal and opened lime quarries (lime is burned and used to improve soil fertility). By keeping his farms reasonably small, the population actually increased.

In Dumfriesshire around 1770, the Duke of Queensberry 'removed no less than 25 farmers from these villages [Torthorwald and Roucan] to the more remote parts of the parish, where good farm houses were erected; for which his Grace gave them considerable assistance and at the same time enclosed almost his whole grounds with stone dykes and thorn hedges'. At Ormiston in East Lothian, the landowner, John Cockburn – known as the father of modern Scottish agriculture – was very keen to introduce to his ancestral estates the improvements he had seen while living in England 'and spared no labour nor expense to accomplish an object so desirable'. In 1732 he remodelled the village of Ormiston and laid out the adjoining fields according to a plan devised by an English surveyor, Lewis Gordon. These 'were all divided into small portions and enclosed with thorn hedges and hedge-row trees'.[56]

The Duke of Hamilton and the Earl of Strathmore also invested thousands of pounds in enclosures, drainage, liming, houses and – most helpfully for generations of subsequent historians – ordering surveys of their estates so as to know how best to proceed, a habit that has left us with many wonderful plans showing what the ground was like before and after Improvement.[57] It is difficult to imagine now what it would have been like to witness such radical change, which even led to the draining and often removal of entire bogs like that on the floodplain of the River Forth at Stirling and of lochs like Spynie near Elgin. From out of these muddy, marshy 'waste' grounds, new grasslands and arable fields sprang up, each with their neat stone farmhouses.

But these enterprising landowners were certainly not the whole story, just as it should also be said that John Cockburn of Ormiston bankrupted himself in his zeal for new agricultural methods and had to sell the estate he had worked so hard to improve. Elsewhere proprietors were criticised for not doing enough. As the minister of Dornock in Dumfriesshire put it:

It is certainly unlucky for this district, as well as for many others in Scotland, that the property of the soil has fallen into the hands of great proprietors, who draw their rents annually away, and spend them either in London or in foreign parts. Whereas smaller

Mertoun House, Berwickshire
The River Tweed meanders through the modern, intensively farmed landscape that was created in the eighteenth century around Mertoun House: a classic example of a lowland country estate and improved rectilinear fields and farms.
HES. DP082552

proprietors, living and residing on the spot, would lay out their rents at home, and uniting their stock and influence with men of activity in business, in promoting manufactories, commerce and improvements of every kind, would soon prove of essential service both to the district itself, and to the kingdom in general.[58]

To be fair, it did not seem to matter whether they were resident or lived elsewhere; many looked no further than the fact that, in getting rid of runrig, they could raise rents by auctioning off tenancies to the highest bidder. To compound the problem, the thought of being able to hike the rent up again at the end of a lease also encouraged landowners to keep them short. This might then leave the new tenant with neither the cash nor the incentive to improve (because he might not be able to stay long enough to get the benefit), though where they did have either sufficient independent means or encouragement, they too could bring about a transformation. Indeed, some fourteen years before John Cockburn began to experiment at Ormiston, one of his tenants, Robert Wight, had 'ditched and hedged and planted hedgerow trees at his own proper charge'. Needless to say, Wight was chosen by Cockburn to be first to hold a 38-year improving tenancy.[59]

The size and shape of Improvement fields very much depended on whether changes happened piecemeal or in one fell swoop, as well as how resistant the ground was to being neatly parcelled up – the drumlins of Galloway, for example, were entirely unwilling to be squared off, 'the fields being stony, interspersed with knolls, and most of them lying on an ascent'.[60] Here the Improvers had no choice but to accommodate what nature was unwilling to concede; but we know these are modern fields because they were not there before the 1st edition OS maps.

Beyond Galloway, however, straight lines were very much *de rigueur*. To begin with, as at Ormiston, these rectilinear* fields were often very small, only two or three acres, but it was soon discovered that bigger plots (around 20 acres) were much more efficient and they became common. In Lothian, where (as with elsewhere in the south-east) Improvement often came early, this process occurred somewhat organically, as and when money became available.

In parts of the north-east, on the other hand, fields were sometimes laid out on a single axis so that they lay together in a straight line. Such unnatural symmetry is, unsurprisingly, the product of a deliberate policy on the part of a landowner willing and able to move to the new system almost overnight and was more usual in the nineteenth rather than the eighteenth century. The island of Shapinsay on Orkney was transformed in this way by its owner, Lord Balfour, in the 1840s. These co-axial field systems are relatively rare, numbering only 4 per cent of the total land area covered by rectilinear fields; they are almost unheard of in the central Lowlands and Galloway.

Not everybody liked straight lines, however; some actively wanted to see aesthetically pleasing curves in the landscape, a preference that was also reflected in the more 'natural' grounds designed around the 'big houses' in the later eighteenth century. Others may have decided, from a financial point of view, to go with the curving lines of the head-dykes that had long separated arable fields from the rough pasture in the runrig system, even if straight dykes or hedges were put in to divide the fields internally.

In the southern uplands, especially Galloway, and the Highlands, these Improved fields (whether straight or curved) may have been imposed, more in hope than expectation, upon land of limited agricultural value, arable oases in seas of rough grazing. Not surprisingly, these fields did not necessarily repay the money spent on them and so were abandoned, the remains of the earthen head-dykes often still visible. If, on the other hand, such efforts did prove a worthwhile investment, the old boundaries might eventually be straightened and their origins lost forever unless captured on a map or a plan. Occasionally straight rig can be found on hillsides without any sign of a dyke or fence, implying that it became so swiftly obvious that the land wasn't worth ploughing that there wasn't even time to build boundaries.

We have already witnessed the revolution caused by the arrival of the mouldboard plough pulled by large teams of heavy oxen. Replacing the primitive ard, this new type of plough turned the soil over, mechanically creating ridges that, over time, formed broad high-backed rigs. This certainly made farming easier and more effective.

A lot of ground went to waste, however, when oxen plodded side by side and turned in such a wide circle; what was needed was a much lighter plough that could be pulled by a small team of horses. Given that this was an era of great scientific endeavour, a technological solution soon arrived in the shape of lighter swing ploughs. James Small, who was born about 1740 at Upsettlington in Berwickshire, developed his revolutionary implement after spending some time in Doncaster as a mechanic. There he came across the 'Rotherham', probably the first factory-made plough. Returning home in 1764, Small persuaded a local landowner, John Renton of Lamberton, to set him up in business and started work on a much better shape of mouldboard. In the end, he decided that iron (rather than wood) was needed to turn over the sod more deeply and easily, a decision made considerably more practical thanks to the founding of the Carron Ironworks near Falkirk five years earlier. Alas, like John Cockburn, James Small was no businessman and he too faced financial ruin, dying in 1793 at the age of only 53. Nevertheless, his invention became so ubiquitous that it was known as the Scots plough.

* * * *

… for the common, or rather universal, method of inclosing this fertile part of the country, where stones are scarce, is by ditches with hawthorn hedges planted in the sides, or on the top of the banks. This method was little known and still less practised till about 35 or 40 years. Before that period no inclosure was to be seen except, perhaps, one or two about a gentleman's seat, in all the wide, extended, beautiful plain of Cunningham. Hence at the end of harvest, when the crop was carried from the fields into the barn-yard, the whole country had the appearance of a wild and dreary common …[61]

Old Statistical Account,
Kilmarnock, Ayrshire, 1792

The question of enclosure is a vexed one, because, once again, we must sift through a morass of prejudice and cultural assumptions in order to get to the bottom of the plethora of opinions offered on the state of Scottish farming and what could be done to improve it. There is certainly much that is contradictory – if you remember, only a few pages ago, Daniel Defoe was really rather impressed with the state of hedging in the Carrick part of Ayrshire in the 1720s, whereas the minister writing the quote above about the Cunningham part of the same county is adamant that enclosure only started to become fashionable there in the 1750s.

We have already touched upon the extent to which fences, hedges and walls were, or had been, part and parcel of the Scottish landscape, which showed that Scottish farmers in some places at certain points in time could and did enclose. Elsewhere, at other times, beasts were supposed to have an eye kept on them, a task often assigned to young men or children, given that there were plenty of them available for work before the invention of factories, chimneys, pits and mandatory full-time education. There were often grave penalties for the trespass of animals, as Edmund Burt noted:

It is a common thing for the poorest sort hereabouts [near Inverness] to lead their horses out in summer, when they have done their work, and attend them while they graze by the sides of the roads and edges of the cornfields, where there is any little grass to be had without a trespass; and generally they hold them all the while by the halter, for they are certainly punished if it be known they encroached ever so little upon a field, of which none are enclosed. In like manner, you may see a man tending a single cow for the greatest part of the day …[62]

Nevertheless, it would be foolish to deny the many voices raised in outcry against the general lack of enclosure in Scotland, a sin compounded, especially in the eyes of shocked visitors from the south, by the lack of trees. Daniel Defoe was characteristically trenchant, though his concern was mainly with grazing:

The greatest thing this country wants is more enclos'd pastures, by which the farmers would keep stocks of cattle well fodder'd in the winter, and which again, would not only furnish good store of butter, cheese, and beef to the market, but would, by their quantity of dung, enrich their soil, according to the unanswerable maxim in grazing, that stock upon land improves land.

Thomas Pennant's remark that: 'Near Achline [west of Killin] the eye begins to be relieved by the

Talla Reservoir, Peebles-shire
Talla Water became a reservoir in 1899, at which time the surrounding hills were home to sheep and black cattle. But in the twentieth century some of the hills were instead covered in fast-growing conifers. More recently, the Borders Forest Trust purchased 4,500 acres of this land, intending to restore it to its 'natural state'. HES, DP033547

Tyninghame, East Lothian
Designed landscapes were a feature of estates in the eighteenth century, such as this planned forest with riding paths radiating from a central viewpoint. HES, DP058328

Deforested conifer plantation, the Borders
Scottish foresters needed to find fast-growing conifers suitable for water-logged, peaty soils, such as the Sitka Spruce from North America. ATStockFoto/Alamy

Tree felling squad, Bowmont Forest, Kelso, 1908
In the early twentieth century, tree felling was done by muscle power, which required a large number of (usually) men.
National Museums Scotland, licensor Scran

Lumbering in Glen Orchy, Argyll, 1950s
Horses helped to transport timber out of difficult-to-access forests and still do today.
National Museums Scotland, licensor Scran

Chapter Two – Farming

Forestry in the Great Glen at Loch Lochy
Straight lines are typical of twentieth century plantations up to 1989, when there was a change in planting policy.
HES, DP111929

Second World War 'Lumberjills', 1942
Like the Land Girls who kept agriculture going during the Second World War, women were given jobs in forestry.
National Museums Scotland, licensor Scran

Plantation, Camptown, Roxburghshire
Monotonous blocks of plantations are now often masked by more varied trees, such as here at Camptown.
Chris Strickland/Alamy

Forestry, Glenbranter, the Cowal peninsula, 1950s
Just as the cross-cut saw displaced the axe, the latter was also replaced – firstly by steam-powered felling and then the chainsaw.
The Scotsman Publications Ltd, licensor Scran

A History of Scotland's Landscapes

sight of the enclosures; and some plantations begin to hide the nakedness of the country' is typical of English expectations when it came to landscape aesthetics. Dorothy Wordsworth, too, did not hesitate to express her chagrin on the subject at every opportunity. 'The country [at Douglas Mill in Lanarkshire] for some time now had been growing into cultivation … trees in clumps, no hedgerows, which always make a country look bare and unlovely'; or 'Further up [Loch Awe], though the plantations on the hills are noble, the valley was cold and naked, wanting hedgerows and comfortable houses.'[63]

But this was not just about aesthetics; it was also about protection from 'the violent westerly winds' that were, according to the minister of the burgh of Ayr, the cause of the stunted thorn bushes and the absence of trees in his parish. His colleague in neighbouring Kilmarnock was more fortunate, for here 'the common, or rather universal, method of inclosing this fertile part of the country, where stones are scarce, is by ditches with hawthorn hedges planted in the sides, or on the top of the banks'. He certainly felt this made a difference, for 'the ground is, in some degree, sheltered by the hedges from the severity of the winter cold and storms. … In consequence, however, of this method of inclosure with thorn hedges, sheep are nearly banished from this country …' The minister at Pettie in Inverness-shire went even further in 1845, complaining that the soil was frequently lost by strong westerly winds, to the detriment of the turnip crops, 'which can be shrivelled and washed away in one hour. A stone dyke about four feet high saved a field on the Brae side for 100 yards from it.'[64]

But opinion was divided as to whether it was better to plant hedges or construct stone walls. The Scots were generally extremely well furnished with stone. On the other hand, the influential English liked their hedgerows, presumably in large part because they were used to them and missed finding them in Scotland. Overall, in the first century of Improvement, the preference seems to have been for hedges, mostly of thorn, usually accompanied by a ditch, though Improvers in the north-east, which is renowned for its stone, generally went for dykes.

It did all depend on what was available – in Torthorwald near Dumfries, 'The thorns have generally succeeded but the stone of which the dykes were built, being of the slatey kind, they have fallen down very much.' On the other hand, at Kirkden in Forfarshire, the minister noted that the 'lack of hedges, notwithstanding that trees are seldom absent, greatly impedes that luxuriance and warmth which the country would otherwise assume.' But he went on to say that the local farmers preferred stone dykes, because they are 'more cheaply and expeditiously brought to perfection, on account of their easy access to material' and also 'because hedges harbour birds, which destroy crops'.[65] Only in the far north and west was there no real attempt as yet to put walls or hedges in, either because farming was still communal or because it was easy enough to find herders for their animals. Or both.

Putting in straight lines through enclosure did not just make the land look less cold, naked or whatever else the Improvers thought hedgerows in particular would add to the view; it helped to completely redefine the look of farms that were used to sitting much more chaotically in the landscape, whilst getting rid of some altogether. Once upon a time, there were four farms whose names – Woodside, Righead, Underbank and Hillend – tell us quite a bit about where they were situated in pre-Improvement South Lanarkshire. But at the end of the eighteenth century, they were each divided into neat parcels of land. Woodside got off lightly with only a straightening of its boundaries; Underbank lost its south-west corner to Hillend, whilst Righead disappeared altogether. Now there were three farms of roughly the same size, all subdivided into straight-sided fields.

The invention of wire for fencing in the middle of the ninteenth century provided a cheaper alternative to hedges and stone dykes, which were both expensive and time-consuming to maintain. However, since stone was still plentiful in the north-east, dykes continued to be built not only where they were needed, but also specifically in order to get rid of the boulders clogging up the fields. Finally, in the decades following on from the Second World War, when a key government objective became the production of cheap food, horses, like the oxen before them, found themselves increasingly redundant. This time it was machines like tractors and combine harvesters that replaced them, their power and speed prompting a desire for even bigger fields. Internal fences, hedges and dykes were removed to create the vast 'prairie fields' of the fertile south-east in particular.

But if you look carefully at many of the fields of lowland Scotland, you can often see the different types of enclosure that farmers have had to choose from over the last 250 years. Stone walls lie beneath or alongside post-and-wire fences; the remains of thorn hedges might be spotted straggling nearby or marooned in the middle of a field that was once split in two. Lines of trees, perhaps with gaps where individuals have died, are also a common sight, again hinting at the fact that there was evolution as well as revolution to Improvement.

But trees played a far greater role in the Improvement plan than merely marking boundaries. The perception, noted above, was that the Scottish landscape was 'naked', particularly in the Lowlands. It is best, in the circumstances, to let Dr Johnson speak on the subject, though he is a man whose low opinion on almost everything and everyone is exceeded only by his even lower opinion of Scotland and the Scots.

A tree might be a show in Scotland as a horse in Venice. At St. Andrews Mr. Boswell found only one, and recommended it to my notice; I told him it was rough and low, or looked as if I thought so. This, said he, is nothing to another a few miles off. I was still less delighted to hear that another tree was not to be seen nearer. Nay, said a gentleman that stood by, I know but of this and that tree in the county.

The good doctor went on to remark that 'Forests are everywhere gradually diminished, as architecture and cultivation prevail by the increase of people and the introduction of arts. But I believe few regions have been denuded like this, where many centuries must have passed in waste without the least thought of future supply.'[66]

In fact the Scottish government had long wrestled with the problem, producing a regular stream of legislation designed to deal with those who peeled bark, 'destroying woods', or stole green (growing) wood. By the mid fifteenth century, steps were also being taken to reverse what was obviously becoming a serious shortage of timber in the Lowlands, ordering all tenants to 'plant woods and trees'. A prohibition was also placed on making fences from anything other than 'lying wood' (wood that had fallen off naturally from the tree).

But it was not enough. In 1505, James IV's parliament lamented that 'because the woods of Scotland are utterly destroyed, the penalty for it being so small, therefore it is decreed and ordained that the penalty for living woods for any man by selling or burning [it] in the future is to be £5 and that is both of regality and royalty, the old penalty for living woods for those who destroy them in other ways remaining in effect as before'.

That too made little difference, presumably because, as with any legislation, it was only as good as the numbers and commitment of those intended to police it. By 1535, the Scottish government tried a new tack, ordering that everyone with £100-worth of land, whether in the Church or a layman, was to 'plant woods and forests and make hedges and enclosures for himself extending to three acres of land, and above or under as his heritage is more or less in places most suitable'. Their tenants were also enjoined to plant at their 'dwelling site' one tree for every merk* of land they rented.[67]

The fruits of this ancient edict, or adaptations of it, do seem to have become an intrinsic part of the farming landscape over many centuries – it was stated in 1792, for example, that: 'By the oldest leases on the Barr estate [in Galston parish, Ayrshire], the tenants were bound to plant at least twelve ash yearly.'[68] Even today, if you see a small clump of trees in an area of rough grazing with no obvious signs of habitation, the chances are that it was once the site of a farmhouse.

But this was scarcely a programme of massive reafforestation. Part of the problem lay in the fact that timber was needed for so many facets of life, from building materials (including the costly hammerbeam roofs that had once enjoyed such popularity among the elites) to tools and domestic goods. Equally, planting around houses, castles and stately homes was unlikely to make a huge difference in terms of replacing the forests that had once covered much of the country. Management practices designed to, for example, preserve trees from the depredations of the animals that were often sent to graze in the shelter of local woods were practised at both an official (ie landowner) level and as part of less formal countryside culture, though the 'cutting high' practised by peasants (probably a form

Black-faced sheep

The black-faced sheep was one of the improved breeds from northern England which replaced the smaller, very woolly, native Scottish sheep in the eighteenth century. The robust black-face proved ideal for hill country exposed to the chill of Atlantic storms and was soon one of the most popular breeds throughout the country. Wayne Hutchinson/Alamy

of pollarding, which is explicitly designed to keep growing shoots away from hungry animal mouths) could be frowned upon by their masters.[69] The other great problem was that the timber resource was not generally owned by most of those who used it and therefore they had no incentive to look after it.

Though this was equally true in the Highlands, comparatively large semi-natural woodlands were still in reasonable supply a number of centuries after scarcity struck the Lowlands. Given the weight of opinion decrying the treeless landscapes of the south, it might seem somewhat ironic that the closer relationship between England and Scotland after 1603 and, particularly, the Union of 1707, brought English (and Irish) entrepreneurs north to chop down many of the remaining forests in the Highlands for industries such as charcoal- and iron-smelting, and tanning, as well as timber for building.

However, that did not necessarily mean that the incomers were responsible for destroying the woodlands, though they were often blamed for it. In 1772 Thomas Pennant described what he found around Loch Tulla near Bridge of Orchy in Argyll, some decades after a contingent of Irish 'adventurers' had been given a contract by the owner, the Earl of Breadalbane (originally the laird of Glenorchy), to cut both pine and oak there: 'A few weather-beaten pines and birch appear scattered up and down, and in all the bogs great numbers of roots, that evince the forest that covered the country within this half century.' Dorothy Wordsworth saw something similar 30 years later: 'A forest – now, as it appeared, dwindled into the small grove bordering the lake – had, not many years ago, spread to that side of the vale where we

114   Chapter Two – Farming

Cheviot sheep

The Cheviot white-faced sheep, which was not as hardy as the black-face, was another improved breed that spread north during the eighteenth and nineteenth centuries. Since the 1970s, however, the Texel breed of sheep from the Netherlands has been preferred for the lean quality of its meat.

Designer Pics Inc/Alamy

were: large stumps of trees which had been cut down were yet remaining undecayed, and there were some single trees left alive …'[70]

These particular Irish entrepreneurs were certainly cavalier in their attitude to the woods and the spirit, if not the letter, of their contract with Breadalbane, not to mention their own creditors and even each other. But the truth is that the estate managers were negligent – often out of ignorance – in putting in place, and enforcing, proper safeguards that would have ensured the long-term future of what must have once been a most impressive forest. This was compounded by the fact that Breadalbane mostly lived in England, and, when he did come to Scotland, usually stayed on his eastern estates on Loch Tay; he was asked to send proper expertise to Glenorchy, but did not realise until it was too late just how serious the situation was.

But even that does not get to the bottom of this sorry tale. According to the contract with the Irish, they were not to cut any pine tree less than 24 inches in girth at breast height, a sensible stipulation that should have guaranteed the next wave of mature trees. As it turned out, however, there were very few of that size, which implies that regeneration was an issue long before the Irish started cutting them. Certainly other pinewoods in the area that they had nothing to do with disappeared too.[71]

Nevertheless, there is no doubt that a far more responsible attitude prevailed among the English ironmasters who set up the Lorn Furnace Company in 1752, constructing the famous Bonawe Iron Furnace on the banks of Loch Etive (though Pennant did fear that it would 'soon devour the beautiful woods of the country').[72] Though considerable amounts of timber were indeed cut

A History of Scotland's Landscapes

down, the instigation of coppicing* and other effective aspects of forestry – not least because it was in their own interests to maintain the supply – meant that, more than 70 years after they began, their 'beneficial effect on the woods was held up for admiration'.[73] Indeed, some of their former sites are lauded today for their ecological value, as at Strone near Dalmally and Glen Nant at Taynuilt, both in Argyll, and Ariundle Oakwood near Strontian, the last two of which are now National Nature Reserves and include charcoal platforms indicating their former role as coppices. The remnants of platforms built in the eighteenth and nineteenth centuries in order to transform timber cut down from the surrounding woods into charcoal (needed for industries such as iron-smelting, glass-making and tanning) are to be found at over one hundred sites in Argyll, Dumfries and Galloway, Moray, and Perthshire. Within each site, individual platforms might number only one or two up to dozens spread over several acres. They might also form part of a much deeper historic environment stretching back millennia.[74]

The introduction of large-scale sheep grazing (and also deer for sport) could have had disastrous consequences just at the point when it seemed the need to plant trees was being taken seriously again, but land managers were by then well aware of the need to protect what was there, usually with dyke and ditch boundaries that can still be seen today, often surmounted by modern post and wire fencing.

Large-scale planting began in the seventeenth century – Defoe reported that 'the gentlemen of Scotland are now set upon planting forest trees, as well for ornament as profit.' He singled out the 'old' Earl of Tweeddale (John Hay, 1st Marquess and 2nd Earl of Tweeddale, 1626 – 1697), who was inspired by King Charles II's plans to create Greenwich and St James's parks in London. The Earl and his son, also John, reputedly 'planted above 6000 acres of land all full of firr-trees; and that, where-ever it was found that any tree fail'd, they were constantly renew'd the next year'.[75] However, the principle of planting far beyond the confines of their own parks and vistas in order to provide both protection for the soil and serviceable timber only became more common as improving principles began to be applied more generally from the latter half of the eighteenth century.

* * * *

***… when any tenant wishes to have his farm improved in any way, he has only to carry the tiles to the field to be drained and to furnish straw to cover them in cases where it is necessary and the whole work is performed without any farther expense to him, except the payment of a yearly sum proportioned to the distance at which the drains are placed.*[76]**

New Statistical Account,
Galston, Ayrshire, 1845

I never imagined I would develop an interest in field drains, but in these past few years I have become slightly fascinated by them. At the back of our village hall sits a tennis court, beyond which is the playpark and football pitch, while even further beyond is a grassy field that usually hosts a flock of sheep and the annual agricultural show. Once upon a time (at least into the 1930s), what is now the football pitch was used for curling, which will immediately alert you to the fact that water accumulates there, running gently down from the sheep field.

Though the curling club disbanded, the puddle/small pond remained and, in particularly wet seasons, it would creep across the park, through the tennis court, and on into the village hall. After investigations, it was discovered that some of the existing field drains were blocked, so a local farmer was paid to clear them out and put a few more in. For the last two winters, we have had nothing more than a soggy football pitch. But I like to keep a close eye on it.

As Improvement gathered pace in the first decades of the nineteenth century, to the point where most farms, certainly in the Lowlands, were reasonably well enclosed, attention turned to fine tuning the condition of the land. Drainage became a hot topic from Dunoon on the Clyde to Banffshire in the north-east. The Duke of Portland, who held estates in Ayrshire but was essentially an English landowner, set up a tile-making factory at Galston near Kilmarnock, bringing in experts from down south to assist his Scottish tenants, who were, as mentioned in the quote at the beginning of this section, given every assistance to introduce the drains into their own fields. The innovation proved very popular, 'because, in winter, the western rains are not taken away by the sun but stagnate on the ground.' Indeed, in Kilmarnock parish alone, it was reckoned that 800,000 tiles were made locally every year, with a further 500,000 brought in from neighbouring Moorhouse.[77]

The drains – which were usually made of clay – were laid out about eighteen feet apart, with various modifications adopted for different types of ground. If the field was more than 250–300 yards long or if there were hollows within it, a main drain two feet deep was put through the middle to prevent choking. Another big drain was then put across the end of the field to take away all the water. It was reckoned that at least £500 (over £40,000 today) was needed to remove water from a 100-acre farm, a sum so extravagant that it certainly required the kind of incentives offered by the Duke of Portland for tenant farmers to think of taking them up. On the Loudoun estate, also in Ayrshire (which seems to have been the field drainage capital of Scotland), one million tiles were manufactured in a single year to draw off water from 250 acres of land.[78]

But such a glorious application of science and technology went well beyond fields. Draining lochs and bogs and turning them into farmland was an intrinsic part of the whole rationalisation of agriculture, since such natural features were regarded as existing in that worst of all conditions – 'waste'. Analysis of General Roy's maps from the eighteenth century once again provides a base-line for the extent of this wholesale drainage and it is has been estimated that some lochs in the Lowlands, and especially eastern Scotland, lost between 40 and 90 per cent of their surface area.[79]

Sometimes they more or less disappeared, as at Spynie near Elgin (which once stretched over an area roughly twelve square kilometres), Loch of Park near Drumoak in Aberdeenshire which has been planted and is now a nature reserve, Loch Auchlossan, also in Aberdeenshire, Restenneth Loch in Forfar, Loch of Kinnordy near Kirriemuir in Angus (which is also a nature reserve) and Rossie Loch in Fife where the Rossie drain, dug in 1806, is still clearly visible along the edge of Heatherhall Woods near Ladybank.

Others have been reduced in size – Loch Leven in Fife, currently thirteen square kilometres, was once nearly half as broad again. Forfar Loch, though never particularly large, lost nearly half of its 140 acres; apparently, 'the vast quantity of the fine marl* at the bottom was the temptation'. By 1845, just about all of this valuable fertiliser had been retrieved from the drained areas and, not wanting to lose any more of the loch, the rest had 'for many years been dredged up from below the water by an apparatus attached to a boat, and many thousands of pounds of this useful manure have been obtained out of this loch'.[80]

Many small lochs have also been drained for farmland, sometimes leaving only a name, as at Loch Brown near Mossgiel in Ayrshire. As late as 1845 it still covered about 60 acres of ground, having escaped being drained, 'for the sake of two corn mills which it supplies with water'. But it is entirely gone now, though the curving north-east boundary of one of the modern fields that lies over the top of it surely retains part of its outline.[81] Such profound changes to the landscape have had a fundamental impact on our understanding of archaeological sites. Around 80 fortified places or crannogs have been located on the Roy maps surrounded by bodies of water that have now completely disappeared, including Lochore Castle near Lochgelly in Fife.

Some of these reclamation projects, like the one at Spynie, were major feats of engineering, but so too were those designed to push back rivers and even the sea, though the process could be made much easier (and cheaper) if the water body in question was already silting up. It is hard to imagine that these places were not always farmland, but if you take a closer look, their origins are sometimes given away by high water marks on maps with suspiciously straight lines. This was the case at Eden croft near Guardbridge, where drains enclosed by a dyke visible on aerial photographs provide further proof that the land here was once under water.

Land reclamation was an urban phenomenon too; in the nineteenth century, new sites were brought into existence for harbours and industrial areas in the large cities. These areas may have

been transformed again in the last few decades as recreational, commercial and residential uses replace industrial and older commercial ones, as has happened at Leith at Edinburgh.

Nevertheless, the most famous reclamation project was the draining of the carse of Stirling, once a bog up to twenty feet deep. The process was begun by a number of local landowners, led by Lord Kames, whose wife inherited the Blair Drummond estate in 1766. Using a waterwheel and a great drainage ditch linked to the River Teith to wash the peat away, the hard labour was provided by the so-called 'Moss lairds' – farmers enticed down from Balquidder (whose most famous resident, Rob Roy MacGregor, reputedly once skulked in the carse's impenetrable morass) by reduced rents for up to nineteen years, wood for houses and free food for a year.

[A typical] eight-acre plot was marked off and behind it ran a drainage channel connected with the complex of waterways. [In the] summer the whole family set to work stripping the top three-foot layer of sphagnum moss which they flung into the ditch. Then came their house. On a small area beside the road, they proceeded to clear the next three-foot layer which consisted of swamp grass and rotting vegetation. Once down to the layer of peat, they cut four trenches about five feet deep right down into the clay sub-strata. Then they scooped out the interior like a turnip lantern. The outside walls dried and shrank, and the estate timber was used to form a roof over this pit which was covered with turf.

More than 10,000 acres were turned into very valuable farmland this way and in 1811 it was recorded that 764 men, woman and children had taken up residence on the carse, along with 264 cows, 166 horses, 375 hens, 30 pigs, 168 cats and 8 dogs. However, the volume of peat sent down, ultimately, into the Forth began to silt up the river so that

Edinburgh Castle and the Nor' Loch, Alexander Nasmyth, 1824

For those of us who approach Edinburgh via Waverley Station, it may be a surprise to learn that the land it occupies was once under water – the Nor' (North) Loch, to be precise. Of the 200 lochs identified in eastern Scotland from mid eighteenth century maps, most have been reduced by between 50 and 100 per cent. National Galleries Scotland. Presented by Mrs E Pringle, 1948

A History of Scotland's Landscapes

Stacked peat, Duirinish peninsula, Skye
Peat was an effective source of fuel in much of Scotland for thousands of years until coal became cheaper in the nineteenth century. Paul Marshall/Alamy

Carrying peat, Eilean Fladday, near Skye, c1965
Cutting, stacking, drying and transporting peat was a back-breaking and time-consuming business for farming communities over the summer. Gairloch Heritage Museum

Peat cuttings, Aird Thunga, Isle of Lewis
Though peat undoubtedly served many communities well as fuel, as it still does today, its spread after 1000 BC acted as a severe impediment to farming, the water-logged soils often proving impossible to cultivate. HES, SC1007539

Haymarket Coal Depot, Edinburgh, 1972
Men fill bags with peat at the Haymarket Coal Depot during a miners' strike. The Scotsman Publications Ltd, licensor Scran

Cut peat, North Uist, Outer Hebrides

Over several seasons a peat bank can reach a depth of two metres. Lynne Evans/Alamy

sea-going ships could no longer reach Stirling (as they still can't). The clearing of the carse stopped in 1865, leaving patches of the old peatbog at Blair Drummond Moss, Drip Moss and the celebrated Flanders Moss.[82]

The development of drainage technology was not just used to create ever more farmland out of aspects of the landscape that were viewed as useless (though which might well be valued now for their biodiversity); it was also put to work in saving existing farmland from flooding. Embankments were one method of control, though they did not necessarily prove sufficient. Those put in to stop the inundations caused by the River Dee near Drumoak in Aberdeenshire had still not worked by 1845, though, further north, the River Don was generally held captive by embankments on the farm of Bedlieston, apart from during exceptional floods, such as the one in 1829. Embankment failure on the Mein Water in Dumfriesshire was put down to 'the gravelly nature of the soil'. It was noted in some places that the field drains caused some of the rivers and streams into which they flowed to rise far higher than they used to, but any extra volume of water did not necessarily last long.[83]

Rather more successfully, the landowner at Lathrisk near Cupar in Fife 'caused a spacious canal [on the River Eden] to be made for the water, twelve feet wide at the bottom and thirty feet at the top, secured on the sides by embankments and hedges, which include a space seventy feet in breadth, so that in time of a flood there is sufficient space for containing the water, and preventing its overflowing and damaging the adjacent grounds'. The unusual straightness of the river that still runs through Lathrisk suggests it is the canal that has survived rather than the original course of the Eden. The Rossie Drain mentioned above falls into the same river a short distance away.[84]

At the same time, farmers may also have wanted to encourage flooding on their haugh lands (so long as the water was not in the habit of carrying off the soil), 'for fattening his meadows with a rich alluvion'.[85] Even more technically challenging were attempts, from at least the early seventeenth century, to control water in order to improve rough grazing on hillsides or to nurture arable fields and plantations. Though these water meadows were known in the Middle Ages as far north as Orkney, where Earl Ronald sat beside the bed of his wife, 'the sick goddess of the fishes of the island-watermeadows',[86] they then seem to have disappeared, probably because the amount of rainfall generally kept the land well-watered. Nevertheless, they were a common feature of the grazing regimes of southern England and, after a failed attempt at the end of the eighteenth century on the Buccleuch estates, English methods were introduced across the Lowlands, especially in the upper reaches of the River Tweed, from the 1820s to the 1840s.

The meadow was laid out in gently sloping ridges separated by drains, while water from a nearby river or stream, controlled by a weir, was brought to it via a lade*. Small sluices and hatches were then used to send the water into a small channel at the crest of each ridge which, when full, would overflow into the ridge itself. This was usually done for a few weeks towards the end of the winter, so that the water could warm up the soil and encourage grass to grow early for sheep to nibble on once the ground had dried out. The process would then be repeated and the grass left this time until summer, when it was cut as hay to be saved for winter fodder.

By the end of the nineteenth century, new fodder crops and mechanisation overtook the need for such meadows; however, many survived as rough grazing right up until the 1940s. They are hard to spot now, without their sluices and drains, their ridges almost invisible at ground-level, though occasionally traces of the grooves marking the line of the water-feeders on their crests can be found. Aerial photographs have revealed over 200 water meadows through the remains of their weirs, lades, sluices, rig, conductors and drains, a testament to yet another optimistic application of human strength and ingenuity that, alas, has not stood the test of time.

* * * *

The means of bettering their situation seem to be chiefly these, 1. Taking high duty off English coals; as much time, labour and expense are consumed in cutting, winning and carting peat, which operates as a very great discouragement to manufactures …[87]

Old Statistical Account, New Abbey, Kirkcudbrightshire, 1792

We have already come across this opinion on the excessive labour required to 'win peats' when we were delving deeper into Dorothy Wordsworth's shocked reaction to the dirt left on the windows and doorways of the houses of the new town of Inveraray. In fact, it was a view held by many in Scotland, for how could the benefits of Improvement be fully realised if the labour force spent so much of its time engaged in an activity that was, given the existence of alternatives for fuel and light, essentially unnecessary?

There were other concerns over peat, not least that, in the second half of the eighteenth century, it was beginning to run out in some parts of the country.[88] The levy on the shipping of English coal was, in fact, repealed for Scotland in 1793 (though not in England and Wales),[89] which helped to tip the balance in favour of its use in the Lowlands, where it was also mined locally. In the Highlands, where peat was still plentiful, transportation costs continued to make coal prohibitively expensive for many, though not all, of the inhabitants. There is also some evidence that the concern felt by visitors at the sheer drudgery of cutting peats, especially when confronted by Highland women most indelicately lugging home huge creels of them on their backs, was not necessarily shared by those engaged in it. In Stornoway parish as late as 1845, 'the peat-cutting season is one of joy and hilarity. Eggs, butter, cheese and whisky are brought to the peat bank.'[90]

It was a back-breaking job, of that there can be no doubt; but sharing it with friends and family made lighter work of it, as was the case for so many aspects of communal farming life, or even a farming life with many hands still needed to perform its necessary tasks. Specially designed spades varied in their shape and length from region to region, but were all designed to deal with the wetness of the ground.

First of all, the turf would be stripped back, exposing the peat, which would be cut into long blocks that left great rectangular scars in the landscape. The diggers needed to make sure that the inevitable rainwater could drain away rather than pooling in the freshly cut area, which would then be ruined. Once the peat had been dug, it needed to dry, either by laying it out in straight lines across the moor or in blocks laid on their ends in a pyramid shape; if this was not done sufficiently – and many seasons must have made that exceedingly difficult – then it simply would not burn properly.

Eventually, however, the blocks could be brought down off the moorland. The farmers were lucky if the ground was suitable for carts pulled by ponies. But in many places it was too uneven and so the women loaded up their creels, caring so little for the weight of them, 'that, while walking with it, they are engaged either at spinning on the distaff or knitting stockings'. Sometimes, as at Ben Lawers in Perthshire, stone stances were built by a tenant to stack the peats temporarily before taking them down to the steading.[91]

In the twentieth century peat cutting remained popular with crofters, many of whom might have been allocated a particular piece of ground from which to get their fuel. The tradition continues down to the present day, particularly in the Northern and Western Isles, though thankfully wheelbarrows and tractors can now be used to bring the fuel in. From the nineteenth century, too, peat has been sold commercially, mostly in the Western Isles, but also along the Central Belt. It was – and still is – most commonly used as fuel and compost, but distilleries have also long burned it to dry the barley, giving some whiskies their distinctive smoky taste.

To begin with these commercial peats were still dug with spades, but from the late nineteenth century machines were invented that allowed distilleries to harvest it from the bogs in granulated form. These days a large machine cuts it out and fashions it into briquettes. Such moorlands look quite different from those cut by spades because of the complete removal of vegetation in a uniform pattern of parallel strips and drains usually put in to prevent water-logging. Narrow gauge railways were sometimes also used to take the peat straight to processing plants, as at the Mossmorran Peat Works in Fife, which – along with many others – closed in the 1970s amid growing environmental concerns.[92]

Once these sites were abandoned, they were soon transformed into industrial wastelands before eventually becoming scrubland. An application to reopen the Mossmorran site, this time on behalf of a company from the north-east of England, was rejected in 2015 amid a plethora of objections from environmental organisations. Peat is now recognised as playing a role in keeping carbon in the ground, which is far better than burning the peat and releasing carbon into the atmosphere.[93]

Bell's improved reaping machine, c1840
Throughout the nineteenth century, efforts were made to invent a mechanical reaper to speed up the harvest. In 1828 Patrick Bell, a Church of Scotland minister, put to work a machine comprising a revolving reel that pulled the crop over a cutting knife, which was then pushed to the side on a canvas conveyor. He did not patent it, believing it should be of universal benefit, but others soon did.
World History Archive/Alamy

Around half a per cent of Scotland's land surface shows traces of peat cutting, the rectangular scars clearly visible from the air in, for example, the haggs* situated in the moss to the north of the crofting township of Aird Thunga on Lewis. However, once the turf begins to grow back, it is almost impossible to be sure it was once cut, though meandering tracks marked on Ordnance Survey maps that seem to peter out into nothing on rough ground might be evidence for recent peat cutting.

Equally, this rough ground might now be used for forestry. Although the private planting projects that were popular between the seventeenth and the nineteenth centuries did make considerable progress in reversing the decline of previous centuries (if not millennia), the military requirements of the First World War devastated their stocks. Deeply concerned about the nation's ability to supply itself with this crucial resource, Lloyd George's coalition government set up the Forestry Commission in 1919 to oversee the buying up of land and the planting of new state-owned forests. In Scotland it proved particularly easy (and cheap) to acquire large areas of rough grazing, particularly on hillsides that were of little interest to farmers at the time. By 1939 the Commission was the largest landowner in Britain, but the onset of the Second World War again severely depleted timber stocks.

With the advent of the nuclear age after the war, however, it was believed that conventional warfare had had its day. The Commission now came under considerable pressure to justify its activities on economic grounds, rather than the need to maintain a strategic reserve of timber. At the same

Combine harvester, Scottish Borders
Though Bell's invention helped to revolutionise agriculture, the use of hand implements continued in many parts of Scotland until the middle of the twentieth century. By then, however, the continuously advancing technology had begun to take hold almost everywhere, leading to another decline in the numbers of people needed to perform what had once been highly labour-intensive tasks.
Jason Baxter/Alamy

time agriculture began to expand, pushing forestry into more and more marginal land, the very areas in which much of the evidence for the land-use of previous centuries was to be found. Modern planting methods, using large machinery, have obliterated many of these ancient landscapes, but, as we see, forestry can also protect older remains.

By the 1960s, concern was developing both within the Commission and among the wider public over the aesthetic impact of commercially preferable monocultures*, often of Sitka Spruce, which grew quickly and well in peaty soils, but tended to look bleak and boring when planted en masse in the landscape.

It is easy enough to recognise the forests planted in this period thanks to their uncompromising straight edges, the tendency to plant single species and the lack of clearings other than equally straight fire breaks. However, some foresters did manage to bend the rules a little, softening the edges of their woods with other species, as at Strathyre north of Callander (which have mostly been clear-felled in recent years), long before they were encouraged to create more fluid and aesthetically pleasing edges, as well as to plant native species, which has been the case since the 1990s.

The Countryside Act of 1968 reflected a growing awareness throughout society of the need to care for the environment and the desire of many, especially in the towns and cities, to have access to the great outdoors. The Forestry Commission moved with the times, slowly but surely making their own vast holdings accessible to campers,

Prairie farmland, Greystone, Angus
In the aftermath of the Second World War, UK agriculture focused on producing substantial quantities of cheap food. Large and expensive machinery aided the task, prompting the creation of even bigger fields to accommodate them. This in turn led to the amalgamation of more farms and the creation of the modern prairie-like farming landscape, with few hedges surviving from earlier phases of Improvement. The village of Greystone in the centre left of the image is a rare relic of a settlement of medieval origin in the modern farming landscape. HES, DP255362

walkers, picnickers and, most recently, mountain-bikers. There has also been a concerted effort, up to and including the appointment of archaeologists to the Commission staff, to record, preserve and publicise the remains of previous land-use to be found within the Forestry estate. Given that conifers cover up to 15 per cent of the total land in Scotland, 9 per cent of which is owned by the Commission, this is much to be welcomed.

Archaeological evidence from the last eight thousand years lies hidden within the depths of semi-natural woodlands and modern plantations; these remains include prehistoric hill-forts, groups of shieling huts, rig and enclosures, abandoned rectilinear fields and remnants of past industrial activity. At the same time, the wider landscape contains traces of the managed woodlands that were once to be found there, such as the original wood dyke boundaries, or, as with field systems, the outline of borders retained by whichever land-use replaced them, their existence corroborated by old maps.

This is also true for the remains of historic orchards, evidence for which is hard to find on the ground, despite the fact that they were once almost everywhere. Fruit trees at least a century old do survive on rig and furrow cultivation in the largely post-Improvement landscape of rectilinear fields in the Carse of Gowrie between Perth and Dundee. The gardens and fields of the nineteenth century planned village (and surrounding cottages and farms) of Hazelbank in Lanarkshire are still covered in fruit trees, some old and dying but others young and thrusting. However, most of the other orchards that once flourished in these prime fruit-growing regions have become overgrown with other vegetation or grubbed up altogether.

As we have already seen, orchards could be found in all parts of the country from at least the Middle Ages, but with the Union and Improvement, commercial opportunities beckoned, not least thanks to better transportation. The Clyde Valley has always been well-known for its fruit, a fact supposedly celebrated by Merlin the poet as far back as the fifth century, though to begin with, as in the rest of Scotland, the trees were planted in the gardens of local houses, 'for the accommodation of the occupants'.

It is claimed, however, that orchards began to be cultivated for profit from the seventeenth century, especially on the north bank of the Clyde, which benefits from a southern exposure. In those days the trees were planted on sloping ground that was no use for anything else (other than forest trees). Even when there was a suitably hospitable climate, there were considerable risks in such ventures. At Hamilton it was noted that 'upon the whole this is a very precarious article of produce, subject to many injuries from spring-frosts, the depredations of caterpillars, summer's blights etc so that there is scarcely one year in three in which the orchards turn to good account'. Nevertheless, only eight miles away, at Dalserf, large orchards had been planted 'and every hedge and fence filled with plum trees; even the tenants all along the Clyde have all large orchards near their houses'. The crop, which included gooseberries and currants, was sold in the teeming metropolises of Glasgow and Paisley and was worth £400 a year (over £40,000 today).[94]

During the 'good' old days of the Napoleonic Wars (1803–15), however, sales exploded to around £1,400 a year (over £120,000 now), prompting fertile ground to be given over to fruit even by small farmers. After 1815 (when the war ended), unsurprisingly, prices plummeted to half their wartime value, thanks to steam-boats bringing in more competitively priced goods from England and Ireland, 'to the indifference of many with regard to the quality of the fruit used – if not also in some degree to the decay of patriotic feeling'.

The main fruits along the Clyde were gooseberries, pears, plums and apples, especially large baking ones. If planting from scratch, great care was taken to make sure that excess water was removed from the ground 'either by open or covered drains'. These newer orchards were neater than the older ones, with the trees set out in rows 10–30 feet apart with 10–20 feet left between each one. Potatoes were often planted while the trees were young or the ground needed to be cleaned, while crops were planted in rotation in the larger orchards.

The fruit used to be harvested by shaking the tree, a strategy likely to produce quick but badly bruised results. By 1845 they were pulled carefully by hand and packed onto carts in hampers and baskets cushioned with straw for their journey to the Glasgow market, which opened at 5pm. The merchants set off at noon, selling their wares in the towns and villages en route. They took their fruit to Edinburgh at the beginning of winter, when supplies were likely to be running low and prices would therefore be higher. These industrious Clydesdale entrepreneurs led a precarious life, often having to deal in other commodities such as wood or survive on extra cash they might earn as labourers. Nevertheless, fruit-growing, for all its arduousness, seemed to breed enthusiasts.[95]

But enthusiasm was not enough in the face of hard economics. By the early twentieth century most orchards had been grubbed up so that a more profitable crop might be planted, though a few places, especially round Blairgowrie in Perthshire, continued to grow fruit commercially. By the beginning of the twenty-first century, however, a growing interest in biodiversity and food miles, as well as an appreciation of the joys of horticulture, has led to a desire to know more about this undervalued aspect of the historic landscape and the lives of our predecessors.[96] The story goes on.

View Towards the Clyde by George Frederick Buchanan, c1850
Smoke from mills and factories along the Clyde interrupts this otherwise typical Victorian landscape painting – the industrialisation of Scotland has become the backdrop even for rural life.
Crown copyright: Government Art Collection, UK

Chapter Three

Industry and Infrastructure

Our very hands and bodies, under the lash and in the midst of insult, are worn down by the toil of clearing forests and morasses ... We have neither fruitful plains, nor mines, nor harbours, for the working of which we may be spared.

Calgacus, as represented by Tacitus in
On the Life and Times of Julius Agricola, cAD 98

In his biography of his father-in-law Agricola, Roman governor of Britain between AD 77 and 85, the historian Tacitus put these sympathetic words into the mouth of Calgacus, the first named Scot, having already given the Caledonian the first memorable Scottish slogan – 'they [the Romans] create a wilderness and call it peace'.[1] The main target of Tacitus's impassioned oratory was the tyranny that he often detected at the heart of Roman power politics, but he also bears witness – presumably through Agricola's own testimony - to the undeveloped 'state of nature' in which the peoples of northern Britain still lingered, in the good company of other Celtic tribes who had not yet been introduced to what the Romans could do for them by way of aqueducts, sanitation, roads, irrigation, etc, etc.

Given that even the Greeks were found lacking by the Romans, we have no reason to imagine that Tacitus (through Agricola) was misrepresenting Caledonia's comparative lack of a sophisticated infrastructure; so far as even the average Roman legionary was concerned, whatever was already there was

A History of Scotland's Landscapes

Ardoch Roman Fort, Perthshire
The Romans were only fleeting visitors to Scotland, but they had planned to stay. This fort is one of the largest remaining examples of their military endeavours in Scotland.
HES, DP229032

bound to struggle to reach even woefully inadequate. Having said that, we already know that the early peoples of Scotland could and did create public and ceremonial spaces every bit as structurally challenging and awe-inspiring as a Roman forum* or temple. Indeed, these monuments are testament to the centralising of local power in the hands of the few, but such a rudimentary hierarchy could never generate the funds and labour needed to build aqueducts, sanitation, roads, irrigation, etc, etc. For that, you needed the concentrated power and bureaucracy of a great city at the heart of a vast empire.

It is also fair to say – as anyone who has slogged up a Scottish mountain or across a Scottish bog away from the well-trampled slopes of the most popular hills will agree – that many a Scottish landscape has a variety of wiles at its disposal to resist being tamed. Even the straightforward determination of a Roman road might well have faltered in the face of the peat spreading across the north and west of the country before, during and after the legionaries' arrival.

There is certainly evidence that the early inhabitants of Scotland knew how to build thoroughfares long before the arrival of the legionaries. As we have already seen, Thomas Pennant recorded the discovery of a prehistoric road at Priestside near Ruthwell in Dumfriesshire.[2] Nevertheless, roads were in short supply before the Romans arrived and for a long time after. In part, it may have been that waterways – which Scotland had in abundance – were, and continued to be, an overwhelmingly easy and culturally important means of transporting people and goods through and around difficult terrain. From the canoes that brought the earliest settlers back to Scotland after the Ice Age to the birlinns* that helped the Lords of the Isles to command the western Highlands and

Rough Castle Fort, Antonine Wall, Stirlingshire
The Antonine Wall, now a UNESCO World Heritage Site, was a major border and communication route, linking the Clyde to the Forth.
HES, DP0014298

Islands, as well as the hundreds of smaller craft used for everyday needs, including fishing, we should not underestimate the seamanship of our predecessors, however few traces we have of their activities.

The Romans, of course, did build roads during the temporary occupation of southern Scotland. The line that they followed – from Carlisle in the north-west of England and Corbridge in the north-east up beyond the Firths of Forth and Clyde – often underpinned much later networks, traces of which still survive today. The remains of their great forts and smaller marching camps are also sometimes still visible across southern Scotland and the Highland fault-line, a testament to the might and sheer determination of the Romans and the character of the land that they ultimately failed to tame.

The Antonine Wall is still the most extensive Roman part of the landscape. 'It begins', says the chronicler John of Fordun, compiling his history over a thousand years later, 'on the east, upon the southern shore of the Scottish sea [the River Forth], near the town of Carriden [near Bo'ness in West Lothian]; then stretches on across the island, for twenty-two miles, with the city of Glasgow to the south of it, and stops on the bank of the river Clyde, near Old Kilpatrick in Dunbartonshire.'[3] Around a third of it – including remains of the forts and fortlets regularly inserted into the wall – can still be detected, often as a ditch or earthwork, while even more is visible as a cropmark from the air.

Built on the orders of Emperor Antoninus Pius around AD 142, this marked the second major attempt at conquering Scotland after the withdrawal of the 80s and the construction of Hadrian's Wall around AD 122 at the northern limit of the Empire in Britain. The new border took twelve years to complete, despite the fact that it was made of turf on stone footings rather than entirely of stone. Only eight years later, however, the legions were again pulled back beyond the southern wall, trashing the Antonine forts and taking anything portable or valuable away with them (but turfing into wells some of the things they couldn't carry, to be found eventually by grateful archaeologists).[4]

Later writers were rather sniffy, as well as confused, about the crucial difference between the two great barriers. Bede, the eighth century Northumbrian historian, commenting on the northern one, states that it was the Emperor Severus[5] who built not a *wall*, for that should have been in stone, but a *rampart*, which was made of sods 'cut out of the earth', with a great ditch (handily made from digging out the sods) in front and strong timber stakes of wood set above it. 'Thus Severus drew a great trench and strong rampart, fortified with several towers, from sea to sea.'

Seven chapters later, however, to confuse things still further, Bede asserts that, once the Romans finally left, the native Britons, suffering the onslaughts of Picts and Scots from the north, sent to Rome for help. A legion duly arrived, sent the Picts and the Scots packing and advised the Britons to put up a wall. 'But the islanders building the wall which they had been told to raise, not of stone, since they had no workmen capable of such a work, but of sods, made it of no use.'[6]

Bede's *Ecclesiastical History of the English People* was hugely influential over succeeding centuries and, having erroneously ascribed the wall's construction not once but twice, he confused many future historians.[7] It was perhaps easier to credit the use of such flimsy materials to the natives rather than the Romans and there is no doubt that, despite some of the Antonine Wall having survived the best part of two millennia, it has not done as well as Hadrian's. It has also been pointed out that: 'Perhaps one of the surprising features about the Wall is that it has not dominated the later landscape layout except in a few areas where the ground is now utilised as rough grazing, such as at Croy Hill in Stirlingshire, or as recreational areas such as Bar Hill, Dunbartonshire, and Kinneil in West Lothian.'[8] It may be that its largely organic construction material proved relatively easy to ignore or destroy, the more equivocal nature of the Antonine Wall, certainly compared to its southern predecessor, perhaps providing us with a metaphor for the Roman presence in Scotland more generally.

Nevertheless, it certainly contained some enduring aspects, though the one that most excited earlier antiquarians is no longer with us. The monument later known as 'Arthur's O'on' (Oven) was first discussed in the fourteenth century (though there was a reference to it as early as 1293) when John of Fordun gathered together a number of stories about it:

Caesar determined to sail across to Gaul, but being uncertain as to his return, he hastily caused a small round chamber, like a pigeon house, and of no use, apparently, but as a landmark, to be built, of large smooth stones, without mortar, not far from the mouth of the river Carron; and he wanted to build this little chamber as marking the extreme limit of the Roman possessions to the north-west, almost at the world's end, and as a lasting monument of his military renown … Another version, especially of common report, is that Julius Caesar had this chamber carried about with him by the troops, with each stone separate, and built up again from day to day, wherever they halted, that he might rest therein more safely than in a tent; but that when he was in a hurry to return to Gaul, he left it behind, with the intention of coming back without delay; and it was built up with one stone merely laid upon another, as can be seen to this day. On the east side of this chamber, there is an entrance so large that an armed soldier on horseback can pass in, without touching the top of the doorway with the crested helmet on his head.[9]

In the sixteenth century, the historian Hector Boece acknowledged the general belief in Caesar's connection to Arthur's O'on, remarking that the alleged portable headquarters mentioned in the last story 'was supposedly called Iulis hoff, or Julius' Palace, a name that has come down to us, since the locals call it such'. He himself, having read books based on the Commentaries, Caesar's own works, which make no mention of the great Roman general fighting against the Scots and the Picts, preferred 'to pass over in silence an expedition of this kind and the things which are commonly said to have transpired in its course, including nothing here that can justly be refuted'. But he did think that it looked more like a temple than anything military, a view corroborated by more recent scholarship, which also asserts that 'the building is unique'.[10]

By the time Thomas Pennant was in the vicinity in 1772, however, Arthur's O'on had been gone for nearly 40 years – 'its barbarous owner [Sir Michael Bruce of Stenhouse in Stirlingshire], a Gothic knight, caused it to be demolished, in order to make a mill-dam with the materials, within less than a year, the Naiades, in resentment of the sacrilege, came down in a flood and entirely swept it away'.[11] Some 50 years later, the local minister provides some insight into Sir Michael's reasons for sweeping away 1,500 years of history:

He certainly was no dilettante, neither real nor pretended. He was not one of the admirers of the beautiful and of the rare in the material world, but a country gentleman who had other things to mind, and never moved much out of the parish where he was born and died there an octogenarian. Notwithstanding all this, the building might have escaped demolition had he not been poor, possessed of a numerous family of children, his income small, and a considerable amount of it derived from the mill. These circumstances moved him to employ the stones, and turn them to profit in repairing his dam … that he might avoid the expense of quarrying stones from the sandstone rock, only two or three miles distant.[12]

This certainly sheds some light into the financial circumstances and the mindset of a small Scottish landowner and, lest we imagine that Sir Michael was an unfortunate aberration, the scholar George Buchanan mentions as early as 1582 that other Roman remains in the area 'are now rendered indistinct, partly in consequence of the progress of agricultural improvement, and partly by gentlemen carrying away the square stones for the construction of villas in the neighbourhood'.[13]

Sir James Clerk of Penicuik, on the other hand, was so incensed by Sir Michael's philistine act of barbarism that he built a dovecot on top of the stable block on his own estates south of Edinburgh in 1763 based on drawings of the lost temple. The replica was preserved when the stable block was converted into a mansion house in 1900.[14] Progress has not always been kind to the relics of the past, especially during the centuries of Improvement and Industrialisation, ancient landmarks that would have been familiar to generation upon generation of Scots often swept away in a rising tide of activity.

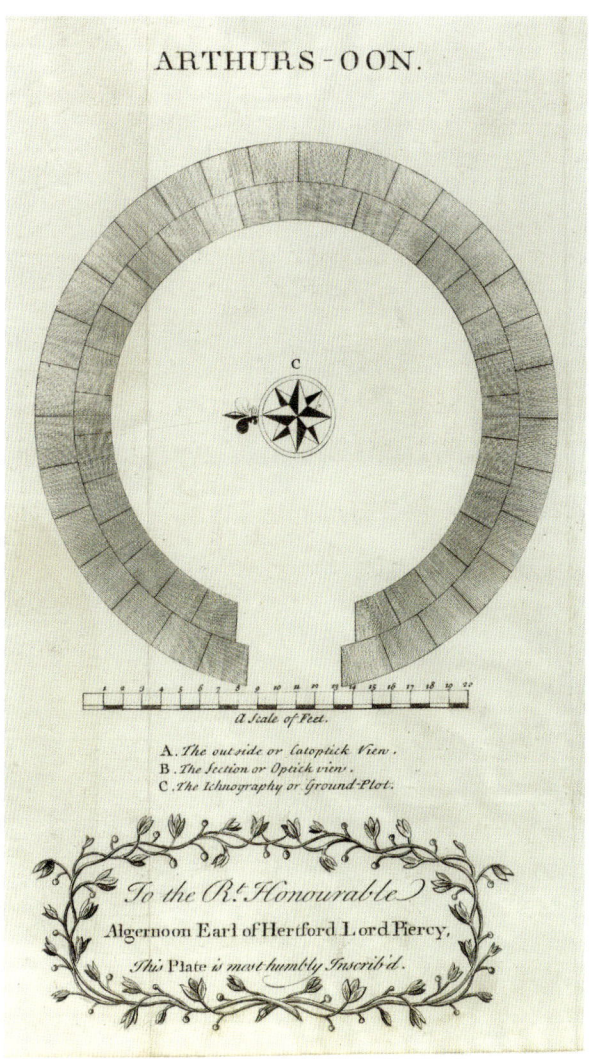

Arthur's O'on, Stenhouse, Stirlingshire
Demolished by the landowner in 1743, Arthur's O'on was a rare surviving example of a Roman temple in Britain.
HES, DP266263

A History of Scotland's Landscapes

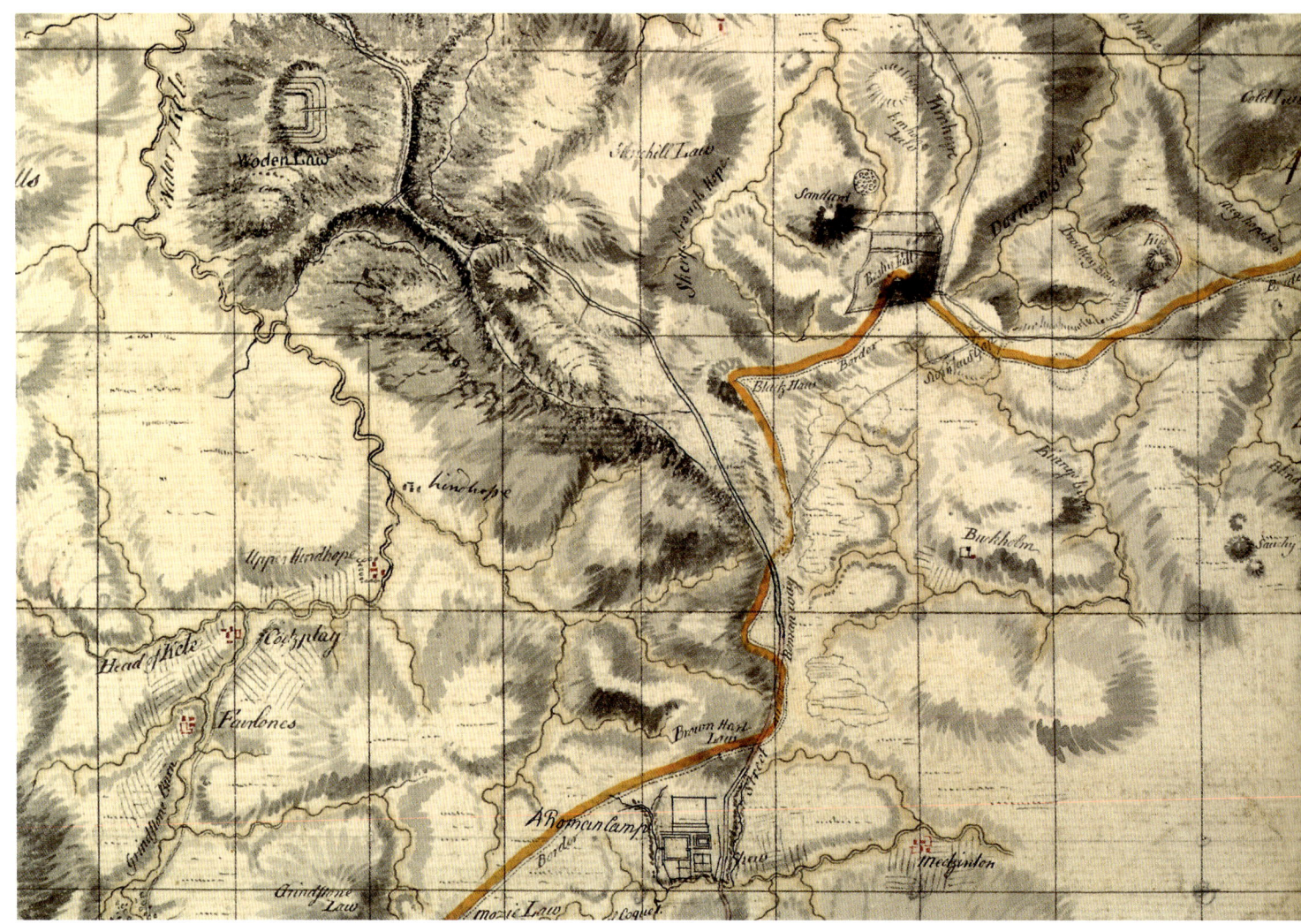

Dere Street, detail from General Roy's Map (Lowlands), 1752–55

Dere Street, that portion of the Roman road system that, throughout the Middle Ages, remained the main route between Scotland and England in the east, crosses the border on Roy's map as it runs between the Roman camp at Chew Green and Woden Law.

British Library, licensor Scran

* * * *

Near this spot must have passed the Roman road, which extended from the wall of Severus[15] (which crosses the country at Newcastle) to the Roman camp in the vicinity of St Abb's Head, where it terminated … for long subsequently to the retiring of the Romans it would be the best, if not the only great, thoroughfare of the country.[16]

New Statistical Account,
Ayton, Roxburghshire, 1845

There was very little point in spending all that time and money building walls, watch-towers, camps and forts (not to mention bath-houses, aquaducts and the other paraphernalia of Roman life) if you had to stumble over tussocky, muddy ground to get from one to the other. The Romans do not seem to have viewed nature as anything other than a temporary impediment, a confidence no doubt based on an apparently unlimited supply of manpower (until it began to run out) and a formidably efficient bureaucracy.

Unlike the rest of Britain, however, Scotland beyond the line of the Antonine Wall was not crisscrossed by a network of Roman roads, proverbially straight or otherwise, for the simple reason that the legions did not get far enough or stay long enough. The one major exception is a 70 mile highway running north-east from Camelon up to Kirriemuir in Angus (through my own village), the most northerly road in the Empire.

However the best-known, most enduring and convenient northern Roman road was (and, to some

Dere Steet, near Jedburgh, Roxburghshire
Portions of Dere Street, such as this stretch at Whitton Edge, are still both visible and usable today. The road, known as the Via Regia (royal way) served medieval pilgrims from central Scotland journeying to the great Border abbeys. Indeed, the hospital at Soutra was founded half-way along its route in part to give shelter to poor travellers.
HES, SC1264046

extent, still is) the one that eventually connected the medieval kingdoms of Scotland and England. For many centuries it continued, as it began, to allow land armies from both sides of the border to cross easily into the other's territory. But for most people, it was a blissfully easy way of getting themselves and their goods – from geese to olives – about. Known in English as Dere (or Deere) Street (so-called because it ran north from Deira, the southern part of the Anglo-Saxon kingdom of Northumbria), it made its way north from York over high passes and through fertile valleys, crossing Hadrian's Wall at Corbridge, beyond which lay the transition zone between the Empire and the 'barbarians'. Reaching the Anglo-Scottish border over the rolling heights of Brownhart Law in Roxburghshire, it ploughed on to the fort at Trimontium near Melrose in the same county, continued up over Soutra Hill in the Lammermuirs towards the eastern end of the Antonine Wall, where it connected with the main route west. Though not every Roman road was built to last, the main ones had stone foundations over which smaller cobbles were laid before being covered with gravel. And when the legions encountered rivers, burns or streams – as they must have done on a regular basis – they built bridges and culverts.

Edward I could be forgiven, when trying to conquer Scotland between 1296 and temporary success in 1303, for wishing never to see Dere Street again, so often did he ride back and forth on it with his armies. But before and after this particularly fraught period of Anglo-Scottish history, its northern section was also a popular pilgrimage route to the great border abbeys and monasteries of south-east Scotland. The hospital at Soutra Aisle in Midlothian was explicitly founded in 1164 by the Scottish king Malcolm IV as a convenient half-way point to provide shelter for pilgrims, and Dere Street can still be seen running past the hospital's remains.[17] The destruction of the border abbeys after the Protestant Reformation of 1560 brought an end to the road's regular use and it began to fall into disrepair; however, once London began to consume large quantities of Scottish beef from the seventeenth century, Dere Street was given a new lease of life as a drove road.

More does survive; it runs alongside the A68 north of Jedburgh, as well as underlying minor roads and bridleways further off the beaten track, as at Cappuck and Whitton Edge, all in Roxburghshire. It can even be identified as the boundaries of fields or estates, though often only in the words of a charter or the lines of an estate map rather than on the ground. Having said that, some of the parishes of the south-east are also bounded by it, as at Oxnam and Hownam; Oxnam, Jedburgh and Eckford; Ancrum, Crailing and Maxton; Crichton and Cranston; and Newton and Edinburgh, testifying to the extent to which this ancient highway loomed large in the lives of Scots many centuries after the legionaries had slipped back to sunnier climes.

After the Roman retreat, therefore, Scotland, like Ireland and unlike England and Wales, could not rely on a basic network of Roman roads and bridges. Nevertheless, as we have already seen, Scotland's early urban centres were partly defined by the tracks and roads surrounding them, as well as the highways between them.[18] But when push came to shove (as it no doubt often did), there is no doubt that much of the kingdom remained untouched by the firm contours of even a half-decent road. For much of Scottish history, it was far easier to transport goods and people along rivers that had not yet been lowered to accommodate the needs of reservoirs and hydro-electric schemes.

Most people, however, spent their lives walking from A to B as a matter of course, and the pressure of feet – human and animal – would eventually create a pathway through grass and moorland, just as walkers and sheep do on hillsides today. Once that route had been worn away – by rain, erosion or just sheer use –another one would emerge alongside it, creating what are called braided trackways, a phenomenon perfectly visible today on popular Munros (mountains generally over 3,000 feet) and other much-loved local walks. In time, some became well-defined, broad trackways, though most – especially in the Highlands – were far more discrete, as Edmund Burt discovered during his own road-building exploits:

The former ways along these slopes were only paths worn by the feet of the Highlanders and their little garrons. They ran along upwards and downwards, one above another, in such a manner as was found most convenient at the first tracing them out … To these narrow paths the passenger was confined (for there is seldom any choice of the way you would take in the Highlands) by the impassability of the hollows at the feet of the mountains.[19]

Remains of early trackways can still be found, especially on the rough hillsides of Perthshire and Angus (and occasionally down the east coast towards the border), where they bear a close resemblance to dried-up riverbeds with which they can easily be confused. The one on the east slope of Meall Odhar in Glenshee in Perthshire criss-crosses over old riverbeds to create a veritable maze of ridges and hollows on the hillside.

There was little point in using carts on such rough terrain and few farms had more than one or two before proper roads began to be built from the eighteenth century. Horses and ponies were still used as beasts of burden, usually with willow baskets, or creels, hanging off both flanks, or pulling a rough sledge. This last was 'formed of two parallel trams, about four feet asunder, joined at the further end by cross bars. The horse was yoked in it as in a cart, but the trams, instead of being on wheels, slid on the ground. On these creels were fixed, in which they put whatever they had to carry.'[20]

But beyond the major towns of the south, it was notoriously difficult, if not downright scary, to go travelling in the rest of the country, especially if you weren't used to it. The Londoner and self-styled Water Poet John Taylor, who walked to and through Scotland in 1618 with no money (who said the Scots were mean?) and wrote his *Pennyless Pilgrimage* by subscription, was impressed with the streets of Edinburgh, but most perturbed by the terrain further north. He learned very quickly that there was no point in trying to hurry. 'Up and down, I think this hill [Mount Keen, on the boundary between Angus and Aberdeenshire] is six miles, the way so uneven, stony, and full of bogs, quagmires, and long heath, that a dog with three legs will out-run a horse with four; for do what we could, we were four hours before we could pass it.'[21] But tediousness wasn't the worst of it:

I did go through a country called Glen Esk, where passing by the side of a hill, so steep as the ridge of a house, where the way was rocky, and not above a yard broad in some places, so fearful and horrid it was to look down into the bottom, for if either horse or man had slipped, he had fallen without recovery a good mile downright …

Both Daniel Defoe and John Macky were terrified by 'a famous pass cut out on the side of a rock, called Entrokin [Enterkin] Path' near Drumlanrig in Dumfriesshire when they passed that way in the 1720s. Defoe almost seems to shudder in remembering that:

… you mount the side of one of those hills, while, as you go on, the bottom in which that water runs down from between the hills, keeping its level on your right, begins to look very deep, till at length it is a precipice horrible and terrifying; on the left the hill rises almost perpendicular, like a wall; till being come about half way, you have a steep unpassable height on the left, and a monstrous calm or ditch on your right; deep, almost as the monument is high, and the path, or way, just broad enough for you to lead your horse on it, and, if his foot slips, you have nothing to do but let go the bridle, least he pulls you with him, and then you will have the satisfaction of seeing him dash'd to pieces and lye at the bottom with his four shoes uppermost. I pass'd twice this hill after this, but the weather was good, and the way dry, which made it safe.

Macky was more prosaic, but clearly felt the same: 'This path or pass is near a mile to the top, and is very steep. There cannot above two go abreast; and the precipice is much more dreadful than Penmaenmawr in Wales. This path brought me into the wildest, poorest Country I ever saw, worse by far than the Peak at Derby …'[22] It is easy to presume – though rather harder to know – that the natives sometimes found their home turf discomfiting – at the 'Maiden's Leap' between Fort Augustus and Loch Oich in Inverness-shire, for example, 'there the rocks project over the lake, and the path so rugged and narrow that the Highlanders were obliged, for their safety, to hold by the rocks and shrubs as they passed, with the prospect of death beneath them'.[23]

Nevertheless, their facility as guides for unwary travellers is well attested (providing they could speak some English, since few, if any, of their clients would have considered learning any Gaelic); Dorothy Wordsworth was much 'astonished at the sagacity with which our Highlander discovered the track, where often no track was visible to us … the more surprising as when he was there before it must have been a plain track, for he told us that fishermen from Arrochar in Argyll carried herrings regularly by that way to Loch Katrine in Stirlingshire when the glens were much more prosperous than they are now'.[24]

After a serious Jacobite uprising in 1715, followed by an abortive one in 1719, the British government began to look closely at the inaccessibility of the Highlands, which was seen by George I, his ministers, most English and many Lowland Scots as a barrier to law and order, not to mention a gift to those tempted to foment disorder and sedition. The truth behind Jacobitism is, as ever, far more complicated, but there can be little doubt as to the consequences of making it easier for outsiders to penetrate these precipitous, boggy tracts. The man who did much to make it happen was the capable and energetic Irish general George Wade, who spent nearly a decade (1725–32) overseeing the most ambitious road- and bridge-building programme since the Romans, and over far more consistently difficult terrain. Thomas Pennant even described Wade as 'another Hannibal, [who] forced his way through rocks supposed to have been unconquerable'.[25] It is surely no coincidence that both endeavours were conducted by the military.

Edmund Burt, as part of Wade's team, is obviously not an impartial witness to this herculean task, though he does provide us with an (ultimately flattering) account of just how outlandish and incredible the locals sometimes found the project.

A History of Scotland's Landscapes **139**

Whilst he was supervising work at Slochd Muic (south of Inverness), the soldiers came across a particularly large and apparently immovable piece of rock.

A very old wrinkled Highland woman … standing over-against me, when the soldiers were fixing their engine, seemed to sneer at it, and said something to an officer of one of the Highland companies. I imagined she was making a jest of the undertaking, and asked the officer what she said. 'I will tell you her words,' said he: 'What are the fools a-doing? That stone will lie there for ever, for all them.' But when she saw that vast bulk begin to rise, though by slow degrees, she set up a hideous Irish yell, took to her heels, ran up the side of a hill just by, like a young girl, and never looked behind her while she was within our sight. I make no doubt she thought it was magic, and the workmen warlocks.[26]

The roads – which began in Crieff in Perthshire and ultimately connected the garrisons at Ruthven (Kingussie) in eastern Inverness-shire, Fort George in Nairnshire, Fort Augustus and Fort William in western Inverness-shire – were indeed a phenomenal achievement. The soldiers were given extra pay for their labours (though only for the days when they were actually working, as opposed to sheltering from a violent rainstorm), but from it had to pay for food, temporary accommodation and anything else required in their 'wild situation'.

Like their Roman predecessors, these Hanoverian roads went straight 'till some great necessity has turned them out of the way', but, when going uphill, they 'must have their circuits, risings, and descents accordingly'. Wade ordained that they should be sixteen feet wide, but Burt says they were wider if the ground was easy; where it was particularly difficult, they were reduced to ten.

As well as using engines to remove stones, the engineers sometimes employed gunpowder. When dealing with water-logged bogs, they removed the ground cover down to the rock, then applied a layer of stones of diminishing size to provide a firm base, followed finally by gravel to bind it all together. A bank was built on either side to protect the road from

Wade Bridge, Aberfeldy, Perthshire
This bridge across the Tay, designed by William Adam in 1734, was a key link in the military road from Crieff to Dalnacardoch and then on to Inverness. John Davidson Photos/Alamy

A History of Scotland's Landscapes

ditches built to carry off the water, a precaution also taken on uphill sections 'to receive rains, melting snows and springs, which last are in many places continually issuing out of the sides of the hills'. At the famously challenging section through the Corrieyairack Pass between Loch Laggan and Fort Augustus in Inverness-shire, the road 'is carried on upon the south declivity of the hill, by seventeen traverses, like the course of a ship when she is turning to windward, by angles still advancing higher and higher; yet little of it is to be seen below, by reason of flats, hollows, and windings that intercept the sight; and nothing could give you a general view of it, unless one could be supposed to be placed high above the mountain in the air'.[27]

Whatever one thinks of government policy towards the Highlands in this period, countless hundreds, if not thousands, had reason to be grateful to those who designed and built what are still known as Wade's roads (though many of them were constructed by the general's successor, Major William Caulfeild). Dorothy Wordsworth was one: 'At the top of the road [the A83 from Loch Lomond to Arrochar in Argyll] we came to a seat with the well-known inscription, "rest and be thankful." On the same stone it was recorded that the road had been made by Col. Wade's regiment.' In fact, it was Caulfeild and his men who built it in 1753, more than twenty years after Wade had moved on to greater things.

Not everyone was uncritical, however. Thomas Pennant, whose credentials as an engineer are far from clear, thought that the roads were generally excellent, 'but from Fort William to Kinloch Leven in Inverness-shire, very injudiciously planned, often carried far about, and often so steep as to be scarce surmountable; whereas had the engineer followed the track used by the inhabitants, those inconveniences would have been avoided'. It was rare for the Welsh naturalist to praise native nous, so he must have had a very rough ride indeed.[28]

And certainly even this colossal effort brought only the bare bones of a road network to northern Scotland, leaving huge swathes of the country untouched. And it wasn't much better in the south, as John Macky found in 1723 near the village of Barr in Ayrshire: 'I passed through the foggy road, nigh the Nick of the Ballock; a road so stony and uneven, that I was obliged to alight and with much ado led our horses to the King's ford of Minnock.'[29] An act to encourage local landowners to raise the money to build turnpike roads, on which the traveller had to pay a toll, had been passed as early as 1713 (for Midlothian), with work progressing throughout the country, particularly in the second half of the century.

Another important development was the abolition of statute labour – a service owed by many small tenants – which had been used for road repairs. It was very difficult to get those that owed it to turn up and, not surprisingly, the quality of the work often left something to be desired even when they did. The service was commuted into money, though the process evolved slowly, on a county by county basis – Perthshire was well ahead of the game, abolishing it in 1754, with Dumfriesshire following suit in 1777, while Aberdeenshire only got there in 1800.[30] At the same time, a levy was imposed on local landowners. As well as renovating the major highways, some of which were already quite old, this allowed the authorities to begin tackling the 'crossroads' in between.

The impact of all this road-building on Scotland's economic development was considerable. The minister of Colmonell in Ayrshire, for example, noted in 1792 that: 'The price of wood here twenty or thirty years ago was a mere trifle, as there was then very little consumption of it in the country, and no good roads to convey it to other places; but now it gives a better price … Being remote from markets without good roads until recently has been a disincentive to raising more grain for export.' He even went so far as to assert that, so long as statute labour was being used, 'nothing to purpose either was, or could be, done in this part of the country'.[31]

It was now worth moving goods around by cart – impossible, as we've seen, on some of the surfaces that once passed for roads. The minister of Whittinghame in Roxburghshire reckoned that eight or ten times the amount could be sent to market on a cart than on horseback.[32] This also helped to bring down the price of coal, which soon began to replace peat as the main source of fuel. On the other hand, making it easier to travel also helped migration – the minister of Dunoon in Argyll complained in 1792 that the 'great road being carried by Lochlomond round the head of

Lochlong and through Glencroe to Inverary' had greatly diminished the population of his village.

It was a slow process nonetheless, with pockets of execrable roads continuing well into the nineteenth century even in the south-east, but especially in the north and north-west – in Barvas parish on Lewis in 1797 'the poor people are under the necessity of carrying every article almost, to and from Stornoway, upon their backs' across twelve to eighteen miles 'of a broken swampy moor'. Two roads were built soon after, which must have been a wonderful improvement, even though the one to Stornoway was described 40 years later as being 'now much out of repair', a state replicated elsewhere on the island.[33] Nevertheless, most parishes throughout the country reported an infinitely improved state of affairs on the roads between the first and second *Statistical Accounts*.

Though many, from great landowners to their smallest tenants, could see the benefits of these roads (even if they had been most reluctant, initially, to pay for them), there were downsides. As Edmund Burt so eloquently put it: 'The middling sort say the roads … have turned them out of their old ways; for their horses being never shod, the gravel would soon whet away their hoofs … To this I have been inconsiderately asked, "Why then do they not shoe their horses?" … But where is the iron, the forge, the farrier, the people within a reasonable distance to maintain him? And lastly, where is the principal requisite – money?' The process of Improvement could, as ever, be a painful one.[34]

The horse, with its stronger pulling power, began to replace oxen in front of the cart or plough, and remained a ubiquitous part of both farming and the transportation system well into the twentieth century. However, the advent of Henry Ford's Model T (1908–27) – the first mass-produced car – would eventually bring an end to living and breathing horsepower (even if I can still remember the coal being delivered on a horse-drawn cart in 1970s Dunfermline, Fife). Between 1930 and 1970 the number of licensed cars owned in the UK shot up to ten million. It soon became apparent that the road network would need to be modernised to accommodate this growing army of automobiles. In 1938 plans were drawn up to build a motorway between Glasgow and London. The war got in the way, but on 5 December 1958 the first 8.25 mile stretch of this new, *double*-laned kind of highway was opened (otherwise known as the M6 by-passing Preston). The first Scottish motorway (the M8 (Edinburgh–Glasgow) Harthill Bypass between junctions 4 and 5) opened in November 1965 and by 1980 the basic motorway network was open for business.[35] Mind you, it would be fair to say that the state of the roads is still an ongoing financial headache, not to mention a source of chagrin to road users.

But no road network would be worth a groat* if it did not also include bridges over the country's many water-courses. In fact, Scotland had a number of fine examples long before the arrival of General Wade and his men, though originally not always of stone. The most famous early Scottish bridge was surely at Stirling (see page 102), which gave the town its command over the main land route crossing from the Lowlands into the Highlands (or vice-versa); it also dictated the site of William Wallace and Andrew Moray's famous victory against an English force in 1297, given that the opposing armies had been marching towards each other from the north and the south. This bridge was wooden, with eight piers (as depicted on the burgh's seal) and was destroyed in the battle; it was not rebuilt until the end of the fourteenth century, still in wood. A stone one was finally constructed only around 1600.

By the time Daniel Defoe turned his penetrating gaze on Scotland in the 1720s, there was a sufficient number of impressive stone bridges to make an unusually good impression. At Aberdeen, the bridge across the Don consisted of an 'immense arch of stone, sprung from two rocks, one on each side, which serve as a buttment to the arch, so that it may be said to have no foundation, nor to need any. The workmanship is artful, and so firm, that it may possibly end with the conflagration only. The other bridge is upon the River Dee, about a mile west above New Aberdeen, and has seven very stately fine arches.'

Defoe described the single-span bridge across the River Doon in Ayrshire, reputedly built in the later fifteenth century and certainly by 1512, as 'the largest I ever saw, much larger than the Rialto at Venice, or the middle arch of the great bridge at York'. This is the bridge immortalised by Robert Burns as the place where Tam O'Shanter narrowly

A History of Scotland's Landscapes

Uist Causeways, Outer Hebrides

A series of causeways and bridges link the islands of the South and North Uists. HES, DP221877

The Friarton Bridge over the Tay, Perthshire

The River Tay presents a major impediment to traffic. While Perth boasts four bridges, traffic wishing to bypass it can, since 1978, enjoy the views from the Friarton Bridge. HES, DP220515

The Skye Bridge, Ross and Cromarty

The bridge opened in 1995 amid controversy, especially over the tolls (which are no longer in place). Recent debate has focused on the island's status now that one is no longer transported 'over the sea to Skye'. HES, DP109900

The Kylesku Bridge, linking Sutherland to Assynt

Opened in 1984, Kylesku Bridge is part of 'Scotland's answer to Route 66', the North Coast 500. HES, DP212192

144   Chapter Three – Industry and Infrastructure

General Wade's Road at Glen Clunie, Perthshire
Built under the direction of Major Caulfeild between 1748 and 1757, the Military Road (on the right bank of the river) through Glen Clunie provides a route from the Lowlands to the centre of the Highlands, linking Coupar Angus to Braemar and Fort George near Inverness. HES. DP0144757

A History of Scotland's Landscapes

The Forth Bridge, the Forth Road Bridge and the construction of the Queensferry Crossing, connecting the Lothians and Fife
The Forth is spanned by three major bridges since the opening of the Queensferry Crossing (seen here under construction) in August 2017. The first was the now iconic rail bridge, completed in 1890 and described by one of its engineers, Wilhelm Westhofen, as 'A discordant feature in a pastoral landscape'. Seventy-four years later the first road bridge was built slightly upstream, replacing the Queen's Ferry which had crossed the Forth for 900 years.
HES, DP233152

missed being caught by the witches thanks to the heroic efforts of his horse, Meg. Even the decaying town of Ayr had 'a handsome stone bridge of four arches', surely a symbol of better days, while the 'magnificent' one at Glasgow unleashed a paroxysm of delight, 'especially when I saw three of the middle arches so exceeding large and high, beyond all the rest, I could not but wonder, hardly thinking it possible, that where the passage or channel is so exceeding broad, for the bridge consists of eight arches …'[36]

But there was much still to do, as Edmund Burt knew at first-hand. The problem was the sudden torrents of water that sometimes came hurtling down the rivers, sweeping away all in its path, as can still happen. He describes the construction of one bridge, whose arch, founded on rocks, 'was elevated much higher above the highest water that had ever been known by the country people' (the engineers had clearly done their homework). Yet it did not last long, having been placed 'too near the issue of water from between two hills'. He reckoned that the military had built 40 bridges in total, 'some of them single arches, of forty or fifty feet diameter, mostly founded upon rocks; others are composed of two; one of three, and one of five, arches. This last is over the Tay [at Aberfeldy in Perthshire], and is the only bridge upon that wild river … It is built with astler-stone [ashlar], and is 370 feet in length.' But what is most illuminating is the reason he says some of the Highland chiefs were against them, namely that the bridges 'will render the ordinary people effeminate, and less fit to pass the waters in other places where there are none'.[37]

Not all chiefs felt the same, however – the Campbell Earl of Breadalbane, for example, paid for the building of a picturesque road between his own estate at Taymouth (beside Kenmore on Loch Tay in Perthshire) on to Tyndrum and ultimately Inveraray in Argyll that required no fewer than 32 stone bridges.[38] In any case, as a species they were here to stay, even if individuals sometimes disappeared in a fighting, kicking maelstrom of water and debris. The crowning glory, designed to open 'a communication with all the different great roads of the kingdom' and described by Thomas Pennant as 'the most beautiful structure of the kind in North Britain', was the bridge at Perth.

Completed only a year before Pennant's arrival, it was designed and executed by John Smeaton, an English civil engineer who also built the Eddystone lighthouse, and was 900 feet long with nine arches.[39]

The history of Scottish bridges over the following decades pursues a similar pattern to that of the roads they carried across water – some were deemed good, while others needed repaired; some places desperately cried out for more or any at all. The commutation of statute labour helped, though, as ever, times changed and users became more demanding, forgetting (if they ever knew) how far they had already come. 'The bridge over the Allan', so the minister of Aithrey near Stirling complained, 'is one of those narrow, old-fashioned, dangerous bridges so common in this part of the country, which one would hardly expect to find at the present day on a great public road …'[40]

But right until the twentieth century, the mighty River Forth could still only be crossed by road at Stirling, until, at last, in 1936, a second bridge was built between Kincardine in Fife and the mudflats of Airth in Stirlingshire, which, at the mouth of the River Pow, had once housed James IV's royal dockyard. Thirty years later, in 1964, another new road bridge was opened to replace the ferry that had linked Fife with Lothian for the best part of a millennium. Like motorways, the Forth Road Bridge was a product of its time, the first long-span suspension bridge in the UK and the fourth longest in the world (the other three were all in the USA).[41] Half a century later, there are now five bridges across the Forth with the completion of the elegantly winged Queensferry Crossing in 2017.

* * * *

… the two firths, from the Firth of Clyde to the Firth of Forth, have not an interval of above twelve or fourteen miles, which, if they were join'd as might easily be done, they might cross Scotland, as I might say, in the very centre. Nor can I refrain mentioning how easy a work it would be to form a navigation, I mean a navigation of art from the Forth to the Clyde, and so join the two seas …[42]

Daniel Defoe, *A Tour through the Whole Island of Great Britain*, 1724–7

In 1681 Louis XIV of France partly realised a project that had been dear to the hearts of his predecessors since at least 1539, namely to build a canal over the phenomenal distance of 100 miles between Toulouse and Narbonne. Although the ultimate dream was to connect the Atlantic Ocean with the Mediterranean (that took another two centuries to fulfil), Louis' canal caused quite a stir on the other side of the Channel long before hordes of British holiday sailors and cyclists thought to descend on it.

Daniel Defoe had the Canal Royal de Languedoc (the Canal du Midi is the name it took after the French Revolution) explicitly in mind when he penned the above piece of heartfelt advice on the efficacy of building one to link the Forth with the Clyde. So far as he was concerned, if the French could do it 'in a place five times as far, and five hundred times as difficult', the Scots could surely manage over the paltry distance of fourteen miles. 'What an advantage in commerce would this be, opening the Irish trade to the merchants of Glasgow, making a communication between the west coast of Scotland, and the east coast of England, and even to London itself … it would take up a volume by itself, to lay down the several advantages to the trade of Scotland …'

But for all his enthusiasm, there were considerable barriers: '… it is too much to undertake here, it must lye till posterity, by the rising greatness of their commerce, shall not only feel the want of it, but find themselves able for the performance'. However, he also said that: 'Those gentlemen who have seen the royal canal in Languedoc … as many in Scotland have, will be able to support what I say in this case.' There was clearly a willingness to consider these major infrastructural projects, but it was no easy task to raise the significant finance involved nor, perhaps more importantly, to get agreement among the landowners through whose lands the canal would go.

In fact, the Forth–Clyde canal was not the first such enterprise proposed for Scotland. A survey of 'certain parts of the Highlands' in 1661 – just as Louis' project was gaining momentum – noted that 'in this Tarbart [on Loch Fyne in Argyll] … there is one little loch which does come from the east and another loch foregainst, which does flow from the west, And these two loch heads they are but one short mile betwixt them. It is thought that with great charges this passage might be cut so that boats might pass from the east seas to the west without going about the Mull of Kintyre, which were very profitable for such as travel to the north islands.'[43]

This narrow isthmus had already played a curious – if probably fictional – role in Scottish history, when King Magnus Barelegs of Norway reputedly had himself dragged in a boat from one loch to the other. This was a ruse devised to gain Kintyre, temporarily at least, because he and the Scottish king Edgar were dividing up the western Highlands and Islands between them in 1098 – it had been agreed that the Norwegian could take those parts that he could sail around.[44] Be that as it may and however pressing the need in 1661, nothing was done.

By the second half of the eighteenth century, however, there were definite plans afoot to build no less than five large canals in Scotland in order to make it even easier to transport various raw materials, such as coal and iron ore, as well as agricultural and commercial products, than along the new roads. The cost of such a worthy endeavour remained prohibitive, however; as Thomas Pennant remarked with regard to the Crinan Canal, it was 'an expense beyond the power of North Britain to effect, except it could realise those sums which the wishes of a few of its sons had attained in idea',[45] a sentiment with which Defoe would no doubt have agreed. At the end of the century, a company of investors was set up by act of parliament, but financial problems right from the start meant that public money was also needed. The canal finally opened across the peninsula some eleven miles north of Tarbert in 1801, though, as the minister of South Knapdale pointed out, it was too small to attract the Baltic and West Indian trade that some had set their hearts (and wallets) on and too large for the local trade that would have been a more realistic opportunity.[46]

It was a similar story when a canal was being considered to connect Loch Oich with Loch Ness in Inverness-shire to save ships from having to sail round the British Isles; for a long time cutting through fourteen miles of sheer rock was also deemed far too difficult and costly.[47] Though James Watt undertook a survey for a waterway in 1773, it was not until parliament again stepped in to finance it that the Caledonian Canal was finally built, opening in 1822. By then, however, the navy

The Caledonian Canal, Inverness-shire, 1950
Completed in 1822, the Caledonian Canal is around 60 miles long, including 22 miles of man-made sections joining a line of lochs from Fort William to Inverness. HES, SC1269532

Corpach Sea Lock, Fort William, Inverness-shire, 1883
This lock marks the point at which the Caledonian Canal meets the seawater of Loch Linnhe. HES, SC1112919

The Caledonian Canal and Loch Ness, Fort Augustus, Inverness-shire, 1954
Conceived to avoid the hazardous route around the top of Scotland, the Caledonian Canal never really proved useful to commercial shipping. HES, DP048367

SS *Linnet* on the Crinan Canal, Argyll, c1923
'Britain's most beautiful shortcut', the Crinan Canal, allowed boats to bypass the Kintyre peninsula. HES, SC714919

The west end of the Crinan Canal, Crinan, Argyll
The Crinan Canal ends at Crinan – previously known as Port Righ (King's Port) – where it merges into the Sound of Jura. HES, DP017931

The Union Canal, Lochrin Basin, Edinburgh, c1914
Linking Glasgow to Edinburgh, the Union Canal was intended to bring goods into the capital, but it was soon superseded by the rail network. HES, SC1071699

The Crinan Canal and Loch Gilp, Argyll
By 1854, 33,000 passengers had been taken through the Crinan Canal. HES, DP112115

Fort Augustus Locks, Caledonian Canal, Inverness-shire, 1979
The Caledonian, Crinan, Union and Forth–Clyde canals are now open for locals and visitors to enjoy once again.
John R Hume, HES, SC554298

A History of Scotland's Landscapes

no longer needed to use it and the newer steamships were much too big. In the end it was tourism – in which Queen Victoria played a major part – that saved it in both the nineteenth century and at the end of the twentieth.

The Forth–Clyde Canal finally began life after an act of parliament of 1768, though this time funds were to be raised by subscription. Thomas Pennant saw it being cut through a bog at Kilsyth in Stirlingshire when he passed by a year later.[48] However, the project ran out of money in 1775 with six miles still to go to reach the Clyde; after an injection of public funds, it was finally completed in 1790. Within only a year, its impact was being felt throughout the country, for both good and ill:

The trade upon it is already great, and is rapidly increasing. One of its first effects has been to equalise in a great measure, the price of grain throughout all the corn-countries of Scotland; to the temporary loss of the landholders in the southern, and to the gain of those in the northern districts.[49]

The Monklands Canal, which carried coal from Lanarkshire into Glasgow, was eventually linked to the Forth–Clyde canal, as was the Union Canal, which then could take coal into the capital. This integrated water-based transport system was hugely important in aiding the development of the great industries of the Central Belt, which in turn stimulated other economic activity, including farming in order to feed the great numbers of migrants pouring into the towns and villages of the south.

Indeed, so much did canals inspire dreams of the economic benefits that would reputedly follow in their wake that everybody wanted one. One minister talked about Kilmarnock in Ayrshire becoming 'the most eligible and flourishing manufacturing town in the west of Scotland' if its distance to the sea could be overcome (and, even better, if it could then be linked to Glasgow); the minister at Crailing in Roxburghshire pinned his hopes on yet another proposal, this time for a navigable route to reach 'the German Ocean' (North Sea): 'it will necessarily lead to the establishment of manufactures and thereby increase the population, extend the improvements and double the value of estates in this part of the kingdom'.

There was widespread and general hope in Aberdeenshire that a canal might be built on the River Don and in the 1790s a subscription was raised to pay for a survey, which came back positive. This produced such enthusiasm that even the local farmers were willing to purchase shares, in the firm belief that each one of them 'along the banks, and to the distance of two or three miles along the banks, and to the distance of two or three miles from these, might, at a cheap rate, and in a few days, lay in his winter-fuel of coals, and have abundant leisure to attend to the improvement of his land'. The local proprietors were less sure, however, which led to accusations of a lack of public-spiritedness by some who were more than willing to spend other people's money.

But the landowners may have had a point. An eighteen-mile canal was finally opened between Aberdeen and Inverurie in 1805, but, though 'it has been of considerable advantage to a large tract of country', the proprietors still hadn't made any money out of it over 40 years later.[50] In part the sheer speed at which technology changed often rendered these big, expensive projects out-of-date even before they opened. And, while the railways did sometimes help in bringing goods and passengers to the canals, in most cases the harnessing of steam made the artifical waterways old before their time. There were plans from 1754, for example, to build a canal to Kirkmahoe parish in Dumfriesshire from the Solway Firth, but a century later, hopes were being pinned on the building of a railway from Sanquhar.

Nevertheless, the first concerted application of steam to transport was again water-based; steamboats were very much in vogue for a while because of the formidable speeds they could reach compared with wind and manpower. They certainly transformed a number of sleepy hamlets within easy reach of the Clyde; Kilmun in Argyll, for example, though ancient in origin, was effectively built in 1829 by an enterprising man from Glasgow, David Napier, who purchased a feu along the eastern shore of the Holy Loch to attract his fellow Glaswegians 'doon the watter' in the summer. It was a similar story for neighbouring Dunoon.[51]

The Crinan Canal did well out of the steam packet boats (as opposed to larger vessels, which were too big for its dimensions), increasing the number of passengers almost tenfold (from 2,400 to 21,406) between 1820 and 1837; while the launch in 1845 of a passage boat on the canal 'greatly promotes the speed of the passage between Greenock in Renfrewshire and Oban in Argyll, and Inverness'.[52] The steamboats were also used to transport goods quickly – 'any uncommonly fine beast [cattle]' was sent to Smithfield on the London–Inverness steamer.[53] Another 'excellent and powerful steamer' connected Orkney with Leith.[54]

But the railways were certainly the first land-based form of transport to achieve unprecedented speeds thanks to the power of steam. Transporting coal was the main rationale behind the construction of many of them, but all kinds of goods – timber, grain, slates and lime – could be sent to markets at distances that were once quite inconceivable. As with canals, they were the products of considerable engineering prowess, not least in the building of tunnels, with a hefty price tag to match.

Some were intended purely for conveying iron or coal. From 1824 the Monkland and Kirkintilloch Railway connected supplies coming in from the rich coal and mineral districts of Lanarkshire – via the Ballochney and Glasgow and Gurnkirk railways – with the Forth–Clyde Canal near Kirkintilloch in Dunbartonshire at a cost of £52,000. In 1835 it was estimated that about 49,000 tons of coal and 3,325 tons of pit-iron were shipped on the canal from the railway.[55]

This time – perhaps encouraged by the earlier benefits of canal-building – investors were often quicker off the mark. Shares for a railroad planned between Ayr and Glasgow and another between Glasgow and Edinburgh had already raised the desired amount by 1845; they were just waiting for parliamentary approval.[56] Conversely, the *lack* of a railway was viewed, with good reason, as an impediment to further economic development. Roxburghshire was desperate for one, despite a veritable revolution in the state of local roads, in part to further lower the price of coal, which many of the poor still struggled to afford.[57]

As the railway network spread its web across the country, even the River Forth ultimately proved no barrier. On 4 March 1890 the future Edward VII drove in the last rivet of the new and soon to be iconic Forth Rail Bridge. Nearly 40 years later, H V Morton mused on how thrilling an experience it was just to see it, never mind to cross on it:

The Forth Bridge flings its three double steel cantilevers across the water to the Kingdom of Fife. It is the most familiar bridge in the world. It is seen on posters, framed in railway carriages and in all kinds of books. To see the Forth Bridge is rather like meeting a popular actress, but with this difference. It is a memorable sight. It is more impressive than its pictures. Its proportions are so tremendous that you do not realize how vast they are until a train crosses over, skied above you in an intricate tracery of girders. Then you are astonished. It is even higher than it appeared without the train, and therefore longer and in every way more stupendous. The sound of trains crossing the Forth Bridge is a queer fascinating and peculiar sound: something between a roar and a rumble, and with a hint of drums.[58]

But with the rise in the number of private cars and buses in the first half of the twentieth century, the need for railways began to decline. Lines began to be closed from the 1920s, until over 6,000 miles of track were removed in the aftermath of the Beeching report of 1963. And as railways began to disappear, freight too was encouraged on to the roads. Nevertheless, the re-opening of the Alloa line from Stirling in 2008, followed by the Borders railway in 2015, makes clear that there is still a healthy appetite for rail travel, while the smooth remains of many a former track have proved perfect for conversion into walking and cycling paths.

* * * *

1769. Carron ironworks lie about a mile from Falkirk, and are the greatest of the kind in Europe: they were founded about eight years ago, before which there was not a single house, and the country a mere moor. At present, the buildings of all sorts are of vast extent, and about twelve hundred men are employed. The iron is smelted from the stone, then cast into cannons, pots, and all sorts of utensils made in foundries. This work has been of great service to the country, by teaching the people industry and a method of setting about any sort of labour, which before the common people had scarce any notion of. Carron wharf lies on the Forth, and is not only useful to the works, but of great service

even to Glasgow, as considerable quantities of goods destined for that city are landed there. The canal likewise begins in this neighbourhood, which, when effected, will prove another benefit to these works.[59]

Thomas Pennant
A Tour in Scotland, 1769

At the beginning of this chapter, Tacitus laid bare Scotland's more or less complete lack of infrastructure and industry in the first century AD from a Roman point of view; 1,600 years later, Daniel Defoe seemed to think that little had changed, certainly in the north (though, as we have already seen, he wasn't much more impressed with the south):

Some people tell us they have both lead, copper, and iron in this part of Scotland [the north], and I am very much inclin'd to believe it: but it seems reserv'd for a future, and more industrious age to search into; which, if it should happen to appear, especially the iron, they would no more have occasion to say that nature furnish'd them with so much timber, and woods of such vast extent to no purpose, seeing it may be all little enough to supply the forges for working up the iron stone, and improving that useful product: And should a time come when these hidden treasures of the earth should be discover'd and improv'd, this part of Scotland may no longer be call'd poor, for such a production would soon change the face of things, bring wealth and commerce to it; fill their harbours full of ships, their towns full of people; and by consuming the provisions bring the soil to be cultivated, its fish cur'd, and its cattle consum'd at home, and so a visible prosperity would shew itself among them.[60]

Glenfinnan Viaduct, Inverness-shire
The Glenfinnan railway viaduct is most famous now for helping to convey Harry Potter to Hogwarts. Most of Scotland's railways were built from the 1840s, their bridges and viaducts creating dramatic engineering structures in the landscape. Though their heyday lasted much longer than the canals they effectively replaced, economic realities prompted the loss of a third of them in the 1960s. HES, DP095070

It would be easy to assume, from such reports, that the Scots were not particularly interested in commerce or innovation, but that would fly in the face of much evidence. Since at least the Middle Ages, when monasteries showed the way with technical know-how, salt had been panned, coal had been mined, bog iron had been smelted and stone had been quarried. We can also point to a number of individuals who dedicated themselves to science and engineering, not to mention the potential profits to be made by applying technological innovation to the extraction and processing of Scotland's natural resources. From 1575 Sir George Bruce of Carnock's colliery at Culross in Fife, for example, employed techniques well in advance of anything known in Britain at the time to allow him to extract coal from *under* the Forth. Building an artificial island out in the river from which a 40-foot vertical shaft connected, via a horizontal tunnel, with another vertical shaft on the shore, he used an Egyptian wheel, on which an endless supply of buckets rotated thanks to the power provided by three horses, in a third shaft to drain the whole miraculous enterprise.

John Taylor, the Pennyless Poet, visited Culross in 1618, a year after the Scottish king, James VI – on his only trip to his northern kingdom after he took the English throne in 1603 – had ventured nervously into the shaft beneath the sea-bed. Taylor was most impressed with his own visit to the mine, gushing that 'for myself neither in any travels that I have been in, nor any history that I have read, or any discourse that I have heard, did never see, read, or hear of any work of man that might parallel or be equivalent with this unfellowed and unmatchable work'. He also noted approvingly that: 'Many poor people are there set on work, which otherwise through the want of employment would perish.'[61] Indeed, it has been estimated that Sir George employed well over 1,000 men in his various enterprises, which amounted to three collieries and 40 salt-pans by the time of his death in 1625. He also oversaw the expansion of Culross itself, which was made a burgh in 1592, making it one of the earliest industrial villages in Britain.[62]

Bruce was by no means the only entrepreneur. In 1610, Sir George Hay of Nether Liff (north-west of Dundee) was granted a commission by James VI, valid for 31 years, 'to make iron and glass within the said kingdom of Scotland'. This followed on from an edict of the previous year, which banned any private free-for-all that might deprive the crown of a share of the profits (as well as seeking to protect Scotland's precious timber):

Forasmuch as it has pleased God to discover certain veins of rich metal within this kingdom, as also certain woods in the highlands, which woods by reason of the savageness of the inhabitants thereabouts were either unknown or at the least unprofitable and unused; and now the estates* presently convened, being informed that some persons, upon advantage of the present general obedience in those parts, would erect iron mills in the same parts to the utter wanting and consuming of the said woods, which might be reserved for many better uses and upon more choice and profitable metals, for the honour, benefit and estimation of the kingdom …[63]

Hay set up his ironworks in 1611 at Loch Maree in Ross and Cromarty, using the timber of the surrounding woods up to four miles from the shore, as well as those around nearby Loch Alsh, Loch Carron and Loch Duich. It thrived for over a decade, with the help of English partners from Sussex, who brought with them new blast-furnace technology (and some of whose workers were reputedly interred on the eastern shore of Loch Maree at a place called 'Cladh nan Sasunnach' – burial-ground of the English). In 1621, Hay was allowed to send his iron to any Scottish burgh, regardless of existing regulations, but by 1624 it was claimed that the furnace had gone out as he focused on climbing ever higher in public office, becoming the first Earl of Dupplin in 1633. Though he remained a sleeping partner in continuing efforts to exploit the ironworks (masterminded by the canny Highland nobleman, Colin Mackenzie of Kintail, newly created Earl of Seaforth), there does not seem to have been much activity beyond the 1630s.[64]

The reasons behind Scotland's apparent technological regression until the later eighteenth century in the face of these promising beginnings are hard to pin down and are certainly not straight-forward. The topography was not easy to overcome; it could (and sometimes still does) make it difficult to reach more mountainous regions, never mind get materials out in a cost-effective manner. The problem of creating jobs in these more remote places is one that has bedevilled governments well into the twentieth century, never mind at a time when there were, as we have already seen, hardly any roads or other basic forms of infrastructure.

But that was true when George Hay and his partners ventured up to Loch Maree. Perhaps it was partly the strange constitutional position which the kingdom found itself in after 1603, with its king ensconced in London and – after James VI – far less concerned with, and personally knowledgeable about, Scotland. It would be simplistic to suggest that royal policy was dictated by the most powerful Scottish nobles, but certainly the king was vulnerable to their fluctuating and (inevitably) self-interested opinions. At the same time, Scottish trade was profoundly disrupted by England's perennial Continental wars.

This situation only got worse after 1689, when William of Orange and his wife, Mary Stuart, became joint monarchs in place of the latter's father, James VII and II. The northern kingdom slipped even further down the king's list of priorities, with the commercial interests of both England and his original Dutch provinces coming first. This helps to explain the disastrous decision to launch the Darien Scheme (an attempt to found the first Scottish colony in the swamp-ridden Isthmus of Panama in Central America in the 1690s) – not only did the Scots have no official support to harness their expansionist energies (which might have produced a better-informed, less rash decision), but they were positively hindered by other interests (particularly the English and the Dutch East India Companies).

However, the whole sorry incident highlights the fact that the appetite for taking and making economic opportunities was still alive and kicking in Scotland, whatever we might think about these colonial ventures today. Alas, the Darien Scheme lost a total of £232,884 (at least £31 million today), representing the life savings of many Scots.[65] This, combined with the long-term indebtedness of a nobility intoxicated by the conspicuous consumption they witnessed south of the border (as Macky said in 1723, 'the nobility have of late run into parking, planting and gardening, which are great improvements of their estates; but what is this to the bulk of the nation, which (if encouraged) has as many natural commodities for exportation as any whatsoever, and more than South Britain?')[66], perhaps explains why getting large-scale infrastructural or industrial projects off the ground was a problem in the early eighteenth century.

Despite a high opinion, both at home and beyond, of Scotland's industrial and commercial potential, it is remarkable how many larger-scale schemes to exploit the nation's natural resources were run by non-Scots as the century progressed, so that, while individual landowners might earn large sums of money by selling timber or iron ore, much of the profits went elsewhere. In part this was down to a lack of native skill, as yet, in new technologies. Even the mighty Carron Ironworks near Falkirk, then in Stirlingshire – founded in 1759 and, as mentioned above, 'the greatest of the kind in Europe'[67] – was founded by two Englishmen, a chemist and a merchant, as well as the Scottish shipping tycoon, William Caddell.

However, although skilled English workers were initially brought north, the works did create local jobs, employing 1,000 men at the end of the century to staff its five blast furnaces, sixteen air furnaces, clay mill, the engine raising water that consumed sixteen tons of coal a day, three cupola furnaces, four boring mills, smiths' forges and the forge for stamping iron. Dorothy Wordsworth was struck by the fact that 'the sky above them was red with a fiery light', the only remarkable sight, so she said, between Stirling Castle and Falkirk. Edwin Muir, 130 years later, was assailed by an even more Stygian prospect: 'As I neared Stirling I could see on my right a cloud of dense darkness, which showed where Falkirk lay round its furnaces.'[68]

Though mainly benefiting from local coal and iron ore, the vast complex also stimulated entrepreneurs across almost the entire country to look for anything they could sell to feed its apparently insatiable demand. Lime was brought to the ironworks from Burntisland in Fife in 1792 – 40 years later, the field from which it came was described as the property of the Carron Company, named as a major landowner in the parish; a sample of iron ore found on the estate of Lealty near Alness in Ross and Cromarty was duly dispatched to the ironmasters 'at their own desire'; in 1845, blocks of ironstone were sent from Culsalmond deep in Aberdeenshire, which, 'it is said, produced good iron'. It was just as well, as the ironstone wrought by the company in the parish of Polmont, which bordered the works, was nearly exhausted.[69]

By then, industry and commerce had spread through much of the Lowlands. Thomas Pennant was impressed by the fact that, on the Clyde below Dumbarton 'there is scarcely a spot on its banks but what is cultivated with bleacheries*, plantations and villas'; while upstream in Glasgow, near the bridge over the Clyde 'is a large almshouse, a vast nailery, a stone-ware manufacture, and a great porter brewery, which supplies some part of unindustrious Ireland. Within sight, on the south side, are the collieries; and much coal is exported into the last-mentioned island and into America.' There were also vast tanneries, 'chiefly for the use of the colonists, whose bark is found unfit for tanning'.[70] At Neilston in Lanarkshire, manufacturing was soon out-competing agriculture. 'Farmers now complain that their servants desert them, and engage in manufactures, where they receive higher wages and have left laborious employment.'[71]

Industry was certainly not confined to Glasgow or even the Central Belt, however. Pennant noted in 1769 that, on Loch Tayside in Perthshire: 'The country within these thirty years is grown very industrious, and manufactures a great deal of thread. They spin with rocks, which they do while they attend their cattle on the hills.' At the same time there were about a hundred weavers of coarse brown linen in Meigle in Angus, though 'since a great proprietor has thought proper to debar the inhabitants from the use of a large peatmoss, it is feared that the manufacturers must remove (as many have already done) for want of that essential article, fuel'. By 1845, an iron foundry at Tain in Ross and Cromarty produced 'the various descriptions of cast-iron ware used in the country round', while a brewery on the Morangie burn – a precursor of the famous whisky distillery there now – 'supplies the neighbourhood with excellent ale'.[72]

A commercial use might also be found for what had long been an established domestic activity, as we have already seen with peat. At the end of the eighteenth century, Loch Kindar near New Abbey in Kirkcudbrightshire produced 'bull-rushes and reeds; the first gathered by chair-makers, and the last by the weavers'. But at that time reeds – still plentiful in undrained lochs and bogs – were more generally used to make thatch. As Improved types of housing became more common over succeeding decades, tiles and slates began to replace them as a roofing

John Brown & Co Shipyard, Clydebank, Dunbartonshire

The ships under construction show the impact of industry on this estuarine and rural location. HES, SC1451860

Gutting herring, Peterhead harbour, Aberdeenshire, c1890

The herring industry was a major employer in Scotland for around 200 years. HES, SC860770

Killoch Colliery, Ochiltree, Ayrshire

Modern coal mining had a massive impact on the farmland of Ayrshire in the 1960s. It is now all gone, leaving nothing but scars on the landscape. HES, SC1438549

Canderigg Colliery, Lanarkshire, 1951

Miner John Monie crawls along a coal seam, the roof held up by wooden pit props.
Scottish Mining Museum, licensor Scran

Beardmore's Parkhead Forge, Glasgow, 1947
Beardmore's was founded in 1886, but was struggling by the mid twentieth century. The massive steelworks closed in 1976. A shopping centre opened on the site in 1988. HES, SC1437789

Ranco Motors Factory, Livingston, West Lothian
Despite a recession in the 1970s, Ranco Motors factory opened in 1973, with a predominantly female workforce.
West Lothian Archives and Records Centre, licensor Scran

Singer Factory, Clydebank, Dunbartonshire, 1934
The Singer Sewing Machine Factory was once the largest in the world, but falling orders led to it closing in 1980.
HES, SC1257700

Rootes Factory, Linwood, Glasgow, 1977
Workers watch the first Chrysler Sunbeams roll off the production line.
The Scotsman Publications Ltd, licensor Scran

A History of Scotland's Landscapes

Reedbeds at Seaside House, Perthshire
Reeds, once an important raw material for roofs and baskets, grew in many boggy areas. This habitat has declined with modern drainage, and the distinctive beds on the Tay are the last in use. HES, DP209603

material, which was just as well as the places where the reeds grew were often now being targeted for draining.

The exception was the Carse of Gowrie between Perth and Dundee, where reeds from beds originally planted to protect reclaimed arable land from erosion were used even in the new buildings of the surrounding parishes.[73] The reedbeds were planted south-east of the village of Errol in Perthshire in 1830; more recent commercial harvesting by the Tayreed Company ceased only in 2005 after 30 years, due to cheaper imports from Eastern Europe. Around half of the 410-hectare site is now managed by the RSPB as a nature reserve, since mudflats and reedbeds are a vital habitat for wild birds, including reed buntings and sedge warblers and the rare bearded tit, which is only found on wetlands planted with reeds.[74] The beds are managed in the old-fashioned way to protect the birds; instead of the large 'lawnmowers' used in commercial reed production, they are cut by hand with a scythe, gathered together, fastened with twine and the loose debris raked out. The bases of the reeds are then knocked on a board to create a tight parcel which is taken elsewhere to dry.

In general, however, very little survives of early industrial activity, because of the overwhelming nature of the mines, factories, smelters and power stations that came after. Nevertheless, the villages of Wanlockhead and Leadhills in Lanarkshire – founded or expanded in the seventeenth century for the exploitation of their mineral resources – are surrounded by the small bings and tramways of that early period of industrialisation. Pennant was appalled by Leadhills in 1769:

… the place consists of numbers of mean houses, inhabited by fifteen hundred souls, supported by the mines; for 500 are employed in the rich sous terrains of this tract. Nothing can equal the barren and gloomy appearance of the country round; neither tree nor shrub, nor verdure, nor picturesque rock …

But by 1803 the village was much improved; Dorothy Wordsworth even found its stone houses – 'single, or in clusters, or rows as it may chance' – rather picturesque, certainly compared with Wanlockhead's thatched huts. But in both places: 'Every cottage seemed to have its little plot of

160   Chapter Three – Industry and Infrastructure

ground, fenced by a ridge of earth', the outline of which can still be seen today.[75]

Mills of various kinds began to spring up in remarkable numbers along river banks across the country, up to and including the Outer Hebrides. At Blantyre in Lanarkshire the cotton magnate David Dale (who sold his mills at New Lanark to a consortium led by his son-in-law, Robert Owen), founded two large cotton mills, again using Clyde water power. By 1845 spinning, weaving and dyeing all took place there, employing 362 men and 558 women who worked five days a week from 6 am to 7.45 pm with 45 minutes for breakfast and one hour for dinner. On Saturdays they were 'only' required to be there for nine hours, which brought their total weekly service to the 69 prescribed by the Factory Act of 1833. A village, 'pleasantly situated on rising ground overlooking the Clyde', was built for them, the minister stressing that the workers were generally 'as healthy as their neighbours in other parts of the parish' (which may not necessarily have been saying much).[76]

Fish traps were another method of manipulating water-courses – in this case, by constructing roughly built stone walls or putting in lines of timber poles with nets strung between them at the mouths of small rivers or on the intertidal mudflats of estuaries. Surviving examples were placed near settlement sites during the last 200–300 years. Because some continued to be in use right up until the 1990s, we know that off-shore fishermen were sometimes allowed to use and maintain fish traps for their retirement. Sometimes, too, the traps were built, maintained and used by generations of the same family, ensuring that knowledge of, for example, which fish species could be caught, what form the trap should take and the construction techniques needed to maintain it were passed on.[77]

This was, however, the last gasp of an ancient and well-regulated practice. Thomas Pennant observed salmon cruives* on the River Don near Tillydrone, now a part of Aberdeen. He was informed that their owners were legally obliged (allegedly by a law dating back to the reign of Robert I 'The Bruce' in the early fourteenth century), to make their rails no wider than two inches, so that the young fishes could pass through. By the time Pennant saw them, however, this sensible stipulation 'is neglected'; instead it was now the practice to 'pay an annual sum to the owners of the fisheries which lie above, to compensate the loss'.[78] Though far easier and cost-effective, it was a practice unlikely to prove sustainable.

* * * *

There is no furnace to cause a nuisance and contaminate the pure air, as in the vicinity of many populous and manufacturing towns.[79]

New Statistical Account,
Moffat, Dumfriesshire, 1845

The drive to commercialise and industrialise was certainly not universally praised. Dorothy Wordsworth, true to form, lamented it on aesthetic grounds. At Galashiels in Selkirkshire, she complained that 'a pretty place it once has been, but a manufactory is established there; and a townish bustle and ugly stone houses are fast taking place of brown-roofed thatched cottages, of which a great number yet remain, partly overshadowed by trees',[80] And as the nineteenth century advanced, so did the repercussions of industrialisation, including pollution of both the air and the water, something the minister of Moffat was clearly well aware of when he expressed his relief that there was no furnace in his parish.

The rivers, their waters now in so much demand, were bound to be affected. 'Salmon formerly abounded in the Carron, but that valuable article of food has been banished by the Carron works and other works, which have dammed up the water, and diverted the stream from its natural course, and thereby prevented the salmon from going up the river to spawn.' At least the slag from the blast furnaces, called *danders* locally and which 'was long an encumbrance', proved useful in road building. At the Levern Water near Neilston on the outskirts of Glasgow, the bleachfields poisoned the river with dye. Though the trout did return to unpolluted places, the salmon were reportedly gone forever.[81]

The remains of these many and various industries are often still to be found throughout Scotland, from urban hinterlands to the banks of rivers to far-flung hillsides and forests – former ironstone and limestone quarries hinted at by scooped-out hollows

Broxburn Oil Works, West Lothian, 1927
From the mid nineteenth century, West Lothian lay at the heart of Scotland's shale oil industry, distilling shale rock to produce oil and other chemicals on an industrial scale. However, by 1927 the Broxburn Oil Works, shown here, had closed. Now only their great bings survive as a well-kent landscape feature. HES, SC1315377

Site of lead mining, Wanlockhead, Dumfriesshire
Lead has been mined at Wanlockhead for over 500 years, but its exploitation began in earnest in the later seventeenth century, lasting until the 1930s. Here we see the scars that this industrial heritage inflicted on the landscape, serving, along with its famous museum, as a reminder of this important aspect of Scottish history. HES, DP095366

The Sloy-Awe Hydro-Electric Scheme, Loch Lomond, Dunbartonshire

Highland topography, not to mention its generous rainfall, made the area ideal for hydro-electric schemes from the later nineteenth century. Today man-made and altered water-bodies account for nearly 1 per cent of modern land-use. The Sloy-Awe Hydro-Electric Scheme is currently used to generate electricity only during unusual spikes in demand.
Jim Gibson/Alamy Stock Photo

on hillsides and piles of waste products; lades and reservoirs betraying the long-gone might of water-wheels and steam engines serving mills and factories and pits; a plethora of tracks, tram roads, slopes, railways and canals laid down to carry raw materials to the furnaces of the ironworks and beyond; and the foundations of the housing built for workers and their families.

It had been known for centuries before the Industrial Revolution that Scotland possessed all manner of naturally occurring metals, minerals and useful rocks. As early as the fourteenth century, it was noted that in the Highlands: 'Marble of two or three colours, that is black, variegated, and white, as well as alabaster, is also found there. It also produces a good deal of iron and lead, and nearly all metals.'[82] However, as George Buchanan somewhat acerbically pointed out two centuries later when discussing alabaster in Sutherland, it was 'almost of no use, the refinement which requires this luxury not yet having spread thus far.' However, he also observed that there was 'a great deal of good white and black marble' being worked at the village of Torrin on Skye, as well as 'large quarries of freestone in several parts of this isle, as at Suisnish in Strath, in the south of Borreraig and the isle of Raasay' and 'an abundance of

164 Chapter Three – Industry and Infrastructure

Loch Meig Dam, Inverness-shire

These photographs of the Loch Meig dam west of Contin taken before, during and after its completion in the 1950s show just how much of an impact hydro schemes have had on the landscape. The dam holds back water from the River Meig catchment, which is then piped to Loch Luichart and on to the Loch Luichart Power Station. Of the 145 hydro schemes in Scotland, generating about 12 per cent of Scottish electricity, more than half are in the Highlands and Islands.

HES, clockwise SC1315114, SC1438413, DP024943, DP024942

A History of Scotland's Landscapes

limestone in Strath and Trotternish.' He and Martin Martin both referred to the lead mine on Islay.[83]

Daniel Defoe described the promise of metal and occasionally its working in the Lowlands, though that, as ever, depended on the whim and finances of the landowners on whose land these precious substances might be found. As we have already seen, he was firmly of the opinion that only by making a concerted effort to dig out and work these 'treasures of the earth' would Scotland escape poverty.[84] Edmund Burt saw the 'great granite quarries' near North Queensferry in Fife, 'which help to supply the streets of London with paving stones', while Thomas Pennant saw not only those, but others near Aberdeen, which had built that town and also helped to satisfy the British capital's insatiable need for slabs. He had previously visited 'the noted slate island' of Easdale in Argyll, where gunpowder was used to blast it out:

… the greater pieces are then divided, carried off in wheelbarrows, and lastly split into merchantable sizes, from eighteen by fourteen inches, to nine by six: and put on board at the price of twenty shillings per thousand. About two millions and a half are sold annually to England, Norway, Canada, and the West Indies … There are many other good slate quarries in this neighbourhood, as, on the isles of Suil, Luing, Balnahua and Kerrera, and some few opposite to them on the coast of Nether Lorn.[85]

There were quarries everywhere, mostly for local use as houses were slowly but surely turned into stone. However, some – as at Easdale – produced materials of a quality that gained a reputation much further afield. The marble worked at Port Soy in Banffshire was used for some of the chimney-pieces of no less exalted a place than the palace of Versailles, where it was 'known by the name of Scottish marble'; 50 years later the quartz from nearby Hill of Durn was being sent for use in the English potteries, because – so the minister proudly asserted – 'It is considered to be peculiarly suitable for this purpose and to be much superior to the English quartz'; sandstone from the Orcadian island of Eday was sent to London for a few years before 1845; and in the 1820s green marble from Glen Tilt in Highland Perthshire 'found its way to the principal towns of Britain and is now frequently met with as mantel-pieces, etc., in many modern mansions'.[86]

With the founding of the great ironworks of the south, limestone was needed in vast quantities to remove the waste elements (slag) from the ironstone. At the Carron Ironworks, the limestone quarries ringed the site in the south, while the resulting slag heaps made those produced by coal mines look puny in comparison. But nothing lasts forever. Once the quarries were exhausted or markets changed to make them unprofitable, there were a limited number of options for these great gouged-out spaces. Many smaller local quarries have been swallowed up by the vegetation of the surrounding moorland or hillside, where they are identifiable only as a roughly round, grassy indentation, whilst others are still open wounds. Some of the bigger ones have been filled in, but many have taken on a new lease of life as open-air rock-climbing venues, as at my old haunt at Auchinstarry in Dunbartonshire or 'Europe's largest indoor climbing arena' (which some claim is the largest in the world) at the former Ratho Quarry outside Edinburgh.

But it was coal and its extraction that has arguably left the biggest mark on the landscape of central Scotland, as well as in the hearts of the close-knit communities left behind when the pits closed. The increasing size and complexity of these operations over the course of the nineteenth century and into the twentieth can still be detected around Shotts in Lanarkshire and Slamannan near Falkirk, from the extensive rail network, now largely abandoned, to the ever-expanding bings, and from the pock-marked bell pit mounds and crow's-foot shaped ones made by successive dumps of spoil brought by tramways, to the great conveyor mounds of more recent times. Edwin Muir, writing of his journey round Scotland in 1934, was appalled by what seemed to him the dereliction of these industrial landscapes:

Nuclear power station, Chapelcross, Dumfriesshire

Scotland's first commercial nuclear power station was completed in 1959 on the site of an old airfield at Chapelcross. With its vast cooling towers and heroic Modern architecture, it was very much a product of its time. After the site was slated for decommissioning and the cooling towers blown up in 2007, some local people (including ex-employees) objected to the removal of such a potent symbol of Scotland's industrial heritage and a highly visible local landmark.
HES, SC624638

The forlorn villages looked like dismembered parts of towns brutally hacked off, and with the raw edges left nakedly exposed. The towns themselves, on the other hand, were like villages on a nightmare scale, which after endless building had never managed to produce what looked like a street, and had no centre of any kind … there was no visible sign of anything holding them together; the houses merely stood side by side; of every shape and size, they crowded upon each other so hard that they seemed to be squabbling in a slatternly, apathetic dejected way for their places.
Round these bloated and scabbed villages there are ranges of slag-heaps, miniature mountain ranges which, though they have no more connection with the green fields round them than the villages themselves, give one the illusion of being geological in formation, so convincing are their contours. These black slag peaks and valleys make up a toy landscape which is not enchanting like the toy landscape of the Tweed Valley, but dwarf-like and sinister, suggesting an immeasurably shrivelled and debased second-childhood.[87]

During the final decades of coal production in Scotland (give or take a couple of opencast mines still in operation), the industry underwent significant change with a move from shaft to opencast mining and the preparing of pits in Fife, the Lothians and Ayrshire to provide coal to generate electricity. But the days of the coal-fired power station came to an end in 2016 with the closure of Longannet near Kincardine in Fife, though it remains a major landmark, standing proud on the north bank of the Forth. I still remember lying in my tent at a Guide camp on a nearby farm and wondering what the rumbling beneath me might be, only to discover that it was the coal being transported to the power station by underground conveyor belt from Longannet Colliery.

As with quarries, the closure of opencast mines has brought still more landscape change in recent times, their extensive acreage sometimes heralding opportunities for artistic landscaping and recreation, or for landfill. But most have gone back to agriculture. The abandoned remains of former collieries can sometimes still be found above ground, as at Kingshill Forest near Carluke in Lanarkshire, where a ruined building and the line of a tramway that took the coal to be washed are still visible at the edge of the woodland. The Lady Victoria Colliery, set beside the planned mining village at Newtongrange in East Lothian, has been the National Mining Museum since 1984, topping an online poll 'in a thrillingly close competition' to become Scotland's most treasured place in 2008,[88] while the Museum of Lead Mining at Wanlockhead in Lanarkshire is set around the remains of a pit dating back over three hundred years.

Some relics of Scotland's industrial heyday are truly enormous. The Greendyke oil shale bing – another well-kent landmark near Edinburgh Airport (oil shale mining was particular to West Lothian, booming first in the 1860s) – has, despite, or perhaps because, it was reputedly once vast enough to be visible from space, been left to go where nature wishes. From trips along the M9, I have watched it slowly transform from monotonous sterility to blossoming hillside, home to over 80 plant species, as well as foxes, hares, red grouse and laverocks (skylarks), which have colonised the alkaline soils over the decades.[89]

At the moment, Scotland's electricity needs are supplied by the nuclear power stations at Hunterston B (North Ayrshire) and Torness (East Lothian), commissioned in the 1970s and 1980s; two pumped-storage hydro-electric power stations (Foyer/Loch Mhor south of Loch Ness and Cruachan in Argyll; the latter was the first of this kind in the world); 81 conventional hydro-electric plants, some of which were built originally to serve the aluminium-smelting industry; over 80 on-shore wind farms plus two off-shore; and a number of others using, amongst other methods, wave and biomass power.

The Kinlochleven hydro scheme, power station and aluminium works in Argyll was a huge enterprise which, it was hoped, would create sufficient employment in the Highlands to stem emigration. Construction on the scheme, which created the Blackwater Reservoir, began in 1905 and was one of the last major projects to use 'navvys' (from navigational engineer, but essentially manual labourers), who built just about everything from canals to railways to reservoirs. The aluminium plant with

Anti-tank barriers, Longniddry Bents, East Lothian
During the Second World War, the nation held its breath in the expectation that enemy craft would land somewhere on the 11,000 mile coastline of Britain. To combat this eventuality, every possible landing point was protected with anti-tank barriers. HES. DP054831

its 76 smelters was opened in 1909; in its heyday, it employed over 700 people, some of whose company housing still survives, though the plant itself closed in 1996 and was largely demolished.[90]

The power station at Kinlochleven, which is still in operation, was built a back-breaking four miles from its water supply at Blackwater; not surprisingly, it is far more usual for these stations to be situated right next to their reservoirs, as at Pitlochry in Perthshire, which opened in 1950 on the south-east side of Loch Faskally, the dammed water engulfing the local golf course. Since their launch in 1943, these large-scale hydro-electric schemes have swallowed up farms and even villages.

Reservoirs were also built to provide clean drinking water, once the link with infectious diseases such as cholera had been made by the middle of the nineteenth century. The most famous is surely Loch Katrine, then in Perthshire – already well-known as the setting of Sir Walter Scott's famous romantic poem of 1810, *The lady of the Lake* – opened by Queen Victoria in 1859 to supply Glasgow 'at a cost of £1.5 million, which gave it the best public supply of water in the UK'. When cholera broke out again in 1865–6, only 53 people died in the city, persuading Edinburgh and Dundee to get on with building their own reservoirs.[91]

* * * *

What is thought to be the world's best preserved non-flying Spitfire now resides suspended aloft at the Kelvingrove Art Gallery and Museum in Glasgow. LA198 was operated by No 602 (City of Glasgow) Squadron in the late 1940s until suffering a heavy landing at Horsham St Faith on July 22 1949. The aircraft subsequently travelled around various airfields in Britain for many years until being gifted to the city almost 50 years later.[92]

Airfields of Britain Conservation Trust

A concerted military presence in Scotland had, as we've already seen, made a fundamental difference to the nation's transportation networks on two occasions, the first during the intermittent Roman presence between AD 71 and AD c211, and the

170   Chapter Three – Industry and Infrastructure

Lochs wind farm, Lewis
The Lochs wind farm is one of the newest sources of power in Scotland. In the foreground are the remains of peat cutting on either side of the road, and one of the few conifer plantations on Lewis. HES, DP111266

second some 1,500 years later when General Wade set about blasting a series of roads and forts through the north and west. The twentieth century heralded a completely new infrastructural dimension, however, once humans managed to harness the power of flight.

To begin with, the development of airfields, which largely swept away evidence for previous land-use, was a military affair, encouraged by the new technology's potential in both World Wars, but especially the Second. After 1945, however, most were abandoned or occasionally amalgamated into upgraded military bases, as at Leuchars in Fife, Kinloss in Moray and Machrihanish in Argyll, though the Cold War against the USSR, with its explicit threat of nuclear war, prompted the construction of new facilities at Faslane in Dunbartonshire, and in the Outer Hebrides at St Kilda and along the western seaboard of the Uists.

The civilian airports still in operation today owe their existence to the exponential expansion of military flight capability in the Second World War. Most of them have, of course, grown much bigger since, with new or extended runways needed to cope with the advent of jet engines and bigger terminals to house expanding passenger numbers (not to mention retail outlets), as well as a growing fleet of maintenance and service buildings. A number of smaller airports have also been built to serve commercial needs and the desire to fly for fun.

Given that over 90 Second World War airfields, from small landing strips to large bomber bases, have been abandoned, as well as a number from the Great War, there are many to find. Lenabo, west of Peterhead in Aberdeenshire, was built in 1915 as the most northerly station in mainland Britain, housing airships that would patrol the North Sea for German submarines. It was not rebuilt after 1939 and the footprint of its enormous airship sheds (one of which measured 216m by 45m and 32m high) survives as unplanted clearings within a modern forestry plantation.[93]

The standard arrangement of Second World War runways was roughly a letter A formed by the intersection of three runways. They were generally much bigger than First World War airfields (give or take the airship sheds), with hangers, workshops, bomb depots, dispersal areas, large accommodation blocks housing up to 2,000 servicemen and women, and defensive buildings such as pillboxes. Before the war, these buildings tended to be grouped together, as at Lossiemouth in Moray, Montrose in Angus and Turnhouse (now Edinburgh Airport); during the war, they were built around the edge of the airfield, as at Tain and Fearn in Ross and Cromarty.

Because such sites tend to be so vast and are often situated in isolated places, many have not been developed since they were abandoned. Hangars might find a new use as agricultural buildings, while paved runways still lurk in the grass. One or two have been taken over and given a completely new lease of life; the control tower at Fearn near Tain, which has just been turned into a highly unusual B&B, even featured on Channel Four's *Restoration Man* in 2015.

Airfields are not the only surviving testament to the huge impact that the military presence – army, navy and airforce – has made on the Scottish landscape throughout the twentieth century. The coastline is still littered with defences designed to protect these islands from invasion, from massive concrete pillboxes to anti-glider poles. There are also the remains – usually the concrete bases of Nissen huts* – of depots, radar sites and barracks, as well as prisoner-of-war camps, to be found mostly in rural locations in the Central Belt.

The camp at Cultybraggan near Comrie in Perthshire held Hitler's deputy, Rudolf Hess, for one night after his capture in 1941, as well as nineteen-year-old Heinrich Steinmeyer for rather longer. Mr Steinmeyer was overwhelmed by the kindness of the locals during his incarceration, a number of whom even went so far as to smuggle him out for the day so that he could go to the cinema for the first time. He came back to Scotland on a number of occasions after the war and, when he died in 2016, he left £384,000 to the Comrie Development Trust to be spent on improving facilities for the village's older inhabitants.[94] Cultybraggan itself has been in community ownership since 2007, when it was sold off by the Ministry of Defence, the striking red and white Nissen huts now rented out to 'an eclectic mix of people and businesses'.[95]

In recent years, defence cuts have led to the closure of a number of military establishments in Scotland. However, there are still large naval bases on the Clyde, where the UK's nuclear deterrent is housed, and at Rosyth on the Forth, as well as refuelling bases at Campbeltown in Argyll and Loch Ewe in Ross and Cromarty. Elsewhere other services have taken over these facilities, as at the former airfields at Kinloss in Moray and Leuchars in Fife, which are now home to the army personnel previously deployed on the Rhine in Germany. Large training areas lie next to existing barracks at Fort George in Nairnshire, Barry Buddon near Carnoustie in Angus, Pentlands (Castlelaw and Dreghorn) near Edinburgh, and Kirkcudbright in the south-west.

The impact of military activity on natural landscapes has recently become better understood – these large-scale, comparatively undeveloped sites can, perhaps contrary to expectations, be a haven for biodiversity.[96] But they might also be marvellous places for preserving the historic landscape. The 19km^2 of the Kirkcudbright Training Area has fossilised the farming landscape of the nineteenth and twentieth centuries (though some older farm buildings have been obliterated during target practice or demolished when they became unsafe), as well as important earlier survivals such as three prehistoric forts, a newly discovered hut circle and homestead, a medieval moated site and a few examples of post-medieval rig.[97]

But there can be no doubt that the many and often supremely impressive – in terms of human ingenuity and sheer hard work – industrial and infrastructural endeavours we have encountered over these pages have cost us dear in terms of the eradication of centuries of previous human activity. It is, of course, a price that we are generally happy to pay for, among many things, heat and light at the flick of a switch, cheap food and the ability to live in one place and work in another or to move quickly across the country in our leisure time.

The good news is, as we have been discovering, that there are more remnants of the past out there than was previously thought – so long as we know what to look for and where – and that new discoveries are still being made. It is also now beholden upon us by law to preserve important elements created by our predecessors for the present and the future. We are infinitely more adept at incorporating older structures and features into ultra-modern restorations and renovations, as well as refashioning sites originally constructed for entirely practical purposes, such as canals, former railways and quarries, into places to be used and enjoyed anew.

Sometimes, however, the price that was paid feels too much and the site too precious and iconic to be renewed while memories are still raw. The Ravenscraig hot strip steel mill near Motherwell in Lanarkshire, south-east of Glasgow, was once the largest in Western Europe. For the men employed there, these were good jobs; despite the dangers inherent in working with such high temperatures, they brought in a wage decent enough to settle down, bring up kids, buy a house and a car, and go on holiday. But in 1992 the mill was closed with the loss of over 10,000 jobs, directly and indirectly. It was one of Scotland's worst employment disasters, in an area then reeling from the closure of the Gartcosh steelworks six years earlier.

Not surprisingly, given that the steel mill covered 1,000 acres, efforts to clean it up have created the largest brownfield site in Europe. In 2006, however, a consortium was set up to redevelop the site in the hope of kick-starting economic regeneration. Although the original proposals did not come to fruition, this consortium is once again making plans for the future, over a quarter of a century after Ravenscraig closed its mighty doors. If these developments make it onto the ground, it will, as usual these days, be housing and leisure facilities that take the place of heavy industry.

In 2012 – the twentieth anniversary of the closure – Jim Fraser, a former engineer at the mill whose skills made it comparatively easy to find another job after he was made redundant, was adamant nonetheless that the area had still not recovered. 'Closing Ravenscraig has ripped the heart out of the community and it ripped many families apart too.' The then local MP, Frank Roy, still thought fondly of the close-knit community of steelmen he used to work with. 'It's the thing that I miss the most, the real patter and laugh you find in heavy industry.'[98] Those that lived and worked across the country over preceding millennia might recognise that sentiment; tasks that may have been time-consuming, laborious and even dangerous might still bring 'joy and hilarity' thanks to the camaraderie of a community.

Hermitage at Dunkeld, Perthshire, artist D McKenzie, engraver Thomas Watt, c1840

Ossian's Hall was built in 1757–8 as part of the pleasure grounds attached to Dunkeld House. It provided an ideal viewing platform for the spectacular falls on the River Braan but its name also testifies to the interest in Celtic mythology at the time, a fascination brought to a head in 1761 when James Macpherson claimed to have discovered the works of the poet Ossian.

HES, SC1462979

Chapter Four

Leisure

A gap in the wall showed where the door had once been, so I entered, and as I did so found myself nodding an acknowledgment to the woman of the house, which was silly really. Of course there was no-one there. The interior was very small, maybe ten or twelve feet from one end to the other; it was just a little plain ruin, in an empty glen …
Now my eye was in, I could see the other shielings. The green knolls were a giveaway, and I counted – as the map had suggested – first one, then another humble little hut, until there were fourteen, and a little field system too, just a few undulations on the ground. There were seven or eight huts straggling along the riverside, forming not a street exactly, they were too spaced out, but the suggestion of one, of neighbourliness …
… The people would come up from the farmsteads below around the beginning of July – 'the girls went laughing up the glen' as the poem says – and return at harvest time. Up here they made milk, butter and cheese, and it was women's work. What a loss that seems now: a time when women were guaranteed a place in the wider landscape, our own place in the hills …[1]

Kathleen Jamie
Sightlines

Our feelings about landscape are similar in nature to our spiritual or religious beliefs, which are shaped by the knowledge and cultural norms to which we are exposed, our own experience, and personal inclination. Attitudes to the remains still cradled in the landscape come, it seems to me, from a similar place – for some, like the poet Kathleen Jamie, above, there is great pleasure to be taken in reminders that empty glens once teemed with life; for others, it is the lack of any obvious human presence that inspires them with the promise of a peace and quiet often missing from these busy modern times. On the other hand, those whose lives and sense of self were turned upside down by the closure of pit, mill or factory will obviously have very different feelings towards their derelict remains, or the housing or out-of-town malls or leisure centres that have replaced them, than those to whom Ravenscraig or Bilston Glen or Singer are, at best, just names.

I like to think, though, that we are especially fortunate in Scotland. Thanks to our particular history, troubled and contentious though it has often been (and whose history hasn't?), we can often have our cake and eat it, enjoy tranquil scenery *and* explore the traces of long-gone human activity that bring a different context and perspective to these beautiful places. And while economic regeneration in the present and the future is key to breathing new life into communities blighted by the comparatively swift and certainly painful demise of heavy industry and traditional manufacture, the fact that the footprint of many of these places lingers in new developments means that they are with us still, if we care to look, if we take the trouble to remember.

Though recent generations are the first to have the leisure time, the books, TV series and internet, the protected sites and objects to help us explore the history and archaeology of our own backyards and further afield, our predecessors have, almost as far back as we have been able to study them, valued their connections with the past. Most were interested in their own ancestors or their immediate surroundings, the physical remains that they lived and worked amongst, and the stories, songs and poetry passed down to them (though members of the educated elites over the last six hundred years or so have also been keen to examine the truth of 'bigger' stories, such as the Roman presence in Scotland).

When the Gododdin, the British tribe living in the Edinburgh area around AD 600, rode to war on their 'swan-white steeds, war-harness drawn tight', it was important to them in the aftermath of a cataclysmic battle to remember that it was fought in a place presided over by a 'Standing stone on cleared ground, on cleared ground a hill On Gododdin's border'.[2]

Many centuries later, stories that had no doubt been spoken or sung for generations to explain the rationale behind similar ancient monuments, began to be written down. According to Hector Boece in 1527, Mainus, a legendary early Scottish king (who supposedly lived around 290 BC), realising that it was both wise and prudent to be nice to the gods:

… commanded that huge stones be set up in circles at various places, as the matter required, with the largest stone set at the south of the circle to be employed as an altar, where burnt-offering might be offered to the gods. As evidence of this, such great stone circles exist to our own day, and are commonly identified as ancient temples of the gods. And whoever has seen these will be bound to wonder by what art or physical strength stones of such size were brought together.[3]

The details may be suspect, but the basic premise is not wildly different from our understanding of these stone circles today.

Boece also noted that Reuda, another legendary Scottish ruler (who supposedly led the Irish Scots across the Irish Sea to Dalriada, now Argyll, around AD 500) 'was the first of all our kings who commanded that the feats of brave men and those who had done fine things for their nation's sake should be memorialized'. Those of Reuda's men who died fighting the Romans were to be honoured with obelisks placed over their tombs 'to match the number of men they had killed', monuments that the historian said could still be seen in parts of the Highlands.

Later, Boece asserted, 'the tombs of the most famous and distinguished men' were venerated by the building of stone cairns and the erecting of great stones 'on which were inscribed the shapes of fish, snakes, and birds (that age used these instead of letters of the alphabet for writing arcane things), to advise passers-by who they were and what fair things they had achieved in life'.[4] In identifying, to some extent, that these ancient monuments belonged to different time periods, the sixteenth century historian was again on the right lines, even if these ancient Scottish kings and their doings are entirely fictitious.

On the other hand, the historian George Buchanan, writing half a century after Boece, exposes the limitations of the age, despite his careful consideration of the available evidence and avowed intention 'to free our ancient history from the uncertainty of fable and rescue it from unmerited oblivion'. He asserts categorically that two earthen mounds on the left bank of the River Carron in Stirlingshire were 'evidently artificial'. They were known locally as Dunipace, which he – a Classical scholar of some renown – confidently translated as Hill of Peace from an amalgamation of Gaelic (*Dun*) and Latin (*pace*), weaving possibilities out of the various stories he knew were associated with the mounds.

Ultimately, however, he concluded rather conventionally that such mounds were 'consecrated as everlasting memorials, reared, by untaught and uncultivated hands, after the fashion of the smaller edifice, which is erected on the banks of the Carron'. (Arthur's O'on, which we met in Chapter Three). In fact, geologists have identified the 'Hills of Dunipace' as the remains of a raised beach (literally left behind when sea levels fell after the last Ice Age) and not artificial at all.[5] But, to be fair, that is a mistake that most of us are likely to make looking at them even now.

There were similarities and fascinating differences across the country in the stories told about each community's ancient monuments, but, in my opinion, North Uist in the Outer Hebrides had some of the best. Martin Martin, visiting in the 1690s, was told that three standing stones, each five feet high and about a quarter of a mile apart, were apparently placed 'on eminences about a mile from Loch Maddy to amuse invaders; for which reason they are still called false sentinels'. An enormous chunk of rock (24 feet long and 4 feet wide) on a hill called Criniveal was, according to the natives, the burial place of 'a giant of a month old'. A twelve foot whopper on the quay opposite Kirkibost was where 'delinquents' were tied during church services. Another one at St Mary's Church near Hougharry was known as the Water Cross because 'the ancient inhabitants had a custom of erecting this sort of cross to procure rain, and when they had got enough they laid it flat on the ground'.[6]

Martin was told that this last practice was discontinued, though that may say as much about rainfall at the time as lack of faith in the cross, given the other 'superstitious' customs that he came across on his travels. Certainly the general belief throughout Scotland, but most enduring in the Highlands, that cairns and standing stones were built to remember warriors killed in nearby battles (the size and number of the stones reflecting the status of the individual) persisted well into the eighteenth century. Thomas Pennant was told on the island of Arran in Ayrshire that: 'as long as the memory of the deceased endured, not a passenger went by without adding a stone to the heap'. There was even a proverb 'allusive to the old practice: a suppliant will tell his patron, "*Curri mi cloche r do charne*", "I will add a stone to your cairn", meaning "when you are no more I will do all possible honour to your memory"'.[7]

We must be careful, though, not to assume that vestiges of the truth were preserved in oral traditions over many centuries, if not millennia, though they might well be. In 1684 a report on Galloway stated that it was said locally that a small ruined chapel 'was the first that was built for the service of Almighty God, in this part of the kingdom, yea, as some say, in the whole kingdom'. In fact, this chapel, at Whithorn in Wigtownshire, dates from around 1300 with slightly older elements, but it was long believed to stand on the site of St Ninian's original Candida Casa (White House), although modern excavation has found no traces of it. There has been considerable debate as to who Ninian really was, current thinking identifying him as the Irish missionary Finnian of Moville (County Donegal), teacher of Columba and student at Whithorn, which would make Candida Casa one of the earliest Christian establishments in Scotland and certainly older than Columba's Iona.[8]

In the course of the eighteenth century, with its growing commitment to rational, scientific modes of inquiry, scepticism about the knowledge held by wise and venerable local men became more pronounced. The problem was what to replace it with. Daniel Defoe summed up the dilemma when confronted with stories about the various relics of St Andrew which supposedly made their way to Scotland 'from Patras in the Morea, near the Gulph of Lepanto' (now the Peloponnese peninsula in Greece). Such stories were, he crisply acknowledged, 'too antient and sound too much of the legend for me to meddle with'.[9]

A century later, the old beliefs were dying out even in the Highlands, partly due to the work of organisations like the Society for the Propagation of Christian Knowledge, founded in 1709, whose schools – which taught in English – were intent on bringing 'civilisation' to the north and west.

However, it cannot have helped that many of the younger generation were soon spending part of the year in the Lowlands, where they were presumably exposed to very different ways of thinking than they had learned from their parents' generation, as well as encouraging them to drop English words into their Gaelic when they got home.

In Aboyne and Glentanar in Aberdeenshire, it was noted in 1845 that the local people had ditched their kilts, plaids and other homemade 'stuffs' for 'the dress and habits' of all the other rural districts. And instead of listening to the old tales that they had enjoyed 50 years before, they 'now take an interest in reading standard works on history and general science, and have provided themselves with a pretty extensive parochial library'.[10] Such an attitude to education is entirely admirable, but it is a pity that so much old knowledge was rejected quite so quickly and comprehensively, though we must be grateful to anyone who thought to write these stories down before they were lost.

Still, the advantages of wider reading and a growing desire to look for comparisons across different time periods and cultures could lead to some interesting, if extravagant, conclusions. In 1845 David Harris, the minister of Fearn near Brechin in Angus, waxed lyrical in his account of the cairn or motte on the nearby Law of Windsor. First of all, he asserted that:

Perhaps it may startle the admirer of ancient Gothic architecture to insinuate a supposition that traces may still be found of a permanent human abode, which can be referred to an age prior by many generations to that in which the foundation of the first Gothic structure was laid in our land.

Referring to himself in the third person, Reverend Harris went on to make an even more startling observation:

Engraving by Charles Cordiner, 1780, of the Shandwick Stone, Ross and Cromarty

The Shandwick Stone or Clach a' Charridh ('stone of the grave plots') sits to the south of the village of Shandwick and about a mile from the site of another incredible Pictish stone at Hilton of Cadboll. This carving shows a hunting scene with stags pursued by dogs and hunters on horseback and on foot.
HES, SC806469

He considers them to be the remains of the wigwam of the country – a conjecture which he is the more disposed to cherish by a notice of Captain Ross in his Arctic Voyage, that he had seen a resemblance of the same in what he considered the deserted summer residences of the Esquimaux.[11]

Though the good minister would have considered his comments to be rooted in rational, scientific reading and observation, there is also a hint of Romanticism about them. Devotees of the Romantic Movement, with its focus on the artistic potential of untrammelled emotions, often sought out foreign or remote landscapes to unleash them. They were also interested in folklore, leading to a Celtic Revival, which in Scotland was brought feverishly into being by James Macpherson's 1761 discovery of an ancient epic poem about the mythical Irish hero, Fionn mac Cumhaill (Finn McCoul), written by one Ossian. Though quickly denounced as largely a fabrication of Macpherson's own devising, the poem's sympathetic treatment of an ancient legend and the natural world inspired many Romantics well beyond Scotland.

Just over a decade after the Ossian sensation, Thomas Pennant noted sniffily that: 'It is but of late that the North Britons became sensible of the beauties of their country.'[12] Leaving aside whether or not that was likely to be true, there is no doubt that, thanks to the road-building programme begun by Wade and continued by Caulfeild, as well as the brutal ending to the Jacobite rebellions in 1746, the Highlands were now accessible to tourists, providing they didn't mind roughing it a bit (and that was exactly what card-carrying Romantics wanted to give them an authentic experience).

But Pennant was wrong. As we have already seen, a number of Scots (and others) had toured their country long before the Welsh naturalist got there. They sometimes even made it clear that they were entirely sensible of its beauties; Macky, for example, described the hills near Melrose in Roxburghshire as 'the prettiest downs in the world'.[13] But generally speaking, they had quite different, more practical reasons for exploring Scotland, usually seeking to establish current practices or future economic potential in soil and sea. In pre-Industrial times the land was there first and foremost to produce, not to look pretty.

But once the furnaces began to glow and the chimneys to belch, those that had the wealth and leisure to do so began to look to nature for escape and meaning. At Loch Maree in Ross and Cromarty, Pennant was entirely charmed by what he saw:

We found ourselves seated in a spot equalized by few in picturesque and magnificent scenery. The banks of the river that rushes by the house [Dundonnel] is fringed with trees; and the course often interrupted by cascades. At a small distance the ground begins to rise: as we mount, the eye is entertained with new objects; the river rolling beneath the dark shade of alders, an extent of plain composed of fields bounded by groves; and as the walk advances, appears a deep and tremendous hollow, shagged with trees, and winding far amidst the hills.

Of course, nature could always be improved upon. Pennant also lauded the Duke of Atholl's efforts to create a suitably idealised landscape at Dunkeld in Perthshire: 'The gardens extend along the side of the river [Tay], and command from different parts the most beautiful and picturesque views of wild and gloomy nature that can be conceived.'[14]

But there can have been few more Romantic travelling companions than Samuel Coleridge and Dorothy and William Wordsworth, who came to Scotland in 1803, paying homage to two Scottish literary giants in the Romantic tradition at the beginning and end of their tour. Robert Burns had, unfortunately, died seven years earlier, and Dorothy had to work hard to keep her prejudices in check when she visited his house in Dumfries where his wife and children still lived. You will not be surprised to learn that she thought: 'It has a mean appearance … dirty about the doors, as almost all Scotch houses are.'

Nevertheless, she was heartened, on entering the parlour, to see 'on one side of the fire was a mahogany desk, opposite to the window a clock, and over the desk a picture from the "Cotter's Saturday Night", which Burns mentions in one of his letters having received as a present'. It presumably came as a considerable relief that: 'The house was cleanly and neat in the inside, the stairs of stone, scoured white'. In the end, though, she was not impressed with Dumfries, 'which is no agreeable place to them who do not love the bustle of a town that seems to be rising up to wealth'. She could not help but pity 'poor Burns and his moving about on that unpoetic ground'. I can only imagine that the bard would have been bemused by such a sentiment.

A month later, she and her brother arrived in Melrose, where they were met by Walter Scott. Scott was still in the early stages of his literary career, having so far only published translations of German poetry and a collection of Border ballads, but he liked to entertain poets and writers. His usefulness to the Wordsworths lay in his avowed knowledge of the area – 'we scarcely passed a house for which he had not some story'.

He joined them as often as he could, in between his duties as local sheriff, treating them on at least two occasions to recitations of parts of *The Lay of the Last Minstrel*, though Dorothy refrained from saying whether or not she liked it. Nevertheless, when they did finally part a few days later on a high hill near Hawick, she admitted that: 'We wished we could have gone with Mr Scott into some of the more remote dales of this country, where in almost every house he can find a home and a hearty welcome.'

They had enjoyed at least one conversation along Romantic lines. Walking through a wood near the old castle at Ferniehurst, she exclaimed 'What a life there is in trees!', as the wind tossed the branches and sunshine danced among the leaves. But she was shocked when Scott said this reminded him of a young woman from Orkney who, on spending a summer in Kelso and Edinburgh, declared herself most disappointed in trees and woods, complaining 'that they were lifeless, silent, and, compared with the grandeur of the ever-changing ocean, even insipid'. To be fair, Dorothy gave this proper consideration and concluded that such feelings were 'natural', that all-important Romantic attribute![15]

As the nineteenth century progressed, tourism – until recently the preserve of a small, and reasonably hardy, elite – began to open up to ever greater numbers. Even the working classes might venture a short distance – from Glasgow to the Clyde resorts, for example, or from Edinburgh along the coast to Portobello – but these precious moments of freedom were not spent seeking out alarming, gloomy scenery or sublimely assembled vistas. As a letter written in 1881 by Mary Allison, wife of a Glasgow storekeeper, poignantly illustrates, holidays were counted in days, not weeks, were often spent with family, and permitted the glorious luxury of sleeping in (till 8 o'clock!). Even climbing the hills of the Arrochar Alps in Argyll was all about the exertion and the simple pleasure of looking for blaeberries.[16]

While rising incomes and more free time played their part, new modes of transport were crucial in making holidays feasible for almost all sections of society. Unlike in England, where it was the railways that proved decisive, steamships also played a vital part in helping the Scottish tourist to get quickly and comparatively comfortably to his or her destination. 'Their service opened up in particular the West Coast firths and islands, making – as handbooks dubbed it – Oban in Argyll the "Charing Cross" of the Highlands.'[17]

But Scotland was attractive to visitors from much further afield too, especially once Sir Walter Scott had, almost single-handedly (with help from James Macpherson), made the Highlands and its dramatic scenery Romantic. The young Queen Victoria was an avid reader of his novels and, soon after her accession, made plans to visit her northern kingdom, spending two weeks there in the autumn of 1842. She was not disappointed, noting in her diary on her return to the south that 'The English coast seemed terribly flat.' She had become particularly attached to the Highlands, missing its 'fine hills', but swore there was more to it than just lovely scenery; 'there was a quiet, a retirement, a wildness, a liberty, and a solitude that had such a charm for us'.[18] By June 1852, she and Prince Albert had become the delighted owners of the Balmoral estate some 50 miles west of Aberdeen.

Where Victoria led, it was incumbent on the rich and powerful – whether of old or new money – to follow. Scotland played its hand expertly and the money flowed in as southern aristocrats and wealthy industrialists turned to fishing, hunting and shooting with determined fervour. 'Contemporaries called this sporting flow "a golden stream".'[19] In giving many northern estates a new lease of life, these Victorian hunters with their uniform tweeds, caps and plus fours, harked back to an ancient pastime, one that had also been treated with deadly seriousness and with an eye to showing the world just what kind of men its participants were.

* * * *

When your daddy went off to hunt,
Spear on his shoulder, club in his hand,
He'd call the hounds so swift of foot:
'Giff, Gaff – seek im, see 'im; fetch, fetch'.
He'd strike fish from a coracle
As a lion strikes a small animal.
When to the mountain your daddy would go,
He'd bring back a stag, a boar, a roe,
A speckled mountain grouse,
A fish from Derwennydd Falls.
Of those your daddy reached with his lance,
Whether a boar or a fox or a lynx,
None could escape unless it had wings.[20]

This seventh century British poem is remarkable, not least because it may well be the first in the history of these islands to be written from a woman's perspective and surely by a female poet. From it, we learn much about how a nobleman went hunting and how his warrior identity was enhanced by his prowess as a hunter – 'None could escape unless it had wings' is a tribute that would be just as applicable on the battlefield.

From the early Middle Ages (and doubtless well before that), hunting lay at the heart of the social and cultural life of the nation's elites. In part, of course, it was about providing for the table, but for many aristocrats of both sexes it was nothing short of a passion. Here was an opportunity to relax, but also to impress in a similar way to modern businessmen taking clients to the golf course (but with rather more energy and risk). Scenes depicted on carved Pictish stones suggest that 'stag-hunting with hounds was the top-ranking thrill', while they also tell us that the Picts were superb horse-breeders, their bridles and harnesses decorated with silver and deep black niello* fittings.[21]

Later historians had a lot to say about earlier hunting practices, though on what evidence, goodness only knows. It is highly likely that they were reflecting some of the methods and certainly the assumptions of their own times. Hector Boece, writing in 1527, was keen to stress the relationship between hunting and honour during the reign of the legendary Scottish king Ethodius. (Here, again, the term Scottish is used to describe the Irish in Argyll.) He promoted ancient ordinances designed to ensure that the balance of power between man and prey was a fair one by restricting which weapons could be

Scott's View, River Tweed, Melrose, Roxburghshire

This view of the River Tweed with the Eildon Hills in the background is the kind of Romantic image that charmed the Victorians in general and Sir Walter Scott in particular. Scott was the father of Scottish Romanticism, not to mention tourism, transforming attitudes towards rural landscapes away from the miserable and unproductive wastelands disapproved of by earlier commentators into awe-inspiring and picturesque visitor attractions. James Smith Photography

used, when to hunt and which deer to go after. 'For he hated nothing so much as to have the hunt, a fair thing for noble and high-born spirits, to be sullied by such offenses, and to have himself and the nobles of his kingdom cheated out of this praiseworthy solace.'

Boece also described the supposed differences between Pictish and Scottish methods of hunting, claiming that the former engaged in exactly the kind of dishonourable methods banned by Ethodius.

… hounds drove stags and does into nets stretched out for the purpose in meadows hard by woods. If any game escaped, they would give pursuit, covering themselves with tree-branches so that they would be unseen by their quarry, and when the beasts were exhausted and had gone to ground, they would attack them with arrows and slingshots. The Scots disliked this manner of

provided gives some idea of the creatures found or bred throughout the kingdom; these included venison, rabbit, partridge, plover, crane, bristle-cock (whatever that might be), peacock (called bristle-pawnie), black cock, muirfowl and capercaillie, as well as fish such as salmon, trout, pike and eel. The total cost was estimated to be £1,000 (over half a million today) for three days of royal hunting.

The papal ambassador was apparently most impressed 'that such a thing could be in Scotland, considering that it was named The Arse of the World'; he was even more astonished when, as the guests were preparing to leave, the whole edifice was torched, the king nonchalantly saying that 'It is the use of our Highland-men, though they be never so well lodged, to burn their Lodging when they depart.'[25] There is no need to take this statement too seriously; it was almost certainly for effect.

Some 30 years later, in 1563, King James's daughter, Mary, Queen of Scots, went hunting in the north-east. This was an enormous affair, with 2,000 Highlanders (disparagingly called 'wild Scottish') employed for two months to drive in deer from all over Atholl, Badenoch, Mar and Moray. By skilful work they managed to gather 2,000 deer, red, roe and fallow.

But such large numbers proved dangerous. When the Queen ordered one of her best dogs to be set on the herd, the lead stag took fright, launching what became a stampede off the ridge of the hill, straight towards a large group of waiting Highlanders – 'they had nothing for it but to throw themselves flat on the heath, and to allow the deer to pass over them'. Needless to say, many were injured and a number killed outright, but they still managed to prevent those at the back from escaping with the main herd. The dogs were then set upon them, killing '360 deer with five wolves, and some roes'.[26]

But the most fascinating account of a great hunt was penned by the Water Poet, John Taylor, in 1618. Once a year, Taylor says, during 'the whole month of August, and sometimes part of September, many of the nobility and gentry of the kingdom [for their pleasure] do come into these Highland Countries to hunt'. On this occasion, the Earl of Mar and his son, the Earl of Moray, the Marquis of Huntly's son and the Earl of Buchan turned up, as well as their various countesses and 'hundreds of others Knights, Esquires, and their followers'.

There was a price to be paid, however, by Lowland gentlemen, in that they could only hunt or let their dogs loose if they wore Highland dress, described as:

… shoes with but one sole apiece; stockings [which they call short hose] made of a warm stuff of divers colours, which they call tartan: as for breeches, many of them, nor their forefathers never wore any, but a jerkin of the same stuff that their hose is of, their garters being bands or wreaths of hay or straw, with a plaid about their shoulders, which is a mantle of divers colours, of much finer and lighter stuff than their hose, with blue flat caps on their heads, a handkerchief knit with two knots about their neck; and thus are they attired.

They had to use Highland weapons too: 'long bows and forked arrows, swords and targets, harquebuses [an early type of long gun supported on a mount], muskets, dirks, and Lochaber axes.'

The hunt itself took place eight miles from Braemar in Aberdeenshire (presumably in towards the Cairngorm Mountains) where a temporary camp was set up, including houses called lonchards or lunkarts (probably similar to shielings) with kitchens:

being always on the side of a bank, many kettles and pots boiling, and many spits turning and winding, with great variety of cheer: as venison baked, sodden, roast, and stewed beef, mutton, goats, kid, hares, fresh salmon, pigeons, hens, capons, chickens, partridge, moor-coots, heath-cocks, capercailzies, and termagants [presumably ptarmigan, rather than the devil or a shrewish woman]; good ale, sack [white fortified wine], white, and claret, tent, (or Alicante) with most potent Aquavitæ [whisky].

Needless to say, most of the meat was easily found on the surrounding hills and moors, 'caught by Falconers, Fowlers, Fishers' or brought up by Mar's tenants and purveyors (supposedly numbering a staggering 14–1500) for whom this was a wonderfully lucrative, if temporary, captive market.

The hunt itself followed a familiar pattern. Five or six hundred tinchels got up very early, spreading out up to ten miles from the camp to drive herds of deer (estimated at up to five hundred per herd) to a pre-appointed spot. The noble hunters and their attendants then rode or walked there, 'sometimes wading up to their middles through burns and rivers', before lying in wait for some three hours. At last, the deer arrived, 'their heads making a show like a wood'. Immediately, Taylor wrote, around two hundred Irish greyhounds (although they were surely Scottish deerhounds, which look very similar to their Irish counterparts), stationed on either side of the glen, were let loose, 'so that with dogs, guns, arrows, dirks, and daggers, in the space of two hours, fourscore fat deer were slain, which after are disposed of some one way, and some another, twenty and thirty miles, and more than enough left for us to make merry withal at our rendezvous'.[27]

Over a century later, Edmund Burt witnessed a similar event, presumably in the mountains beyond Inverness, where he was based. This one was on a much smaller scale, however, for the average Highland chief (as opposed to great earl) could only summon three or four hundred vassals, who, nonetheless, displayed considerable skill.

With these he surrounds the hill, and as they advance upwards, the deer flies at the sight of them, first of one side, then of another; and they still, as they mount, get into closer order, till, in the end, he is enclosed by them in a small circle, and there they hack him down with their broadswords. And they generally do it so dexterously, as to preserve the hide entire.

Different tactics were employed in different settings. If the hunt took place in the midst of trees in the mountains, 'the tenants spread themselves as much as they can, in a rank extending upwards; and march, or rather crawl forward, with a hideous yell. Thus they drive everything before them, while the laird and his friends are waiting at the farther end with their guns to shoot the deer. But it is difficult to force the roes out of their cover; insomuch that when they come into the open sight, they sometimes turn back upon the huntsmen, and are taken alive.'[28]

The days of the great Highland hunt were numbered, however. Pennant, who knew about Taylor's hunting extravaganza at Braemar, put it down to Jacobitism, for such gatherings 'were often the preludes to rebellion … which at length occasioned an Act of Parliament prohibiting such dangerous assemblies'. Though visiting Scotland only some 25 years after Bonnie Prince Charlie's doomed campaign of 1745–6, he noted that 'Most of the ancient sports of the Highlanders, such as archery, hunting, fowling and fishing, are now disused.'

But relics of them remained scattered across the countryside. The island of Inchmurrin in Loch Lomond on the border between Dunbartonshire and Perthshire was 'a deer park, and has on it the ruins of a house once belonging to the family of Lennox'. On the island of Skye in the Outer Hebrides, travelling past Loch Slapin to the south, he saw 'a stone dike or fence called Parainam Fiadh, or "the enclosure of the deer", which seems once to have been continued up a neighbouring hill. In one angle is a hollow, in the days of Ossian, a pitfall covered with boughs for the destruction of the animals chased into it.' However, on Jura in the Inner Hebrides, which, as we saw above, was once a proper deer hunting forest, Pennant found only 'some stunted woods of birch and hazels, giving shelter to black game'.[29]

The hills surrounding Loch Laggan in Inverness-shire also used to be 'famous for hunting' with a local story claiming that ancient Scottish kings used to spend their summers there and that a ruined building on an island on the loch was where they 'retired from hunting and feasted on their game.' By the end of the eighteenth century, however, the hills were covered in sheep, which had 'chased the deer away.' Drum in Aberdeenshire, the property of the Irvine family for 650 years from 1325, also supposedly attracted Scottish kings, albeit later ones. 'The park of Drum formed part of the chase and a powerful spring at the north-east end of the loch is still known by the designation of the King's Well.'[30]

As we have already seen, however, it was arguably the Scottish nobility who hosted the best hunting. The Earls Marischal (whose family name was Keith) reputedly once had a park at Garvock, south-east of Laurencekirk in Kincardineshire. 'There is the more ground to credit this tradition, as the remains of a dyke, which surrounding the parish (which, to this day, is called the *Deer-dyke*, because, as people affirm, it inclosed a forest in which plenty of those animals were then found), are still perceptible.' On the hill of Little Tulloch west of Aboyne in Aberdeenshire, the earls of Mar had 'My Lord's House', where they could supposedly get a good (and comparatively comfortable) view of deer hunts in the surrounding forest of Glen Tanar. Over in the west, Benmore, a hill above Dunoon in Argyll, was

Hunting party, Glen Tilt, Perthshire, c1900
A returning deer-stalking party at Forest Lodge. From the 1870s, deer forests began to replace the sheep-farming and cattle ranching that had dominated Highland landscapes for over a century. National Museums Scotland, licensor Scran

Duke of Buccleuch's Christmas Eve Hunt at Maxpoffle near Melrose, Roxburghshire, 1968
Though much of the surrounding countryside is hills and moorland, the hunting area also took in arable land.
Robert Clapperton Photographic Trust, licensor Scran

Otter hunting, c1895
A party of women and men gather for the hunt with dogs and otter poles. HES, DP007394

Stag hunting, Kinloch Castle, Rum
By the end of the nineteenth century, around 3 million hectares of Highland land was given over to deer. HES, SC1081002

Ardverikie House, Loch Laggan, Inverness-shire
James Hamilton, Second Marquess of Abercorn, remodelled Ardverikie House as a hunting lodge in the 1840s. The house found fame as the setting for *Monarch of the Glen*.
HES, SC686519

Rabbit hunting
This hunting party is after rabbits, not deer, their much smaller dogs at the ready. HES, SC1226210

Fishing, Kyle of Sutherland, c1910
This peaceful scene would have been very different one hundred years earlier, when the residents of the surrounding valley were forcibly removed. HES, DP093897

Deer-Stalking, Knoydart, Inverness-shire
Once the preserve of the wealthy, the estate is now owned by the Knoydart Foundation and is managed 'for the well-being of the environment and the people'. Gerry McCann

A History of Scotland's Landscapes

once a deer forest belonging to the earls of Argyll. 'The remains of mounds erected for the purpose of driving the deer into certain passes are still visible on this hill and it continued to be preserved as a forest till near the close of the last century [c1800].'³¹

By then, with improvements in shotguns, the game on the moors might well be enjoyed by local sportsmen 'in the shooting season', as at Kirkpatrick west of Dumfries, assuming the land was not earmarked for draining by the Improvers. But as such sport became increasingly lucrative for estate owners, it was soon noted, as at Stenton near Haddington in East Lothian, that: 'Poaching in game is beginning to show itself, from the strict system of preserving adopted by the surrounding landed proprietors.'³² At Blair Atholl in Perthshire, the local minister went so far as to suggest that this was only to be expected:

*If a young man be occasionally found in our distant and extensive moors with a gun in his hand, it need not be wondered at. Sportsmen from the south train them either as servants or guides or sacketmen to a fascinating amusement and which, when their masters leave off their sport, it is not easy for them to relinquish.*³³

By the 1840s, too, there are hints that the panoply of creatures worthy of being hunted was in flux. Though pheasants may have come to Britain with the Romans and were certainly a colourful feature of royal forests and parks at the end of the seventeenth century (when James VI legislated to protect them and other wildfowl and venison), they only seem to have spread across the country in the early nineteenth century. At the same time, 'grouse, the favourite of the sportsman, is rapidly disappearing', certainly in southern Ayrshire, while deer, once native, had been gone for nearly a century in Moffat parish in Dumfriesshire (the last hart was shot in 1754). On the other hand, game – black and red grouse and partridges – were still to be found here, though they were 'liable to fluctuations', depending, so it was supposed, on muir-burning* and the eradication of birds of prey.³⁴

By this time, hunting no longer had to involve a cast of hundreds. But, in keeping with the hardy athleticism displayed by the Scottish nobility in previous centuries, at New Year 1800, a local man, Captain McP---, and four attendants made their way to an unoccupied lodge house in the Gaick Forest in the lower reaches of the Cairngorms, south of Kingussie in Inverness-shire. They intended to go deer-stalking and took enough provisions to last four or five days. A few days in, however, the weather deteriorated with gale force winds and drifting snow blowing in from the south-east.

The Captain's friends did not worry for they knew that the lodge was a substantial stone building; however, when he did not return on the allotted day, a party of twelve went in after him, the storm having abated. But as they approached, they were shocked to find 'the stones which had formed part of the walls, along with the wood and divots of the roof … among the snow between the house and the bottom of the valley, at various distances, some of them from two to three hundred yards from the house'.

The five bodies were found in and around the place where the lodge had been, and 'it appeared that the unfortunate men had been retiring to bed, or at least reclining, when the sad event befell them'. Though local people put it down to 'some supernatural agency, or at least the shock of an earthquake or to lightning', it was, of course, an avalanche, a phenomenon that does not seem to have been as well known then as it is now that skiing and mountaineering are popular leisure pursuits.³⁵

Captain McP---, being a military man, might be expected to rough it, but the Scottish nobility, not to mention their sporting friends and clients, were now generally keen on home comforts when they went to shoot. In 1844, for example, the Marquess of Abercorn leased the estates of Benalder and Ardverikie and proceeded to embellish the Ardverikie shooting lodge on Loch Laggan in Inverness-shire. The end result, as the local minister pithily put it, 'may be inferred from the fact that it is taxed for sixty windows'.³⁶ It is now known as Ardverikie House.

But that was nothing compared with what the Duke of Atholl's estate in Perthshire had to offer the outdoor enthusiast. In 1845 it was said that:

The park contains many hundred acres of excellent arable land, exclusive of its extensive plantations; the garden is large and productive; the gravel walks along the Tilt, the Banvie, and the Fender, the Bruar, and the Garry; the various and well-conducted carriage drives; all afford the advantage of active exercise with the pleasure of admiring magnificent scenery; and if the whole be viewed in connection with the forest and its lodges, its lakes and its rivers, Blair may be justly said to be one of the most splendid hunting chateaux in Europe.[33]

Perhaps such grandeur was only to be expected – the owner, John Murray, 5th Duke of Atholl, was, after all, the great-great-great-great-great-great-great-grandson of John Stewart, Earl of Atholl who had so lavishly entertained James V 300 years earlier. In the 1840s, as in the 1530s, such sport was the preserve of the upper classes and the very wealthy; 170 years later, anyone with a bit of cash can go and shoot grouse, stalk deer or fish on the Atholl estates.

Though most people living in Scotland have little to do with hunting, it is nevertheless the only activity that humans have undertaken, and often enjoyed, from the moment the first canoes carried people here after the last Ice Age right up to today. And while there is no doubt that farming has had a far greater impact on the landscape, the needs of sport have also contributed to the way it looks now, from the grouse moors with their intermittent drystone shooting butts and burnt patches, to wooded plantations providing cover for pheasants, to the many and varied lodge houses scattered throughout the Highlands in particular, some of which are now available for holiday-makers to rent.

* * * *

Panmure new built and as is thought by many, except Holyroodhouse, the best house in the kingdom of Scotland, with delicate gardens with high stone walls, extraordinary much planting, young and old, many great parks about the new and old house with a great deal of planting around the old house, brave hay meadows well ditched and hedged and in a word, is a most excellent sweet delicate place …[38]

Landscapes have, to some extent, been designed since at least the Middle Ages, with deer parks and herb gardens flanking many a castle. But from the Renaissance*, these landscapes began to be arranged on straight lines leading from the house, with plots laid out on a grid and often arranged into a knot design. They might also include various man-made features such as grottos and groves, statues and sculptures, and spectacular water features. Even in Scotland, some noble houses came to be as well-furnished outdoors as inside, their gardens, orchards and pleasure grounds forming an integral part of the overall show.

The garden at Edzell Castle near Brechin in Angus, first laid out in 1604, is a unique Scottish survival from this period, though even it was replanted in the 1930s; another at Gordonstoun near Elgin in Moray lasted long enough to be recorded on General Roy's map in the eighteenth century and traces of it may linger in cropmarks south of the current gardens belonging to the school there.[39] The remains of the pleasure grounds constructed in the 1630s for Charles I's only visit to his Scottish kingdom are also still visible to the south of Stirling Castle:

Beneath, on the flat, are to be seen the vestiges of the gardens belonging to the palace, called the King's Knot; where, according to the taste of the times, the flowers had been disposed in beds and curious knots, at this time very easily to be traced in the fantastic form of the turf. Above these walks is the Ladies Hill; for here sat the fair to see their faithful knights exert their vigour and address in the tilts and tournaments, performed in a hollow between this spot and the castle.[40]

Though the Italians were the master Renaissance gardeners to begin with, it was the French who took these ideas to a new level, particularly at Versailles, begun by Louis XIII in the 1630s but primarily associated with his son, Louis XIV (1638 – 1715). Charles II, who was Louis' first cousin, spent a number of years on the Continent, including in France, during the civil wars of the mid seventeenth century; on his return to Britain in 1660, he was able to indulge his 'love of managing what we call forest trees, and making fine vistas and avenues'.

As mentioned in Chapter Two, he passed on this passion to one of his favourites, John Hay, Earl of Tweeddale, whose estate lay at Yester, south of Haddington in East Lothian. 'This occasion'd his lordship, as soon as he went down into Scotland, to lay out the plan and design of all those noble walks and woods of trees, or, as it might be call'd, forests of trees, which he afterwards saw planted.' It was a similar story at the Duke of Buccleuch's

castle of Drumlanrig in Dumfriesshire where the gardens were 'truly magnificent, and all in a wild, mountainous country'. They took up the whole south and west side of the house, 'the park and avenues completely planted with trees. At the extent of the gardens there are pavilions and banqueting-houses, exactly answering to one another, and the greens trimm'd, spaliers* and hedges are in perfection.'[41]

But while Renaissance gardening principles were clearly known in Scotland, the hints and brief descriptions of upper-class gardens from the seventeenth century suggest that most were planted for largely practical purposes. Thus, for example, the castle at Inveraray in Argyll possessed 'sundry yards [the Scottish word for an enclosed area of ground next to a house, planted with grass or trees, or used as a garden or orchard], some of them with divers kind of herbs growing and set thereunto. And other yards planted with sundry fruit trees very prettily set, and planted, and there fair greens to walk upon, with one wall of stone and lime built lately about said green'; Ardkinglas on the opposite bank of Loch Fyne, boasted 'fair yards planted with sundry kinds of fruit trees therein and sundry kinds of herbs'; Walkingshaw House in Renfrewshire possessed 'mightily pleasant fine orchards and gardens and excellent regular avenues of barren timber', whilst neighbouring Houston was 'most excellently adorned with fine orchards and gardens with wood hard by and vast number of barren timber, with which this country abounds'.[42]

In Kyle and Cunningham in Ayrshire, 'every gentleman has by his house both wood and water orchards and parkes', while at Cassilis, the main house of the Kennedy family near Maybole, 'there be large plots of ground cast into Gardens, fenced about with stone walls exceeding high which yields good store of Apricocks, peaches, cherries, and all other fruits and herbage which this Kingdome produces'. Though the grounds are still extensive, there doesn't seem to be anything left, alas, of the walled gardens.

At Coif or Cove on the Ayrshire coast, the laird of Culzean did not live in the grand Robert Adam-designed castle we can visit today; instead he had a 'Mansion house standing upon a rock above the sea, flanked on the south with very pretty gardens and orchards adorned with excellent Tarrases [terraces] and the walls loaden with peaches, apricotes, cherries and other fruit.'[43]

And so it goes on throughout much of the country, even in places abandoned by their original owners, as at Dunfermline in Fife, where, in 1618, John Taylor, the Water Poet, discovered 'the ruins of an ancient and stately built Abbey, with fair gardens, orchards, meadows belonging to the Palace'; a century and a half later, Thomas Pennant visited Kinloss Abbey near Forres in Moray, next to which still flourished 'an orchard of apple and pear trees, at least coeval with the last monks [around two hundred years earlier]; numbers lie prostrate, their venerable branches seem to have taken fresh roots, and were loaden with fruit, beyond what could be expected from their antique look'. A few years later he went to Lincluden Abbey, near Dumfries, which still had 'the vestiges of a flower garden, with the parterres and scrolls very visible; and near that a great artificial mount, with a spiral walk to the top, which is hollowed, and has a turf seat around to command the beautiful views'. This is presumably the earthwork shaped like a poppy and restored in recent decades.[44]

Daniel Defoe was, as ever, quick to point out where the Scottish nobles were going wrong when it came to their gardens and orchards, having seen an exceptional example at the Marquess of Annandale's house in Edinburgh in the early 1720s.

And here I observ'd his lordship was making bricks, in order to build walls round his garden; a thing hardly to be seen in Scotland, except there. On the other hand, it is for want of brick walls that the wall-fruit in Scotland does not thrive so well there as it would otherwise do. And whereas they have no peaches or nectarines or but very few, it is evident had they brick walls they might have both; but the stone will not do it. The reflexion of the sun is not equally nourishing, nor does the stone hold the warmth of the sun, after it is gone, as the bricks do.[45]

The King's Knot, Stirling Castle, Stirling

Clearly visible as a grassy feature beyond Stirling Castle, the King's Knot is probably of early seventeenth century date and may have been created as part of the welcome home package designed for Charles I during his only visit to his Scottish kingdom in 1633. The area had long been a playground for monarchs, having once formed part of a hunting park where kings, courtiers and visitors jousted, hawked and hunted.

HES, DP051058

Balcaskie House, Fife
One of the most visible trends of the seventeenth century (inspired by what the Scottish nobility saw in England after the Union of the Crowns of 1603 and Louis XIV's Versailles) were the designed landscapes that took root next to castles and stately homes. Here at Balcaskie, the notable architect Sir William Bruce laid out terraced gardens with a central axis focused on the Bass Rock out in the River Forth.
HES, DP050894

Presumably the abundance of good building stone in Scotland (which England lacked) meant that few felt the need, as yet, to develop a brick-making industry.

By the eighteenth century, horticultural tastes had moved on, particularly in England under the influence of Lancelot 'Capability' Brown (c1715–1783) and other proponents of the 'style anglais'. As Improvement ideas took hold and the agricultural landscape, particularly on lower ground, became more and more regimented, the desire for a 'natural' look in upper-class gardens took hold.

Parterres (regimented flowerbed arrangements) and formal avenues gave way to lawns with softer, rounder lines, lakes were made bigger and trees were carefully arranged to help create what was deemed an ideal rural landscape, often inspired by neo-classical painting. As the style evolved during the later eighteenth and early nineteenth centuries, natural features such as waterfalls, rivers and striking rock formations were also brought into the designed landscape. Often surrounded by the real countryside, these carefully planned 'wildernesses' also included paths through densely planted trees to provide a little frisson of fear and exhilaration beloved of a Romantic soul.

But, for a while at least, the Scottish nobility were still playing catch-up with Versailles-influenced style. Thus, while Thomas Pennant was very impressed with the grounds of Hopetoun House near Edinburgh in 1769, he qualified his praise:

The great improvements round the house are very extensive; but the gardens are still in the old taste: trees

Drumlanrig Castle, Dumfriesshire

The Duke of Queensberry's castle at Drumlanrig, completed in 1691, sits amid a truly vast garden that dominates the landscape, with local rivers and streams even diverted to create a waterfall. Early visitors, including John Macky and Daniel Defoe, admired the results but disliked the wild mountains that formed the backdrop. As tastes changed, later visitors often preferred the natural surroundings to the formality of the gardens.

HES, DP104033

and shrubs succeed here greatly; among others were two Portugal laurels thirty feet high. Nothing can equal the grandeur of the approach to the house, or the prospect from it.[46]

It was the same with the gardens at Alloa Tower in Clackmannanshire and at Barncluith near Hamilton in Lanarkshire. Barncluith was once 'much resorted to by strangers' attracted by a landscape laid out in the seventeenth century – a series of five terraces cut into a steep bank above the River Avon, decorated with topiary and planting. By the end of the eighteenth century, however, the place was falling into ruin; 'the taste for this artificial species of gardening having become less fashionable, the place is not now held in so much repute'.[47] Still, Dorothy Wordsworth liked it:

The house stands very sweetly in complete retirement; it has its gardens and terraces one above another, with flights of steps between, box-trees and yew-trees cut in fantastic shapes, flower-borders and summer-houses; and still below, apples and pears were hanging in abundance on the branches of large, old trees, which grew intermingled with the natural wood, elms, beeches, etc. even to the water's edge. The whole place is in perfect harmony with the taste of our ancestors and the yews and hollies are shaven as nicely, and the gravel-walks and flower-borders kept in exact order, as if the spirit of the first architect of the terraces still presided over them ... [it] ... is one of the most elaborate old things ever seen, a little hanging garden of Babylon ...[48]

The exception, for Pennant, was Dunkeld in Perthshire, where, by 1769, 'The great ornament of this place is the Duke of Athol's extensive improvements, and magnificent plantations, bounded by crags with summits of a tremendous height. The gardens extend along the side of the river, and command from different parts the most beautiful and picturesque views of wild and gloomy nature that can be conceived.' Dorothy Wordsworth agreed that newer principles were at work here, enjoying the Romantic surroundings:

The walks are quaintly enough intersected, here and there, by a baby garden of fine flowers among the rocks and stones … We left the Braan [a river that joins the Tay at Dunkeld] and pursued our walk through the plantations … They are already no insignificant woods, where the trees happen to be oaks, birches, and others natural to the soil; and under their shade the walks are delightful.[49]

Needless to say, styles changed again; by the middle of the nineteenth century, formal and regimented gardens were back in fashion, along with a craze for exotic species, especially trees, reflecting the thirst for exploration inspired in men like the botanist David Douglas. The straight avenues and parterres of Drummond Castle near Crieff in Perthshire belong to this period and still prove popular to this day.

But with, among other things, changes to the tax system, including the introduction of death duties in the later nineteenth century, some estates began to be sold off for other uses, in whole or in part. The sheer size of many of the designed landscapes within them meant that they were often separated off (to be sold or used for something else) from the big houses that were meant to form an integral part of their design. Sometimes the houses themselves proved too expensive or old-fashioned and have disappeared. But many of these impressive designed landscapes have simply been buried beneath urban sprawl, fields, forestry or other types of cultivation. Occasionally they might be used for another form of recreation completely, particularly golf courses, which are ideally suited to these great well-designed spaces. But their origins are still hinted at by nicely structured clumps of trees or unexpected water features.[50]

Such transformations are part-and-parcel of modern life, when change can strike quickly and potential uses of the land are so much more diverse than they were in the past. Now, too, leisure is, quite justifiably, viewed as a right, not a privilege; the things we can do with our free time are surely well beyond the wildest dreams of early working-class holiday-makers like Mary Allison. And our activities are likely to make far more of a mark on the landscape than going blaeberry-picking on the Arrochar Alps.

* * * *

1669. Just opposite to this Vennel there is another that leads North West from the chiefe street to the Green which is a pleasant plot of ground enclosed around with an Earthen wall wherein they were wont to play at football but now at the Gowffe and Byasse bowls.[51]

Personally, I find it reassuring to know that the gentlemen of Maybole in Ayrshire were playing golf and bowls 350 years ago. I think of them when I watch our own bowlers from the kitchen window, resplendent in white during a match or in 'auld claes' when they set to mowing and rollering their pristine grass (as they do with impressively fanatical regularity). Byasse – or bias – bowls (so-called because the bowls are shaped with a 'bias' to make them travel an elliptical path) is the same as lawn bowls and, while the game did not originate in Scotland, its popularity here means that its world headquarters is in Edinburgh.

On the other hand, golf as we know it is indeed something that Scotland can claim to have given to the world. It is a much older game than bowls, being first mentioned in 1458 (in order to ban it and football so as to encourage men to practise archery),[52] while Mary, Queen of Scots was the first celebrity enthusiast – 'She played a round on the links* at Seton [east of Edinburgh] a few days after the murder of Darnley [her husband], a game her enemies were not slow to notice.'[53] The earliest golf courses tended to be on rough ground by the seashore, but a few could be found inland next to cities like Perth and Edinburgh. Martin Martin even saw golf being played on St Kilda:

196 Chapter Four – Leisure

They use for their diversion short clubs and balls of wood; the sand is a fair field for this sport and exercise, in which they take great pleasure and are very nimble at it; they play for some eggs, fowls, hooks, or tobacco; and so eager are they for victory, that they strip themselves to their shirts to obtain it …[54]

Often located next to medieval burghs or villages and characterised by sandy soils and brown grass during long dry summers (no sprinklers here!), these were clearly little more than convenient flat spaces to play, rather than dedicated courses with artificial features – the golfers had to share them with anyone else who wanted to use them for whatever purpose. As a result, many of these early golf courses have disappeared, though the footprints of links at Bruntsfield and Leith in Edinburgh are still preserved in the outline of the public parks that succeeded them.

By the time Thomas Pennant visited St Andrews in Fife in 1772, the town was already well-known for golf. Indeed, the manufacture of golf balls was its only industry, 'which, trifling as it may seem, maintains several people'. This was, believe it or not, a dangerous occupation. 'The trade is commonly fatal to the artists, for the balls are made by stuffing a great quantity of feathers into a leather case, by help of an iron rod, with a wooden handle, pressed against the breast, which seldom fails to bring on a consumption.' Early clubs were reputedly made in Perth by the 'bowyers' whose trade was suffering as archery went out of fashion with the advent of guns.[55]

By the end of the eighteenth century, the game was becoming sophisticated and organised, with courses designed, at last, with the kind of interesting physical features integral to the modern game. At Burntisland in Fife:

To those who enjoy the healthful and manly diversion of golf there is adjoining one of the finest pieces of links, of its size, in Scotland. A great part of it is like velvet with all the variety of hazards necessary to employ the different clubs used by the nicest players. A golfing club was instituted lately by the gentlemen of the town and neighbourhood.

But the game really took off with the expansion of the railways in the mid nineteenth century, which allowed wealthier golfers to visit courses all over the country. Increasing leisure time and spare cash also brought about demand for facilities in the middle-class suburbs. By the end of the century, the number of new golfing societies was exploding.

These societies were committed to making proper golf courses, some buying or leasing good quality land to create flat, tree-lined fairways. Such genteel, manicured parkland courses were very different to the traditionally windswept links or those dug out of barren moorlands, as at Braemar in Aberdeenshire (the highest 18-holer in Scotland, apparently), which nonetheless rely on good drainage to keep the fairways puddle-free on peaty ground. Estate owners sometimes also created their own private courses as part of their designed landscapes.

Before the Second World War, the impact of these courses was minimal, using the existing topography and moving earth around as little as possible. Modern technology has, however, allowed designers to create whatever landscape they desire, with artificial mounds and lochs abounding. On the other hand, some of the courses on far-flung Scottish islands make imaginative use of natural features or abandoned buildings, as at Stroma, an island en route to Orkney, which was created in 1996 'by simply cutting some tees and greens – the sheep keep the rest of the course "manageable" and … well fertilised'.[56]

In cities and towns, the only land available for golf tended to be hilly areas unsuitable for housing, which in turn has helped to create oases of biodiversity within the urban environment. However, as with many other leisure pursuits, golf is not as popular as it once was and many clubs, such as Torphin Hill and Lothianburn in Edinburgh, have closed in the last few years. But even if these courses are slowly sinking beneath the grass, the dips and folds of their bunkers, tees and greens are still there to tempt us to duck, just in case.

The leisure pursuits discussed this far have been almost unremittingly upper or middle class in terms of the people enjoying them. While links courses, generally owned by local authorities, were open to anyone, the parkland golf clubs were certainly middle- or upper-class affairs – in the 1920s H V Morton described St Andrews, not entirely surprisingly, as 'full of men in plus fours and women with golf bags on their tweed shoulders'.[57] But there

Gairloch Golf Course, Ross and Cromarty

Golf, which Scotland claims to have invented, was banned by Scottish kings between 1457 and 1502 to encourage archery. But in the sixteenth century James IV, his granddaughter, Mary, Queen of Scots, and great-grandson, James VI, were players. Scotland can also boast of some truly fabulous courses. At Gairloch you can tee off above a beautiful sandy beach with views of Skye, Harris and Lewis to the west and the Torridon mountains to the south.
HES, DP109997

Ladybank Golf Club, Fife
Established in 1879, Ladybank was designed by the famous greenkeeper and golfer Old Tom Morris, who was the first to deliberately place hazards in his designs. HES, DP100735

Royal Tarlair Golf Course, Aberdeenshire
This modernised early twentieth century course still retains its notorious thirteenth hole, the 'Clivet', situated on a rocky headland. HES, DP193193

Carnegie Golf Course, Skibo, Sutherland
Carnegie Golf Course sits on a prime site on the Dornoch Firth within the grounds of Skibo Castle, which was owned from 1898 by the industrialist Andrew Carnegie. HES, DP191757

King James VI Golf Course, Perth
The James VI Golf Course, which lies on Moncrieffe Island, is probably the only inland island course in Britain.
HES, DP103418

A History of Scotland's Landscapes

are features still forming part of the landscape that were explicitly designed for, or by, working-class families. As part of the general drive to provide for returning soldiers after the First World War, as well as those cramped in difficult conditions in the inner cities, timber summer huts were built to provide cheap holiday accommodation. This formed part of a broader movement championing the benefits of healthy outdoor living in many parts of Europe (including Nazi Germany), aimed in part at the urban poor.

To begin with, a few landowners permitted those ex-servicemen or deprived families they deemed deserving to camp on their estates; over time, rudimentary timber huts sometimes began to appear, often using recycled timbers and to a design entirely at the behest of the builder, who paid only a modest rent to the landowner. Most were constructed in the early 1930s, though those in the Scottish Borders were put up after the Second World War. Since then, however, numbers have been in decline.

In 1999 703 huts were recorded over thirty-six sites, only seventeen of which occupied more than a hectare of ground. Most are near cities or at the seaside, as in Dumfries and Galloway, Renfrewshire, East Lothian and Ayrshire. As with the huts themselves, the sites are equally idiosyncratic, having spread organically and fitting in with local topography, vegetation, water, access and the landlord. Some are in groups, while others are all on their own; many are surrounded by fences and have had extensions tacked on as and when they were needed.

The largest and best-known summer huts are the 180 located at Carbeth in Stirlingshire, north-west of Glasgow. In 2013, the Carbeth Hutters Community Company bought 90 acres of the surrounding estate to become the first community-owned site, but their example has so far proved the exception rather than the rule. Since the publication of a Scottish Executive report in 2000, however, attempts have been made to revive the hutting movement, which, with similar beginnings, is still extremely popular in Scandinavia. Planning regulations have been amended in part to encourage low-impact rural retreats to be built, which would give people the benefit of even a few days out in nature. By April 2017 the 'A Thousand Huts' campaign, run by Reforesting Scotland, had a list of over 850 people looking to build one. It is now a question of matching them up with landowners willing to let them go ahead.[58]

While the number of summer huts is tiny (and any developments are explicitly intended to minimise the impact of future ones), they form an important part of the history of leisure in Scotland, not least because they were unusual in developing largely on the initiative of those who intended to use them. Like thousands of ordinary Scots before them putting up simple houses with their neighbours in townships or farmtowns, these 'hutters' have worked with both the landscape and often the limited resources available to them, though few would pretend that the similarity goes much deeper.

Carn Dearg, Inverness-shire

This image of Carn Dearg, a remote peak above Loch Ossian, encapsulates the emptiness and raw nature that is often most prized about the Highlands. Nevertheless, even here there is evidence that this landscape has been lived and worked in throughout the centuries, from medieval or early modern shielings and settlements to an old hunting lodge that served as an isolation hospital in the early twentieth century.

Walkhighlands

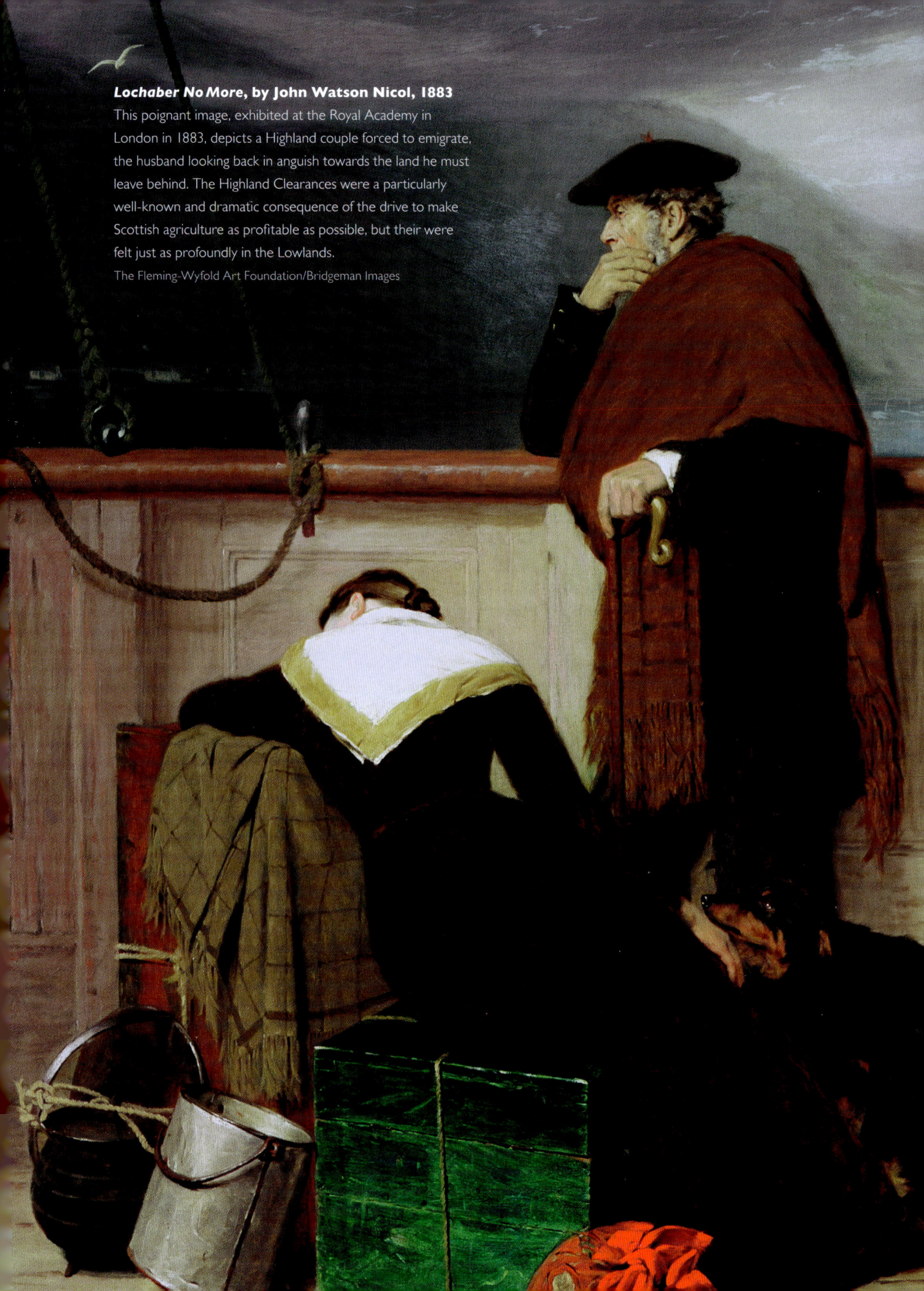

***Lochaber No More*, by John Watson Nicol, 1883**
This poignant image, exhibited at the Royal Academy in London in 1883, depicts a Highland couple forced to emigrate, the husband looking back in anguish towards the land he must leave behind. The Highland Clearances were a particularly well-known and dramatic consequence of the drive to make Scottish agriculture as profitable as possible, but their were felt just as profoundly in the Lowlands.
The Fleming-Wyfold Art Foundation/Bridgeman Images

Conclusion

We have wandered long and far in the course of this book, traversing centuries, hills, glens and urban streets. On the way, we have witnessed great upheavals and stagnation, phenomenal achievement and terrible failure, the remains of which have now been much more fully revealed by recent research. But this has not been a straightforward journey from the depths of prehistory to the heights of modernity; it is often clear that aspects of land-use and management viewed as novel and desirable had been implemented decades or even centuries before and abandoned for many different reasons. At the same time, as reactions to the fundamental changes heralded by Improvement reveal – at a time when we have much more evidence to study – there were winners and there were losers. That goes for communities as much as individuals and has surely been true whenever such transformations took place.

Lewis Grassic Gibbon sums up in one paragraph what the writers of the *Old* and *New Statistical Accounts*, other contemporary analyses of Improvement, along with hundreds of books like this one, have spilled countless vats of ink over.

Maybe there were some twenty to thirty holdings in all, the crofters dour folk of the old Pict stock, they had no history, common folk, and ill-reared their biggins clustered and chaved amid the long, sloping fields. The leases were one-year, two-year, you worked from the blink of the day you were breeked to the flicker of the night they shrouded you, and the dirt of gentry sat and ate up your rents but you were as good as they were … the boy Cospatric … he was douce and sensible and set putting the estate to rights. He threw out half the little tenants, they flitted off to Canada and Dundee and parts like those, the others he couldn't move but slowly. But on the cleared land he had bigger steadings and he let them at bigger rents and longer leases, he said the day of the fine big farm had come. And he had woods of fir and larch and pine planted to shield the long, bleak slopes, and might well have retrieved the Kinraddie fortunes but that he married a Morton quean with black blood in her, she smitted him and drove him to drink and death, that was the best way out.

Grassic Gibbon knew that life was hard before the arrival 'of the fine big farm' and he does not sentimentalise the lives of those who toiled on the 'twenty to thirty holdings'. And yet he surely means us to feel that 'the boy Cospatric' got his just deserts with his 'Morton quean'. When we read about the migration in the eighteenth century of thousands of farm workers into the towns and villages of southern Scotland and the heartless clearance of families for sheep that even the authorities knew was scarcely just, we can lament – as many did at the time – the destruction of community and the pre-eminence given to the profit of the few over the livelihoods of the many.

And yet Grassic Gibbon's main concern in his A Scots Quair trilogy – and *Sunset Song* in particular – was with the sweeping changes that once more blew through farming life in Scotland in the dark days of the Depression in the 1930s. 'Going down the rigs this morning,' he said, 'my head full of that unaccustomed smell of the earth, fresh and salty and anciently mouldy, I remembered the psalmists voice of the turtle and instinctively listened for its Scots equivalent – that far cooing of pigeons that used to greet the coming of Spring mornings when I was a boy. But the woods have gone, their green encirclement replaced by swathes of bog and muck and rank-growing heath, all is left bare in the North wind's blow.'[1]

If any of us return to our childhood homes, having moved elsewhere, we see changes that are not always discernible to those who have stayed behind. In that case, memory keeps us rooted in the past, whether we like it or not, even if we know that change is inevitable and often desirable. But Grassic Gibbon was not lamenting the cutting down of a wood here, or the building of new houses there; he was mourning the passing of an entire way of life. Some farms remained, 'but they are fewer, the cultivated lands. Half of them are in grass – permanently in grass – and browsed upon by great flocks of sheep, leaving that spider-trail of grey that sheep bring to pastures.'[2]

Perhaps it is the pace of change that is really so unsettling, the discarding of whole lifetimes of experience, and expectations within those lifetimes. But such revolutionary whirlwinds are not particular to the recent past; they have stalked the land in the aftermath of invasions and migrations, the arrival of the Black Death, or enclosure, or sheep.

And their effects are written there long after the people who experienced them have gone, bearing witness to their lives. If you should find yourself on the slopes of Chatto Craig in Roxburghshire, for example, you can stand alongside the countless generations who have been there before you, loosening the bonds of time so that the past fans out in front of you rather than shooting away like an arrow. At the very top is a hill-fort set within a field system that was most probably cultivated at the same time. Just below, on the upper slopes, the serpentine pattern of rig and furrow attests to the balmier climatic conditions that allowed their medieval successors to plough to such heights, that essential division between the arable fields and the rough grazing still clearly marked on the south by an earthen head-dyke.

Further down, modern farming with its neat, straight fields has removed much of the surviving archaeology. But in the field beside the farm of Upper Chatto, the platforms on which the houses of a deserted village once stood have been preserved, along with the rig and furrow furlongs of their fields running down to the burn, alongside the moated manor from where the lord of these lands once gave justice, went to war and received the many and various fruits of the labours of those who toiled above. In these ruins of the past, or even their vague footprints, we are able to reach out, however imperfectly, to those whose lives were vastly different from our own. And doesn't it give our own lives – and the landscape – far greater depth, if now and again we say hello?

MARE DEVCALIDONIVM

Rona

SCHIA LEVISSA

HEBRIDES INSVLAE
XLIII

Dungisby
Cathenesia
SOTHERLANDIA
Straverma
Dorno
Lindorna f.
Nardus f. Canoria
Sinus salutis
Enuernes Elgen
MORAVIA
Roßia
Rozmai
Shea f.
Stermaggi
MARIA
Aberdo
Dea f.
MVLA
IONA
ILA
Hilana f.
IAT DAC
Couc
CVMBRA
GRAM PIVS
MARN
Tauf. Dunkel
Erna f. S. Ioanes
ARGADIA
Don f.
Lacus Lemnus
Dumblam
Porthea Donfermilg FIFA
Arana
Lacus
Kinghorn
Dombroton Sterling
Air Glasco Lizhco
Pastei Hamelton Edingburg
GAL LOVI DIA
Dus
HVLTONIA
Galeis Ken f. Solueus f. Tueda f.
S. Ninianus Wigton Kirko bro Dunfres Norham
Armacana metrop. Bambrog
Agremont
CVM BRIA Coker month

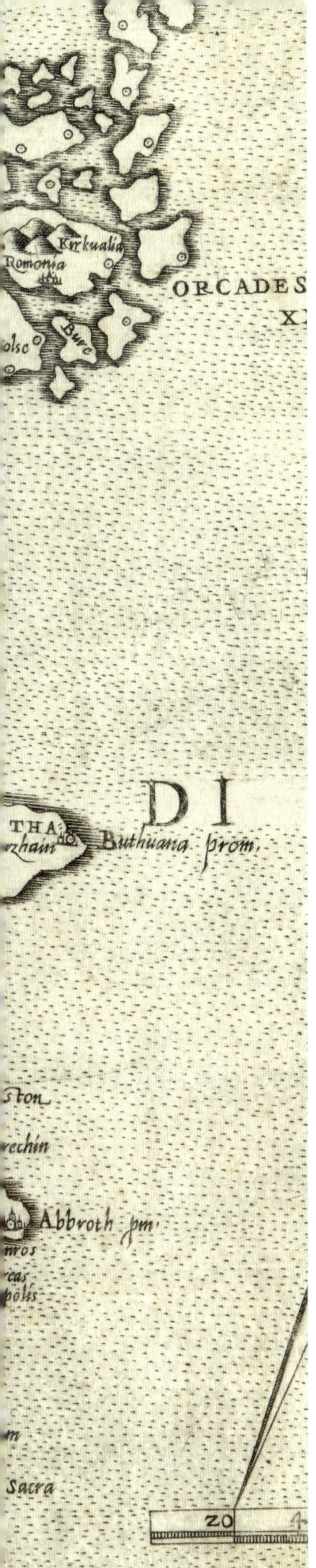

Land-use Maps

Over its eighteen-year span, the Historic Land-Use Assessment project researched and recorded land-use types throughout Scotland with the aid of maps, survey records and photography. The entire country has been mapped using these methods, with comprehensive information on every hectare available via the HLAmap website. As HLA's categories encompass both current and historical land-use, a picture of life in Scotland – from prehistory to the present day – can be extracted from this extensive analysis.

Through interpretation of the HLA data, these distribution maps present a snapshot of various land-use types across Scotland. In keeping with the aims of HLA, the maps purposefully show the land-use types visible on the ground today – if one has superseded another, then the new category is recorded. Using the information uncovered by the underlying research, these maps display patterns, gaps and regional variations in land-use across Scotland's landscape.

Scotia by Paolo Forlani, Venice, c1560
The first ever printed map of Scotland, issued in Venice by Paolo Forlani in 1560. Maps from this time were often based upon written descriptions rather than measured surveys. It depicts the Highlands with rows of conical mountains and the Lowlands with settlement symbols and place-names reflecting the essential geography of Scotland at that time.
Reproduced by permission of the National Library of Scotland

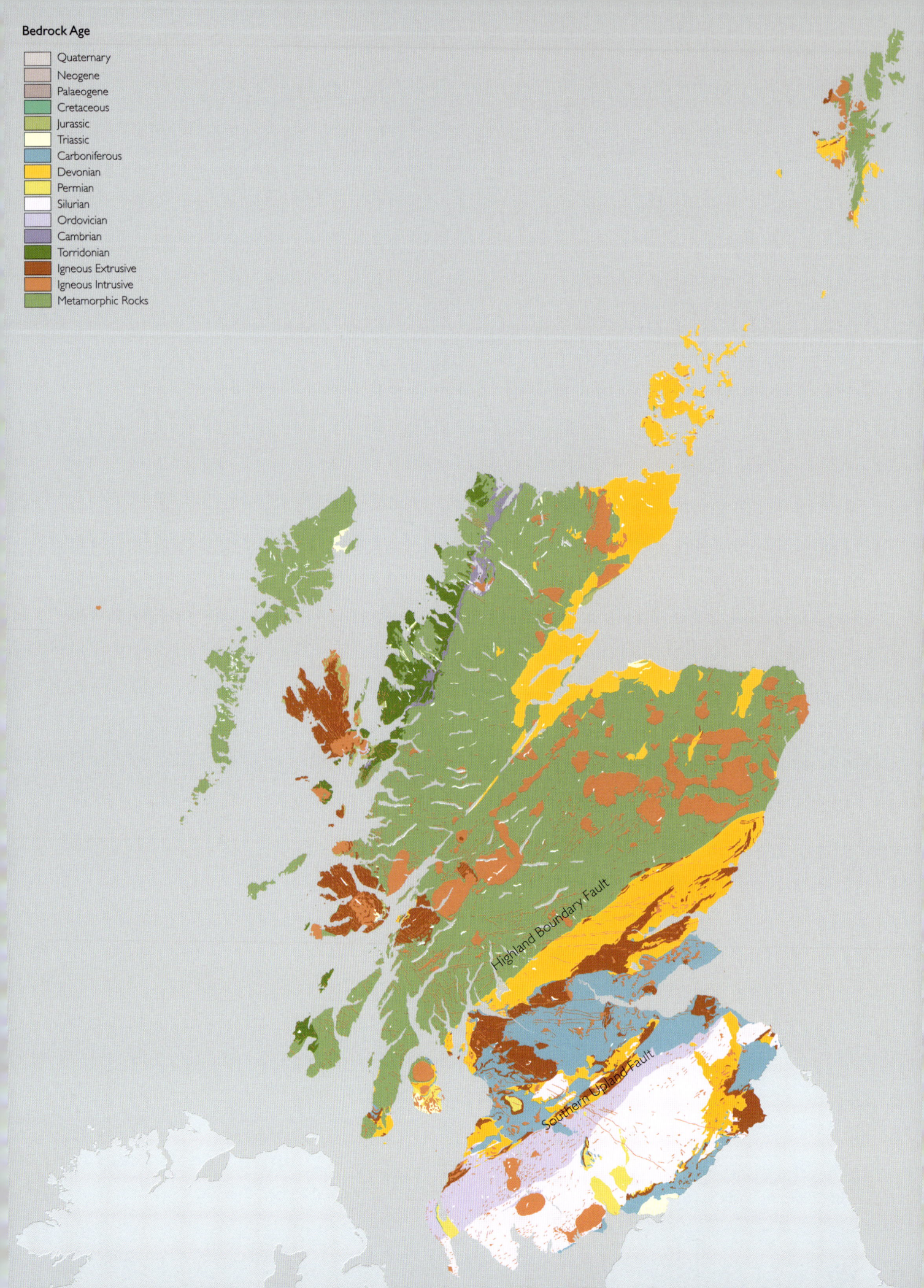

Geology

Land-use in Scotland has adapted and evolved over the millennia in response to climate, resources and requirements. But underpinning the story of the landscape is geology.

Scotland's most iconic geological feature is the Highland Boundary Fault, or Highland Line, which has transcended solid rock to become an easy metaphor for perceived divisions in the Scottish character. The Highland Line runs from Bute in the south-west to Stonehaven in the north-east, and is formed by the fault line between the softer sedimentary rocks of the Lowlands (Devonian and Carboniferous), and the largely hard and metamorphosed rocks of the Highlands.

Within the Lowlands there are significant ranges of hills, usually based on the igneous rocks which make large tracts of hillside suitable for grazing. However, the Southern Uplands, perhaps the best known range of hills in southern Scotland, are instead mostly made up of hard metamorphic Silurian-greywacke sandstones. The Southern Uplands are bounded on the north by the Southern Upland Fault, which is most recognisable by the steep edge of the Lammermuirs skirting the Lothian plain. These rocks have been moulded and smoothed by episodes of glaciation, which left debris along the Tweed Valley and drumlins spread along the Solway coast of Galloway.

This geology is reflected in the pattern of settlement and agriculture with scattered farms and squared fields predominating in the eastern and southern Lowlands, whereas in the Highlands of the north and west and in the Southern Uplands, grazing is the dominant land-use. In addition, geology was an important determiner of land-use during the Agricultural and Industrial Revolutions of the eighteenth and nineteenth centuries when the division between lowland farming and upland grazing became starker. The contrast was further exacerbated by the coal-bearing Carboniferous rocks of the central lowland plain, which led to industrial exploitation of that area.

Prehistoric

The Ring of Brodgar on Orkney. The standing stones of Callanish on Lewis. The Hill o' Many Stanes in the Highlands. These ceremonial sites date back over 3,500 years, but our fascination with them shows no sign of fading. However, not only large ritualistic monuments have survived our prehistory. More obscure sites can be found scattered across Scotland's lower lying countryside, which is remarkable considering that some were constructed of earth and timber rather than stone. Viewed together, these are markers of a well-used prehistoric landscape, and other sites, too small to be recorded on this map, fill in many of the apparent gaps.

Not all prehistoric remains are grand or ceremonial. Extensive evidence of early prehistoric agriculture and settlement can be found on Shetland and in lower Deeside. The stone structures and field dykes of Shetland's Scord of Brouster have not been swept away by later farming activity, as is often the case elsewhere. In contrast, while the timber halls of Deeside are long gone, the pits that once held their massive upright timbers survive, masked by top soil and only exposed by aerial survey during dry summers. Indeed such sites generally only survive as these cropmarks. Further evidence of land-use from this period is rarer, but shell midden mounds and flint scatters that are large enough to cover more than a hectare do occur in a few places around the coast, particularly on the tidal island of Oronsay and by the rivers Forth and Tay. These are the last fragments of Mesolithic coastal settlements, situated along raised beaches that have been left high and dry by post-glacial changes in sea level.

In comparison to the early period, the density of surviving land-uses from the later prehistoric time is significant. Settlement and agriculture as well as fortified sites appear across much of mainland Scotland. All of the forts and duns noted on this map are more than a hectare in size, but there are numerous others too small to be recorded which, if added, would give the map a dense speckling of sites on ridges and hills up to 300m above sea level. Located on grassy tops and rocky knolls, some of these larger sites are still clearly visible. Others have been flattened by more recent agricultural activity but have been subsequently recorded by aerial photography.

Today, later prehistoric round houses, field systems and clearance cairns are a feature of areas of rough grazing and hills that were suitable for cultivation in prehistory but have long since been turned to pasture due to climatic change and peat growth. The relative absence of sites in the west is directly related to peat growth and the mountainous terrain that had limited the potential for settlement. Future work will no doubt reveal even more later-prehistoric farming activity across Scotland's upland landscapes.

Prehistoric land-use

Roman

When the Roman military withdrew from Scotland, they left behind the outline of their invasion. The routes taken by the advancing legions – primarily in the east – during the various campaigns of the first, second and early third centuries AD are clear, with the forts and marching camps like beacons along their way. The line across central Scotland from the Firth of Forth to the Firth of Clyde indicates the Antonine Wall, which was a turf rampart fronted by a wide and deep ditch and punctuated by forts. For a time this was the most northern boundary of the Roman Empire. Although a significant portion can still be seen today, the active lifespan of the Antonine Wall was short – built in the early 140s, it was abandoned little more than twenty years later. Further south, Dere Street, built by occupying Romans troops from AD 79 to AD 81, ran from Edinburgh to the Scottish border and to York beyond. This road continued to be a major route into the medieval period and in places is still used as a public road today.

There has long been a strong interest in researching the Roman presence in Scotland, and as a result it is possible to highlight most of the original Roman features in the landscape. However, only a few are upstanding forts or camps – most are instead revealed through archaeological aerial survey, the shape of their enclosing ditches appearing bright green in fields of ripening yellow crops or parched pasture, while the network of roads that connected the Roman forts still impinges on the road and field patterns of the modern landscape in the Scottish Borders.

Roman military sites

Medieval and Post-Medieval

Medieval or post-medieval land-use, dating variously from the twelfth to the early nineteenth century, has had a more major impact on the Scottish landscape than may be immediately apparent. Although there are numerous examples, their characteristics are often subtle, and it can be difficult to pinpoint evidence of day-to-day life exclusively to the medieval period. Without accurate dates for the creation and development of certain features, such as open fields of rig, or indeed deserted settlements, they must be assigned to both the medieval and post-medieval periods – a sign of the cultural continuity across these centuries. Examples include the ruins of small stone and turf dwellings associated with lazy beds in the north-west, reverse-S-shaped ridges in eastern Scotland (now often only recognisable from the air as a consequence of being flattened by modern agriculture), and summer shielings on the higher ground. Their density brings the blank areas of the map into focus – the parts of Scotland where agricultural improvements, industrialisation and urbanisation have almost cleared the countryside of the once more widespread evidence for this pre-modern land-use.

There are certain elements of the landscape that we can more confidently date specifically to the medieval period. Due to their sheer scale, buildings and features which grew from religious or royal connections, such as cathedrals, castles and monasteries, have often endured as significant landmarks. Medieval burghs can still be identified in the heart of certain towns and cities, and medieval villages have also occasionally survived. The majority of these medieval focal points are dispersed across the most fertile parts of the country.

But these stone-built representations of power and privilege are not the only medieval elements in the landscape. The deer forests, which provided the Crown with exclusive hunting rights, can easily be overlooked. They were associated with regal and baronial progresses, where kings and barons travelled around the country staying at their castles, manors and hunting lodges. Within these hunting forests, activities that were detrimental to the hunt, such as grazing, farming or felling trees, were limited, and the small nearby farms were enclosed to provide protection from the deer.

- ■ Medieval and post-medieval towns and villages
- ■ Medieval and post-medieval land-use
- ■ Medieval and post-medieval reverse-S-shaped fields and rig – cropmarks only

Urban Areas and Motorways

The majority of Scottish people today live and work in built-up urban areas. However, as is immediately obvious from this map, in terms of land coverage the physical presence of these areas is very small – around 1.4 per cent. Unsurprisingly, the largest and most concentrated urban areas lie across the Central Belt and around the east coast up to the Dornoch Firth. Throughout the whole country there are examples of modern built-up areas, although on a smaller scale.

Certain urban environments can be traced back through our history, but the existence and scale of many areas are a consequence of the past few hundred years (where the specific origins of an earlier settlement are still present today, such as a medieval burgh, these are identified by HLA as having their own origins and development). The early decades of the nineteenth century saw a sudden and significant migration of the rural population to the expanding towns in search of work. This trend continued through to the end of the century, by which time nearly 60 per cent of people lived in towns with populations over 5,000. As heavy industries emerged, the demand for workers rapidly reached unprecedented levels and resulted in the massive growth of urban settlement, particularly in and around Glasgow.

Those who benefited economically from manufacturing and industry increasingly desired to reflect their success in the appearance and location of their homes. To achieve this elevated status, new housing was built along the approaches to many towns, and suburbs were developed throughout the Victorian and Edwardian eras.

As the initial industrial boom began to decline, the expansion of urban areas slowed. But after the Second World War the need for new housing, often to replace aging poor-quality homes dismissed as slums, became crucial. This led to large social housing programmes, including low and high rise blocks and the building of new towns in rural locations, especially to home those cleared from the Glasgow slums. These New Towns of East Kilbride, Cumbernauld, Glenrothes and others were designed to combine housing with schools, shops, community centres and parkland. More recently, new housing developments have included the conversion or replacement of former industrial sites, and retail and industrial developments have become common on the outskirts of many towns.

Scotland's main cities are linked by a motorway network that runs for over 380km, and carries more than 5,300 million vehicles each year. Despite stretching from Inverness to Gretna Green, as the map shows, the road coverage is not comprehensive and much of the country is not in fact connected by major roads.

- Nineteenth century to present urban, industrial and commercial areas
- Late twentieth century motorways and major roads

A History of Scotland's Landscapes

Crofting

At the turn of the nineteenth century landowners in the Highlands and Islands instigated a rearrangement of the landscape – which in practice meant the redistribution of people who had lived on the land for generations. Rather than continuing to squeeze an income from these small tenant farmers who were often unable to pay their rent, landowners were instead drawn to the financial ease promised by agricultural improvements, such as enclosed fields farmed by a single tenant, and sheep farming. These improved farms typically absorbed all of the best available land.

As the long tradition of communal farming became increasingly marginalised, the landowners, with varying levels of compassion and success, had to decide what to do with their surplus tenants. Some were evicted without any support. Others were channelled into crofting townships or re-homed in smallholdings along the edges of the large modernised farms. This reorganisation of the land was subject to cultural and geographical contraints, with crofting townships mostly in the west and smallholdings dominating the east. The term 'croft' can be used to refer to a residence on either a crofting township or a smallholding, and the inhabitants of both are known as crofters.

These new crofting townships were often along the coast on poor land that the crofters struggled to cultivate. The houses and steadings were set out in a linear pattern on long thin strips of land. The developments resulted in a particularly distinctive landscape – across the north and west of the Highlands and the Western Isles today, settlements have inherited the shape of the crofting townships. With a few exceptions, they are found in the crofting counties (Argyll, Caithness, Inverness, Orkney, Ross and Cromarty, Shetland, and Sutherland), and gaps in their distribution can generally be explained by either the priorities of the landowner or the inhospitable environment.

While these crofting townships were being populated by new residents, individual smallholdings were spreading throughout Scotland. Their purpose was the same – relocating communities to free up the land for greater profitability. Usually located on the fringes of nineteenth century farms, where they provided a convenient labour force, the majority consisted of a cottage with small irregular fields for farming or grazing. Smallholdings are notable for being found in the north-east outside the crofting counties included in the Crofting Act of 1886. They extend over 1 per cent of Scotland and in some cases they are now part of larger modern farms, others have been reinvented as houses or outbuildings, and sometimes only the ruins remain.

- Eighteenth to nineteenth century crofting townships
- Nineteenth to twentieth century smallholdings

Mining and Quarrying

The development of the Scottish economy from the start of the Industrial Revolution can be read in the landscape of central Scotland. Remote rural communities across the central Lowlands were thrust into the forefront of industrial development by entrepreneurs and landowners exploiting the local geology, with fortunes fluctuating as resources were won, abandoned and exhausted. The remains of these once dominant industries can be found throughout the region – the shafts and spoil tips of old coal mines; the scars and overburden dumps from disused ironstone and limestone quarries; the lades and reservoirs that served long-vanished water wheels and steam engines; the successive networks of tracks, roads, railways and canals that carried material to the furnaces of the ironworks and beyond; and the footings of the miners' rows which were home to the workers and their families. The remains of early workings predating the nineteenth century rarely survive as they were overtaken by the continuous development and modernisation of coal mining and its related industries in the subsequent centuries.

In the late twentieth century, opencast mining began to supersede shaft-mining, and great swathes of Fife, Lothian and Ayrshire were completely modified by the drive for coal to fire power stations. Some scars are too large to fill, but land formerly used for mining has recently provided opportunities for landscaping or been converted to landfill, although more commonly it has been returned to agriculture. Today, the only mine still worked is the gold mine high on the hillside above Tyndrum, and opencast is itself falling out of use with the closure of the coal-fired power stations.

Modern large-scale quarrying for gravel, roadstone and lime continues wherever resources occur such as the superquarry at Glensanda on Loch Linnie in the Western Highlands.

- Eighteenth century to present opencast and mining
- Nineteenth century to present quarry sites

A History of Scotland's Landscapes

Peat

Peat has been sustaining life in Scotland for countless generations, used for heating, cooking, lighting and even industrial processes. The cutting and drying of peat is labour intensive and traditionally involved the whole family or community working together.

Traditional methods involved digging peat with specially designed spades that varied from region to region. Turf would first be stripped back to expose the peat, which would be cut in long vertical or horizontal blocks that left sharp scars in the landscape. The peat then had to be dried. Two methods were popular: either the peat was laid out in straight lines or the blocks would be placed on their end to form pyramid shape mounds. The peat blocks were then removed from the moorland, often over difficult terrain, on carts pulled by ponies or by hand. Today, instead of these techniques, some crofters use modern peat-cutting machinery and tractors to extract peat from the land.

Peat was widely cut throughout the country until supplies began to become scarce in Lowland Scotland at the end of the eighteenth century. In the Lowlands, wood and coal were readily available alternatives, and these quickly became the preferred options. In the Highlands, however, where peat was still cheap and plentiful, peat cutting continued throughout the eighteenth and nineteenth centuries. It remained popular with crofters in the twentieth century, when it was not unusual for a croft to be allocated a patch of land for peat cutting.

Today, as much as 0.5 per cent of Scotland shows traces of peat cutting, and it is especially evident in the north and west. However, it can be impossible to accurately date abandoned areas of peat cutting to before the modern period once the top layer of turf has regrown. Modern peat cutting is easier to decipher, leaving rectangular strips on the landscape, especially the commercial extraction around the Central Belt.

Although domestic use is of course much reduced today, peat is still used as compost and burnt on open fires for its warmth and distinctive smell. Another important market is the distilling industry where peat is burnt to dry barley grain and give whisky its smoky flavour. Spade-dug peats would have originally been used by the distilleries but now the peat for fuel and whisky distilling is harvested by a large machine.

- Late twentieth century to present commercial peat cutting
- Eighteenth century to present traditional peat cutting

Rough Grazing

In the twenty-first century, much of the Scottish population experiences their country from an urban perspective. But a remarkable 51 per cent of the landscape can be categorised as rough grazing, making it the most typical environment in Scotland (and prior to the 1919 creation of the Forestry Commission and the resulting programme of plantation, rough grazing covered two-thirds of the country).

Rough grazing exists in many forms – essentially it is those areas that are too poor in quality for the ground to be used for anything but grazing sheep, cattle or deer. It includes the coastal salt grass and the machair on the north-west coast. It extends to the high mountain tops where only a limited range of wild flowers and scrub grass flourish in the short growing season. On the north-west, where there is often exposed rock and peat growth, the patches of rough grazing are further hemmed in by the wind. In the central Highlands the relatively lighter rainfall spawns high grassland plateaux, such as that of the Monadhliath mountains in the Highlands with its lime-rich rocks, and the distinctive patchwork of grouse moors. In this environment shepherds' huts and hunters' bothies are common on the spots where shieling huts once stood, many now converted to shelters for hikers. Although frequently isolated now, these areas of rough grazing were once economically significant. They led to the post-medieval cattle droving trade based on the long tradition of transhumance and summer grazing, while at the same time being used by monasteries and landowners to graze sheep for the wool industry.

Owing to the lack of recent human activity in areas of rough grazing, deserted remains of prehistoric and medieval settlements have often survived. In fact, around half of the traces of past land-use visible today lie in this terrain.

Rough grazing

Fields

From the end of hunter-gatherer times, humans have been tied to the land by farming. In Scotland, this early agriculture developed into a system of communal farms, where peasant farmers grew crops and grazed animals on irregularly shaped strips of land.

By the end of the eighteenth century, agricultural improvements caused a shift away from the common field systems to large enclosed fields with straight boundaries – forming rectilinear fields and farms. The improvers realised these new fields, cultivated by a single farmer, increased output and profit. Improved farming methods incorporated diverse planting, boundaries of hedges or stone, crop rotation and pioneering technical developments, such as the lighter swing-plough. Estate owners would pay for the changes, and new farmhouses and outbuildings were often built as part of the plan.

A further development in field patterns was due to the mechanisation of agriculture after the Second World War and the economies of scale that could be achieved with large fields, leading to the creation of so-called 'Prairie' fields, especially in the drier eastern Lowlands where arable crops are most productive.

Rectilinear fields and farms remain a vital part of our landscape and account for about 23 per cent of current land-use in Scotland, although the vast majority of this farmland was created prior to the twenty-first century.

Eighteenth to twentieth century rectilinear fields and farms

Conifer Plantations

Britain was heavily reliant on timber during the First World War. The importation of supplies was severely restricted, which resulted in the intensive felling of British woodlands. Consequently, in 1919 the Forestry Commission was created, with a remit not only to buy up land for planting new trees, but also to develop best practice in woodland management and promote the timber industry. In the early decades of the twentieth century the oversight of the Forestry Commission remained vital as considerable new woodlands were established and heavy industries demanded increasing amounts of timber.

The woodland stock was once again diminished by the unparalleled requirements of the Second World War, and rebuilding the timber reserves remained a priority. After the war, commercial returns on timber became the focus of planting policies instead. Over the years huge areas of land were taken into the forestry estate as governments sought greater returns from timber production. The competing demands of agriculture led to fast-growing coniferous forestry increasingly being planted on ever more marginal ground. New techniques in planting, felling, pest control, mechanisation and fertilisation were developed, improving the efficiency and resilience of coniferous forest management. Forests planted in this period are recognisable by their uncompromising straight edges and near 100 per cent conifer planting with few clearings.

Interest in the environment and its care grew from the mid twentieth century, which was reflected in the Countryside Act of 1968. Within its provisions, the Act outlined the need to provide public access, with facilities for recreational pursuits, such as campsites and picnic areas. In recent years, plantations have been adapted to include more fragmented boundaries – as opposed to the previous regimented blocks – and broadleaf trees are also often included to provide more variety.

The current National Forest Estate, in the care of the Forestry Commission Scotland, represents some 9 per cent of the country's land cover, and conifer plantations in general are widespread, covering almost 15 per cent of Scotland's landscape. However, approximately one third of the National Forest Estate is unplanted open ground encompassing mountainous areas, moorland and coastal stretches. Examples of earlier land-use lie within many of these areas, reflecting all eras of human presence in Scotland. Prehistoric forts, groups of shieling huts and rectilinear fields are among the broad array of archaeological remains that HLA has recorded within the estate. It is likely that in future the National Forest Estate will continue to expand, in part to contribute to the alleviation of the effects of climate change.

Twentieth century to present conifer plantations

End Notes

Preface

1. J Macky, *A Journey through Scotland* (1729), p154
2. *NSA*, Muthill, p317; www.drummondcastlegardens.co.uk/garden-history/
3. F R Coles, 'Report on stone circles in Perthshire principally Strathearn, with measured plans and drawings (obtained under the Gunning Fellowship)', *Proceedings of the Society of Antiquaries of Scotland*, 45 (1910–11), p74

Introduction

1. T Pennant, *A Tour in Scotland and Voyage to the Hebrides, 1772* (1998), p87
2. B Finlayson, *Wild Harvesters. The First People in Scotland* (1998), p17 onwards; T C Smout, A R Macdonald and F Watson, *A History of the Native Woodlands of Scotland, 1500–1920* (2005), pp10–13; T C Smout and M Stewart, *The Firth of Forth: An Environmental History* (2012), Chapter 1; *OSA*, Borrowstowness, p443; R P J McCullagh and R Tipping, eds, *The Lairg Project 1988–1996. The Evolution of an Archaeological Landscape in Northern Scotland*, Scottish Trust for Archaeological Research Monograph 3 (1998), pp58–64
3. Lynn White Jr, Professor of Medieval History at Princeton, argued this strongly and controversially in his 1962 book *Medieval Technology and Social Change*. Still in print, the book continues to be hugely influential.
4. P Dixon, 'Mukked and folded land: medieval cultivation techniques in Scotland', in J Klapste, ed, *Agrarian Technology in The Medieval Landscape*, Ruralia X (2016), p14
5. C Skovsgaard, 'The heavy plough and the European agricultural revolution of the middle ages: Evidence from a historical experiment', Economic History Society Conference, York (2013)
6. W Shakespeare, *Macbeth*, Act 4, Scene 3
7. See D Broun, 'Attitudes of Gall to Gaedhil in Scotland before John of Fordun' in D Broun and M D MacGregor, eds, *Miorun Mòr Nan Gall, 'The Great Ill-Will of the Lowlander'? Lowland Perceptions of the Highlands, Medieval and Modern* (2009), pp49–82
8. E Muir, *A Scottish Journey* (1935), p243

Chapter One

1. D Wordsworth, *Recollections of a Tour made in Scotland AD 1803* (1874), p126
2. Wordsworth, *Recollections*, pp126–8
3. *OSA*, Inveraray, pp296–7. The spinners would work at home, the finished wool then being transported to the mill. Even if the women in fact had no interest in this knitting opportunity, it doesn't alter the basic point that they were, for much of the year, engaged in the back-breaking work at the peats, which almost certainly lay some distance away.
4. K Jamie, 'Diary', *London Review of Books*, vol 38, no 19, 6 October 2016, p43. The poet is describing taking part in an archaeological dig on Westray, part of the Orkney Isles.
5. There are two sites – one near Biggar (12,000 BC) and the other on Islay (c10,000 BC) – that attest to the presence of humans here before this period (*The Scotsman*, 9 April 2009; *The Guardian*, 9 October 2015), but it's hard to argue – yet – that this represents widespread colonisation.
6. B Finlayson and K J Edwards, 'The Mesolithic' in K J Edwards and I B M Ralston, eds, *Scotland after the Ice Age* (2005)
7. K Paton, 'The evolution of settlement at Roslin from prehistory to the 21st century', *History Scotland*, vol 17, no 2 (March/April, 2017), p14
8. K Brophy, *Reading Between the Lines: The Neolithic Cursus Monuments of Scotland* (2016)
9. canmore.org.uk/site/28473/cleaven-dyke; Pennant, *A Tour, 1772*, pp432–6. The Picts are not known to have built towns.
10. K Brophy, 'Seeing the cursus as a symbolic river', *British Archaeology*, 44 (1999), pp6–7; I Ralston, *Scotland's Hidden History* (1998), pp55–6; G J Barclay, 'The Neolithic', in Edwards and Ralston, *Scotland after the Ice Age*, pp134–7
11. M Martin, *Description of the Western Islands of Scotland, c1695* (1999), p18
12. A Welfare, *Great Crowns of Stone: The Recumbent Stone Circles of Scotland* (2011)
13. Barclay, 'The Neolithic', p139
14. H Fairhurst and D B Taylor, 'A hut circle settlement at Kilphedir, Sutherland', *Proceedings of the Society of Antiquaries of Scotland*, 103 (1970–71), pp65–103
15. T G Cowie and I A G Shepherd, 'The Bronze Age', in Edwards and Ralston, *Scotland after the Ice Age*; I Armit and I B M Ralston, 'The Iron Age', in Edwards and Ralston, *Scotland after the Ice Age*, p188
16. 'Grisly human trophies at East Lothian hill-fort', *Scotsman*, 8 August 2013, www.scotsman.com/heritage/people-places/grisly-human-trophies-at-east-lothian-hill-fort-1-3034036
17. W S Hanson, 'The Roman presence: brief interludes' in Edwards and Ralston, *Scotland after the Ice Age*, p214
18. *NSA*, Ayton, p134
19. www.treasuredplaces.org.uk/gallery/detail/.php?id=40
20. Martin, *Description*, pp33, 99–100
21. Pennant, *A Tour, 1772*, pp207–8; Sutherland, Sheet LXXIX (includes: Kildonan; Latheron), survey date: 1871, publication date: 1879 (National Library of Scotland, maps.nls.uk/view/74431070)
22. K Jamie, 'Glacial', *The Bonniest Companie* (2015), p4
23. 'Five Year Project to investigate the "lost kingdoms" of Northwest Europe', Past Horizons (2016), www.pasthorizonspr.com/index.php/archives/12/2016/five-year-project-to-investigate-the-lost-

kingdoms-of-northwest-europe; 'Who was Scotland's "Rhynie Man"?', *Daily Mail,* 27 August 2015, www.dailymail.co.uk/sciencetech/article-3212596/; online.aberdeenshire.gov.uk/smrpub/master/detail.aspx?refno=NJ42NE0047; canmore.org.uk/site/17199/rhynie-craw-stane

24 *Annals of Ulster*, 538.3; Adomnan, *Life of St Columba*, ed William Reeves (1874) p138. These were probably still confederations of kingdoms, with one dominant king; Pictland was certainly at least two kingdoms, the most powerful one (Fortriu) based around Inverness and the other(s) south of the Grampian mountains.

25 I Armit, *Scotland's Hidden History* (1998), pp130–2; 'Dunadd', Canmore, canmore.org.uk/site/39564/dunadd

26 M Carver, *Portmahomack: Monastery of the Picts* (2008), pp23–4. Portmahomack was even founded in the same century as Columba's famous visit to King Bridei.

27 *Annals of Ulster*, 658.2

28 canmore.org.uk/event/698083

29 I B M Ralston and I Armit, 'The Early Historic Period' in Edwards and Ralston, *Scotland after the Ice Age*, pp226–7

30 G C Homans, 'The Frisians in East Anglia', in *Sentiments and Activities* (2013); Carver, *Portmahomack*, p139

31 *Annals of Ulster*, 900.6

32 Ralston and Armit, 'The Early Historic Period', p229

33 See N Aitchison, *Forteviot: A Pictish and Scottish Royal Centre* (2006)

34 'An elegy for Earl Thorfinn the Mighty' (d.1064/5) (Thorfinnsdrapa) in Clancy and Markus, *The Triumph Tree* (2008), p172

35 H Boece, *Historia Gentis Scotorum* (1527), Book 1, 16

36 A Crone and F Watson, 'Sufficiency to scarcity: medieval Scotland, 500–1600', in T C Smout, ed, *People and Woods in Scotland: A History* (2002), p80

37 It has been argued that there was a stone keep at Edinburgh by the late eleventh century, but since no evidence has been found for it or any stone defences from that period, it is still possible that these royal dwellings were made of timber: see S T Driscoll and P A Yeoman, *Excavations within Edinburgh Castle in 1988–91* (1997), p232. There were two stone buildings on Edinburgh castle rock from at least as early as the twelfth century, but these were a chapel and a church.

38 S Smith, 'Notes on an artificial mound near Bonnybridge', *Proceedings of the Society of Antiquaries of Scotland,* 68 (1933–4), pp66–7

39 H Boece, *Historia Gentis Scotorum*, Book 6, 60

40 J Macky, *A Journey*, p189

41 Burt, *Burt's Letters from the North of Scotland* (begun in 1726) (1998), p27

42 G D Raeburn, 'The Long Reformation of the Dead in Scotland', PhD thesis, Durham University (2012), p58 onwards, etheses.dur.ac.uk/6926/; *NSA*, Dairsie, p773

43 Macky, *A Journey*, pp31,48, 49–50, 59. The King William referred to was William, Duke of Orange, who became, along with his wife, Mary Stuart, ruler of England and Scotland in 1688/9 after Mary's father, James VII and II, was deposed.

44 Burt, *Letters*, p3

45 Quoted in Martin, *Description*, pp178–9

46 The other two were the clergy and the nobility.

47 canmore.org.uk/site/58422/roxburgh; C Martin and R Oram, 'Medieval Roxburgh: A preliminary assessment of the burgh and its locality', *Proceedings of the Society of Antiquaries of Scotland*, 137 (2007), pp357–404. If you want to see what *Time Team* found, you can watch the episode (which aired in 2004) at www.youtube.com/watch?v=yKBZ9F418Wk

48 J Taylor, *The Pennyless Pilgrimage* (1618), pp19–20, 25

49 Description of Carrick by Mr Abercrombie, minister of Maybole (1696), in *Macfarlane's Geographical Collections*, vol 2, p17

50 Presbytery of Brechin, *Macfarlane's Geographical Collections*, p42; Macky, *A Journey*, p101

51 Macky, *A Journey*, p81

52 D Defoe, *A Tour through the Whole Island of Great Britain* (1727), letters 12 and 13

53 Taylor, *Pennyless Pilgrimage*, p25

54 O Lelong, 'Finding medieval (or later) rural settlement in the Highlands and Islands: the case for optimism', in S Govan, ed, *Medieval or Later Rural Settlement: 10 Years On* (2003); R A Dodgshon, 'Changes in Scottish township organization during the medieval and early modern periods', *Geografiska Annaler B,* 59 (1977), pp51–65

55 G Buchanan, *History of Scotland* (1827), vol 1, p44

56 Martin, *Description,* p25

57 canmore.org.uk/event/656528

58 Martin, *Description*, p241

59 Macky, *A Journey*, p334

60 Martin, *Description*, p179

61 J A Atkinson, 'Ben Lawers: An archaeological landscape in time', *Scottish Archaeological Trust Internet Reports,* 62 (2016), Chapter 9

62 Pennant, *A Tour, 1772*, p204

63 Wordsworth, *Recollections*, p228

64 D Campbell, *The Lairds of Glenlyon: Historical Sketches Relating to the Districts of Appin, Glenlyon and Breadalbane* (1886) pp108–9

65 *OSA,* Durness, p577

66 T Pennant, *A Tour in Scotland 1769* (2000), p31

67 James Gray, ed, *Scottish Population Statistics* (1952), pxvii

68 *OSA*, Stonehouse; *NSA*, Kincardine

69 Pennant, *A Tour, 1772*, p276

70 *OSA*, Kilmarnock, pp104–5; *OSA*, Maybole, p221; *OSA*, Liberton, p244; *OSA*, Fortingall, p457

71 Burt, *Letters*, pp176–7

72 *NSA*, Stornoway, pp128–9

73 See mygarden.rhs.org.uk/forums/t/29498.aspx

74 *NSA*, Kilmuir, Skye, p268; *NSA*, Stornoway, Lewis, p129

75 *OSA*, Dornock, pp22–3

76 *NSA*, Tongue, p185

77 Wordsworth, *Recollections*, p224

78 Defoe, *A Tour*, Letter 12

79 For example, *OSA*, Kilmarnock, p105; *OSA*, Galashiels, p307; *OSA*, Dalserf, p374; *OSA*, Chirnside, pp55–6; *OSA*, Cockburnspath, p100; Wordsworth, *Recollections*, p131, 247

80 *NSA*, Dyce, p124. See also M Glendinning and S Wade Martins, *Buildings of the Land: Scotland's Farms, 1750–2000,* (2009)

81 Muir, *A Scottish Journey*, p181; L Grassic Gibbon, *Sunset Song* (2015), pp14, xi

82 *OSA*, Libberton and Quothquan (1792), p238

83 See, for example, Pennant, *A Tour, 1772,* p551, *OSA*, Galston, p80; *OSA*, Kirkpatrick-Durham, p255; *OSA*, Galashiels, p307; *OSA*, Cockpen, p318; *OSA*, Glencairn, pp340–1

84 Wordsworth, *Recollections*, pp15,17

85 *OSA*, Eaglesham, pp120–1; *NSA*, Eaglesham, p401

86 'Toft', *Dictionary of the Older Scottish Tongue*, www.dsl.ac.uk/entry/dost/toft_n_1; 'Croft', *Dictionary of the Older Scottish Tongue*, www.dsl.ac.uk/entry/dost/croft

87 *RPS*, 1681/7/109; 1645/1/233. The first reference (1681/7/109) clearly shows just how many might be situated within a relatively small area.

88 'Pendicle', *Dictionary of the Older Scottish Tongue*, www.dsl.ac.uk/entry/dost/pendicle. The most famous pendicles (those of Collymoon) are actually in Stirlingshire and featured heavily in Iain Banks' 1996 novel *Whit*.

89 *OSA*, Farr, pp73, 80

90 Wordsworth, *Recollections*, p141

91 *NSA*, Lochs, Lewis, p167

92 *NSA*, Kilmuir, Skye, pp270, 273; *NSA*, Barvas, Lewis, p147; *NSA*, Gairloch, p95; *NSA*, Durness, p97

93 Crofters Holdings (Scotland) Act, 1886, www.legislation.gov.uk/ukpga/Vict/49–50/29/part/VI/enacted

94 E A Cameron, *Land for the People? The British Government and the Scottish Highlands, c1880–1925*, (1996), Chapter 5

95 'A grant and loan scheme supporting young crofting families to access homes', *Review of Croft House Grant Scheme: SCF response to Scottish Government consultation*, March 2015 – Supporting Paper, www.crofting.org/uploads/consultations/cghs-supportingpaper.pdf

96 canmore.org.uk/site/11381/skye-erisco

97 L Forrest, '"Gairloch" settlements in the 19th century: Wester Ross and the Canadian Maritimes', thesis, University of Aberdeen (2011), pp46–8, www.kinlochewe.com/documents/GairlochandCanadianMaritimes-Copy.pdf

98 Scottish Land and Estates, The Modern Face of Scottish Landownership, www.scottishlandandestates.co.uk/index.php?option=com_attachments&task=download&id=1219

99 Atkinson, 'Ben Lawers', pp195–6

100 *OSA*, Monymusk, p73

101 This was during the Seven Years War fought among the European powers at home and across their various colonial spheres of interest.

102 A M Smith, 'The Forfeited Estate Papers, 1745: A Study of the work of the commissioners for the forfeited annexed estates, 1755–1784, with particular reference to their contribution to the development of communications in Scotland in the eighteenth century', PhD thesis, University of St Andrews (1975), pp 62–4

103 Pennant, *A Tour, 1772*, p453; Smith, 'The Forfeited Estates Papers', p64

104 Muir, *A Scottish Journey*, p7

105 Pennant, *A Tour, 1769*, p40

106 Defoe, *A Tour*, letter 12, part 2; Macky, *A Journey*, p291; Burt *Letters*, p13; Pennant, *A Tour, 1769*, p154

107 Muir, *A Scottish Journey*, p21

108 Wordsworth, *Recollections*, pp52–55; Muir, *A Scottish Journey*, pp95,163

109 Muir, *A Scottish Journey*, p12

110 H V Morton, *In Search of Scotland* (1932), p250

111 www.visitbanchory.com/heritage/nordrach-on-dee/

112 M Jay, 'I'm not signing', review of John Foot's *The Man Who Closed the Asylums: Franco Basaglia and the Revolution in Mental Health Care*, London Review of Books, vol 38, no 17, 8 September 2016, pp11–14

113 www.visitbanchory.com/heritage/nordrach-on-dee/; Historic Scotland, *Building up our Health: the Architecture of Scotland's Historic Hospitals* (2010)

114 R Scot, *Death by Design: The True Story of the Glasgow Necropolis* (2005)

Chapter Two

1. Buchanan, *History of Scotland*, vol 1, p156
2. See Introduction, p6; D Broun, 'Attitudes of Gall to Gaedhil in Scotland'
3. John of Fordun, *Chronica Gentis Scotorum*, ed W F Skene, trans F J H Skene (1872), Book II, Chapter 9
4. A W R Whittle et al, *Scord of Brouster: an Early Agricultural Settlement on Shetland* (1986)
5. Armit and Ralston, 'The Iron Age', in Edwards and Ralston, *Scotland After the Ice Age*, p189–191; *Chalcolithic and Bronze Age Scotland* ScARF Panel Report (2012), 3.4 Agriculture, pp62–6
6. *NSA*, Aboyne and Glentanar, p1065
7. Taliesin, 'The War-Band's Return' and 'In praise of Gwallawg', in Clancy and Markus, *The Triumph Tree*, pp83, 92
8. Aneirin, 'The Gododdin', in Clancy and Markus, *The Triumph Tree*, p75
9. 'The Miracles of St Nynia the Bishop', in Clancy and Markus, *The Triumph Tree*, p131
10. John of Fordun, *Chronica Gentis Scotorum*, Chapter 39, p232; Chapter 43, p236
11. See Dixon, 'Mukked and folded land', p15. As pointed out here, there is, however, some tantalising evidence that, around Nynia's church at Whithorn, this revolutionary new technology arrived several centuries earlier.
12. 'Arran' (mid–late 12th century), in Clancy and Markus, *The Triumph Tree*, p187; William, clerk of Glasgow (fl.1164), 'Song on the death of Somerled', *ibid*, p212
13. A Woolf, *From Pictland to Alba* (2007), p346
14. A D Ross, 'The Province of Moray, c1000–1230', PhD thesis, University of Aberdeen (2003), Chapter 2 and conclusion.
15. D Dalrymple, *Annals of Scotland* (1776). It is not clear on what authority Dalrymple, writing nearly 450 years after these events, is basing this assertion, but, given that Scotland was (temporarily) emerging from a period of intense warfare, particularly in the fertile lowlands of the south-east, it does seem plausible. According to the website Measuring Worth (www.measuringworth.com/ukcompare/), two shillings would be worth around £67 today.
16. Pennant, *A Tour, 1772*, pp168–9
17. *RPS*, 1235/1. The word used for hedge was 'sepium', from 'sepes', meaning anything planted to form a barrier.
18. 'Northside of the coast of Buchan' (1683), *Macfarlane's Geographical Collections*, vol 2, p141
19. D Cowey and J Harrison, '*Well shelter'd and Watered*': *Menstrie Glen, a Farming Landscape Near Stirling* (2001)
20. See Dixon, 'Mukked and folded land' for a full discussion of prehistoric, medieval and post-medieval field systems in Scotland.
21. J Bain, ed, *Calendar of Documents relating to Scotland*, vol 4 (1888), p451
22. 'Poem to Aenghus Mor Mac Domhnaill, King of the Isles' (c1250), in Clancy and Markus, *The Triumph Tree*, p291
23. Boece, *Historia Gentis Scotorum*, Book 13, 83
24. *RPS*, A1504/3/113
25. *RPS*, 1424/21; *RPS*, 1458/3/33
26. *Chronicle of Lanercost Priory*, trans H Maxwell (1913), p10; A A M Duncan, *Scotland: The Making of the Kingdom* (1992), p421
27. *RPS*, 1368/6/16
28. A Grant, *Independence and Nationhood: Scotland 1306–1469* (1984), pp77–84
29. *RPS*, 1458/3/28
30. See for example, *RPS*, 1645/1/224; *RPS*, 1696/9/157; *RPS*, 1686/4/37
31. *OSA*, Libberton, pp240, 242
32. *Liber Insule Missarum* (1847), no 8, p12, pxxvi (Inchaffray's waterlogged situation is amply attested by its Latin name, which means Island of the Masses); *RPS*, 1696/9/158; *RPS*, 1641/8/430; www.parliament.scot/parliamentarybusiness/CurrentCommittees/pow-of-inchaffray-committee.aspx
33. GD160/2/13; *RPS*, A1625/10/1; *RPS*, 1704/7/55
34. Defoe, *A Tour*, letter 11
35. Burt, *Letters*, pli
36. A MacKillop, 'Clans of the Highlands and Islands 2' in M Lynch, ed, *The Oxford Companion to Scottish History* (2001), p96
37. D Monro, *A Description of the Occidental ie. Western Islands of Scotland* (1549), in Martin, *Description*, pp324, 321
38. Martin, *Description*, p111
39. Burt, *Letters*, p213; *OSA*, Kilmuir, Skye, p240; *OSA*, Kirkwall, Orkney, pp559–60
40. See, for example, M Zimecki, 'The lunar cycle: effects on human and animal behaviour and physiology, *Postepy Hig Med Dosw* (Online), 60 (2006) pp1–7
41. P Dixon, J B Stevenson and G S Maxwell, *Waternish, Skye and Lochalsh District, Highland Region: An Archaeological Survey (Afforestable Land Survey)* (1993), canmore-pdf.rcahms.gov.uk/wp/00/WP003828.pdf
42. R A Armstrong, *Gaelic Dictionary in Two Parts* (1825), vol 1, p92, quoting Sinclair's Statistics: Edderrachylis
43. Monro, *Description*, pp338, 335, 322; Martin, *Description*, pp64, 182; Pennant, *A Tour, 1772*, p210
44. Buchanan, *History of Scotland*, vol 1, p35
45. canmore.org.uk/site/6710/learable
46. Geographical Collections relating to Scotland, ed W Macfarlane, J T Clark, vol ii, Edinburgh (1907), p17. Though published in the twentieth century, the collections themselves mostly date to the later seventeenth and early eighteenth. Macky, *A Journey*, pp138, 111, 119; Burt, *Letters*, pp27, 176
47. MacKillop, 'Clans of the Highlands and Islands 2', p96
48. Pennant, *A Tour, 1772*, pp495–6. In this instance, Pennant was travelling south.
49. www.legislation.gov.uk/aosp/1695/69/paragraph/p1
50. See T M Devine, *Clearance and Improvement: Land, Power and People in Scotland, 1700–1900* (2006), Chapters 2, 4, 5 and 6
51. *OSA*, Dunoon, p391; *OSA*, Laggan, p149
52. Pennant, *A Tour, 1772*, p391
53. See, for example, J Hunter, *Set Adrift Upon the World: The Sutherland Clearances* (2016)
54. www.electricscotland.com/history/articles/sheep.htm
55. Defoe, *A Tour*, letter 12
56. *OSA*, Loudoun, pp103–9; *OSA*, Torthorwald, p4; *NSA*, Ormiston, pp137–8
57. T M Devine, *The Transformation of Rural Scotland: Social Change and the Agrarian Economy* (1994)
58. *OSA*, Dornock, p19
59. Pennant, *A Tour, 1772*, p169; J C Loudon, *An Encyclopaedia of Agriculture* (1825), p128
60. *OSA*, Lochrutton, p37
61. *OSA*, Kilmarnock, p98
62. Burt, *Letters*, p44

63 Defoe, *A Tour*, letter 11; Pennant, *A Tour*, 1772, pp392–3; Wordsworth, *Recollections*, pp27, 132
64 *OSA*, Newtown-upon-Ayr, p265; *OSA*, Kilmarnock, p98; *NSA*, Pettie, p416
65 *OSA*, Torthorwald, p4; *NSA*, Kirkden, p389
66 S Johnson and J Boswell, *A Journey to the Western Islands of Scotland* (1984), p39
67 *RPS*, 1425/3/11; *RPS*, 1425/3/12; *RPS*, 1458/3/28; 1458/3/31; 1504/3/116; 1535/16
68 *OSA*, Galston, p77
69 F Watson, 'Need versus greed?: Attitudes to woodland management on a central Highland estate, 1630–1740' in C Watkins, ed, *European Woods and Forests: Studies in Cultural History*, CAB International (1998), pp135–56
70 Pennant, *A Tour*, 1769, p141; Wordsworth, *Recollections*, p182
71 Smout, Macdonald and Watson, *A History of the Native Woodlands*, Chapter 13
72 Pennant, *A Tour*, 1769, p145
73 Smout, Macdonald and Watson, *A History of the Native Woodlands*, p248
74 See, for example, C Ellis (Argyll Archaeology) with T B Ballin and S Ramsay, *Activities in the Woods: Platforms and a Lithic Scatter, Loch Doilean, Sunart, Lochaber*, Archaeology Reports Online no 20 (2016), www.archaeologyreportsonline.com/PDF/ARO20_Loch_Doilean.pdf
75 Defoe, *A Tour*, letter 11
76 *NSA*, Galston, p184
77 *NSA*, Galston, p184; *NSA*, Kilmarnock, p547
78 *Ibid*; *NSA*, Loudoun, p849
79 P Dixon and L Macinnes, *The Historic Land-use Assessment of Scotland, 1996–2015* (2018)
80 *OSA*, Glamis, p125; Pennant, *A Tour*, 1772, p522; *NSA*, Glamis, p341. 140 acres is just over half a square kilometre.
81 *OSA*, Mauchline, p116; *NSA*, Mauchline, p159. This is exactly the same entry and I had to check more than once that I wasn't getting confused.
82 A McKerracher, *Perthshire in History and Legend* (1988), pp134–42
83 *NSA*, Drumoak, p875; *NSA*, Dyce, p127; *NSA*, Hoddam, p290; *NSA*, Kirkmahoe, pp62–3; *NSA*, Chirnside, p124
84 *NSA*, Drumoak, p875; *NSA*, Collessie, p32
85 *NSA*, Drumoak, p875
86 Earl Rognvald Kali (St Ronald of Orkney, d.1158), in Clancy and Markus, *The Triumph Tree*, p199. As ever in early heroic literature, this is in fact a metaphor, specifically to a serpent, believe it or not. But it does not alter the fact that the metaphor would not work if readers or listeners were unfamiliar with its core image.
87 *OSA*, New Abbey, p140
88 *OSA*, Ellon, p101; *OSA*, Fintray, p238
89 hansard.millbanksystems.com/commons/1819/may/20/coal-duties
90 *NSA*, Stornoway, p140
91 *NSA*, Kilmuir, p278; S Boyle, 'Ben Lawers: An Improvement-period landscape on Lochtayside, Perthshire', in S Govan (ed), *Medieval or Later Rural Settlement in Scotland: 10 Years On* (2003), pp17–29
92 canmore.org.uk/collection/525018
93 See, for example, www.dunfermlinepress.com/news/13592402.Mossmorran_peat_extraction_plan_rejected/ or scottishwildlifetrust.org.uk/news/trust-calls-for-rejection-of-peat-extraction-appeal/
94 *OSA*, Hamilton, p191; *OSA*, Dalserf, p377
95 *NSA*, Dalziel, pp457–64; *NSA*, Dalserf, pp745–6. If you are at all interested in orchards, including the various old species of fruit that used to be grown, then there is a lot of valuable information to be found here.
96 See, for example, scottishorchards.com, orchardrevival.org.uk/inventory-scotland/ and clydevalleyorchards.co.uk

Chapter Three

1. Tacitus, *Agricola*, Book 1, 29–32, written in AD 98. The Latin is *ubi solitudinem faciunt, pacem appellant*, the second word being variously translated as solitude, wilderness or desert. Calgacus himself is also called Galgacus or Calgacos.
2. Pennant, *A Tour, 1772*, p87
3. Fordun, *Chronica Gentis Scotorum*, Chapter 4, p82
4. www.antoninewall.org/about-the-wall/the-romans-in-scotland; www.antoninewall.org/about-wall/wall-after-romans
5. Septimius Severus attempted the third conquest of Caledonia in AD 208, strengthening Antonine's wall in the process. But he did not build it.
6. Bede, *Ecclesiastical History of England*, Book 1, Chapters 5,12. In Chapter 12, Bede is basically quoting from *De Excidio et Conquestu Britanniae* (*On the Ruin and Conquest of Britain*) written by the sixth century monk Gildas. They were both right, though, about the Antonine Wall being made of turf.
7. See, for example, Fordun, *Chronica Gentis Scotorum*, Book 3, Chapter 3, p80. Among other errors, later writers began to believe that Hadrian's Wall was also made of turf. See Boece, *Historia Gentis Scotorum*, Book 5, 13
8. Dixon and Macinnes, *The Historic Land-use Assessment of Scotland,*
9. Fordun, *Chronica Gentis Scotorum*, Chapter 16, p46; Derek Hall, *Scottish Monastic Landscapes*, (2006), p61
10. Boece, *Historia Gentis Scotorum*, Book 3, 14; canmore.org.uk/site/46950/arthurs-oon-stenhouse
11. Pennant, *A Tour, 1769*, p164
12. *NSA*, Larbert, pp357–62
13. Buchanan, *History of Scotland*, vol 1, p25. Buchanan insisted that these remains marked the site of the small city called Guidi by Bede, who 'places it in the angle of the wall of Severus' (that is, the Antonine Wall). Much debate surrounds the site of this place, which is most likely to have been one of the forts on the wall, but the essential point is still that, in Buchanan's day, local gentlemen were pillaging stone from ancient sites near Camelon.
14. canmore.org.uk/site/51638/penicuik-penicuik-house-stables
15. Total confusion now! This is clearly Hadrian's Wall.
16. *NSA*, Ayton, p134. By now Severus's wall has become Hadrian's.
17. Sir James Hunter, *Fala and Soutra, Including a History of the Ancient Domus de Soltre* (1892) pp30–1
18. *Macfarlane's Geographical Collections*, vol 2, p74 (Galloway, 1684)
19. Burt, *Letters*, p287
20. *NSA*, Kilmorie, Bute, p62
21. Taylor, *Pennyless Pilgrimage*, pp25–6
22. Macky, *A Journey*, p16; Defoe, *A Tour*, letter 12
23. Burt, *Letters*, p295
24. Wordsworth, *Recollections*, p228
25. Pennant, *A Tour, 1769*, p142
26. Burt, *Letters*, p296
27. Burt, quite understandably, devotes a considerable section of his *Letters* from p278 to describing his 11-year stint on the Scottish roads from 1726.
28. Pennant, *A Tour, 1769*, p142
29. Macky, *A Journey*, p325
30. *OSA*, Hoddam, p352; *OSA*, Fortingall, p458; www.genegenie-scotland.co.uk/Roads_in_Aberdeenshire_1750-1900.pdf, p2
31. *OSA*, Colmonell, pp59, 64, 63
32. *OSA*, Whittinghame, p353
33. *OSA*, Barvas, p272; *NSA*, Barvas, p149; *NSA*, Stornoway, p136
34. Burt, *Letters*, p298
35. pathetic.org.uk/
36. Defoe, *A Tour*, pp6–7
37. Burt, *Letters*, pp286–7, 297–8
38. Pennant, *A Tour, 1769*, p65
39. Pennant, *A Tour, 1772*, pp472–3
40. *NSA*, Airthrey, p231
41. www.forth-bridges.co.uk/forth-road-bridge/facts-figures-road
42. Defoe, *A Tour*, letter 12
43. *Macfarlane's Geographical Collections*, vol 2, p150
44. See Duncan, *Scotland: The Making of the Kingdom*, p127
45. Pennant, *A Tour, 1772*, pp158–9
46. *NSA*, South Knapdale, p267
47. Burt, *Letters*, p293
48. Pennant, *A Tour, 1769*, p159
49. *OSA*, Kirkintilloch, pp279–80. See also *OSA*, Denny, p422; *OSA*, Larbert and Dunipace, p335
50. *OSA*, Kilmarnock, pp89–90; *OSA*, Crailing, p332; *OSA*, Keithhall, p529; *OSA*, Aberdeen, pp226–7; *OSA*, Rhynie and Essie, p295; *OSA*, Aboyne and Glentanar pp99–300; *NSA*, Kinnellar, p118
51. *NSA*, Dunoon, p606, pp607–8
52. *NSA*, South Knapdale, p270
53. *NSA*, Pettie, p405
54. *NSA*, Kirkwall, p9
55. *NSA*, Kirkintilloch, pp201–2
56. *NSA*, Ayr, p66
57. *NSA*, Maxton, p126; *NSA*, Galashiels, pp24, 28; *NSA*, Crailing, p187
58. Morton, *In Search of Scotland*, pp75–6
59. Pennant, *A Tour, 1769*, pp163–4
60. Defoe, *A Tour*, Letter 13, part 2
61. Taylor, *Pennyless Pilgrimage*, pp23–24
62. D Adamson, 'A Coal Mine in the Sea: Culross and the Moat Pit', *Scottish Archaeological Journal,* 30:1–2 (2008), pp161–99
63. rps.ac.uk/trans/1612/10/66; rps.ac.uk/trans/A1609/1/10
64. Smout, Macdonald and Watson, *A History of the Native Woodlands*, pp229–35
65. www.bbc.co.uk/history/british/civil_war_revolution/scotland_darien_01.shtml
66. Macky, *A Journey*, p271
67. Pennant, *A Tour, 1769*, pp163–4
68. *OSA*, Larbert and Dunipace, pp334–5; Wordsworth, *Recollections*, p242; Muir, *A Scottish Journey*, p177
69. *OSA*, Burntisland, p432; *NSA*, Burntisland, p405, p412; *OSA*, Alness, p239; *NSA*, Culsalmond, p730; *NSA*, Polmont, p193
70. Pennant, *A Tour, 1769*, pp152,155; *A Tour, 1772*, p127
71. *OSA*, Neilston, p162
72. Pennant, *A Tour, 1769*, p66, 527; *NSA*, Tain, p295
73. *OSA*, New Abbey, p127; *NSA*, Forgandenny, p956
74. www.rspb.org.uk/groups/aberdeen/reports/250445/ (2015)
75. Pennant, *A Tour, 1772*, p111; Wordsworth, *Recollections*, pp15–17
76. *NSA*, Lochs, p164; *NSA*, Blantyre, pp322–3
77. T D Bathgate, 'Ancient fish-traps or yairs in Scotland', *Proceedings of the Society of Antiquaries of Scotland,* 83 (1948–9), pp98–102; A Hale, 'Fish traps in Scotland: construction, supply, demand and destruction' in J Klaptse, ed, *Water Management in the Medieval Rural Economy*, Ruralia V (2005), pp119–26
78. Pennant, *A Tour, 1769*, p89
79. *NSA*, Moffat, p105
80. Wordsworth, *Recollections*, p255

81 *NSA*, Larbert, pp342, 375; *NSA*, Neilston, pp321–2
82 Fordun, *Chronica Gentis Scotorum,* Chapter 8, p37
83 Buchanan, *History of Scotland*, vol 1, p36; Martin, *Description*, pp44, 89, 202
84 Defoe, *A Tour*, letter 12; letter 13, part 2
85 Burt, *Letters*, p47; Pennant, *A Tour, 1772*, pp86, 363, 560
86 *OSA*, Fordyce, p87; *NSA*, Fordyce, pp180, 190; *NSA*, Stronsay and Eday, p158; *NSA*, Blair Atholl, p561
87 Muir, *A Scottish Journey*, pp168–9
88 www.treasuredplaces.org.uk/gallery/winning_image.php
89 See www.theguardian.com/commentisfree/2013/sep/07/industrial-waste-pride-community
90 canmore.org.uk/site/76800/kinlochleven-aluminium-works
91 W W Knox, *A History of the Scottish People*, 'Health in Scotland, 1840–1940', www.scran.ac.uk/scotland/pdf/SP2_3Health.pdf, p4
92 www.abct.org.uk/airfields/airfield-finder/abbotsinch-glasgow/
93 canmore.org.uk/site/81604/lenabo-longside-airship-station-forest-of-deer
94 www.theguardian.com/world/2016/dec/03/former-german-pow-leaves-384000-to-scottish-village-in-will
95 comriedevelopmenttrust.org.uk/working-groups/cultybraggan
96 See www.bristol.ac.uk/history/militarylandscapes/
97 D C Cowley, *Kirkcudbright Training Area: An Archaeological Survey* (2003), www.academia.edu/29934393/Kirkcudbright_Training_Area_an_archaeological_survey
98 canmore.org.uk/site/70181/motherwell-ravenscraig-steelworks; B Mciver, 'Closure of Ravenscraig steel works still causing pain twenty years on', *Daily Record*, 23 June 2012, www.dailyrecord.co.uk/news/real-life/closure-of-ravenscraig-steel-works-still-1130067

Chapter Four

1 K Jamie, 'Markings' in *Sightlines* (2005), pp121–2
2 'The Gododdin' in Clancy and Markus, *The Triumph Tree*, p72
3 Boece, *Historia Gentis Scotorum*, Book 2, 11
4 Boece, *Historia Gentis Scotorum*, Book 2, 23
5 Buchanan, *History of Scotland*, Book 1, p1, pp23–24; canmore.org.uk/site/47049/hills-of-dunipace
6 Martin, *Description*, p46
7 Pennant, *A Tour, 1772*, pp173–4
8 *Macfarlane's Geographical Collections*, vol 2, p84; canmore.org.uk/site/63096/isle-of-whithorn-st-ninians-chapel; T O Clancy, 'The real St Ninian', *Innes Review*, 52 (2001), pp1–28
9 Defoe, *A Tour*, letter 13, part 1
10 *NSA*, Kilmuir, p273; *NSA*, Aboyne and Glentanar, p1069
11 canmore.org.uk/site/35112/hilton-of-fern-motte; *NSA*, Fearn, pp313–4
12 Pennant, *A Tour, 1772*, p426
13 Macky, *A Journey*, p21
14 Pennant, *A Tour, 1772*, pp327, 428–9
15 Wordsworth, *Recollections*, p255 onwards
16 A J Durie, *Travels in Scotland, 1788–1881: A selection from contemporary tourist journals* (2012), pp206–33
17 Durie, *Travels in Scotland*, p5 onwards; p7
18 Queen Victoria, *Leaves from the Journal of our Life in the Highlands from 1848 to 1861*, ed A Helps (1868), p75
19 Durie, *Travels in Scotland*, p10
20 'Dinogad's Coat' [anon female, c650?] in Clancy and Markus, *The Triumph Tree*, p94. As Professor Clancy himself admits, it is set in the British kingdom of Rheged (thanks to the reference to Derwennydd Falls, which has been identified as Lodore Falls near Derwentwater), which is believed to have been focused on modern-day Cumbria, but seems also to have extended into Dumfries and Galloway in what is now Scotland. That is good enough for me to include this wonderful, unique poem.
21 M Carver, *Surviving in Symbols: A Visit to the Pictish Nation*, (1999), pp33–5
22 Fordun, *Chronica Gentis Scotorum*, Book 5, Chapter 9, p195
23 canmore.org.uk/site/28801/buzzart-dikes; canmore.org.uk/site/348728/kincardine-park;
24 *OSA*, Blair Atholl and Strowan, p475
25 R Lindsay of Pitscottie, *History of Scotland* (1728), pp146–7
26 William Barclay, *Contra Monarchomachos*, 1563, quoted in Pennant, *A Tour, 1772*, p430
27 Taylor, *Pennyless Pilgrimage*, pp26–7
28 Burt, *Letters*, p222
29 Pennant, *A Tour, 1772*, pp147, 288, 207
30 *OSA*, Laggan, p152; *OSA*, Drumoak, p880
31 *OSA*, Garvock, p545; *OSA*, Aboyne and Glentanar, p1060; *NSA*, Dunoon, p605
32 *OSA*, Kirkpatrick Durham, pp250–1; *OSA*, Stenton, p58
33 *NSA*, Blair Atholl, p570
34 *RPS* 1594/4/31; *NSA*, South Knapdale, p261; *NSA*, Colmonell, p534; *NSA*, Moffat, p108
35 *NSA*, Kingussie, Note, pp68–70
36 *NSA*, Laggan, p427
37 *NSA*, Blair Atholl, pp658–9
38 *Macfarlane's Geographical Collections*, vol 2, Presbytery of Arbroath (1683–1722), p48
39 canmore.org.uk/site/269769/gordonstoun-house

40 Pennant, *A Tour, 1772*, p575
41 Defoe, *A Tour*, letters 11,12
42 *Macfarlane's Geographical Collections*, vol 2, pp145, 146, 206, 207
43 *Macfarlane's Geographical Collections*, vol 2, pp3, 8, 9
44 Taylor, *Pennyless Pilgrimage*, p22; Pennant, *A Tour, 1769*, p98; *A Tour, 1772*, p105
45 Defoe, *A Tour*, letter 11
46 Pennant, *A Tour, 1769*, p166
47 Pennant, *A Tour, 1772*, p570; *OSA*, Hamilton, p209
48 Wordsworth, *Recollections*, pp 46–7
49 Pennant, *A Tour, 1772*, p428
50 M Brown, *Scotland's Lost Gardens* (2012)
51 *Macfarlane's Geographical Collections*, vol 2, Description of Carrick, p17
52 *RPS*, 1458/3/7
53 Morton, *In Search of Scotland*, p63
54 Martin, *Description*, p277
55 Pennant, *A Tour, 1772*, p547; Morton, *In Search of Scotland*, p114
56 www.scottishgolfhistory.org/ (2016); scottishgolfcourses-allofthem.blogspot.co.uk/2012/09/stroma-golf-course-course-no-534
57 Morton, *In Search of Scotland*, p98
58 'Huts' and 'Hutters' in Scotland, Research Consultancy Services, The Scottish Executive Central Research Unit 2000, www.gov.scot/resource/doc/156526/0042031.pdf (2015); www.heraldscotland.com/news/13167016.Hopes_of_a_revival_in_hut_culture_after_legal_milestone/; www.thousandhuts.org/

Conclusion

1 I Campbell, Introduction to L Grassic Gibbon's *Sunset Song* (2015), ppix–x
2 *Ibid*, pxi

Land-use Maps

Urban Areas and Motorways

1 W W Knox, *A History of Scottish People*, 'Urban Housing in Scotland 1840–1940', www.scran.ac.uk/scotland/pdf/SP2_4Housing.pdf (2015)

Mining and Quarrying

1 J Butt, *The Industrial Archaeology of Scotland*, The industrial archaeology of the British Isles series, (1967) pp147–8; RCAHMS, *Forts, Farms and Furnaces: Archaeology in the Central Scotland Forest* (1998)

Fields

1 R Richens, 'Changes in the physical and social landscape of three Lanarkshire farms during the eighteenth-century agricultural reorganisation', *Review of Scottish Culture,* 9 (1995/6); P Dixon, ed, *Buildings of the Land* (2008)

Conifers

1 M L Anderson, *A History of Scottish Forestry*, vol 2; Smout, MacDonald and Watson, *A History of the Native Woodlands* pp258–89

Glossary

Barilla is a blanket term used to cover a number of (unrelated) salt-marsh plants once burned to make soda ash used in glass-making. In Spanish the word means salt wort.

A **barrow** is a prehistoric earthen mound containing a tomb built in a variety of shapes, from long and thin to round. Also known as a tumulus (plural, tumuli).

A **birlinn** was a large wooden boat or barge propelled by sail or oars, used in the West Highlands.

A **blackhouse** is the term given to a thatched house, usually found in the north and west Highlands, and built with thick walls and few windows.

Blockwork in building construction means blocks of a uniform size held together by mortar.

A **bleachery** was a place where cloth was made as white as possible before being printed.

A **boll** is a unit of measurement usually used for grain. It corresponds to 145.145 litres.

A **broch** is a huge circular drystone tower with stairs and chambers built in the cavity between the inner and outer walls. Archaeologists also describe brochs as a type of Atlantic round house. They are found only in Scotland.

Chambered cairns are a prehistoric form of tomb made up of an inner burial chamber and a passage leading to it, set within a stone cairn. Like barrows*, they come in a variety of shapes and sizes, both long and round.

Coppicing is a method of tree management that involves repeatedly cutting fledgling tree stems close to the ground to encourage fresh growth.

A **cottar** was a landless labourer who was given a cottage to live in in return for labour.

A **crannog** is an entirely or partially man-made island in a loch on which dwellings of either timber or stone were constructed. Crannogs are mostly found in Ireland and Scotland, though there is one in Wales. They were inhabited at various periods across Scotland between c800 BC and as late as AD c1700. Connected to the wider landscape, they were elite homes, which, like brochs and hill-forts, were designed to look impressive from a distance. On Loch Tay alone there were eighteen such crannogs. The organic material, including timber, would tend to decay, though if it fell into the water, archaeologists could recover it. Stone remains and other debris on their island bases can be spotted today, though the islands themselves often give their origins away by their suspiciously even roundness and their causeways.

Cropmarks appear in arable fields during particularly dry weather because the crops grow differently if there are archaeological remains below the soil. The outline of the hidden structure is therefore revealed, particularly if seen from the air.

A **cruive** is the Scottish word for a wicker or wooden enclosure used to catch salmon or other fish.

Cursus monuments. The name is derived from the Latin word for course, because the archaeologists who first discovered them in the eighteenth century thought their long, parallel banks with external ditches constituted some kind of Roman race track.

A **dun**, like a broch, is another kind of Atlantic round house, though they are most easily described as a particular type of hill-fort. Indeed, the word *dùn*, which is Gaelic, means fort. Unfortunately many brochs are also called duns, but they are not round towers, although they do have chambers in the walls.

Ecclesiastical derives from the Latin word *ecclesia*, meaning church. This is also the derivation of *Eccles* in Scottish place-names and the Gaelic word for church, *eaglais* (though it is usually the suffix *Kil-* that signifies church in Gaelic place-names).

The **Estates** was the Scottish term for parliament, consisting as it did of three estates – the clergy, the nobles and the burghs.

Feuing land was an ancient way of granting it out on payment of an annual feu duty, as well as a considerable sum when a new holder took possession. However, feuing encouraged new building, because it gave security of tenure (providing the feu duties were paid). See, for example, Pennant, *A Tour, 1772*, p551.

Forfeited estates were properties belonging to those who had opposed the house of Hanover (otherwise known as Jacobites) from 1715 onwards. Taken into government hands, they were viewed as fair game for the application of Improvement techniques in agriculture, industry and planning. They were not necessarily very successful.

A Roman **forum** was the public space at the heart of towns and cities across the Empire, though the most famous is still in Rome itself. It was in essence a market-place, often graced with columns.

The **German Ocean** is the old term for the North Sea.

A **groat** was a Scottish coin (there was an English version too) first minted in the fourteenth century and originally worth four pennies. Later versions were valued at eight pence and a shilling (twelve pence). They were still around into the twentieth century, but were not actually minted for domestic use after 1800.

A **hagg** is that part of a moss or bog which has been cut for peats.

A **haugh** is the Scottish word for the floodplain of a river.

Henges are large circular enclosures surrounded by a bank with a ditch inside it. They form part of the ritual landscape from around 3000 BC.

Heritor is a Scottish term for the owner of a heritable property.

Hip-roofed is a type of roofing that does away with the need for gable ends or other vertical sides; each part of the roof slopes down towards the walls.

Hut circle is the term used for the stone foundations of prehistoric round houses measuring at least 5 metres and up to 12 metres within the walls. They form part of a wider landscape that certainly included field systems and perhaps ritual monuments.

Improvement is a term used to encompass a range of activities associated with major changes in the rural landscape from agriculture to housing. Improvers were intent on using scientific principles and experimentation to improve agricultural productivity and living conditions, based on examples from throughout Europe, but mostly England. Improvement took off as a movement in Scotland around 1750, though examples of improved agriculture could be found much earlier.

Infield was the best land in the communal agricultural system usually lying nearest to the settlement and regularly manured with, for example, dung or the turf roofs of houses that were replaced every year.

Jacobites were supporters of the exiled royal house of Stuart after the expulsion of James VII and II from the thrones of Scotland and England in 1688/89 in favour of his daughter, Mary, and her husband, William of Orange. Jacobite rebellions were launched in Scotland in 1715, 1719 and 1745, though there were English Jacobites too.

A **kale-yard** is a vegetable or kitchen garden (kale is a form of leaf cabbage). The term kale-yard school is used to define a particular type of Scottish fiction produced in the decades around the turn of the twentieth century renowned now for its sentimental portrayal of rural life, though it was very popular at the time.

Kelp are a family of large brown seaweeds, which were harvested then burnt in order to produce soda ash (mostly sodium carbonate), which was used in the manufacture of glass and soap.

Lade is the Scottish word for a man-made watercourse or channel, usually used to bring water to a mill. It comes from the word for a load, pack or burden.

A **laird** is, in effect, a Scottish lord, whose lands officially allow him to be called 'so-and-so *of* somewhere'. The somewhere might not bring in very much income, but his status is still above that of an ordinary gentleman.

Lay comes from the old French word *lai*, meaning not a member of the clergy.

Lazy beds were small spade-dug patches of cultivated ground. The topsoil was piled up into ridges and fertilised with manure or seaweed, while the furrows in between provided access and drainage. This meant that even poor, thin soils could produce crops, with a lot of hard work.

Links is the Scottish word for 'the sandy undulating ground, generally covered with turf, bent grass, gorse, etc, which is frequently found near the sea-shore on a flat part of the coast, and is often common ground belonging to the nearest town' (*Scottish National Dictionary*, www.dsl.ac.uk/entry/snd/links). Many links were converted into golf courses for public use precisely because they did belong to local towns.

Machair is the Gaelic word for field or, more specifically links* land – fertile, low-lying sandy ground often inundated with water in the winter. Although found on Orkney, Shetland, Lewis, Harris and other islands off the west coast, the best machair – renowned for its fabulous biodiversity – is on the Uists, Tiree and Barra, where it was prized as the best arable land.

Marl is a lime-rich sludge (calcium carbonate) often found beneath peat bogs or at the bottom of Scottish lochs. It was found to be very good as a fertiliser, though care had to be taken as to how much was applied, as the lime in it, though beneficial, could become too potent.

A **merk** was a Scottish unit of currency that originally equated to two-thirds of a Scots pound (or 13 shillings and 4 pence in old money). It was not an actual coin until the later sixteenth century. Merklands were also common units of land value.

Middens are rubbish dumps which range from enormous mounds of communal detritus to a household accoutrement forming an essential and valuable part of the farming regime, being spread upon the fields as manure.

A **monoculture** means the growing of a single crop and often refers to the preference for a single species of tree – compared to the range of species and other vegetation to be found in semi-natural woodlands – characteristic of modern forestry plantations.

A **motte and bailey** was a type of castle introduced to Britain after the Norman Conquest of England in 1066. The motte itself was an artificial mound surrounded by a wooden palisade or stone wall on which a wooden or stone keep was built. It was reached via the bailey. The bailey, like the motte, was built on an artificial platform, though not quite so high. It was surrounded by a palisade or stone wall and housed the domestic and industrial activities, from bake-houses to smithies, necessary to life in the castle.

Muir-burning is an ancient form of land management when patches of upland were deliberately set alight in order to burn off old shoots to encourage new, which are far tastier to grazing animals, including sheep, deer and grouse. Muir-burn was carefully managed, with a prohibition placed on the practice after March (see *RPS* 1458/3/39) in order to protect birds which would then be nesting on the ground. It is still practised today, though the cut-off date for burning is mid April.

Niello is an amalgam of sulphur with silver, copper or lead added to designs engraved on metal (usually silver). The contrast of black on silver is particularly attractive.

Nissen huts were prefabricated buildings formed into a distinctive half-cylinder shape made of corrugated steel. Designed by Major Peter Norman Nissen during the First World War, they were used everywhere in the Second World War.

Nolt is the collective noun for cattle, oxen, bulls and cows.

The **outfield** was the area of the communal agricultural system that was only cultivated occasionally, though it was also used for pasturing animals.

The **Reformation** of 1560 transformed Scotland from a Catholic realm to a Protestant one. The Reformation parliament, which met in August of that year, passed legislation that abolished papal jurisdiction over the kingdom, though it did so without the acquiescence of the monarch, Mary, Queen of Scots, who was then living in France. The process by which Scotland ultimately adhered to a Presbyterian form of Protestantism was a long and bloody one, but was ultimately achieved in 1689, when this was made one of the conditions of accepting William of Orange as king in place of the deposed James VII and II. See Jacobites.

Rectilinear generally describes anything made up of straight sides.

The **Renaissance** (literally, rebirth) was a cultural movement in Europe inspired by the rediscovery of classical Greek and Roman texts. It began in Florence, Italy, in the fourteenth century and affected most areas of academic thought, including art, architecture, politics, science, religion and literature.

A **rotary quern** consists of two heavy circular stones, where the top one is rotated (usually by a handle inserted into a small hole) so as to grind the grain placed between them.

Runrig is a system of communal agriculture, whereby the cultivatable land was divided into a series of rigs reallocated on a regular basis among the tenants so that all got a fair share of the good and bad land. The downside was that no-one had any incentive to make improvements as someone else was likely to get the benefit of them.

Spalier, or espalier now, is a horticultural technique for trees (usually fruit trees), whereby they are pruned and tied to a frame. It can also be used to create a particular shape.

Spelt is an ancient form of wheat. It is making something of a comeback as a health food and substitute for more gluten-intense forms of the grain (though it does contain a moderate amount).

Stake and rice is a kind of lattice-work whereby twigs are woven horizontally between vertical stakes to produce a structure that could then (though not necessarily) be plastered.

Stubble is the remains of crops left after harvest and, in the past, put to good use. More recently, it used to be burnt (I remember it when I was young), but the number of road accidents caused by the drifting smoke put paid to that and the practice was banned in England and Wales in 1993.

Subsistence agriculture is geared towards providing enough for those producing it and their families, rather than generating a surplus which could be sold for profit and invested against future shortfalls.

Threshing mills housed machinery which removed the seeds from the rest of the plant as part of the harvesting process. In the past, this job had been done by hand using flails. The job is now done by combine harvesters, so these mills have become obsolete.

Tollbooths were the main municipal buildings in Scottish burghs, usually comprising at least a council meeting room, a court and a prison.

Bibliography

A note on the *Statistical Accounts of Scotland*. I have, like so many researching this period, made extensive use of the *Statistical Accounts*. The idea for this impressive endeavour came to Sir John Sinclair of Ulbster, Caithness, in May 1790. What he wanted was to establish, at a national level, a consistent body of knowledge 'for the purpose of ascertaining the quantum of happiness enjoyed by its inhabitants, and the means of its future improvement'. He therefore wrote to the minister in each of Scotland's 938 parishes with a long list of questions for them to answer. Most did indeed respond, though Sinclair had to pay surveyors to produce twelve of the reports of what is now called the *Old Statistical Account* (*OSA*). The results were published between 1791 and 1799. Some 30 years later it was proposed to repeat the process, resulting in the publication of the *New Statistical Account* (*NSA*) between 1834 and 1845. Given the changes that Scotland underwent in those years, both Accounts have proved invaluable to historians and anyone interested in Scottish history ever since. They can be accessed for free online at stataccscot.edina.ac.uk. References (including books, articles and websites) are in alphabetical order of author, unless there is no obvious author, in which case the title has been used; websites without a named author are also listed alphabetically.

Airfields of Britain Conservation Trust
abct.org.uk

Adamson, D
'A coal mine in the sea: Culross and the moat pit', *Scottish Archaeological Journal* 30 (2008), 1–2

Adomnan
Life of St Columba, ed W Reeves, Edinburgh (1874)

'A grant and loan scheme supporting young crofting families to access homes'
Review of Croft House Grant Scheme: SCF Response to Scottish Government Consultation, March 2015 – Supporting Paper: www.crofting.org

Annals of Ulster
celt.ucc.ie

Aitchison, N
Forteviot: A Pictish and Scottish Royal Centre, Stroud (2006)

Anderson, M L
A History of Scottish Forestry, vol 2, London (1967)

The Antonine Wall: Frontiers of the Roman Empire
antoninewall.org

Armstrong, R A
Gaelic Dictionary in Two Parts, vol 1, London (1825)

Atkinson, J A
'Ben Lawers: An archaeological landscape in time', *Scottish Archaeological Trust Internet Reports*, 62, available at: archaeologydataservice.ac.uk

Bain, J (ed)
Calendar of Documents Relating to Scotland, vol 4, Edinburgh (1888)

Bathgate, T D
'Ancient fish-traps or yairs in Scotland', *Proceedings of the Society of Antiquaries of Scotland* 83 (1948–9), 98–102

Bede
Ecclesiastical History of England, trans A M Sellar, London (1907)

Boece, H
Historia Gentis Scotorum, taken from the 1575 version, available at: www.philological.bham.ac.uk

University of Bristol, History Department
bristol.ac.uk/history

Brophy, K
'Seeing the cursus as a symbolic river', *British Archaeology*, 44 (1999), 6–7

Brophy, K
Reading Between the Lines: The Neolithic Cursus Monuments of Scotland, London (2016)

Broun, D
'Attitudes of Gall to Gaedhil in Scotland before John of Fordun' in D Broun & M D MacGregor, eds, *Mìorun Mòr Nan Gall, 'The Great Ill-Will of the Lowlander'? Lowland Perceptions of the Highlands, Medieval and Modern,* Glasgow (2009)

Brown, M
Scotland's Lost Gardens, Edinburgh (2012)

Buchanan, G
History of Scotland, ed J Aikman, Glasgow (1827)

Building up our Health: The Architecture of Scotland's Historic Hospitals
Edinburgh (2010)

Burt, E
Burt's Letters from the North of Scotland, Edinburgh (1998)

Butt, J
The Industrial Archaeology of Scotland, The industrial archaeology of the British Isles series, Newton Abbot (1967)

Cameron, E A
Land for the People? The British Government and the Scottish Highlands, c1880–1925, Edinburgh (1996)

Campbell, D
The Lairds of Glenlyon: Historical Sketches Relating to the Districts of Appin, Glenlyon and Breadalbane, Perth (1886)

Canmore
National Record of the Historic Environment, available at: canmore.org.uk

Carver, M
Surviving in Symbols: A Visit to the Pictish Nation, Edinburgh (1999)

Carver, M
Portmahomack: Monastery of the Picts, Edinburgh (2008)

Chalcolithic and Bronze Age Scotland
ScARF Panel Report (2012)

Chronicle of Lanercost Priory
trans H Maxwell, Edinburgh (1913)

Clancy, T O
'The real St Ninian', *Innes Review*, 52 (2001), 1–28

Clancy, T O & Markus, B (eds)
The Triumph Tree, Edinburgh (2008)

Clyde Valley Orchards
clydevalleyorchards.co.uk

Coles, F R
'Report on stone circles in Perthshire principally Strathearn, with measured plans and drawings (obtained under the Gunning Fellowship)', *Proceedings of the Society of Antiquaries of Scotland* 45 (1910–11), 46–116

Comrie Development Trust
comriedevelopmenttrust.org.uk

Cowley, D & Harrison, J
'Well Shelter'd and Watered': Menstrie Glen, a Farming Landscape Near Stirling, Edinburgh (2001)

Cowley, D C
Kirkcudbright Training Area: An Archaeological Survey, Edinburgh (2003)

Crofters Holdings (Scotland) Act, 1886
www.legislation.gov.uk

Dalrymple, D
Annals of Scotland, vol 2, Edinburgh (1819)

Defoe, D
A Tour through the Whole Island of Great Britain, 1724–7, vol 3, London (1727)

Devine, T M
The Transformation of Rural Scotland: Social Change and the Agrarian Economy, Edinburgh (1994)

Devine, T M
Clearance and Improvement: Land, Power and People in Scotland, 1700–1900, Edinburgh (2006)

Dictionary of the Older Scottish Tongue
www.dsl.ac.uk

Dixon, P, ed
Buildings of the Land, Edinburgh (2008)

Dixon, P
'Mukked and folded land: medieval cultivation techniques in Scotland', in J Klapste, ed, *Agrarian Technology in the Medieval Landscape*, Ruralia X, Turnhout (2015)

Dixon, P & Macinnes, L
The Historic Land-use Assessment of Scotland, 1996–2015 (2018), available at: hlamap.org.uk/content/historic-landscape

Dodgshon, R A
'Changes in Scottish township organization during the medieval and early modern periods', *Geografiska Annaler* B 59 (1977): 51–65

Driscoll, S T & Yeoman, P A
Excavations within Edinburgh Castle in 1988–91, Edinburgh (1997)

Drummond Castle Gardens
drummondcastlegardens.co.uk

Duncan, A A M
Scotland: The Making of the Kingdom, Edinburgh (1992)

Durie, A J
Travels in Scotland, 1788–1881: A Selection From Contemporary Tourist Journals, Woodbridge (2012)

Edwards, K J & Ralston, I B M (eds)
Scotland after the Ice Age, Edinburgh (2005)

Electric Scotland
electricscotland.com

Ellis, C, with Ballin, T B & Ramsay, S
Activities in the Woods: Platforms and a Lithic Scatter, Loch Doilean, Sunart, Lochaber, Archaeology Reports Online, no 20 (2016), available at: www.archaeologyreportsonline.com

Fairhurst, H & Taylor, D B
'A hut circle settlement at Kilphedir, Sutherland', *Proceedings of the Society of Antiquaries of Scotland* 103 (1970–71): 65–99

Finlayson, B
Wild Harvesters: The First People in Scotland, Edinburgh (1998)

Fordun, John of
Chronica Gentis Scotorum, ed W F Skene, trans F J H Skene, Edinburgh (1872)

Forrest, L
'"Gairloch" settlements in the 19th century: Wester Ross and the Canadian Maritimes', thesis, University of Aberdeen (2011)

The Forth Bridges
forth-bridges.co.uk

Gene Genie Scotland
www.genegenie-scotland.co.uk

Gibbon, L G
Sunset Song, Edinburgh (2015)

Glendinning, M & Martins, S W
Buildings of the Land: Scotland's Farms, 1750–2000, Edinburgh (2009)

Govan, S (ed)
Medieval or Later Rural Settlement: 10 Years On, Edinburgh (2003)

Grant, A
Independence and Nationhood: Scotland 1306–1469, London (1984)

Gray, J (ed)
Scottish Population Statistics, Edinburgh (1952)

Hale, A
'Fish traps in Scotland: construction, supply, demand and destruction' in Klaptse, J, ed, *Water Management in the Medieval Rural Economy*, Ruralia V, Turnhout (2005)

Hall, D
Scottish Monastic Landscapes, Stroud (2006)

Hansard Millbank Systems
hansard.millbanksystems.com

Historic Scotland
Building up our Health: the Architecture of Scotland's Historic Hospitals, Edinburgh (2010)

HLAmap: Scotland's Historic Land Use
hlamap.org.uk

Homans, G C
'The Frisians in East Anglia', in *Sentiments and Activities,* London (2013)

Hunter, Sir J
Fala and Soutra, Including a History of the Ancient Domus de Soltre, Edinburgh (1892)

Hunter, J
Set Adrift Upon the World: The Sutherland Clearances, Edinburgh (2016)

'Huts' and 'Hutters' in Scotland
Research Consultancy Services, Scottish Executive Central Research Unit 2000 (2015), available at: www.gov.scot

Jamie, K
Sightlines, London (2005)

Jamie, K
The Bonniest Companie, London (2015)

Jamie, K
'Diary', *London Review of Books,* vol 38, no 19, 6 October 2016

Jay, M
'I'm not signing' (review of John Foot's *The Man Who Closed the Asylums: Franco Basaglia and the Revolution in Mental Health Care),* London Review of Books, vol 38, no 17, 8 September 2016

Johnson, S & Boswell, J
A Journey to the Western Islands of Scotland, London (1984)

Knox, W W
A History of the Scottish People, 'Health in Scotland, 1840–1940', available at: www.scran.ac.uk

UK Legislation
legislation.gov.uk

Liber Insule Missarum Abbacie Canonicorum Regularium B. Virginis et S. Johannis de Inchaffery Registrum Vetus
Edinburgh (1847)

Lindsay, R, of Pitscottie
History of Scotland, Edinburgh (1728)

Loudon, J C
An Encyclopaedia of Agriculture, London (1825)

McCullagh, R P J & Tipping, R (eds)
The Lairg Project 1988–1996: The Evolution of an Archaeological Landscape in Northern Scotland, Scottish Trust for Archaeological Research Monograph 3, Edinburgh (1998)

Macfarlane, W
Geographical Collections relating to Scotland (otherwise Macfarlane's Geographical Collections), vol 2, ed A Mitchell, Scottish History Society, Edinburgh (1907)

Mciver, B
'Closure of Ravenscraig steel works still causing pain twenty years on', *Daily Record,* 23 June 2012

McKerracher, A
Perthshire in History and Legend, Edinburgh (1988)

MacKillop, A
'Clans of the Highlands and Islands 2' in M Lynch, ed, *The Oxford Companion to Scottish History,* Oxford (2001)

Macky, J
A Journey through Scotland: In Familiar Letters from a Gentlemen Here, to his Friends Abroad, Being the Third Volume Which Compleats Great Britain, London (1729)

Martin, C & Oram, R
'Medieval Roxburgh: A preliminary assessment of the burgh and its locality', *Proceedings of the Society of Antiquaries of Scotland,* 137 (2007), 357–404

Martin, M
Description of the Western Islands of Scotland, c1695, Edinburgh (1999)

Monro, D
A Description of the Occidental ie Western Islands of Scotland (1549), in Martin, *Description of the Western Islands of Scotland*

Morton, H V
In Search of Scotland, London (1932)

Muir, E
A Scottish Journey, London (1935)

Royal Horticultural Society: My Garden
mygarden.rhs.org.uk

National Library of Scotland (maps)
maps.nls.uk

NSA
The New Statistical Account of Scotland, vols 1–15, Edinburgh (1834–1845)

Orchard Revival
orchardrevival.org.uk

OSA
Sinclair, J, *The Statistical Account of Scotland,* vols 1–21, Edinburgh (1791–9)

Past Horizons: Adventures in Archaeology
pasthorizonspr.com

Pathetic Motorways
pathetic.org.uk

Paton, Kevin
'The evolution of settlement at Roslin from prehistory to the 21st century', *History Scotland,* vol 17, no 2 (March/April 2017)

Pennant, T
A Tour in Scotland and Voyage to the Hebrides, 1772, Edinburgh (1998)

Pennant, T
A Tour in Scotland, 1769, Edinburgh (2000)

Queen Victoria
Leaves from the Journal of our Life in the Highlands from 1848 to 1861, ed A Helps, New York (1868)

Raeburn, G D
'The long reformation of the dead in Scotland', PhD thesis, Durham University (2012)

Ralston, I
Scotland's Hidden History, Stroud (1998)

RCAHMS
Forts, Farms and Furnaces: Archaeology in the Central Scotland Forest, Edinburgh (1998)

RPS
The Records of the Parliaments of Scotland to 1707, ed K M Brown *et al,* St Andrews (2007–2017), available at: rps.ac.uk

Richens, R
'Changes in the physical and social landscape of three Lanarkshire farms during the eighteenth-century agricultural reorganisation', *Review of Scottish Culture,* 9, Edinburgh (1995/6)

Ross, A D
'The Province of Moray, c1000–1230', PhD thesis, University of Aberdeen (2003)

RSPB
rspb.org.uk

Scot, R
Death by Design: The True Story of the Glasgow Necropolis, Edinburgh (2005)

Scottish Golf Courses
scottishgolfcourses-allofthem.blogspot.co.uk

Scottish Golf History
scottishgolfhistory.org

Scottish Land and Estates
scottishlandandestates.co.uk

Scottish Orchards
scottishorchards.com

Scottish Parliament
parliament.scot

Scottish Wildlife Trust
scottishwildlifetrust.org.uk

Skovsgaard, C
'The heavy plough and the European agricultural revolution of the middle ages: Evidence from a historical experiment', Economic History Society Conference, York (2013)

Smith, A M
'The Forfeited Estate Papers, 1745: A Study of the work of the commissioners for the forfeited annexed estates, 1755–1784, with particular reference to their contribution to the development of communications in Scotland in the eighteenth century', PhD thesis, University of St Andrews (1975)

Smith, S
'Notes on an artificial mound near Bonnybridge', *Proceedings of the Society of Antiquaries of Scotland*, 68 (1933–4), 59–68

Smout, T C
People and Woods in Scotland: A History, Edinburgh (2002)

Smout, T C, MacDonald, A R & Watson, F
A History of the Woodlands of Scotland, 1500–1920, Edinburgh (2005)

Smout, T C & Stewart, M
The Firth of Forth: An Environmental History, Edinburgh (2012)

Tacitus, C
On the Life and Times of Julius Agricola, trans A J Church and W J Brodribb, London (1877)

Taylor, J
The Pennyless Pilgrimage (1618), ed C Hindley, London (1876): scholarsbank.uoregon.edu

A Thousand Huts
thousandhuts.org

Treasured Places
treasuredplaces.org.uk

Visit Banchory
visitbanchory.com

Dixon, P, Stevenson, J B & Maxwell, G S
Waternish, Skye and Lochalsh District, Highland Region: An Archaeological Survey (Afforestable Land Survey), Edinburgh (1993)

Watson, F
'Need versus greed? Attitudes to woodland management on a central Highland estate,1630–1740' in C Watkins, ed, *European Woods and Forests*, Studies in Cultural History, CAB International (1998)

Welfare, A
Great Crowns of Stone: The Recumbent Stone Circles of Scotland, Edinburgh (2011)

White Jr, L
Medieval Technology and Social Change, Oxford (1962)

Whittle, A W R, Keith-Lucas, M, Milles, A, Noddle, B, Rees, S & Romans, J C C
Scord of Brouster: An Early Aricultural Settlement on Shetland, Monograph 9, Oxford (1986)

Woolf, A
From Pictland to Alba, Edinburgh (2007)

Wordsworth, D
Recollections of a Tour made in Scotland AD 1803, New York (1874)

Zimecki, M
'The lunar cycle: effects on human and animal behaviour and physiology', *Postepy Hig Med Dosw* (Online), 60 (2006) 1–7

Historic Land-use Assessment

A History of Scotland's Landscapes emerged from the Historic Land-use Assessment (HLA). Through mapping the surviving fragments in the present landscape, this project aimed to reveal the changing landscape of Scotland from early prehistory to modern times.

The Historic Land-use Assessment of Scotland was undertaken as a joint project between Historic Scotland and the Royal Commission on the Ancient and Historical Monuments of Scotland (now merged to form Historic Environment Scotland). Its purpose was to establish a national map-based digital data-set that depicted the historic origins of land-use in Scotland. This would enhance understanding of the historic dimension of the landscape, therefore aiding landscape protection and management both in its own right and alongside Land Character Assessment (a descriptive technique for recording elements and influences that make landscapes distinctive, although it does not fully encompass the complex range of historical influences). In addition, HLA would provide a spatial framework for historic environment data and help comparisons with other types of landscape data, allowing the historic landscape to be embedded in wider strategies for land-use change and landscape management. The project began with a pilot study between 1996 and 1998 and continued for the next two decades until national coverage was completed in 2015.

The HLA project divided the landscape of Scotland into fifty-four 'Historic Land-use Types', which are active components of the modern landscape, and forty-three archaeological 'Relict Types' of the prehistoric, medieval and modern periods that are fossilised within them. These are grouped into twelve 'Historic Land-use Categories'. The approach focuses on the time period in which any type of land-use began as well as its function. For example, Designed Landscape is a recognised Land-use Type in HLA that originated in the seventeenth century. However, in the National Land-use Database it is broken down into the constituent parts – woodland, pasture, dwellings and gardens – without reference to their shared historical origins. Furthermore, there is no Vacant or Derelict Land-use group in the HLA interpretation, since the historic land-use does not in effect change until a new land-use is established. This highlights one of the essential elements of this assessment – the importance of change and the impact of past land-use on the present, with the mapping of relict remains wherever they may be seen. This is an archaeological approach, viewing changing land-use as 'stratigraphy' in the landscape, each phase of land-use leaving its mark on the landscape, or being overlain and obscured by new land-uses.

HLA data provides a systematic and rigorous means of analysing the landscape to identify elements that survive from past activities and are recognisable in the patterns of modern land-use. In effect, HLA is a GIS-based (geographic information system) map that depicts the historic origin of land-uses, describing them by period, form and function. The HLA methodology is mainly desk-based and analyses a comprehensive range of sources to identify and interpret historic land-uses. The key sources are historical and current Ordnance Survey maps, the National Record of the Historic Environment, local authority historic environment records and aerial photography. Data held by the Forestry Commission, Macaulay Land Use Research Institute (now the James Hutton institute), Scottish Natural Heritage and other organisations was also consulted wherever relevant.

Annotated HLA land-use types

The HLA research team allocated land-use designations by hand before transferring the detailed information to the online HLAMap. HES

The HLA map was compiled at 1:25,000. At this scale 100m on the ground is represented by 4mm on the map, meaning that the minimum practical recording unit is one hectare. Following interpretation of the sources and digital mapping of individual land-use types, component parts of the data were double-checked and edited to ensure consistency, and selected field-checking was undertaken to authenticate the work. Polygons were used on the maps to denote the modern land-use. Any discernible archaeological landscapes greater than the one hectare cut-off are recorded within the modern land-use polygons. However, smaller sites can be overlaid on the HLA map by importing them from historic environment records, such as Canmore, to create a comprehensive overview of the historic landscape.

While the aim was always to produce a national map, at times the project focused on specific locations to help address strategic management issues. This approach led to reports on Loch Lomond & the Trossachs and the Cairngorms when they were under consideration for National Park status, with the HLA data subsequently being used by the Park Authorities to inform their strategies for landscape management. HLA reporting was also undertaken to assist the development of management strategies for National Scenic Areas, focusing on the three pilot areas on the Solway coast, and in Wester Ross, and for Scottish National Heritage's special qualities assessment of National Scenic Areas. Similarly, it was used to help understand the landscape context of the newly inscribed Antonine Wall World Heritage Site. For each of these areas, HLA raised awareness of their historical development and the degree of archaeological survival within them, which informed deliberations and decisions on their landscape management.

This book offers an insight into what has been discovered about the landscape of Scotland today through the Historic Land-use Assessment. HLA has provided a wealth of new information about the historical development of Scotland's landscape and about the origin of its modern land-uses. It has added to our understanding of the variety, complexity and time depth of the historic landscape and has created an accessible digital record. The HLA data itself is available through the dedicated website HLAmap, where the digital map can be explored directly or the data downloaded for use in GIS platforms. The website contains a detailed explanation of the historic land-use types and provides case studies to help understand the data and its potential for research and for decision-making. We hope that this volume and the resources available via the HLA website will stimulate interest in Scotland's changing landscape and encourage further research.

Acknowledgements

I would like to thank Historic Environment Scotland for giving me the opportunity to work on this fascinating project and to Piers Dixon, Lesley Macinnes and the HLA team for keeping me right. I would also like to thank the HES Publications team – Jamie Crawford, Christine Wilson and Oliver Brookes – for transforming the bare text into a thing of beauty.

Thanks also go to HES staff including Robert Adam, Tahra Duncan-Clarke, Anne Martin, Derek Smart and David Cowley for their work on the photography, to Georgina Brown for the maps and Adam Welfare and George Geddes for their comments on the text. The text was proofread by Mairi Sutherland and indexed by Linda Sutherland.

This book emerged from the extensive and detailed Historic Land-use Assessment project (HLA). The HLA team included Helen Brown, Karen Clarke, Mel Conway, Richard Craig, Stephen Digney, Jonathan Dowling, Lynn Dyson Bruce, Cole Henley, Sine Hood, Allan Kilpatrick, Siobhan McConnachie, Billy Macrae, Kirsty Millican, Chris Nelson, Oliver O'Grady, Caragh O'Neill, Steven Orr and Hannah Smith under the management of Piers Dixon, Sarah Govan, Richard Hingley, Lesley Macinnes, Mike Middleton and Jack Stevenson. The website that provides online access to the HLA data, prepared by Jill Harden and designed by Lisa McGuckin, Keith Rooney, and Gary Wales, is available at hlamap.org.uk.

Index

Page numbers in *italics* refer to captions

abbeys 36, 37, 40, 59, 87, *95*, 96, 122, *137*, 138, 193
Abercorn, Marquess of 190
Abercorn, Second Marquess of *189*
Aberdeen 45, *68*, 70, 100, 143, 152, 161, 166
Aberdeen Royal Infirmary *72*
Aberdeenshire 76
    beef cattle 15
    canals 152
    crofts/smallholdings 66, 67
    farmhouses 56
    farms 67
    flood defences 122
    forest 187
    forts 27, 30
    golf courses 197, *199*
    herring gutting *158*
    medieval rigs 88
    planned villages 57, 67
    roads 142, *145*
    timber halls 21
    see also names of places in Aberdeenshire
Aberfeldy, Perthshire *141*, 148
Abernethy, Perthshire 88
Aboyne, Aberdeenshire 84, 187
Aboyne and Glentanar, Aberdeenshire 83–4, 179
Achline 107, 112
Adam, John *45*
Adam, Robert *45*
Adam, William *45*, *141*
Agricola, Gnaeus Julius 29, 131
Agricultural Revolution 9, 209, 215
    see also Improvement
agricultural workers 15, 101, 157
agriculture *see* farming
Aird Thunga, Lewis, Outer Hebrides *120*, 124
Airfields of Britain Conservation Trust 170
airports/airfields 170, 172
Airth, Stirlingshire 148
Aithrey, Stirlingshire 148
alabaster 164
Alba 85
Albert, Prince 181, *184*
Allan (river) 148
Allison, Mary 180, 196
Alloa, Clackmannanshire 153
Alloa Tower, Clackmannanshire 195
Alness 103, 157
Alt Clut (Dumbarton Rock), Dunbartonshire 30
altar stones 25
aluminium works, Kinlochleven, Argyll 169, 170
Ancrum 138
Anglo-Saxons 29, 30, 31, 85
    see also Northumbria
Angus
    deer parks 184
    farming 56
    trackways 138
    see also names of places in Angus
animal manure 15, 81, 83, 87–8
animals *see* deer; livestock farming; wildlife
Annandale, Dumfriesshire 184
Annandale, Marquess of 193
anti-tank barriers 169
Antonine Wall 29, 133–4, *133*, 137, 213, 249
Antoninus Pius, Emperor 133
arable farming
    at high levels 25, 81, *81*, 83–4
    Highland-Lowland divide 79
    Improvement 53, 56–7, 104
    Lowlands 104, 227
    medieval 84–9
    Northern Isles 83
    Perthshire 8, 9
    prehistoric 14–15, 25, 81, *81*, 82–3
    reedbeds 160
    see also assarts/assarting; crops; cultivation methods; infields
archery 187, 196, 197, *198*
àrd Nev, Rum, Outer Hebrides 184
Ardkinglas, Argyll 193
Ardoch, Perthshire 7–8, *132*
Ardoch Church, Perthshire 7–8
Ardrishaig, Argyll *151*
ards 14, 21, 81
Ardverikie estate, Inverness-shire 190
Ardverikie House, Loch Laggan, Inverness-shire *189*, 190
Argyll
    charcoal industry 116
    crofting 63, 66, 219
    gardens and orchards 193
    iron industry 116
    power stations 169, 170
    roads 143, 148
    sheep farming 103
    steamships, tourism and 181
    see also names of places in Argyll
Argyll, Duke of 20, 56
Argyll, Earls of 190
Ariundle Oakwood, Strontian 116
Arnisdale, Inverness-shire *50*
Arran 16, 66, 85, 86–7, 177
Arrochar, Argyll 139, 142
Arrochar Alps, Argyll 181, 196
Arthur's O'on (Oven), Stirlingshire 134–5, *135*, 176
assarts/assarting 88–9, 183, 184
Atholl 186
Atholl, Duke of 180, 190–1, 196
Atholl, Earl of 184, 191
Auchinstarry, Dunbartonshire 166
Avenel, Richard 87
Avon (river), Lanarkshire 195
Ayr 45, 112, 148, 153
Ayrshire
    bridges 143, 148
    castles 42, 193
    cattle 15, 104
    coal 104, *158*, 169, 221
    corn mills 117
    Duke of Portland's estates 117
    enclosure 107, 112
    farmhouses 104
    field/land drainage 116, 117

grouse in 190
holiday accommodation 200
houses 51, 104
Improvement 56, 104, 107, 112
Kennedy family, Cassilis 193
population 104
quarrying 104
roads 104, 142
sheep 112
shepherds 103
trees 104
weather 112
see also names of places in Ayrshire
Ayton
Berwickshire 50
Roxburghshire 136

Badenoch, Inverness-shire 57, 186, 204
Balbridie, Aberdeenshire 21
Balcaskie House, Fife *194*
Balfour, Lord 106
Balliol, John 89
Ballochney railway 153
Balmoral Castle, Aberdeenshire *184*
Balmoral estate, Aberdeenshire 181
Balquidder 119
Banchory, Aberdeenshire 76
Banffshire 57, 59, 116–17, 166
Bangour General Hospital, West Lothian 76
Banvie (river) 190
Bar Hill, Dunbartonshire 134
barilla 62, 238
Barncluith, Lanarkshire 195
barns 8, 37, 46, 66, 68
Barr, Ayrshire 142
Barr estate, Galston, Ayrshire 113
Barra, Outer Hebrides 63, 99
barrows 22, 238
see also burial mounds
Barry Buddon, Carnoustie, Angus 173
Barvas, Lewis, Outer Hebrides *64*, 143
Basaglia, Franco 76
Bass Rock *194*
Beardmore's Parkhead Forge, Glasgow *159*
Beauly to Denny electricity line 9
Bede 134
Bedlieston farm, River Don flood defences 122
Bell, Patrick, reaping machine *124*, *125*
Ben Lawers, Perthshire 123
Ben-y-Glo, Perthshire 184
Benalder estate 190
Benmore, Dunoon, Argyll 187, 190
Bennachie, Aberdeenshire 27
Bernera Beg, Outer Hebrides 97
Bertha, Perthshire 29
Berwick 41, 42
Berwickshire 26–7, *29*, 30, 50, 67, 81, *104*
Bilston Glen 176
bings
coal 166
oil shale *162*, 169
biodynamics 97
Black Death, the 95, 204

Black Isle, Ross and Cromarty 66
Black Watch 103
black-faced sheep *114*
blackhouses *48*, *49*, *50*, 63, *65*, 238
Blackwater Reservoir 169, 170
Blair Atholl, Perthshire 184, 190–1
Blair Drummond estate 119
Blair Drummond Moss 122
Blairgowrie, Perthshire 21, 129, 184
Blantyre, Lanarkshire 161
bleacheries 157, 238
bleachfields 161
Board of Agriculture for Scotland 63, 66
Boece, Hector 34, 134, 176, 181–2
bogs *see* peat
Bonawe Iron Furnace 115
Bo'ness, West Lothian 14, 133
Borders
abbeys 37, *137*, 138
Anglo-Saxon territory 85
clearances 53
combine harvesters *125*
Dere Street *137*, 138
holiday accommodation 200
palisaded settlements 81
part of Northumbria 31
railway 153
war veterans' smallholdings 68
see also Cheviot Hills; Southern Uplands
Borders Forest Trust *108*
Boswell, James 113
bothies
hunters' 225
see also huts
Bowmont Forest, Kelso 110
Braan (river) *174*, 196
Braco, Perthshire 7, 8, 9
Braco Castle 8
Braemar, Aberdeenshire *145*, 186, 197
Breadalbane, Earl of 62, 66, 114, 115, 148
Breanski, Alfred de, *The Borders of Loch Fyne* *12*
breweries 157
Bridei, son of Maelchon 30
Bridge of Dee/Bridge of Don, Aberdeen 143
Bridge of Orchy, Argyll 114
bridges 8, 137, 138, *141*, 143, *144*, *146*, 148, 153
British Fisheries Society 59
Britons 30, 31, 84, 85, 134, 176
brochs 26, 27, 31, *32*, *33*, *65*, 238
Brora (river) 82
Brown, John, & Co *158*
Brown, Lancelot 'Capability' 194
Brownhart Law, Roxburghshire 137
Broxburn Oil Works, West Lothian *162*
Broxmouth, East Lothian 26
Bruar (river) 190
Bruce, Sir George, of Carnock 155
Bruce, Sir Michael 135
Bruce, Robert *see* Robert I (the Bruce), King
Bruce, Sir William *194*
Bruntsfield, Edinburgh 197
Buaile-mhor, Ronay, Outer Hebrides 46
Buccleuch, Duchess of 40
Buccleuch, Duke of 103, *188*, 193
Buccleuch estates 53, 103, 122, *188*

Buchan 100
Buchan, Earl of 186
Buchanan, George 46, 79, 100, 135, 164, 166, 176–7
Buckhaven, Fife 45
Buckie, Moray 57
buildings
    early farmers 25
    timber for 113, 114
    see also brochs; castles; duns; farm buildings; forts; houses; huts; industrial sites/buildings; palaces; religious buildings; settlements; shielings; timber halls
burgesses *39*, 41
Burghead, Moray 30
burghs 41, 45, *68*, 88, 101, 155, 156, 215, 217
burial grounds 37, 40, 76–7
burial mounds 81
    see also barrows
burials 21, 22, 40, 76, 176
    see also cremations; crypts; mortuary houses
Burns, Robert 143, 180
Burntisland, Fife 157, 197
Burt, Edmund
    on beliefs about moon 97
    on deer hunting 187
    on Glasgow 70
    on grazing control 107
    on Highland chief 100
    on Highland paths 138
    on Inverness churchyard 40
    on Inverness houses 45
    on Macky's work 40–1
    on quarrying 166
    on road bridges 148
    roads and 139, 141, 143
Bute 34, 209
Buttergask 96
Buzzart Dikes, Blairgowrie, Perthshire 184
byres 31, 46

Caddell, William 157
Caerlaverock Castle, Dumfriesshire *34*
Caesar, Julius 134
Cairngorms 47, 184, 190, 249
cairns *32*, 176, 177, 179
    see also chambered cairns/tombs; clearance cairns
Caithness 22, 56, 63, 66, 68, 219
Caledonian Canal
    Inverness-shire 149, *150*, *151*, 152
        see also Great Glen
Calgacus 131
Callander, Strathyre 125
Callanish, Lewis, Outer Hebrides 23, 25, 99, 209
Cambuskenneth Abbey, Stirlingshire 40
Camelon, West Lothian 29, 136
Campbell, John, of Barcaldine 67
Campbeltown, Argyll 173
camping 125, 229
Camptown, Roxburghshire *111*
Canal Royal de Languedoc/Canal du Midi 149
canals 122, 148–9, *150*, *151*, 152–3, 164, 221
    Canderigg Colliery, Lanarkshire *158*
Candida Casa 177
Canongate, Edinburgh *39*

Cappuck, Roxburghshire 138
Carbeth, Stirlingshire 200
Cardross, Dunbartonshire 34
Cargill 96
Carlisle 133
Carluke, Lanarkshire 166, 169
Carn Dearg, Inverness-shire *200*
Carnegie, Andrew 199
Carnegie Golf Course, Skibo, Sutherland 199
Carnoustie, Angus 173
Carrick, Ayrshire 104, 107
Carriden 133
Carron Ironworks 107, *130*, 153, 155, 157, 161, 166
Carron (river) 134, 161, 177
cars 143, 153, *159*
Carse of Gowrie 100, 128, 160
Carse of Stirling *103*, 119, 122
carts 138, 142
cas-chrom (foot-plough/spade) *83*, *91*, 97–8
Caskieben, Aberdeenshire 56
Cassilis, Ayrshire 193
Castle Law Fort, Midlothian *32*
Castle Street, Aberdeen *68*
Castle Sween, Argyll 34
Castle Tioram, Argyll 34
Castlelaw 173
castles 34, 36–7, 40, 100, 215
    Balmoral *184*
    Braco 8
    Caerlaverock *34*
    Culzean 193
    designed landscapes 36, 191, 193, *193*, *194*
    Drumlanrig 193, *195*
    Drummond 9, 36, 67, 196
    Edinburgh *18*, 30, 34, *119*
    Edzell 36, 191
    forts and 26, 34, *34*, *37*, *133*
    gardens 9, 36, 191, 193
    Hermitage 184
    Inverary 56, 193
    Inverlochy 40
    Kincardine 184
    Kinloch *188*
    Lochore 117
    Marchmont 42
    Maybole 42
    medieval 27, 34
    Newcastle 136
    orchards 36, 193
    parks 36, 100, 184, *193*
    Rough Castle Fort *133*
    Skibo *199*
    stables 37, 56
    Stirling 34, 36, *103*, 191, *193*
    trees and 113
    Urquhart *37*
    see also motte and bailey keeps
cathedrals 36, 37, 85, 215
cattle
    Aberdeenshire 15
    Ayrshire 15, 104
    deer forests replace 188
    fodder 87
    Galloway 53
    grazing control 107

hides 95
Orkney 97
Peeblesshire *108*
pens/enclosures for 87–8, 96
raiding for 84, 96, 103
trade in 100, 138, 153
value 84, 85, 89, 95, 100, 103
see also byres; droving/drove roads; grazing; milking; oxen
Caulfeild, Maj. William 142, *145*, 179
causeways, North and South Uist, Outer Hebrides *144*
Celtic Revival 179
cemeteries *see* burial grounds
ceremonial sites *see* ritual spaces
chambered cairns/tombs 22, *22*, 25, *25*, 238
Chapelcross, Dumfriesshire 166
chapels 30, 177
charcoal 114, 116
Charles I, King 95, 191, *193*
Charles II, King 95, 116, 191
Charlie, Bonnie Prince 187
Charlotte, Queen 67
Chatto Craig, Roxburghshire 204
Cheviot Hills
Hut Knowe cord rig cultivation 81, *81*
see also Borders; Southern Uplands
Cheviot sheep 15, 103, *115*
Chirnside, Berwickshire 67
Christianity 30
Christmas Eve Hunt *188*
churches 7–8, 9, 21, 36, 40, 177
churchyards *see* burial grounds
cities *see* urban areas
Clach a' Charridh/Shandwick Stone, Ross and Cromarty *179*
Clackmannanshire 153, 195
Cladh nan Sasunnach, Loch Maree, Ross and Cromarty 156
Clark, John, *The City of Edinburgh 18*
clearance cairns 81, 84, 211
clearances 53, 203–4, 219
Borders 53
Buccleuch estates 53, 103
Dumfriesshire 53, 104
Highlands 16, 52, 59, 62, 63
Liddesdale 53
Lowlands 16
Nicol's *Lochaber No More 202*
Sutherland 16, 53, 62, 101, 103, *189*
Cleaven Dyke, Perthshire 21
cleits, St Kilda *93*
Clerk, Sir James, of Penicuik 135
climate 14, 16, 25, 89, 95, 211
Clyde resorts, tourism 180
Clyde (river) 26, 84, 133, 172
see also Forth-Clyde canal
Clyde Valley/Clydesdale 128–9
Clydebank shipyard *158*
Clydeside industry, Pennant on 157
coal 20, 104, 123, 142, 157
transport 149, 152, 153, 164, 166, 169
coal bings 166
coal depot, Edinburgh Haymarket *120*
coal-fired electricity generation 169
coal-mining 53, 57, 71, 155, 157, *158*, 166, 169, 221
Cockburn, John 104, 106, 107
Coire-chattachan, Skye, Outer Hebrides 97
Coleridge, Samuel 19, 53, 180, *193*

Coll, Inner Hebrides *33*, 51
Colmonell, Ayrshire 142
combine harvesters 112, *125*
Commissioners of the Forfeited Estates 67
Comrie, Perthshire 172
Comrie Development Trust 172
Congested Districts Board 63
conifer plantations 108, 110, *111*, 116, 125, *171*, 229
Constantine, Emperor 30
coppicing 116, 238
Corbridge 133, 137
cord rig cultivation 81, *81*, 84
Cordiner, Charles *179*
corn *see* grain crops
Corpach Sea Lock, Inverness-shire *150*
Corrieyairack Pass, Inverness-shire 142
cotton mills 57, 59, 161
country houses 40–1, 100, 101, 113, 135, 191, 196
see also designed landscapes
Countryside Act 1968 125, 229
Coupar Angus, Perthshire 96, *145*
Cove, Ayrshire 193
Cowal, Argyll *111*
Craig Phadrig, Inverness-shire 30
Craigshill, Livingston, West Lothian *72*
Crailing, Roxburghshire 138, 152
Cramond, Dere Street *136*
crannogs 27, *33*, 34, 117, 238
Cranston 138
Crathes, Aberdeenshire 21
Craw Stane, Rhynie, Aberdeenshire 30
cremations
stone circles and 25
see also burials
Crianlarich, sheep 103
Crichton, Dere Street and 138
Crieff, Perthshire 7, 9, 141
Crinan Canal, Argyll 149, *150*, *151*, 152–3
Criniveal, North Uist, Outer Hebrides 177
Crofters Act 1886 63, 219
Crofters Commission 63
crofts and crofting 55, 59, 62–3, *64–5*, 66–7, *91*, *93*, 117, 123, 219, 223
see also clearances; smallholdings; subsistence agriculture
Cromwell, Oliver 104
cropmarks 21, 31, 42, 84, 133, 191, 211, 238
crops 15
Arran 87
Ayton, Berwickshire 50
climate and 95
failure, 1782 51
grain *see* grain crops
hay *93*, 122, 191
Highlands 66
Improvement 50, 103
Moray 100
in orchards 128
see also fruit
peas, Arran 87
peat's effect on 81
potatoes 52, 128
rotation 82, 128
St Kilda *93*
Taransay 97
turnips 112

war veterans' smallholdings 68
see also cultivation methods
Croy Hill, Stirlingshire 134
Cruachan power station, Argyll 169
cruives 161, 238
crypts 37
Culdees 9
Culross, Fife 155
Culross Abbey/Culross House, Fife *95*
Culsalmond, Aberdeenshire 157
cultivation methods
    Taransay 97
    see also digging; fertilisers; ploughing; rigs
Cultybraggan, Comrie, Perthsire 172
Culzean Castle 193
Cumbernauld, Dunbartonshire *72, 73*, 71, 217
Cunningham, Ayrshire 107, 193
cursus monuments 21–2, 238

Dairsie, Fife 40
Dale, David 161
Dalkeith Palace 40
Dalmally, Argyll 62, 66, 116
Dalriada, kingdom of 29, 30, 31, 85
Dalriadan Scots 29, 30, 31, 79, 134, 176, 181–3
Dalserf, Lanarkshire 128
Dalswinton, Dumfriesshire 57
dams 135, *165*
Darien Scheme 156
Darnaway, Moray 34
Darnley, Henry, Lord 196
David I, King 15, 34, 41, 85
David II, King 36, 40, 86, 95
davochs/*dabhaichean* 85–6
de Breanski, Alfred, *The Borders of Loch Fyne 12*
Dee (river) 122, 143, 211
deer 66, 89, 116, 181–91, *184*, *188–9*, 215
Defoe, Daniel
    on Aberdeen 45, 143
    on burghs and commerce 45
    on Carrick, Ayrshire 104, 107
    on Drumlanrig Castle *195*
    on Enterkin Path 139
    on Forth-Clyde canal 148, 149
    on Galloway 53, 104
    on gardens and orchards 193
    on Glasgow 45, 70
    on industry 155
    on legends 177
    on Lowlands farming 96
    on mining 166
    on road bridges 143, 148
    on tree planting 116
Deira 137
Denny to Beauly electricity line 9
Department of Agriculture (Scotland) 68
Dere Street *136*, 137–138, *137*, 213
designed landscapes 36, *45*, 106, *110*, *174*, 191, 193–196, *193–195*, 197, 248
    see also gardens; orchards; parks; woodlands
digging 15, 97
    see also spades
Dingleton Hospital, Melrose, Roxburghshire 76

Dingwall 97
distilleries 123, 223
ditches
    Antonine Wall remnants 133, 213
    assarts and 183
    Carse of Stirling drainage 119
    cursus monuments 21
    enclosure 107, 112
    forts 26–7, *29*, *32*
    henges 23
    lazy beds 97
    Ormiston, East Lothian 106
    Panmure 191
    shown by cropmarks 84
    Wade's roads 142
    woodland management 116
    see also field/land drainage
Division of Commonties Act 1695 101
Don (river) 122, 143, 152, 161
Donald, King 31
Donald the Hammerer 96
Doon Hill, East Lothian 31
Doon (river), Ayrshire 143, 148
Dornoch Firth 71, *199*, 217
Dornock, Dumfriesshire 52, 104, 106
Douglas, David 196
Douglas Mill, Lanarkshire 112
Douglas Water 20
Douglasmuir, Angus 21
dovecots 89, 135
drainage
    longhouses, Perthshire 31
    see also field/land drainage
Dreghorn barracks 173
Drip Moss 122
droving/drove roads 138, 225
Drum, Aberdeenshire 187
Drumlanrig, Dumfriesshire 139
Drumlanrig Castle, Dumfriesshire 193, *195*
Drummond Castle, Perthshire 9, 36, 67, 196
Drummond, John, Lord 96
Drumoak, Aberdeenshire 117, 122
Duirinish, Skye, Outer Hebrides *120*
Duke of Portland's estates, Ayrshire 117
Dumbarton Rock 30
Dumfries 180
Dumfries and Galloway 68, 116
Dumfriesshire
    clearances 53, 104
    dykes 104, 112
    farmhouses 52, 104
    farming 104
    gardens 160–1
    hedges 104, 112, 193
    holiday accommodation 200
    houses 52, 160–1
    Improvement 104
    industry 160, *163*
    roads 13, 132, 142
    urban areas 41, 45
    villages 57, 104
    see also names of places in Dumfriesshire
Dun Anlaimh Crannog, Coll, Inner Hebrides *33*
Dun Bhoraraig, Islay, Inner Hebrides 27
Dun Carloway, Lewis, Outer Hebrides *32*, *65*

Dunadd, Argyll 30
Dunbartonshire
    Brown's shipyard *158*
    houses 53
    quarry 166
    recreational area 134
    Singer Factory *159*, 176
    Sloy-Awe Hydro-Electric Scheme *164*
    see also names of places in Dunbartonshire
Dundee 45, *73*, *75*, 77, 170
Dundee Law 75
Dundonnel, Loch Maree, Ross and Cromarty 180
Dundrennan Abbey, Kirkcudbrightshire 59
Dundurn, Perthshire 30–1
Dunfermline, Fife 96, 143, 193
Dunfermline Abbey, Fife 36, 37, 40, 193
Dunipace, Stirlingshire 176–7
Dunkeld, Perthshire *174*, 180, 196
Dunkeld House, Perthshire *174*
Dunoon, Argyll 116, 142, 152, 187, 190
duns 26, 211, 238
Dunsinane, Perthshire 31
Dupplin, Earl of *see* Hay, Sir George, of Nether Liff
Durness, Sutherland 63
Dyce, Aberdeenshire 56
dykes
    assarts and 183
    Charles II's laws 95
    deer dykes 183
    Dumfriesshire 104, 112
    Eden croft, Guardbridge 117
    Garvock deer park 187
    head-dykes 88, 97, 106, 204
    hedges and 112
    Improvement 104, 106
    Kirkden, Forfarshire 112
    Libberton, Lanarkshire 95
    Outer Hebrides 96, 97
    removal 113
    St Kilda 93
    woodlands 116, 128
    see also Cleaven Dyke; walls; White Dyke
Dysart, Fife 45

Eaglesham, Renfrewshire 57, 59
Earn (river) 7, 31
earthworks 21, 26, 27, 97, 133, 193
    see also embankments
Easdale, Argyll 166
East Kilbride, Lanarkshire 71, 217
East Lothian
    designed landscapes *110*, 191
    farming 84, 104, 106
    hedges 104, 106
    holiday accommodation 200
    Improvement 104, 106
    palaces 31, 40
    trees 104, 191
    villages 104, 169
    see also names of places in East Lothian
East Warriston House, Edinburgh 77
Eckford, Dere Street and 138
Eday, Orkney 166

Eddystone lighthouse 148
Eden croft, Guardbridge 117
Eden (river) 122
Edgar, King 149
Edinburgh
    after Union of the Parliaments 42
    Bruntsfield 197
    burgh 41
    Canongate 39
    capital city 42
    Clark's *The City of Edinburgh* *18*
    Defoe on 45
    Dere Street and 138, 213
    East Warriston House 77
    fruit trade 129
    gardens *39*, 193
    George Square 70
    golf courses 196, 197
    Gordon of Rothemay's view of *39*
    Haymarket Coal Depot *120*
    High Street 42
    houses 42, 70
    Industrial Revolution's effects 70, 71
    Leith Walk 71
    M8 motorway 143
    Meadows, the 70
    migration to 70
    Muir on 71
    New Town *18*, 70
    Nor' Loch 119
    Old Town *18*, 42, 70
    Orkney woman in 180
    Princes Street 71
    railways 153
    St Andrew's Square 70
    social structures 71
    streets 138–9
    tourism from 180
    Union Canal *151*
    Warriston Cemetery 77
    water supply 170
    see also Leith
Edinburgh Airport 172
Edinburgh Castle *18*, 30, 34, *119*
Edward I, King 88, 137
Edward VII, King 153
Edzell, Angus 46
Edzell Castle, Angus 36, 191
Eglinton, Earl of 57
Eildon Hills *182*
Eilean a'Ghiorr, North Uist *48*
Eilean Fladday, Outer Hebrides *120*
Eithinyn ap Boddw Adaf 84
electricity *see* Beauly to Denny electricity line; hydro-electric schemes; power stations
Elgin, Moray 88, 104, 117
embankments 122, 133, 141–2
    see also earthworks
emigration 50, 62, 66, 77, *202*
enclosure
    Improvement 15, 50, 88, 101, 104, 107, 112–13, 116, 204
    prehistoric farming 25
    Restoration period 95
    war veterans' smallholdings 67
    see also dykes; fences; hedges; walls

enclosures
    Carrick, Ayrshire 104, 107
    deer hunting 184, 187
    grazing control 95–6, 215
    Hut Knowe, Roxburghshire 81, *81*
    livestock 87–8, 89, 96, *98*
    Lunan, Angus 100
    medieval farming 87–8
    prehistoric farming 81
    Rhynie, Aberdeenshire 30
    Southern Uplands 89
    woodland/forest sites 128
    see also cursus monuments; fields; henges; hill-forts; parks
Enterkin Path, Drumlanrig, Dumfriesshire 139
Erisko, Skye, Outer Hebrides 66
Errol, Perthshire 160
Estates, the 41, 238
Ethodius, legendary king 181–2
Ettrick, Selkirkshire 184
evictions *see* clearances

factories *see* industrial sites/buildings
Fair Isle, Shetland *90*
Falkirk, Stirlingshire 14, *130*
    see also Carron Ironworks
farm buildings 53, 56, 68, 70, 101, 172, 173, 227
    see also barns; byres; cleits; farmhouses; hen house; shielings
farm workers 15, 101, 157
farmhouses 8
    Aberdeenshire 56
    Ayrshire 104
    Dumfriesshire 52, 104
    Improvement 53, 56, 101, 104, 227
    modern uses 57
    trees and 113
farming 14–16, 79–129, 227
    abbeys and 36
    Angus 56
    at higher elevations 25, *81*, 95
    designed landscapes and 194
    geology and 209
    Improvement 50–1, 53, 56–7, 88, 101, 103–4, 106–7, 112–17, 194, 219
    industry and 157
    Kirkcudbright Training Area 173
    Lowlands 68, 88, 96, 104, 227
    mechanisation 56, 68, *90*, 112–13, 122, *124*, *125*, 227
        see also prairie farmland
    medieval 84–9
    Mertoun House, Berwickshire *104*
    monasteries 15, 36, 85
    moon's influence 97
    prehistoric 14–15, 20–3, 25, 79, 81, *81*, 82–3, 211, 227
    water transport and 152
    see also arable farming; crofting; field systems; fields; grazing; livestock farming; subsistence agriculture
farms 8, 77
    Aberdeenshire 67
    Bedlieston 122
    Caithness 66
    Grassic Gibbon on 204
    Highlands 46, 67
    Improvement 50, 104

    layout 15
    Lowlands 66, 209
    Mertoun House, Berwickshire *104*
    Upper Chatto, Roxburghshire 204
    war veterans' smallholdings 68
Farr, Sutherland 59, 62
Faslane, Dunbartonshire 172
Fearn
    Angus 179
    Ross and Cromarty 172
fences 25, 97, 107, 112, 113, 116, 183, 184
    see also dykes; hedges
Fender (river) 190
Ferniehurst 180
fertilisers 15, 52, 81, 83, 87–8, 96, 99, 117, 122
    see also soil improvement; tathing
Fettercairn, Kincardineshire 184
field boundaries 66, 68, 81, 82, 84, 106, 117, 128, 138
    see also dykes; field systems; hedges; walls
field systems
    Chatto Craig, Roxburghshire 204
    cord rig cultivation, hill-forts 81
    crofts *64*, 67
    medieval 88
    medieval settlements erased by 41
    Ormiston, East Lothian 104
    prehistoric 81, 82–3, 211
    Shetland 62
    shielings 175
field/land drainage
    Ayrshire 116, 117
    Carse of Stirling 119, 122
    effect on reedbeds 160, *160*
    effect on rivers 119, 122
    Improvement 103, 104, 116–17, 119, 122
    Loch Spynie 104, 117
    Lowlands 117
    monasteries 96
    orchards 128
    ploughed ridges 15
    Rossie Drain 117, 122
    Stirling 104, 122
    tiles for 117
    see also ditches; land reclamation
fields 84, 101, 227
    farm machinery and 112–13
    Galloway 106
    Highlands 106
    Improvement 106, 219, 227
    increased size 56
    Lanarkshire 112, 128
    layout 15
    Linlithgow, West Lothian *99*
    Lothian 106
    Lowlands 106, 113, 227
    Mertoun House, Berwickshire *104*
    National Forest Estate 229
    Perthshire 8
    Roxburghshire *81*, 204
    St Kilda *93*
    Shapinsay, Orkney 106
    Southern Uplands 106
    war veterans' smallholdings 68, 70
    woodland/forest sites 128
    see also rigs

258 Index

Fife
    bridges *146*, 148, 153
    coal-mining 169, 221
    gardens/orchards *42*, *95*
    golf 197, *199*
    villages *42*, 155
    see also names of places in Fife
Firth of Clyde 29, 133, 148, 213
Firth of Forth 14, 29, 133, 148, 213
Fiscavaig, Skye, Outer Hebrides 63
fish traps 161
fishing 57, *59*, *60*, 62, *68*, 97, 139, *158*
    leisure pursuit 181, *184*, *189*, 191
    see also salmon fishing
Flanders Moss 122
flood defences 122
    see also field/land drainage
Fochabers, Moray 59
foot-plough (*cas-chrom*) 83, *91*, 97–8
Ford, Henry 143
Forest Lodge, Glen Tilt, Perthshire *188*
Forest of Selkirk 88
forestry *111*, 124–5, 128, 172, 229
    see also conifer plantations; timber; trees; woodlands
Forestry Commission 124–5, 128, 225, 229, 248
forests
    Blair Atholl 191
    Bowmont *110*
    Darnaway 34
    deer 66, 184, 187, *188*, 190, 215
    deforestation 113–16
    enclosures/fields 128
    forts in 128, 229
    Gaick 190
    hunting forests 183–4
    industrial sites in 128
    Dr Johnson on 113
    Kingshill 169
    medieval 88
    National Forest Estate 229
    planting 113
    Reforesting Scotland 200
    rigs in 128
    royal forests *87*, 190
    Selkirk 88
    shielings in 128, 229
    Tyninghame *110*
    see also assarts/assarting; trees; woodlands
Forfar Loch 117
Forfarshire 112, 117
forfeited estates 67, 239
Forlani, Paolo, *Scotia* 207
Forres, Moray 193
Fort Augustus, Inverness-shire 141, 142, *150*
Fort Augustus Locks, Caledonian Canal, Inverness-shire *151*
Fort George, Nairnshire 141, *145*, 173
Fort William, Inverness-shire 141, 142, *150*
Forteviot, Perthshire 31
Forth Bridge *146*, 148
Forth Bridges *146*, 148, 153
Forth Rail Bridge *146*, 153
Forth (river) 26, 31, 104, 119, 122, 133, 155, 211
    see also Bass Rock
Forth Road Bridge *146*, 148
Forth-Clyde canal 148–9, 152, 153

Fortingall, Perthshire 59
forts
    Caerlaverock Castle, Dumfriesshire *34*
    Castle Law, Midlothian *32*
    castles and 26, 34, *34*, *37*, *133*
    ditches 26–7, *29*, *32*
    in forests 128, 229
    Habchester 26–7, *29*, 81
    Kirkcudbright Training Area 173
    medieval, Dundee Law *75*
    prehistoric 173, 211, 229
    Rhynie, Aberdeenshire 30
    Roman 8, 29, 133, *133*, 134, 213
    Rough Castle Fort, Stirlingshire *133*
    Trimontium fort, Roxburghshire 137
    Urquhart Castle, Inverness-shire *37*
    White Cathertun, Angus 27
    see also crannogs; hill-forts
Foyer/Loch Mhor power station, Inverness-shire 169
Fraser, Jim 173
Fraser, Rev. Paul 20
Freuchie, Fife 42
Friarton Bridge, Perthshire *144*
Frisian influence, early medieval period 31
fruit 89, *95*, 100, 128–9, 193, 195
    see also orchards

Gaick Forest, Cairngorms 190
Gairloch, Ross and Cromarty 63, 66, *198*
Galashiels, Selkirkshire 47, 56, 161
Galloway 85
    chapel 177
    Defoe on 53, 104
    geology 209
    holiday accommodation 200
    Improvement 56, 104, 106
    livestock 53
    medieval rigs 88
    Normans in 34
    rig and furrow ploughing 15
    see also Dumfries and Galloway
Galston, Ayrshire 113, 116, 117
game 89, 187, 190
    see also grouse; wildlife
Garden, Alexander, of Troup 87–8
gardens 41, 100, 193
    burghs 88
    castles 9, 36, 191, 193
    Edinburgh *39*, 193
    Fife *42*, *95*
    fruit trees 128
    Glasgow Cathedral 85
    Gordonstoun, Moray 191
    Hazelbank, Lanarkshire 128
    Hebrides 99
    Improvement 194
    Lincluden Abbey 193
    medieval 84–5, 89
    medieval rigs become 88
    in National Land-use Database 248
    Panmure 191
    Perthshire 88, 190–1
    planned villages 59, 128

Renaissance *95*, 191, 193
town/village plots 41, 42, 88
Wanlockhead and Leadhills, Dumfriesshire 160–1
see also designed landscapes; orchards
Garry (river) 190
Gartcosh steelworks 173
Garvock, Kincardineshire 187
Gaston III, Comte de Foix, hunting scene *87*
geology 209
see also mining; quarrying
George I, King 139
George II, King 67
George III, King 67
George, Bishop of Dunkeld 96
George Square, Edinburgh 70
Gibbon, Lewis Grassic 56–7, 77, 203–4
Gillies, Sir William, *The Red Field 6*
Giric (Pictish king) 30–31
Glasgow *41*
Antonine Wall and 133
Beardmore's Parkhead Forge *159*
Burt on 70
Defoe on 45, 70
fruit trade 128
Hutchesontown *73*
Industrial Revolution 71
industry 157, 217
Kelvingrove Art Gallery and Museum 170
Knightswood 71
Linwood *159*
Merchant City 70
Monklands Canal 152
motorways 143
Muir on 71
Necropolis 76–7
New Town 70
Pennant on 70, 157
railways 153
road bridge 148
St Kilda man in 41, 47
social structures 71
tourism from 180
Trongate 70
Union Canal *151*
Union of the Parliaments and 42
water supply 170
Glasgow Cathedral 85
glass-making industry 116, 155
Glen Clunie, Perthshire *145*
Glen Esk 139
Glen Nant, Taynuilt, Argyll 116
Glen O' Dee Hospital, Banchory, Aberdeenshire 76
Glen Orchy, Argyll *110*
Glen Tanar, Aberdeenshire 187
Glen Tilt, Perthshire 166, *188*
Glenbranter, Cowal, Argyll *111*
Glencroe 143
Glendochart 47
Glenfinnan Viaduct, Inverness-shire 153
Glenorchy, deforestation 115–16
Glenrothes, Fife *72*, 71, 217
Glensanda, Loch Linnie 221
Gododdin 30, 31, 84, 176
gold mining 221
golf 68, 170, 181, 196–7, *198–9*, 200

goods transport 138, 143, 149, 152, 153, 164, 221
coal 149, 152, 153, 164, 166, 169
grain 142, 152, 153
horses and *110*, 138, 143
iron industry 149, 153
lime/limestone 153
peat 123, 223
timber *110*, 153
see also carts; trade
Gordon, Duke of 103
Gordon of Rothemay, view of Edinburgh *39*
Gordonstoun, Moray 191
Gorizia, Italy 76
grain crops
Arran 87
barley 50, 52, 81, 97, 98–9, 123
beir (bere) 98–9
climate and 95
grinding 81, *91*, 241
Improvement 103
moon's influence 97
Moray 100
oats 50, 81
spelt 81
Taransay 97
wheat 81
grain market 56
grain trade 142, 152, 153
Grampians, shielings 47
granaries, Montrose, Angus 45
Grant, Reverend Samuel 7
gravestones 40, 176
graveyards *see* burial grounds
grazing
assarts and 88, 183
Carrick, Ayrshire 104
common land 101
control of 95–6, 107, 113, 116, 183, 184, 215
enclosure 107
Highlands 14, 209, 225
Lowlands 209
moorland 81
Moray 100
in National Land-use Database 248
outfields 87
peat's effect on 81
Perthshire 46
shown by cropmarks 84
Southern Uplands 209
see also rough grazing; shielings
Great Glen *37*, *111*
see also Caledonian Canal
Greendyke bing, West Lothian 169
Greenock, Renfrewshire 153
Greenwich park, London 116
grouse *184*, 190, 191, 225
Guardbridge 117
gunpowder factory, Braco, Perthshire 8
Gurness broch, Orkney *33*
Gurnkirk 153
Gwallawg, King 84

Habchester, Berwickshire 26–7, *29*
Haddington
    East Lothian 190
        see also Yester
Hadrian's Wall 29, 133–4, 137
Halliday, Strat 26
halls, timber 21, 30, 31, 211
Hamilton, Lanarkshire 57, 128, 195
Hamilton, Duke of 104
Hamilton, James, 2nd Marquess of Abercorn *189*
Harris, Outer Hebrides 27, 66
Harris, David 179
Harthill Bypass, M8 143
Hawick, Roxburghshire 180, 184
hay *93*, 122, 191
Hay, Sir George, of Nether Liff 155–6
Hay, John, 1st Marquis and 2nd Earl of Tweeddale 116, 191
Haymarket Coal Depot, Edinburgh *120*
Hazelbank, Lanarkshire 128
Heatherhall Woods, Ladybank, Fife 117
Hebrides
    crofting townships 55, 63, *64*, 66
    crofts and crofting 62, 63, *64*, *65*, 66, *91*
    deer hunting 184, 187
    dykes 96, 97
    houses 46–7, *51*, 52, 62, 63, *65*, 66
    Improvement 56
    lotters 62, 66
    mills 161
    orchards 99
    peat 66
    shielings 47
    trees 187
    see also names of individual islands
hedges 95
    Dalserf, Lanarkshire 128
    deer dykes 183
    Dumfriesshire 104, 112, 193
    dykes and 112
    Galloway 104
    grazing control 95
    Improvement 15, 104, 106, 107, 112, 227
    Kilmarnock, Ayrshire 107, 112
    Kirkden, Forfarshire 112
    Lowlands 113
    medieval 87, 95, 113
    Ormiston, East Lothian 104, 106
    Panmure 191
    prairie farmland *127*
    removal 113
    wildlife and 112
Helmsdale (river) *32*
hen house, Morar, Inverness-shire *49*
henges 22–3, 25, *25*, 99, 209, 239
    see also stone circles
Hepburn Gardens, St Andrews, Fife 88
Hepburn, John, abbot/prior 37
Hermitage, Dunkeld, Perthshire *174*
Hermitage Castle, Roxburghshire 184
Hess, Rudolf 172
Highland Boundary Fault/Highland Line 209
    see also Highland-Lowland divide
Highland dress 186
Highland-Lowland divide 16–17, 79, 209
Highlands
    bridges 148
    canals 149
    cattle trade 100
    clearances 16, 52, 59, 62, 63
    cord rig cultivation 81
    crofts and crofting 59, 62, 63, 66–7, 219
    crops 66
    deer hunting 186–7, *188*
    education 177, 179
    emigration 50, 62
    farmhouses 56
    farms 46, 67
    fields 106
    in Forlani's *Scotia 207*
    grazing 14, 209, 225
    houses 46, 51, 56
    Improvement 50, 56, 59, 62, 66, 106
    land management 96–7
    livestock 66
    Lowlands, Highlanders in 179
    migration from Highlands 50, 51, 63
    Monadhliath mountains 225
    Norse and 149
    paths/trackways 138, 139
    peat 123, 223, 225
    Pennant on 51, 187
    population 62–3
    power stations *165*
    roads 139, 141–2
    Romanticism and 181
    rough grazing 225
    settlements 46–7, 219
    shielings 47–9
    sporting estates *184*
    sports 187
    tourism 179, 181
    trees 14
    woodland management 114–16
    see also crofts and crofting; Highland-Lowland divide
Hill of Durn, Banffshire 166
Hill o' Many Stanes 211
hill-forts 26–7, *29*, 30–1, 34, 46, *75*, 81, 128, 204
Hillend farm, Lanarkshire 112
'Hills of Dunipace' 176–7
Hilton of Cadboll symbol stone *179*
Historic Land-use Assessment (HLA) project 207, 248–9
holiday accommodation 200
Holy Loch 152
Holyrood Abbey 37
Holyroodhouse, palace of 37, 40, 191
Hopetoun House, West Lothian *45*, 194–5
horses 53, 68, 87, *91*, 95, 106–7, *110*, 112–13, 138, 143, 181
hospitals *72*, *73*, 71, 76, *137*, 138, *200*
Hougharry, North Uist, Outer Hebrides 177
house platforms 71, 204
houses 31, 217
    Arnisdale, Inverness-shire *50*
    assarts and 88
    Ayrshire 51, 104
    Ayton, Berwickshire 50
    in burghs 41, 45
    Carse of Stirling drainage 119
    crofting townships 59, 62, 63, 66, 67, 219
    Dalriadan Scots 31
    Dingleton Hospital, Melrose, Roxburghshire 76

Duke of Hamilton's and Earl of Strathmore's estates 104
Dumfriesshire 52, 160–1
Edinburgh 42, 70
feuing and 53, 57
Galashiels, Selkirkshire 161
Hebrides 46–7, *51*, 52, 62, 63, *65*, 66
Highlands 46, 51, 56
Improvement 50, 51–3, 57, 157
Inchmurrin, Loch Lomond 187
Industrial Revolution and 70, 71, 217
Inverary, new town 19–20
Inverness 45
Kilconquhar, Fife *42*
Lanarkshire 51, 195
Loch Lomondside, Dunbartonshire 53
Lowlands 51, 219
medieval villages 42
medieval/post-medieval 215
in National Land-use Database 248
Northern Isles and Western Isles 31
Perth 45
Perthshire 7, 9, 51
Picts' 31
prehistoric farmers 21
Ross and Cromarty 66, 180
St Kilda 46–7
Tongue, Sutherland 53
trees and 113
urban areas 45, 71, 77
war veterans' 67–8, 70
Dorothy Wordsworth on 19–20, 53, 56, 59, 123, 161, 180, 195
workers' 164, 169, 221
see also blackhouses; country houses; farmhouses; hunting lodges; lonchards/lunkards; longhouses; roundhouses; shielings; wheelhouses
housing estates *73*, 71
Houston, Renfrewshire 193
Hownam, Dere Street and 138
hunter-gatherers 14, 20–1
see also prehistoric communities
hunters' bothies 225
Hunterston B nuclear power station, Ayrshire 169
hunting 34, *87*, 89, 181–4, *184*, 186–7, *188–9*, 190–1, *193*, 215
hunting forests 183–4
hunting lodges *189*, 190, 191, *200*, 215
Huntly, Marquis of 186
hut circles 25, *32*, 173, 239
Hut Knowe, Roxburghshire 81, *81*
Hutchesonstown, Glasgow *73*
huts 20, 21, 25, 30, 31, 200, 225
see also bothies; Nissen huts; shielings
hydro-electric schemes *164*, *165*, 169, 170

Improvement 15–16, 49–53, 56–7, 59, 88, 143, 203
Argyll 56, 103
Ayrshire 56, 104, 107, 112
Berwickshire 50, *104*
Caithness 56
crofting townships 66
crops 50, 103
davochs/*dabhaichean* 86
definition 239
Dumfriesshire 104
dykes 104, 106

East Lothian 104, 106
emigration 50, 62
enclosure 15, 50, 88, 101, 104, 107, 112–13, 116, 204
farm buildings 53, 56, 101, 227
farmhouses 53, 56, 101, 104, 227
farming 50–1, 53, 56–7, 88, 101, 103–4, 106–7, 112–17, 194, 219
field boundaries 106
field/land drainage 103, 104, 116–17, 119, 122
fields 106, 219, 227
Galloway 56, 104, 106
gardens and 194
hedges 15, 104, 106, 107, 112, 227
Highlands 50, 56, 59, 62, 66, 106
houses 50, 51–3, 57, 157
Lanarkshire 56
Linlithgow, West Lothian *99*
livestock farming 15, 16, 49, 53, 103–4
Lothian, fields 106
Lowlands 50, 56, 101, 104, 106, 116
medieval field systems preserved during 88
migration 50–1, 53, 56, 77
Outer Hebrides 56
Pennant on 50, 103
runrig elimination *99*, 101, 104, 106
St Kilda *93*
Shapinsay, Orkney 106
sheep 49, 103, 219
smallholdings 67, 219
Southern Uplands 106
Sutherland 62
trees 15, 104, 113
walls 15, 107, 227
see also Agricultural Revolution; clearances; crofts and crofting; enclosure
Inchaffray Abbey, Perthshire 96
Inchmurrin, Loch Lomond 187
Inchtuthil, Perthshire, Roman fort 29
Industrial Revolution 70–3, 161, 209, 215, 217, 221
industrial sites/buildings 77, 128, 217
industrial villages 155, 169
industry 53, 131–71, 176
farm workers and 15, 101
geology and 209
Glasgow 157, 217
golf club manufacture, Perth 197
gunpowder factory, Braco, Perthshire 8
migration to urban areas 15, 217
planned villages 57
smallholdings and 67, 68
timber for 229
see also charcoal; fishing; glass-making industry; iron industry; kelp; mining; oil industry; quarrying; tanning industry
infields 62, 87, 106, 204, 239
infrastructure 131–71
see also bridges; drainage; motorways; power stations; roads; water supply; waterways
inhumations *see* burials
Inverary, Argyll 19–20, 46, 59, 123, 143, 148
Inverary Castle, Argyll 56, 193
Inverfalla 96
Inverlochy Castle, Argyll 40
Invernahyle, Appin 96
Inverness 40, 45, 104, 153, 217
Inverness-shire
blackhouses *49*

crofting county 63, 219
deer hunting 187
forts 30, *37*
grazing control 107
hen house *49*
sheep 187
Urquhart Castle *37*
see also names of places in Inverness-shire
Inverurie, Aberdeenshire 152
Iona 30, 99, 177
Iron Age *32*, *75*, *81*
see also brochs; crannogs
iron industry 153, 155, 157, 164, 166, 221
Beardmore's Parkhead Forge, Glasgow *159*
burghs 156
ironstone quarries 161, 221
pollution 161
timber for 114, 115–16, 156
transport 149, 153
woodlands 115–16
see also Carron Ironworks
Irvine, Ayrshire 45
Irvine family, Drum, Aberdeenshire 187
Islay, Inner Hebrides 27, 66, 99, 166

Jacobite Rebellions 9, 45, 139, 179, 187
James IV, King 89, 113, 148, *198*
James V, King 184, 186, 191
James VI and I, King 42, 155, 156, 190, *198*
James VI Golf Course, Perth 199
James VII and II, King 40, 95, 156
Jamie, Kathleen 20, 29, 175
Jedburgh, Roxburghshire *137*, 138, 183
John of Fordun 79, 133, 134, 184
Johnson, Dr Samuel 113
Jones, Maxwell 76
Julius' Palace 134
Jura, Inner Hebrides 47, 184, 187
Jura, Sound of *151*

kale-yards 100, 239
Kames, Lord 119
Keir Burn 8
Keith family, Earls Marischal 187
kelp 62, 239
Kelso *110*, 180
Kelvingrove Art Gallery and Museum, Glasgow 170
Kenmore, Perthshire 148
Kennedy family, Cassilis, Ayrshire 193
Kenneth mac Alpin 31
Kilconquhar, Fife *42*
Killin 107, 112
Killoch Colliery, Ochiltree, Ayrshire *158*
Kilmarnock, Ayrshire 51, 107, 112, 117, 152
Kilmuir, Skye, Outer Hebrides 62–3, 97
Kilmun, Argyll 152
kilns, Montrose, Angus 45
Kilphedir Broch, Sutherland *32*
Kilsyth, Stirlingshire 152
Kincardine, Fife 148, 184
Kincardineshire 16, 184, 187, 209

King James VI Golf Course, Perth 199
King's Knot, Stirling Castle 191, *193*
King's Well, Drum, Aberdeenshire 187
Kingshill Forest, Carluke, Lanarkshire 169
Kingussie, Inverness-shire 141, 190
Kinloch Castle, Rum *188*
Kinlochleven 142, 169, 170
Kinloss, Moray 173
Kinloss Abbey 193
Kinnedar, Moray 30
Kinneil, West Lothian 134
Kintyre, Argyll 149, *150*
see also Crinan Canal
Kirkcaldy, Fife 45
Kirkcudbright 45, 173
Kirkcudbright Training Area 173
Kirkcudbrightshire 21, 59, 122
Kirkden, Forfarshire 112
Kirkibost, North Uist, Outer Hebrides 177
Kirkintilloch, Dunbartonshire 153
Kirkmabreck North, Kirkcudbrightshire 21
Kirkmahoe, Dumfriesshire 152
Kirkpatrick, Dumfriesshire 190
Kirkpatrick, Dunbartonshire 133
Kirriemuir, Angus 117, 136
Knaik (river) 8
Knapdale 149
Knightswood, Glasgow 71
Knoydart, Inverness-shire *189*
Knoydart Foundation *189*
Kyle, Ayrshire 104, 193
Kyle of Sutherland 189
Kylesku Bridge, Sutherland/Assynt *144*

lades 122, 164, 221, 239
Ladies Hill, Stirling Castle 191
Lady Hill, Smailholm Tower, Roxburghshire *36*
Lady Victoria Colliery 169
Ladybank, Fife, Heatherhall Woods 117
Ladybank Golf Club, Fife 199
Laggan, Inverness-shire 103
Lammermuirs 137, 209
Lanarkshire
farms 112
fields 112, 128
houses 51, 195
Improvement 56
orchards 128
planned villages 57, 128
railways 153
see also names of places in Lanarkshire
Land Character Assessment 248
land clearance see assarts/assarting; clearances; Improvement
land division 101
land management, Highlands 96–7
land measurement, davochs 85–6
land ownership 101
land reclamation 117, 119, 122, 160
see also field/land drainage
Land Resettlement Act 1919 67
land use 10, 128, 203, 207–29, 248
landscapes *174*, 175–7, 179–81, *182*, 190–1
see also designed landscapes

Larkhall, Lanarkshire 57
Larotoun 96
Lathrisk, Fife, canal 122
Laurencekirk, Kincardineshire 187
Law of Windsor, Angus 179
Lawson, Dr David 76
Lawton, burn of 96
lazy beds 65, 93, 97, 215, 240
lead mining 163, 164, 169
Leadhills, Dumfriesshire 57, 160–1
Lealty estate, Alness 157
Learable, Sutherland 100
leather trade 95
    see also tanning industry
leisure 68, 119, 125–8, 134, 166, 175–200, 229
    see also fishing; hunting; sport; tourism; walking
Leith 42, 77, 119, 153, 197
Leith Walk, Edinburgh 71
Lenabo, Peterhead, Aberdeenshire 172
Lennox family 187
Leuchars, Fife 91, 173
Levern Water 161
Lewis, Outer Hebrides
    Aird Thunga 120, 124
    Barvas 64, 143
    beir (bere) 98–99
    Callanish 23, 25, 99, 209
    crofts and crofting 63, 64, 66
    Dun Carloway 32, 65
    houses 52, 65
    lazy beds 65
    Lochs 171
    peat 98–99, 120, 123, 124, 171
    roads 143
    seaweed as fertiliser 99
    shielings 47, 49
    Stornoway 52, 123, 143
Libberton, Lanarkshire 51, 57, 95
Liddesdale, Roxburghshire 53, 183
lime/limestone 104, 153, 157, 161, 166, 221
Lincluden Abbey, Dumfriesshire 193
linen *see* textile industries
Linlithgow, West Lothian 45, 98, 99
Linwood, Glasgow 159
Little Tulloch, Aboyne, Aberdeenshire 187
livestock farming
    Ardoch estate, Perthshire 8
    crofting townships 66
    enclosures 87–8, 89, 96, 98
    Galloway 53
    Improvement 15, 16, 49, 53, 103–4
    prehistoric 15, 25, 82
    Scord of Brouster, Shetland 81
    trade 89, 95, 100, 138, 153, 225
    war veterans' smallholdings 68
    see also cattle; grazing; sheep; shielings
Livingston, West Lothian 72, 71, 159
Lloyd George, David 67, 124
Loch Alsh, Ross and Cromarty 156
Loch Auchlossan, Aberdeenshire 117
Loch Awe 112
Loch Bi, South Uist, Outer Hebrides 96
Loch Broom 60
Loch Brown, Mossgiel, Ayrshire 117
Loch Carron, Ross and Cromarty 156

Loch Creran 96
Loch Duich, Ross and Cromarty 156
Loch Etive 115
Loch Ewe, Ross and Cromarty 173
Loch Faskally, Perthshire 170
Loch Fyne, Argyll 12, 19, 149, 193
    see also Ardkinglas
Loch Gilp, Argyll 151
Loch Hourn, Inverness-shire 50
Loch Katrine, Stirlingshire 47, 48, 139, 170
Loch Kindar, New Abbey, Kirkcudbrightshire 157
Loch of Kinnordy, Kirriemuir, Angus 117
Loch Laggan, Inverness-shire 142, 187, 189, 190
Loch Leven, Fife 117
Loch Linnhe, Inverness-shire 150
Loch Linnie, Glensanda 221
Loch Lochy 111
Loch Lomond 20, 142–3, 164, 187, 249
Loch Lomondside 53
Loch Luichart 165
Loch Maddy, North Uist 177
Loch Maree, Ross and Cromarty 156, 180
Loch Meig Dam, Inverness-shire 165
Loch Mhor/Foyer power station, Inverness-shire 169
Loch Ness 37, 149, 150
Loch Oich 149
Loch Ossian, Inverness-shire 200
Loch of Park, Aberdeenshire 117
Loch Slapin, Skye, Outer Hebrides 187
Loch Spynie 104, 117
Loch Tay, Perthshire 33, 66, 115
    see also Taymouth
Loch Tayside, Perthshire 47, 157
Loch Tulla, Argyll 114
Lochainn, Perthshire 184
Lochlong 143
Lochore Castle, Lochgelly, Fife 117
Lochrin Basin, Edinburgh, Union Canal 151
Lochs, Lewis, Outer Hebrides 171
lodges *see* hunting lodges
lonchards/lunkards 186
Longannet, Fife 169
longhouses 31
Longniddry Bents, East Lothian 169
Lords of the Isles 132
Lorn Furnace Company 115
Lossiemouth, Moray 172
Lothianburn golf club, Edinburgh 197
Lothians
    Anglo-Saxon territory 85
    coal-mining 169, 221
    fields 106
    Forth Bridges 146, 148
    Gododdin territory 30, 176
    Normans in 15, 85
    part of Northumbria 31
    Southern Upland Fault 209
    Taliesin on cattle raid into 84
    see also East Lothian; Midlothian; West Lothian
lotters 62–3, 66
Loudoun, 5th Earl of 104
Loudoun estate, Ayrshire 117
Louis XIII, King of France 191
Louis XIV, King of France 41, 149, 191, 194
Lowlands

clearances 16
crofts/smallholdings 59, 66, 67
cropmarks 84
cursus monuments 21
emigration from 66
enclosure 101, 116
fallow land 96
farmhouses 56
farming 68, 88, 96, 104, 227
farms 66, 209
fences 113
field/land drainage 117
fields 106, 113, 227
  in Forlani's *Scotia* *207*
fuels 123, 223
geology 209
grazing 209
hedges 113
Highlanders in 179
houses 51, 219
hunting 183, 186
Improvement 50, 56, 101, 104, 106, 116
industry 157
loch drainage 117
migration from 50
mining and quarrying 166, 221
pease-meal year 51
peat 223
roads 142–3
sheep folding 96
shielings 47
timber 113
trees 89, 113
water meadows 122
woodland management 113–14
see also Highland-Lowland divide
Lunan, Angus 100
lunatic asylums 76
lunkards/lonchards 186
lynchets 81

mac Alpin, Kenneth 31
Macbeth, King 31
Macdonald, Angus mor 89
MacDonald, Catherine 49
Macduff, Banffshire 57
MacGregor, Rob Roy 119
Macinnes, Allan 10
Mackenzie, Colin, of Kintail 156
McKenzie, D, *Hermitage at Dunkeld, Perthshire 174*
Mackenzie, Francis, of Gairloch 66
Mackenzie, Dr John, of Gairloch 66
Mackenzie, Kenneth, of Gairloch 66
Maclean and Brodie 57
Macpherson, James *174*, 179, 181
machair 62, 240
Machrihanish, Argyll 172
Macky, John 40–1, 45, 70, 139, 142, 156, 179, *195*
Madderty, Perthshire 96
Maeshowe, Orkney *22*, 25, *25*
Magnus Barelegs, King of Norway 149
Maiden's Leap, Inverness-shire 139
Mainus, legendary king 176

Malcolm III, King 184
Malcolm IV, King 138
malthouses, Montrose, Angus 45
manors 34, 204
manuring *see* fertilisers
Mar 186
Mar, Earl of 40, 186, 187
marble 164, 166
Marchmont Castle, Roxburgh 42
Margaret, Queen (Margaret Tudor) 184
markets, urban areas 41
  see also trade
marl 117, 240
Martin, Martin 23, 25, 27, 46–7, 97, 166, 177, 196–7
Mary, Queen (wife of William of Orange) 40, 156
Mary, Queen of Scots 186, 196, *198*
Masterson, Sir James 8
Maugham, Somerset 76
Maxpoffle, Melrose, Roxburghshire *188*
Maxton, Dere Street and 138
Maybole, Ayrshire 42, 45, 51, 100, 193, 196
Meadows, the, Edinburgh 70
Meall Odhar, Glenshee, Perthshire 138
mechanisation
  farming 56, 68, *90*, 112–13, 122, *124*, *125*, 227
    see also prairie farmland
  forestry 125, 229
  peat cutting 123
medieval period
  castles 27, 34
  churches 36
  Dundee Law *75*
  farming 41, 84–9
  forests 88
  Frisian influence 31
  gardens 84–5, 89
  hedges 87, 95, 113
  houses 215
  hunting 184
  land use 215
  moated site, Kirkcudbright Training Area 173
  orchards 89
  Roxburgh 42
  settlements 41–7, 215, 225
  sheep 89, 95
  urban areas 41–2
  villages 41–2, *42*, 215
  water meadows 122
Meig (river) *165*
Meigle, Angus 157
Mein Water, Dumfriesshire 122
Melrose, Roxburghshire 76, 137, 179, 180, *182*, 188
Melrose Abbey, Roxburghshire 40, 87
Menstrie Glen, Stirlingshire 88
Merchant City, Glasgow 70
Mertoun House, Berwickshire *104*
middens 14, 20, 211, 240
Midlothian 21, *32*, 56, *137*, 138, 142, 166
migration
  from Highlands 50, 51, 63
  from Lowlands 50
  Improvement 50–1, 53, 56, 77
  roads and 142–3
  to urban areas 15, 50, 70, 77, 152, 204, 217
    see also clearances; emigration

military facilities 170, 172–3
    see also forts
milking, Fair Isle, Shetland *90*
mills 8, 37, 67, 96, 117, 135, 161, 221
    see also cotton mills; threshing mills
Mingulay, Outer Hebrides 63
mining 160, 164, 166, 169, 221
    see also coal-mining; lead mining
Ministry of Defence 172
Minnock ford, Ayrshire 142
Mission House, Coll, Inner Hebrides *51*
moated manor, Upper Chatto, Roxburghshire 204
moated site, Kirkcudbright Training Area 173
Moffat, Dumfriesshire 161, 190
Monadhliath mountains 225
monasteries 215
    farming 15, 36, 85
    field/land drainage 96
    industry 155
    Kinnedar, Moray 30
    pilgrim routes *137*, 138
    Ross and Cromarty 30, 31
    sheep farming/wool trade 89, 225
    see also Culdees; Iona
Moncrieffe Island, Perth 199
Monie, John 158
Monkland and Kirkintilloch Railway 153
Monklands Canal, Lanarkshire 152
monocultures 125, 240
Monro, Donald 97–9
Mons Graupius 29
Montrose, Angus 45, 172
Monymusk, Aberdeenshire 67
moon, beliefs about 97
Moorhouse, Ayrshire 117
moorland 25, 27, 81, 229
    see also peat; rough grazing
Morangie burn 157
Morar, Inverness-shire *49*
Moray 104, 186
    charcoal industry 116
    crofts and crofting 66
    cropmarks 191
    crops 100
    grazing 100
    medieval farming 85
    Normans in 34
    orchards 100
    Pictland and 85
    planned villages 57, 59
    see also names of places in Moray
Moray, Andrew 143
Moray, Earl of 186
Morris, Old Tom 199
Morton, H V 71, 153, 197
mortuary houses 21
Moss lairds 119
Mossgiel, Ayrshire 117
Mossmorran Peat Works, Fife 123
motorways 143, 217
motte, Law of Windsor, Angus 179
motte and bailey keeps 34, 240
mouldboard ploughs 14–15, 81, 85, *86*, 90, 106
Mount Keen 139
Muir, Edwin 17, 56, 70–3, 77, 157, 166, 169

muir-burning 190, 240
Mull, Inner Hebrides 57
Murray, John, 5th Duke of Atholl 191
Museum of Lead Mining 169
Muthill, Perthshire 7, 9, 36
My Lord's House, Little Tulloch, Aberdeenshire 187

Nairnshire, Fort George 141, *145*, 173
Napier, David 152
Nasmyth, Alexander, *Edinburgh Castle and the Nor' Loch* 119
National Forest Estate 229
National Land-use Database 248
National Mining Museum 169
Necropolis, Glasgow 76–7
Neilston, Lanarkshire 157, 161
Nether Braco, Perthshire 8
Netherlands 16, 31, 115
New Abbey, Kirkcudbrightshire 122
New Lanark 161
New Towns 72, *73*, 71, 217
    see also planned villages
Newton, Dere Street and 138
Newton Stewart, Wigtownshire 57
Newtongrange, East Lothian 169
Newtyle, Angus 57
Nick of the Ballock, Ayrshire 142
Nicol, John Watson, *Lochaber No More* 202
Nissen huts 172, 240
Nith (river), Dumfriesshire *34*
nolt 95, 240
Nor' Loch, Edinburgh 119
Nordrach-on-Dee sanatorium, Banchory, Aberdeenshire 76
Normans 15, 34, 85
Norse 30, 31, *33*, 34, 85, 149
North Queensferry, Fife 166
North Ronaldsay, Orkney *90*
North Sea oil and gas *68*
North Uist, Outer Hebrides *48*, *121*, *144*, 177
Northern Isles 31, 62, 66–7, 83, 123
    see also Orkney; Shetland
Northumbria 31, 137
    see also Anglo-Saxons
nuclear power stations *166*, 169

Oban, Argyll 153, 181
Ochil Hills 8, *130*
Ochiltree, Ayrshire *158*
oil industry
    North Sea *68*
    shale, West Lothian *162*, 169
Old Scatness Broch, Shetland *32*
open-cast coal mines 169, 221
orchards 36, *42*, 85, 89, *95*, 99, 100, 128–9, 191, 193
Ordnance Survey maps *99*, 101, 106, 124, 248
Orkney
    beliefs about moon 97
    cattle 97
    crofting county 63, 219
    ploughing 15, *90*
    steamboats 153
    water meadows 122

see also names of places in Orkney
Orkney woman in Edinburgh 180
Ormiston, East Lothian 104, 106
Oronsay 211
Ossian *174*, 179
Ossian's Hall, Dunkeld House, Perthshire *174*
otter hunting 188
outbuildings *see* farm buildings
outfields 87–8, 97, 106, 204, 241
Owen, Robert 161
oxen 14, *86*, *90*, 106
Oxnam, Dere Street and 138

Pabay 96
Paisley, Renfrewshire 128
palaces 30, 31, 36, 37, 40, 134, 166, 191, *194*
palisaded settlements 26, 81
Panmure 191
Parainam Fiadh, Skye, Outer Hebrides 187
parks
    Bruntsfield, Edinburgh 197
    castles 36, 100, 184, *193*
    Charles II's legislation 95
    Culross House, Fife *95*
    Drum, Aberdeenshire 187
    Greenwich and St James's, London 116
    Leith 197
    Panmure 191
    Perthshire, Duke of Atholl's park 190–1
    pheasants 190
    Stirling 184, *193*
    Yester, East Lothian 40
    see also designed landscapes
passenger transport 152–3
    see also airports/airfields; cars; railways; steamboats/steamships
pasture
    in National Land-use Database 248
    see also grazing
paths/trackways 138, 139, 153, 164, 194, 221
peas, Arran 87
pease-meal year (1782) 51
peat 123–124, 223
    assarts and 88
    Carse of Stirling drainage 119, 122
    common land 101
    cutting, drying, and transporting 20, 97, *120*, *121*, 122–3, 124, *171*, 223
    effect on crops/grazing 81
    formation 14
    Haymarket Coal Depot, Edinburgh *120*
    Highlands 123, 223, 225
    Inner Hebrides 66
    landscape preservation 13, 14, 25, 81
    Lewis, Outer Hebrides 98–9, *120*, 123, 124, *171*
    linen industry 157
    prehistoric communities 14
    removal 14
    replaced by coal 142
    Shetland 47, 62, 81
    spread 21, 25, 81, *120*, 132, 211
    stacking *120*, 123
    see also moorland
Peeblesshire 30, *91*, *108*

Penicuik 135
Pennant, Thomas
    on abbey orchards and gardens 193
    on Arran cairns 177
    on Arthur's O'on (Oven) 134–5
    on Bonawe Iron Furnace 115
    on Carron Ironworks 153, 155
    on Cleaven Dyke 21
    on Clydeside industry 157
    on Crinan Canal 149
    on deer hunting 187
    on deforestation 114
    on Dun Bhoraraig 27
    on Dunkeld landscape 180, 196
    on earthen dykes 97
    on Edinburgh New Town 70
    on enclosures 100, 107, 112
    on Forth-Clyde canal 152
    on Glasgow 70, 157
    on golf at St Andrews 197
    on Highland politeness 51
    on Highlanders' sports 187
    on Hopetoun House 194–5
    on Improvement 50, 103
    on industry 157
    on Jura shielings 47
    on Kinloss Abbey orchards 193
    on Leadhills 160
    on Lincluden Abbey garden 193
    on Loch Maree scenery 180
    on Perth road bridge 148
    on Perthshire smallholdings for war veterans 67
    on quarrying 166
    on runrig 86–7
    on salmon cruives 161
    on Scots' awareness of landscape 179
    on Wade, Gen. George 139
    on Wade's roads 142
    on wooden road 13, 132
pens *see* enclosures
Pentlands training area 173
Père Lachaise Cemetery, Paris 76
Perth 42, 45, *144*, 148, 196, 197, *199*
Perth, Duke of 67
Perth, Earl of 9
Perthshire
    Agricultural Revolution 9
    arable farming 8, 9
    bridges *141*, *144*, 148
    charcoal industry 116
    crofts and crofting 66
    Duke of Atholl's estate 190–1, 196
    fields 8
    gardens 88, 190–1
    grazing 46
    high-level settlements 25
    hill-forts 46
    houses 7, 9, 51
    longhouses 31
    medieval settlements 46
    paths/trackways 138
    roads 9, 142, *145*, 148
    Roman forts 8, 29
    smallholdings 59, 67
    standing stones 9

stone circles 9
villages 7, 9, 67
see also names of places in Perthshire
Peterhead, Aberdeenshire *158*, 172
Pettie, Inverness-shire 112
Philiphaugh, Selkirkshire 31
Phopachy Crannog, Inverness-shire *33*
Picts 29–31, 34, 79, 85, 86, 134, *179*, 181, 182–3
pigs, grazing control 95
pilgrim route, Dere Street/Via Regia *137*, 138
Pitlochry, Perthshire 170
plague (Black Death) 95, 204
planned villages 8, 57, 59, *59*, 67, 128, 169
see also New Towns
pleasure grounds *see* designed landscapes
ploughing 14–15, 21, 83–4
Carse of Gowrie 128
Fair Isle, Shetland *90*
hill-forts and 26
horses *91*, 106–7, 143
lynchets 81
near Peebles *91*
Orkney 15, *90*
outfields 87
rig and furrow 14, 15, 106, 128, 204
Taransay 97
terraces made by 81
see also ridges/ridging; rigs
ploughs 106–7
ards 14, 21, 81
cas-chrom (foot-plough) 83, *91*, 97–8
mouldboard ploughs 14–15, 81, 85, 86, *86*, *90*, 106
Rotherham ploughs 107
swing/Scots ploughs 107, 227
poaching 190
pollarding 113–14
pollution 161
Polmont, Stirlingshire 157
poorhouses 76
population 20, 25, 50
Ayrshire 104
distribution 71
Highlands 62–3
Kilmuir, Skye 62–3
plague's effects 95
see also clearances; emigration; migration
Port Righ (King's Port), Argyll *151*
Port Soy, Banffshire 166
Portland, Duke of 117
Portmahomack, Ross and Cromarty 30, 31
Portnalong, Skye, Outer Hebrides 63
Portobello 180
Pow of Inchaffray 96
Pow (river) 148
Pow Water 96
power stations *164*, *165*, *166*, 169, 170, 221
prairie farmland 113, *127*, 227
prehistoric communities
farming 14–15, 20–3, 25, 79, 81, *81*, 82–3, 211, 227
Forteviot ritual landscape 31
forts 173, 211, 229
see also hill-forts
houses 21
see also hut circles; huts
peat 14

roads 13, 132
settlements 20, 25–6, 81, *81*, 84, 211, 225
woodland management 14
see also henges; standing stones; stone circles
Priestside, Dumfriesshire 13, 132
Princes Street, Edinburgh 71
Pringle family, Smailholm Tower, Roxburghshire *36*

quarrying 8, 56, 104, 155, 161, 164, 166, 173, 221
Queensberry, Duke of 104, *195*
Queensferry Crossing *146*, 148
Quothquan, Lanarkshire 57

Raasay, Outer Hebrides 97, 99
rabbit hunting *189*
railways 123, *146*, 152, 153, *153*, 164, 166, 173, 197, 221
Ranco Motors Factory, Livingston, West Lothian *159*
Randolph, Thomas 86
Rannoch, Perthshire 51
Rannoch Moor, Argyll 10
Ratho Quarry, Midlothian 166
Ravenscraig, Lanarkshire 173, 176
reaper, Bell's *124*, *125*
recreation *see* leisure
reedbeds 157, 160, *160*
Reforesting Scotland 200
Reformation, the 37, 40, 76, 241
Relict Types 248
religious buildings 36–7, 40, 215
see also abbeys; cathedrals; chapels; churches; monasteries
Renaissance gardens 95, 191, 193
Renfrewshire 57, 59, 128, 153, 193, 200
Renton, John 107
reservoirs *108*, 164, 169, 170, 221
Restenneth Loch, Forfarshire 117
Restoration period 95
see also Charles II, King
Reuda, legendary king 176
Rheged 84
Rhynie, Aberdeenshire 29–30
ridges/ridging 15, 21, 81, 106, 122
see also ploughing; rig and furrow ploughing; rigs
rig and furrow ploughing 14, 15, 106, 128, 204
Righead farm, Lanarkshire 112
rigs *82*, 86, 88, *98*, 128, 173, 215
see also ploughing; runrig
Ring of Brodgar, Orkney 23, *25*, 209
ritual spaces 25, 31, 132, 176, 211
see also cursus monuments
rivers 21, 41, 119, 122, 138, 161, 194
see also names of individual rivers
roads 8, 95, 136–9, 141–3, 153, 172, 221
Aberdeenshire 142, *145*
Argyll 143, 148, 153
Ayrshire 104, 142
Bangour General Hospital, West Lothian 76
Dumfriesshire 13, 132, 142
Perthshire 9, 142, *145*, 148
prehistoric communities 13, 132
slag for 161
statute labour 142, 148

urban areas 41, 138
war veterans' smallholdings 68, 70
wooden 13, 132
see also bridges; droving/drove roads; paths/trackways; Roman roads; Wade's roads
Robert I (the Bruce), King 34, 36, 86, 161
Roman period 26, 29, 31, 170, 172, 176
    Arthur's O'on (Oven) 134–5, *135*, 176
    Buchanan on remains 135
    Christianity 30
    Dalriadan Scots 134
    forts 8, 29, 133, *133*, 134, 213
    hill-forts 26, 81
    infrastructure 131–8, 155
    land use 213
    pheasants 190
    re-use of stones from 135
    St Abb's Head camp 136
Roman roads 29, 132, 133, 136–8, *136*, 137–8, *137*, 213
Romanticism *12*, 19, 56, *174*, 179, 180, 181, *182*, 194
Ronald, Earl of Orkney 122
Ronay, Outer Hebrides 46
Rootes Factory, Linwood, Glasgow 159
Rosemarkie, Ross and Cromarty 30
Roslin, Midlothian 21, 56
Ross, Captain 179
Ross and Cromarty
    crofts and crofting 63, 66, 219
    houses 66, 180
    monasteries 30, 31
    Skye Bridge *144*
    see also names of places in Ross and Cromarty
Rossie Drain 117, 122
Rossie Loch, Fife 117
Rosyth, Fife 173
rotary querns 81, *91*, 241
Rothesay Castle, Bute 34
Roucan, Dumfriesshire 104
Rough Castle Fort, Stirlingshire *133*
rough grazing 8, 27, 122, 124, 134, 211, 225
    see also moorland
roundhouses 211
    see also wheelhouses
Roxburgh 41, 42
Roxburghshire
    fields *81*, 204
    forts 137, 204
    Gododdin territory 30
    Macky on hills 179
    railways 153
    roads 153
    see also names of places in Roxburghshire
Roy, Gen., maps 42, *98*, 101, 117, *136*, 191
Roy, Frank 173
royal forests *87*, 190
Royal Tarlair Golf Course, Aberdeenshire *199*
RSPB 160
Rum, Outer Hebrides 184, *188*
runrig 53, 86–7, *99*, 101, 104, 106, 241
Ruthven, Inverness-shire 141
Ruthwell, Dumfriesshire 13, 132

St Abb's Head, Roman camp 136
St Andrew 177
St Andrews, Fife 88, 197
St Andrews Cathedral, Fife 36, 37
St Andrew's Square, Edinburgh 70
St Columba 30, 177
St Finnian of Moville 84, 177
St James's park, London 116
St Kilda 41, 46–7, *93*, 172, 196–7
St Mary's Church, North Uist, Outer Hebrides 177
St Ninian 84, 177
St Serf's, Fife 36
salmon fishing 161, 181, *184*
salt panning 155
sandstone 166, 209
Sanquhar 152
Scarp, Outer Hebrides *55*
Scord of Brouster, Shetland 81, 211
Scotland proper 85
Scots, of Dalriada 29, 30, 31, 79, 134, 176, 181–3
Scott, Mr, of Gala 56
Scott, Sir Walter 96, 170, 180, 181, *182*
Scottish Crannog Centre *33*
Seaforth, Earl of 156
Seaside House, Perthshire *160*
seaweed, fertiliser 96, 99
Selkirk, Forest of 88
Selkirkshire 30, 31, 47, 56, 161, 184
Seton, golf links 196
settlement 19–77, 209
settlements
    high-level 25, 81, *81*, 83–4
    Highlands 46–7, 219
    Loch Ossian, Inverness-shire *200*
    medieval 41–7, 215, 225
    palisaded 26, 81
    prehistoric 20, 25–6, 81, *81*, 84, 211, 225
    see also townships; villages
Severus, Septimius, Emperor 134, 136
shale oil industry, West Lothian *162*, 169
Shandwick Stone/Clach a' Charridh, Ross and Cromarty *179*
Shapinsay, Orkney 106
sheep 15, 103–4, 204, 225
    Ayrshire 112
    black-faced *114*
    Cheviot 15, 103, *115*
    deer forests replace *188*
    Galloway 53
    grazing control 95, 116
    Improvement and 49, 103, 219
    Inverness-shire 187
    Lowlands, folding 96
    medieval period 89, 95
    monasteries 89, 225
    Peeblesshire *108*
    Southern Uplands 89, 103
    Texel 16, *115*
    Wilkie's *Sheepwashing* 78
    see also clearances; grazing; wool trade
sheep scab 89
shell middens 14, 211
Shetland *32*, 47, 62, 63, 81, *90*, 211, 219
shielings 10, 47–9, 128, 175, *200*, 215, 225, 229
    see also lonchards/lunkards
shipbuilding *68*, 158

shooting 181, *184*, 190–1, 225
Shotts, Lanarkshire 166
Singer Factory, Clydebank, Dunbartonshire *159*, 176
Sitka Spruce plantations *110*, 125
Siward, Earl of Northumbria 31
Skibo Castle, Sutherland 199
Skye, Outer Hebrides 27, 62–3, 66, *91*, 97, 99, *120*, 144, 164, 166, 187
Skye Bridge, Ross and Cromarty 144
Slamannan, Stirlingshire 166
Slezer, John, *View of Culross House, Fife* 95
Slochd Muic, Inverness-shire 141
Smailholm Tower, Roxburghshire *36*
Small, James (Struan factor) 67
Small, James (swing plough inventor) 107
smallholdings 15, 59, 66, 67–8, 70, 71, 219
    see also crofts and crofting
Smeaton, East Lothian 40
Smeaton, John 148
Smout, T C 16
Society of Improvers in the Knowledge of Agriculture in Scotland 101
Society for the Propagation of Christian Knowledge 177
soil improvement 83, 104
    see also fertilisers
soldiers *see* war veterans
Solway Firth *34*, 152, 209, 249
Somerled, King of the Isles 85
South Uist, Outer Hebrides 96, *144*
Southdean, Roxburghshire 183–4
Southern Uplands 25, 89, 103, 106, 209
    see also Borders; Cheviot Hills
Soutra Aisle, Midlothian *137*, 138
Soutra Hill 137
spades 15, 83, 123, 223
    see also cas-chrom (foot-plough/spade)
spinning *see* textile industries
sport 8, 187, 196
    see also archery; fishing; golf; hunting; shooting
sporting estates *184*
Sprouston, Selkirkshire 31
SS *Linnet*, on Crinan Canal *150*
stables 37, 56, 135
Stafford, Marquis of 62
standing stones 9, 25, 176, 177
    see also henges; symbol stones
stately homes *see* castles; country houses
statute labour, roads 142, 148
steam power 152, 153, 164, 221
steamboats/steamships 152–3, 181
steel manufacture *159*, 173
Steinmeyer, Heinrich 172
Stenhouse, Stirlingshire 134–5, *135*, 176
Stenness, Orkney 23, *25*
Stenton, Haddington, East Lothian 190
Stewart, John, Earl of Atholl 191
Stirling
    bridge 143, 148
    burgh 41
    Defoe on 45
    field/land drainage 104, 122
    Gododdin territory 30
    hill-fort 34
    palace 30, 40
    parks 184, *193*
    railway 153

    redevelopment 77
    see also Carse of Stirling
Stirling Castle 34, 36, *103*, 191, *193*
Stirling Royal Infirmary *73*
Stirlingshire
    Carron Ironworks 107, *130*, 153, 155, 157, 161, 166
    see also names of places in Stirlingshire
stone circles 9, 25, 176
    see also henges
Stonehaven, Kincardineshire 16, 209
Stones of Stenness 23, *25*
Stornoway, Lewis, Outer Hebrides 52, 123, 143
Stout, Mrs 90
Straiton, Ayrshire 57
Strath 166
Strath Avon 184
Strathallan, Perthshire 8, 23
Strathclyde, Britons' territory 30, 85
Strathmore 21, 31
Strathmore, Earl of 104
Strathyre, Callander 125
strawberries, Islay 99
Strelitz, Perthshire 67
Stroma, Orkney 197
Strone, Dalmally, Argyll 116
Struan estate, Perthshire 67
subsistence agriculture 50–1, 241
summer huts 200
Sutherland
    alabaster 164
    clearances 16, 53, 62, 101, 103, *189*
    crofts and crofting 59, 62, 63, 219
    emigration 62
    huts 25
    Improvement 62
    mouldboard ploughs 86
    shielings 49
    see also names of places in Sutherland
Sutherland, Countess of 62
Sutherland, Duke of 53
symbol stones 30, 176, *179*

Tacitus 29, 131, 155
Tain, Ross and Cromarty 41, 157, 172
Taliesen 84
Talla Reservoir, Peeblesshire *108*
tanning industry 114, 116, 157
    see also leather trade
Taransay 97
Tarbert, Loch Fyne, Argyll 149
tathing, outfields 87–8
Tay (river) *75*, *141*, *144*, 148, 211
Taylor, John 42, 45, 46, 138–9, 155, 186–7, 193
Taymouth, Perthshire, road 148
Taynuilt, Glen Nant, Argyll 116
Tayreed Company 160
Tayside, reedbeds *160*
Teith (river) 119
Telford, Thomas 60
temples
    Arthur's O'on (Oven) 134–5, *135*, 176
    see also ritual spaces
textile industries 57, 59, 157, 161

see also bleacheries; bleachfields; cotton mills; wool trade
threshing mills 56, 241
Tillydrone, Aberdeen 161
Tilt (river) 190
timber 34, *110*, 113–14, 115–16, 153, 156, 193, 229
    see also timber halls; wood
timber halls 21, 30, 31, 211
timber trade 157
Tobermory, Mull, Inner Hebrides 57
tolbooths 45, 104, 241
tombs
    standing stones and 176
    see also barrows; chambered cairns/tombs; mortuary houses
Tomintoul, Banffshire 59
Tongue, Sutherland 53, 62
Torness nuclear power station, East Lothian 169
Torphin Hill golf club, Edinburgh 197
Torrin, Skye, Outer Hebrides 164
Torthorwald, Dumfriesshire 104, 112
Tough, Rev. George 26
Toulouse-Narbonne canal 149
tourism 152, 179, 180, 181
towns *see* urban areas
townships 46, *50*, *55*, 59, 62, 63, *64*, 66, 67, 219
    see also villages
trackways/paths 138, 139, 153, 164, 194, 221
tractors *90*, 112
trade 77, 100, 156
    Anglo-Saxons 29, 30
    coal 157
    Dalriadan Scots 30
    Frisians 31
    fruit 128–9
    grain 142, 152, 153
    leather 95
        see also tanning industry
    livestock 89, 95, 100, 138, 153, 225
    Picts 29–30
    Roman period 29
    timber 157
    transport and 142, 149, 152, 153
    urban areas 41
    wool 41, 42, 89, 95, 225
    see also burghs; goods transport; markets
tramways, coal industry 164, 166, 169
transhumance *see* shielings
transport *110*, 132, 142, 149, 152, 153, 164, 166, 169, 181
    see also airports/airfields; goods transport; passenger transport; railways; roads; tramways; waterways
tree felling squad, Bowmont Forest, Kelso *110*
trees
    after Ice Age 13–14
    assarts and 88, 89
    Ayrshire 104
    castles 113
    designed landscapes 191, 193, 194, 195, 196
    East Lothian 104, 191
    farmhouses 113
    farming 14, 104
    fruit trees 89, *95*, 100, 128, 193, 195
    Galloway 104
    Highlands 14
    houses 113
    Improvement 15, 104, 113
    Inner Hebrides 187
    Kirkden, Forfarshire 112
    Lowlands 89, 113
    Moray 100
    planting 113, 116, 125
    pollarding 113–14
    protection 95, 113, 116
    see also conifer plantations; forestry; forests; timber; woodlands
Trimontium fort, Roxburghshire 137
Trongate, Glasgow 70
Trotternish 166
Tudor, Margaret (Queen Margaret) 184
turf 83, 88, 101
Turner's Croft, Kirkcudbrightshire 59
Turnhouse airport 172
Turriff, Aberdeenshire 57
Tweed (river) *104*, 122, *182*
Tweed Valley 209
Tweeddale, 1st Marquis and 2nd Earl of 116, 191
Tyndrum, Argyll 148, 221
Tyninghame, East Lothian *110*

Uist Causeways, Outer Hebrides *144*
Uists, Outer Hebrides 62, 172
    see also North Uist; South Uist
Ullapool, Ross and Cromarty 57, *59*, *60*
Underbank farm, Lanarkshire 112
Union Canal *151*, 152
Union of the Crowns (1603) 42, 45, 100, 114, 156, *194*
Union of the Parliaments (1707) 40, 42, 45, 46, 100, 114
Upper Chatto, Roxburghshire 204
urban areas 45–6, 70–7, 215, 217
    castles and 34
    commercial uses 119
    Dumfriesshire 41, 45
    golf courses 197
    houses 45, 71, 77
    Industrial Revolution's effects 70–3
    land reclamation 117, 119
    markets 41
    medieval 41–2
    migration to 15, 50, 70, 77, 152, 204, 217
    Muir on 70–3
    recreational uses 119
    residential uses 119
    rivers 41
    roads and 41, 138
    streets following medieval rigs 88
    trade 41
    see also Aberdeen; burghs; Dundee; Edinburgh; Glasgow; Inverness; Perth
Urbicus, Lollius 29
Urquhart Castle, Inverness-shire *37*

Vatersay, Outer Hebrides 63
Versailles, palace of 166, 191, *194*
Via Regia (royal way) *137*
Victoria, Queen 9, 152, 170, 181, *184*
Vikings *see* Norse
villages
    cattle pens 96
    cottage hospitals 71

Dumfriesshire 57, 104
East Lothian 104, 169
Fife *42*, 155
gardens 41, 42, 88
Gurness broch, Orkney *33*
industrial 57, 155, 169
medieval 41–2, *42*, 215
Perthshire 7, 9, 67
planned 8, 57, 59, *59*, 67, 128, 169
Upper Chatto, Roxburghshire 204
war veterans' 67
see also settlements; townships

Wade Bridge, Aberfeldy, Perthshire *141*
Wade's roads 139, 141–2, 143, *145*, 172, 179
Walker, Rev. James 9
walking 128, 225
Walkingshaw House, Renfrewshire 193
Wallace, William 143
walls
    brochs 27
    deer parks / deer hunting 184
    enclosures 112
    forts 26–7, *29*
    Improvement works 15, 107, 227
    Lowland fields 113
    parks 184
    Perthshire longhouse 31
    prehistoric settlements 20, 25
    St Kilda *93*
    Scord of Brouster, Shetland 81
    see also dykes
Wanlockhead, Dumfriesshire 57, 160–1, *163*, 169
war veterans 67–8, 70, 200
Warriston Cemetery, Edinburgh 77
Water Cross, North Uist, Outer Hebrides 177
water features, designed landscapes 191, 194, *195*, 196
water meadows 122
water supply *108*, 164, 169, 170, 221
Waternish, Skye, Outer Hebrides 97
waterways 132, 138, 149, 152
    see also canals; rivers; steamboats/steamships
Watt, James 149
Watt, Thomas, *Hermitage at Dunkeld, Perthshire 174*
weather *see* climate
weaving *see* textile industries
weirs, water meadows 122
West Cornton Vale, Stirlingshire 88
West Lothian
    shale oil industry *162*, 169
    see also names of places in West Lothian
Wester Ross 66, 249
Western Isles 31, 83, 123, 184
    see also Hebrides
Westhofen, William *146*
wheelhouses 31, *32*
    see also roundhouses
White Cathertun, Angus 27
White Dyke, Hermitage Castle, Roxburghshire 184
'white houses', Arnisdale, Inverness-shire *50*
Whitfield Development, Dundee *73*
Whithorn, Wigtownshire, Candida Casa 177
Whittinghame, Roxburghshire 142

Whitton Edge, Roxburghshire *137*, 138
Whitton, Michael 88
Wight, Robert 106
Wigtownshire 57, 177
wildfowl *see* game
wildlife 13, 14, 89, 112, 160, 169, 186
    see also deer; game
Wilkie, Sir David, *Sheepwashing 78*
William III and II (William of Orange), King 40, 156
wind farms 169, *171*
wood
    assarts and 88
    see also timber
wooden road, Priestside, Dumfriesshire 13, 132
woodlands 113–16, 128, 229
    castles 36
    grazing control 95, 113
    Jura 187
    in National Land-use Database 248
    Pabay 96
    prehistoric period 14
    reduction in 89
    shown by cropmarks 84
    see also conifer plantations; forests; trees
Woodside farm, Lanarkshire 112
wool trade 41, 42, 89, 95, 225
Wordsworth, Dorothy
    on Argyll crofts 62, 66
    on Barncluith 195
    Burns and 180
    on Carron Ironworks 157
    on deforestation 114–15
    on Dumfries 180
    on Dunkeld 196
    on enclosures 112
    on Glasgow 70
    on houses 19–20, 53, 56, 59, 123, 161, 180, 195
    on industrialisation/industry 161
    on Inveraray 19
    on landscape 180
    on Leadhills 160
    on paths/trackways 139
    Scott and 180
    on shielings 47–8
    on Wade's roads 142
Wordsworth, William 19, 47, 180, 193
workers' houses 164, 169, 221

Yester, East Lothian 40, 191